D0834874

READINGS IN GENDER COMMUNICATION

PHILIP M. BACKLUND
Central Washington University

MARY ROSE WILLIAMS
Christopher Newport University

THOMSON
™
WADSWORTH

Australia ▪ Canada ▪ Mexico ▪ Singapore ▪ Spain
United Kingdom ▪ United States

THOMSON

WADSWORTH

Publisher: *Holly J. Allen*
Executive Editor: *Annie Mitchell*
Assistant Editor: *Breanna Gilbert*
Editorial Assistant: *Trina Enriquez*
Technology Project Manager: *Jeanette Wiseman*
Marketing Manager: *Kimberly Russell*
Marketing Assistant: *Andrew Keay*
Advertising Project Manager: *Shemika Britt*
Project Manager, Editorial Production:
  Catherine Morris
Print/Media Buyer: *Doreen Suruki*

Permissions Editor: *Bob Kauser*
Production Service: *Scratchgravel Publishing
  Services*
Art Editor: *Gregory Draus*
Copy Editor: *Margaret C. Tropp*
Cover Designer: *Bill Stanton*
Cover Image: *Denis Felix/Getty Images*
Compositor: *Scratchgravel Publishing Services*
Text and Cover Printer: *Transcontinental
  Printing/Louiseville*

COPYRIGHT © 2004 Wadsworth, a division of
Thomson Learning, Inc. Thomson Learning™ is
a trademark used herein under license.

ALL RIGHTS RESERVED. No part of this
work covered by the copyright hereon may be
reproduced or used in any form or by any
means—graphic, electronic, or mechanical,
including but not limited to photocopying,
recording, taping, Web distribution, information
networks, or information storage and retrieval
systems—without the written permission of the
publisher.

Printed in Canada

1 2 3 4 5 6 7 07 06 05 04 03

For more information about our products,
contact us at:

**Thomson Learning Academic
Resource Center
1-800-423-0563**

For permission to use material from this
text, contact us by:

Phone: 1-800-730-2214
Fax: 1-800-730-2215
Web: http://www.thomsonrights.com

Library of Congress Control Number:
2003111400

ISBN 0-534-58113-7

Wadsworth/Thomson Learning
10 Davis Drive
Belmont, CA 94002-3098
USA

Asia
Thomson Learning
5 Shenton Way #01-01
UIC Building
Singapore 068808

Australia/New Zealand
Thomson Learning
102 Dodds Street
Southbank, Victoria 3006
Australia

Canada
Nelson
1120 Birchmount Road
Toronto, Ontario M1K 5G4
Canada

Europe/Middle East/Africa
Thomson Learning
High Holborn House
50/51 Bedford Row
London WC1R 4LR
United Kingdom

Latin America
Thomson Learning
Seneca, 53
Colonia Polanco
11560 Mexico D.F.
Mexico

Spain/Portugal
Paraninfo
Calle/Magallanes, 25
28015 Madrid, Spain

CONTENTS

PART IV

VERBAL AND NONVERBAL COMMUNICATION

PART V

PERSONAL RELATIONSHIPS

PART VI

EDUCATIONAL AND PROFESSIONAL CONTEXTS

PART VII
MEDIA INFLUENCES ON GENDER COMMUNICATION

PREFACE

Gender is to humans as oxygen is to the atmosphere, or grains of sand to the world's deserts and shores—it is insidiously and thoroughly a part of our being. Gender, the "culturally constructed organization of biology and social life into particular ways of doing, thinking, and experiencing the world" (Rakow, 1986), influences and is influenced by every aspect of being. There is no idea, behavior, or process that is gender-free, for all human action is inseparable from the gender socialization that begins with such questions as "Do you want a girl or a boy?" "Are you having a boy or a girl?" "Is it a girl or a boy?" The degree to which gender factors into an interaction depends on a number of variables, including the message, the context, and the race, ethnicity, and socioeconomic culture of the participants. Regardless of where gender falls on the continuum of influence relative to other variables, it is always present.

As the role of gender socialization in our personal, public, and political lives has become more evident, the impetus to study the construct of gender has become stronger. The purpose of this book is to advance that cause, particularly by shedding light on the nuances of gender as it is reinforced in daily lived experiences. We believe the best way for students to recognize, understand, and appreciate the complexities of gender is through illustrations of gender socialization as revealed and perpetuated in the common activities of people in various contexts. Toward that end, this book is designed as a supplementary text to reinforce theories discussed in gender and communication textbooks by examining various topics in diverse formats. We hope that all readers of the book will find something of personal value and enjoyment as they expand their knowledge of gender and communication theories.

Readings in Gender Communication is a compilation of studies, stories, analyses, and personal testimonies contributed by communication, gender, psychology, and sociology scholars and students. Because the book is designed as a supplementary text, theoretical content is limited, with primary emphasis given to demonstrating gender theory as it applies to students' lives. Readability is also a noteworthy feature of this text, as the articles generally are written for the 100- and 200-level college student who is unfamiliar with sophisticated scholarly prose and is a novice in the studies of gender and communication.

The articles are arranged systematically according to objective and topic focus. For instance, those who are most interested in gender as manifested in interpersonal communication can find relevant pieces in Part V, Personal Relationships. Analyses of the evolution of gender depictions in the media, such as World War II propaganda posters and motorcycle advertisements, are in Part III, Social Change. Articles that theorize about issues of gender identity, change, and fluidity appear in Part II, Theoretical Perspectives. Ideally, the pieces are intended to be read in the order of readers' needs and interests, rather than in a structured or progressive manner.

Readings in Gender Communication is designed to be highly interactive. We preface each article with a brief introduction, including a preview of its thesis, findings, questions for consideration as the piece is read, and suggestions of related topics in gender and communication for further study. Many contributors disburse discussion questions throughout their work; other articles are followed by thought catalysts and project ideas. Students easily can choose those articles that offer topics they find most relevant and interesting.

The editors would like to thank the following reviewers for their comments: Patricia Amason, University of Arkansas; Bernardo Attias, California State University–Northridge; Lori Byers, University of North Texas; Robert A. Davilla, University of Northern Iowa; Steve Duck, University of Iowa; Beverly Graham, Georgia Southern University; Rona Halualani, San Jose State University; Julie Mayberry, North Carolina State University; Elena Strauman, Auburn University; Carol L. Thompson, University of Arkansas at Little Rock; Linda P. Van Buskirk, Cornell University; and Ralph Webb, Purdue University. We also thank Phil's extended family (Judy, Shane, Kari, Ryan, Matt, Emily, and Madison) for their support and encouragement, and Arthur Ranney, University of Wisconsin, Platteville, for technical and research support.

REFERENCE

Rakow, L. (1986). Rethinking gender research in communication. *Journal of Communication*, *36*, 11–26.

INTRODUCTION

N ext time you are in your local grocery store, scan the magazine rack. You are likely to see dozens of article titles such as "How to Tell If He Loves You," "Sex Secrets That Work," and "What Is Your Love Quotient?" Titles such as these do not appear only on the covers of women's magazines; they are common on the front pages of tabloids and the new style of men's magazines such as *Details, Maxim, Men's Health,* and *Men's Journal.* Similarly, dozens, if not hundreds, of talk shows, television shows, and movies focus on romantic communication (both heterosexual and homosexual), relationships, images, and the politics of sex. Clearly, the topic of gender communication continues to be hot. You might think that with all of this talk and advice, no one would have any trouble with gender communication. Problems between males and females, however, abound. Who hasn't had issues, concerns, and dissatisfactions arising from gender differences? Such problems seem to be part of the human condition.

As a student in a gender communication course, you have the opportunity to study this topic in more depth than the average person. Such an opportunity is exciting, but it can also be frustrating. Discussion of gender communication and related issues can provide the means for healthy and productive change in interpersonal relationships. Yet the study of gender communication can be a bit frustrating in that difficulties in gender communication will continue in spite of knowledge and skills gained through study. To use a sports analogy, none of us will ever bat a thousand (getting a hit in baseball every time), but we can improve our average.

People appear to be drawn to the study of gender communication for three reasons. First, many people who inquire into gender communication want to increase the number, quality, depth, and satisfaction of their relationships. These relationships range from the romantic to the professional, from personal friendships to public and political interaction. People drawn to the study in order to improve their relationships are usually looking for advice or strategies for increasing success. Second, some people are drawn to the study as a means of gaining a fuller and clearer understanding of themselves and others. These individuals may recognize their own lack of knowledge, feel an uncertainty in their own gender role, or simply be curious about why and how gender communication evolved and continues. Third, still others are drawn to the study of gender communication for political reasons. Particularly, they want to understand and challenge how communication creates and perpetuates the inequality of the sexes that is very much present in our society. Most courses in gender communication address all three motivations with varying degrees of emphasis. This reader will help support that motivational force.

As instructors of gender communication and as coeditors of this reader, we believe that gender communication as an area of study encompasses a range of theoretical knowledge, a variety of skills, and an examination of the values and emotions surrounding the topic. For the student of gender communication, the advantages of such study include self-development, improved relationships, and political awareness.

Self-Development. Some people are drawn to the study of gender by a desire to understand themselves more fully, which leads, ultimately, to personal growth. For such students, the course functions as a vehicle for self-improvement. Considering the problems present in our society, we support this reason. Thus, possible learning outcomes for this objective could include:

- Developing greater awareness of how social structures, popular culture, race, and discourse related to gender influence a student's own gender role, communication behavior, and the responses of others to that behavior. Understanding how one's own behavior is shaped is the first step in considering change.
- Developing and understanding the concept of personal change and growth. Although one popular book suggests that men and women are from different planets, we do not believe that is the case. As one friend of ours said, "We're from the same planet. Deal with it." Despite the claims of some that change is not possible—men are men, women are women, that is the way it is, biology is destiny—we believe that behavioral change is possible, as well as vital. Individual skill development is a useful goal for everyone. These skills include listening and responding behavior, other-centeredness, questions of power and dominance, and self-expression.

Relationship Goals. Many students enroll in a gender communication course because they have had difficulty in relating to individuals of their own or the other sex. As much of the satisfaction or pain we have in life is based on the quality of our relationships, this can be a particularly powerful motivation for some students. Often these students come to the class hoping to have their problems solved. However, caution needs to be exercised here, as interpersonal problems are multilayered and complex. It is not realistic to believe that any course can offer a complete "cure" for an interpersonal ill. We cannot stress this point too much; in fact, we both include the following nonobjectives for our gender courses: (1) not to fall in love; (2) not to find a mate; (3) not to have all of your cross-gender problems solved; and (4) not to find the perfect answer. Having reasonable objectives in the relationship area is very helpful. But what are they?

- To expand your repertoire of abilities and capabilities in gender communication
- To gain some knowledge of the skills necessary to create and maintain effective relationships with members of the other sex in contexts including friendships, family, romance, and professional
- To understand and analyze the communication behavior similarities and differences between the sexes

Politics. Recorded history attests to the fact that the majority of the world's cultures have valued men over women and masculine style over feminine. The various

U.S. and international women's movements of the eighteenth through twentieth centuries have resulted in much progress toward minimizing inequities. However, sex and gender equality remains an elusive condition. Questions of the definitions of equality, implications of these definitions, societal forces and change, and the role of the individual in encouraging societal change remain to be answered. Some students are drawn to a course such as this as a means toward their own political awakening and activism. Goals in this area may include:

- To understand and reduce privilege based on biological sex
- To analyze and critique social structures and contexts such as education, the professions, industry, and the politics of relationships to discover how they function to maintain the status quo of sex and gender inequality
- To shift the value judgment the culture applies to the concepts of masculinity and femininity so that neither is valued over the other

As editors, we have a series of goals for our own courses and for this reader. We believe it important for you to think carefully about your own goals for a course such as this, and to consider the goals of others. Why do other people think a gender communication course is a good idea? The purpose of such a course is to explore the communication between and about men and women. Although the ability to communicate effectively is not everything, the absence of that ability can and does create problems. The presence of this ability can and does aid in achieving a good deal of satisfaction and success.

A course such as this will help you study, analyze, and understand the theories that explain gender communication outcomes and that support effective communication strategies. We leave this section with a description of two more global goals related to courses in gender communication.

The Lens. Communication researchers suggest that all of our perceptions are filtered through a variety of physiological, psychological, and cultural lenses. We cannot understand anything without interpreting through these filters. Gender constitutes a significant lens, for once we classify another individual as male or female, we begin to draw inferences about that person's psychological attributes based on our own gender socialization. Some men, in looking at a woman, cannot see anything but "feminine." Of course, you might say, that is the most obvious thing. But is it? Or does it have to be? Is it possible to look at someone's sex without seeing their gender? Or to see other qualities, such as friend, coworker, or classmate first? Remember, gender is not the same as biological sex. If feminine attributes are devalued, then the ability to literally see other qualities first may lead to more effective and less biased communication behavior. So, one goal we have for you is to enhance your ability to alter or shift the lenses through which you view people, specifically people of the sex other than your own. Such a perceptual reorientation may have interesting results.

Androgyny. Learning to incorporate communication behaviors of the other gender when useful and appropriate leads to what is referred to as "androgyny." One of the editors of this reader regularly starts his gender communication courses by suggesting that by the end of the course, the men in the class will communicate more like women and the women will communicate more like men. This usually generates an interesting reaction, especially from the men. Some say "I don't want to do that!" However, one goal of our courses is to modify the identification of certain communication behaviors as masculine and others as feminine. Ideally, individual communication behaviors would not be gender linked. Each sex would and could feel free to use whatever communication behavior advanced a particular communication goal and not think about "Well, this is what women (men) do!" Blending the best of gender communication behaviors is our goal for you.

PART I

FOUNDATIONS

YOU'VE COME A LONG WAY, BABY . . . OR HAVE YOU?

A Self-Test

Johnston M. Brendel and Diana K. Ivy
TEXAS A&M UNIVERSITY, CORPUS CHRISTI

Times have changed, but how much? Are we free from sexism and gender bias? Does equal opportunity now exist for women and men? Have women "arrived"? More important, how would we know? What societal indicators should we look to? How can progress or change be measured?

In this article, Brendel and Ivy present twenty different pieces of evidence that point to equality, or the lack thereof. This article is an excellent discussion starter for analyzing just how much things have changed. It is clear that things have changed, but work still needs to be done if equality is to be achieved.

In your class discussions, you might talk about these indicators and then suggest some of your own. In addition, we suggest some possible questions for discussion.

QUESTIONS FOR DISCUSSION

- *In your own opinion, has society changed in the past 25 years? How do you know?*
- *Who or what has been responsible for the changes?*
- *How would you define "progress"?*
- *What is the goal of that progress?*
- *What is left to do?*
- *What would have to happen before we could say, "The goal has been achieved"?*

Reprinted with permission.

It is widely acknowledged that the modern feminist movement began in the late 1950s and early to mid-1960s and that significant gains have been made by women in subsequent decades. One must be cautious, however, in assuming that the struggle for equality is over or that "women have arrived." A common response, when thinking about or discussing the status of women in American culture, is impatience or disdain because we want to believe that the struggle for equality is over, that equality between the sexes has been achieved. Some view gender equality as a "dead issue," or as something that society set out to achieve some decades ago, and the successes of those past efforts should suffice.

Myths and misinformation abound about the roles, status, and opportunities for women in today's American society. From time to time it is useful to perform a "reality check" to expose the hype, rumors, and assumptions that we all make about gender equality. It is particularly helpful for researchers and instructors across various disciplines who focus classroom attention on gender issues to be able to gauge student attitudes and beliefs about the sexes. What beliefs or opinions about men's and women's "place" in our culture do students bring with them when they arrive at our classroom doors? Exercises that can alert students to misinformation and expose the assumptions that lead to faulty or outdated thinking can be extremely useful to educators and valuable for students.

The purpose of this article is to provide one such exercise, a classroom or workshop activity that can spark discussion and offer glimpses into the current status of women in this country. The following twenty questions reflect various topics and concerns related to women in particular, and gender issues in general. This activity can be done in the classroom as a warm-up exercise to determine the level of students' awareness of these issues and to generate discussion. Questions can also be subdivided into specialized topics, such as women in the workforce, women and violence, and personal relationships, for an instructor's use in conjunction with other course material on that specific area. Answers and references pertaining to the questions are also provided.

HOW FAR HAS THE "BABY" ACTUALLY COME? QUESTIONS TO TEST YOUR KNOWLEDGE OF THE STATUS OF WOMEN

1. Does the statistic that women earn 76 cents in comparison to a man's dollar in the United States apply to or reflect all women, across racial and ethnic groups?

Answer: No. U.S. Bureau of Labor statistics show that Hispanic women working full-time earn approximately 55 cents, African American women 65 cents, and European American women 80 cents to men's dollars (all men, combined) (Herman,

2001; U.S. Bureau of Labor Statistics, 1994). This wage gap indicates that the average woman earns $420,000 less in salary over her lifetime ("Wage Gap," 1996). In addition, 2001 U.S. Census Bureau statistics show that the average woman's wage dropped from 76 cents in 1990 to 73 cents in 2000 (Lipson, 2001). The pay gap widens with age: the 73 cents decreases to 70 cents for women ages 45 to 54, and to 64 to 68 cents for women ages 55 to 64 (Lipson, 2001).

2. Are men and women equally represented as elected officials in our federal government?

Answer: No. The U.S. Census Bureau (1999) estimates that women comprise 51% of the total population in the United States, but currently only two of the nine Supreme Court Justices are women, 58 of the 435 members of Congress are women, and 9 of the 100 members of the United States Senate are women.

3. What segment of society has benefited most from affirmative action programs?

Answer: Although many people believe that African Americans have benefited the most from affirmative action programs, actually European American women have been the biggest beneficiaries over the 30 years of the program's existence. European American women are the largest single group to benefit, with much less benefit extended to Hispanic and African American men and women (American Civil Liberties Union, 1995; "Analyzing Affirmative Action," 1995; St. George, 1995).

4. What kinds of unethical questions are women often asked in job interviews?

Answer: Women interviewing for jobs are frequently asked questions about their personal and family lives, often in an attempt to discover if they have children or, more to the point, if they intend to have children while employed at the company or institution with which they are interviewing. Men are rarely asked such questions because of the assumption that their careers or work responsibilities will not be deterred or interrupted by raising a family (Ivy & Backlund, 2000).

5. Is it still legal to include a space for sex (as in male __ female __) on job applications?

Answer: Yes. It is still legal to request that a job applicant indicate her or his sex on an application, but it is illegal to let the response affect a person's chances of being interviewed or hired (Ivy & Backlund, 2000).

6. Given that in 1968 15% of managers were women, then 15% should have risen through the ranks to become senior managers in the decade of the 1990s. What percentage actually represents women in senior management in the 1990s?

Answer: Only 3% of senior management in the 1990s were women, suggesting that the "glass ceiling" in corporations is alive and well. This trend led one team of researchers to conclude: "If women's rate of progress proceeds at the present pace, women will not achieve equitable representation and pay at all management levels for another 75 to 100 years" (Reskin & Padavic, 1994, pp. 95–96).

7. What percentage of women in the workforce choose nontraditional (or traditionally male-dominated) careers?

Answer: Only 6% of women in the American workforce choose nontraditional or male-dominated career paths (American Association of University Women, 1998a, 1998b). Women cluster in only 20 of the 400 job categories provided on questionnaires about career paths. However, more women in the 21st century are entering male-dominated and, typically, higher-paying professions than in recent decades (Lipson, 2001).

8. What percentage of minimum wage earners are women?
   A. One third
   B. One half
   C. Two thirds
   D. One quarter

Answer: Two thirds of all minimum wage earners in the United States are women (American Association of University Women, 1998a, 1998b).

9. Given that girls account for 40% of all high school athletes and women are 37% of all college varsity athletes, what percentage of athletic scholarship dollars do female athletes receive?
   A. 10%
   B. 23%
   C. 41%
   D   50%

Answer: According to the Executive Summary on Title IX, 25 years after the enactment of Title IX, only 23% of college athletic scholarship dollars go to female athletes. Only 27% of recruiting dollars are spent on female athletes (National Coalition for Women and Girls in Education, 1997).

10. Women comprise 73% of elementary and secondary school teachers. What percentage are principals?
   A. 35%
   B. 45%
   C. 55%
   D. 65%

Answer: The correct answer is 35%, according to the Report Card on Gender Equity (National Coalition for Women and Girls in Education, 1997).

11. True or False? Studies show that 60% of 8th through 11th graders have experienced sexual harassment.

Answer: False. Studies show that 81% (85% of girls; 76% of boys) have experienced sexual harassment (American Association of University Women, 1993). Research indicates that sexual harassment is related to female students' reduced academic performance and decreased interest in school.

12. Are Americans ready for a woman president?

Answer: George Gallup first asked citizens in 1936 whether they would "vote for a woman for president if she qualified in every other respect." Sixty-five percent of respondents said they would not. A recent poll shows that 90% of Americans say that they could support a woman for president (Clift & Brazaitis, 2000). Still, when it comes to the qualities that people seek in candidates for public office, men still have the advantage. Leadership and the ability to be decisive are perceived to be male traits, while women are viewed as being more honest and caring (Clift & Brazaitis, 2000).

13. Is there a relationship between pornography and violence against women?

Answer: Common sense suggests that pornographic materials that portray women in humiliating and degrading poses are unhealthy for women. In fact, the 1986 Meese Commission concluded that extensive viewing of pornographic materials leads viewers to believe that rape and other forms of sexual violence are less harmful than they might otherwise believe. Most researchers agree that pornography has not been proven to be a direct cause of violence. Rather, studies show that viewing violence can lead to violent behavior (Starer, 1995). When reviewing the research findings, one must be diligent in uncovering political agendas. For example, the issue of censorship is often intertwined in discussions about pornography. Interested parties in the equation include pro-family lobbies, the religious right, the press, feminists, and the American Civil Liberties Union (ACLU). All parties would receive an incentive if conclusive evidence emerged that pornography directly causes violence (Starer, 1995).

14. What is the economic impact of divorce for men versus women?

Answer: Many women face a decrease in their standard of living following a divorce. For the average woman, it takes five years to recover financially (Gelernter, 1996). On average, divorced men enjoy a 10% increase in their standard of living, but women suffer a 30% drop in their standard of living. Census reports indicate that only half of divorced women who were awarded child support receive it in full each month, about 25% of fathers pay a portion, and about 25% pay nothing. As their children grow older, fathers become less likely to pay in full and more likely to pay smaller amounts (Gelernter, 1996).

15. After a marriage breaks up, is it more beneficial for children to be raised by their father or their mother?

Answer: In a study of more than 22,000 American male respondents, researchers found that children raised by single mothers were nearly as likely to succeed in adulthood as children raised in traditional two-parent homes. When income and job status were taken into account, children who were raised by single mothers were more likely to reach higher professional and educational levels than children raised in households headed by a stepfather or single father (Biblarz, Raftery, & Bucur, 1997). Researcher Timothy Biblarz explains: "On average, mothers tend to sustain a higher level of emotional involvement in children amid spousal conflict and marital disruptions. Compared to a father, a mother has a greater reproductive investment in a particular child. A father's relations with his children tend to diminish as his relations diminish with the children's mother" (Biblarz, in Sullivan, 1997).

16. What percentage of married women will experience marital rape?

Answer: The FBI indicated that 102,555 women were survivors of rape in 1990 (U.S. Department of Justice, 1996), but the Rape in America study estimates that 683,000 women are raped every year (National Victims Center and Crime Victims Research and Treatment Center, 1992). The National Violence Against Women survey reported that nearly 18% of respondents had been raped or had been the target of an attempted rape (Tjaden & Thoennes, 1998). In this study, 8,000 women and 8,000 men shared their experiences with rape, physical assault, and stalking. The findings indicated that violence against women is primarily partner violence: 76% of the women who were raped and/or physically assaulted since age 18 were assaulted by a current or former husband, cohabiting partner, or date, compared with 18% of the men. The women's movement raised public awareness of rape and also facilitated new responses for survivors; however, a great deal remains to be done in this area. At the United Nations Conference on Women in Beijing in 1995, violence against women was identified as one of the most pressing concerns of women worldwide (Winters, 1998).

17. True or False? The majority of American workers are covered by the national Family and Medical Leave Act, which requires businesses to permit up to 12 weeks of unpaid leave annually.

Answer: True. Signed by President Clinton in 1993, the national Family and Medical Leave Act (FMLA) covers approximately two thirds of the U.S. labor force, including private and public sector employees. Employers with 50 or more employees are required to provide up to 12 weeks of unpaid, job-protected leave a year to eligible employees to care for a newborn, newly adopted, or foster child; to care for a child, spouse, or parent with a serious health condition; or for the serious health condition of the employee, including maternity-related disability. Although this is a significant step forward, many U.S. workers are still not covered by the Act. This group includes teachers, employees who work for companies with fewer than 50 employees, and people deemed "key" employees (Family and Medical Leave Act, 1993). Other industrial countries do much better, with Canadian workers receiving 15 weeks of family leave at 60% pay and women in France receiving 12 weeks of maternity leave at full pay (Kenen, 1998).

18. True or False? Women are frequently required to pay higher insurance premiums than men for the same benefits, or to pay the same as men for less protection or benefits.

Answer: True. If women won equality in insurance prices, coverage, and benefits, they would gain more than $2.5 billion annually. This would include $150 million per year in increased annuities paid to retired women and would equal what men receive with the same policies. Life insurance savings paid out to older women would be $140 million per year, equaling what men get with the same policies. Women would gain $2 billion per year in reduced charges for automobile insurance. Current pricing methods are strongly biased against women because they ignore the 2:1 ratio of men's to women's average mileage and, consequently, the 2:1 ratio of accident involvement (Butler, 1993).

19. Is Social Security a woman's issue?

Answer: Yes. Since women live longer than men, they depend on Social Security benefits for more years than men do. Additionally, women are half as likely as men to receive a pension and when they do, the average pension income for older women is $2,682 annually, compared to $5,731 for men (American Association of University Women, 2000). The Social Security system, founded in 1940, reflects the predominant role (homemaker) that women played at that time. The percentage of women in the workforce in 1940 was 14%; the percentage had risen to 59% by 1993 (Social Security Administration, 1993). Sixty-three percent of women on Social Security receive benefits based on their husbands' earnings (wives' or widows' benefits), while only 1% of men receive benefits based on their wives' earnings. Thirty-seven percent of these women had no earnings history, and 26% had a higher benefit as a wife or widow than as an earner. Monthly benefits for women currently average $621, while men receive an average of $810 (National Organization for Women, 1999).

20. How are federal judicial nominations handled differently between sexes?

Answer: In 1999, the Citizens for Independent Courts Task Force on Federal Judicial Selection submitted a nonpartisan blue-ribbon study during the 105th Congress. It reported that the confirmation procedure for women and minority nominees took significantly longer than for white male nominees. On average, the process took 65 days longer for women and 60 days longer for nonwhite nominees. In 1999, six of the ten judicial candidates who waited two years or longer to be confirmed were women or members of minorities. On the federal bench, women and minority members are underrepresented, with less than 21% of the seats belonging to women and less than 17% of the federal judgeships held by members of ethnic minorities (American Association of University Women, 2000).

REFERENCES

American Association of University Women. (1993). *Hostile hallways: The MUW survey on sexual harassment in America's schools.* Washington, DC: AAUW Educational Foundation.

American Association of University Women. (1998a). *Gender gaps: Where schools still fail our children.* Washington, DC: AAUW Educational Foundation.

American Association of University Women. (1998b). *News release: Technology gender gap develops while gaps in math and science narrow, AAUW Foundation report shows.* [Online]. Available: http://www.aauw.org

American Association of University Women. (2000, April). *Federal judicial nominations fact sheet. AAUW Public Policy in Government Relations Department.* [Online]. Available: http://www.aauw.org

American Civil Liberties Union. (1995). *Affirmative action: Still effective, still needed in the pursuit of equal opportunity in the '90s.* New York: American Civil Liberties Union Press.

Analyzing affirmative action. (1995, November 17). *Chronicle of Higher Education,* p. A6.

Biblarz, T. J., Raftery, A. E., & Bucur, A. (1997). Family structure and social mobility. *Social Forces,* 1319–1341.

Butler, P. (1993). *Insurance sex discrimination in the United States: Fact sheet, National Organization for Women.* [Online]. Available: http://www.now.org

Clift, E., & Brazaitis, T. (2000). *Madam president.* New York: Scribner.

Family and Medical Leave Act. (1993). Washington, DC: Government Printing Office.

Gelernter, C. (1996, July 21). Divorce: The impact of a split decision. *Seattle Times.* [Online]. Available: http://seattletimes.nwsource.com

Herman, A. (2001). *Who wears the pants?* Presentation by the U.S. Secretary of Labor, Alexis Herman (1-7-2001). [Online]. Available: http://content.aol.monster.com/experts/herman/

Ivy, D. K., & Backlund, P. (2000). *Exploring genderspeak: Personal effectiveness in gender communication* (2nd ed.). New York: McGraw-Hill.

Kenen, R. H. (1998). Environmental and occupational health. In Boston Women's Health Book Collective (Eds.), *Our bodies, ourselves* (pp. 131–157). New York: Simon & Schuster.

Lipson, J. (2001, Fall). Equity fact or fiction? American Association of University Women's *Outlook, 95,* 15–18.

National Coalition for Women and Girls in Education. (1997). *Executive summary Title IX at 25: Report card on gender equity.* Washington, DC: National Women's Law Center.

National Organization for Women. (1999, Winter). Viewpoint: Women most vulnerable in social security debate. *National NOW Times.* [Online]. Available: http://www.now.org

National Victims Center and Crime Victims Research and Treatment Center. (1992). *Rape in America: A report to the nation.* Arlington, VA: National Victims Center.

Reskin, B., & Padavic, I. (1994). *Women and men at work.* Thousand Oaks, CA: Pine Forge Press.

Social Security Administration. (1993, August). *Social Security bulletin annual statistical supplement, 1993.* Washington, DC: U.S. Department of Health and Human Services.

Starer, D. (1995). *Hot topics: Everything you wanted to know about the fifty major controversies everyone pretends to know about.* New York: Simon & Schuster.

St. George, D. (1995, March 19). Analysts: Affirmative action helps white women. *Corpus Christi Caller Times,* p. A8.

Sullivan, M. (1997, September 15). The powerful force of a mother's influence. University of Southern California Chronicle. [Online]. Available: http://uscnews.usc.edu/detail.php?recordnum=2991

Tjaden, P., & Thoennes, N. (1998, November). Prevalence, incidence, and consequences of violence against women: Findings from the National Violence Against Women Survey. *Research in brief.* Washington, DC: National Institute of Justice, U.S. Department of Justice.

U.S. Bureau of Labor Statistics. (1994). [No title]. Washington, DC: Government Printing Office.

U.S. Census Bureau. (1999). *USA statistics in brief.* Washington, DC: Government Printing Office.

U.S. Department of Justice. (1996). *Uniform crime reports for the U.S.* Washington, DC: Government Printing Office.

The wage gap. (1996, March–April). *Ms.*, pp. 36–37.

Winters, K. I. (1998). Violence against women. In Boston Women's Health Book Collective (Eds.), *Our bodies, ourselves* (pp. 158–178). New York: Simon & Schuster.

THERE'S A RAINBOW IN THE CLOSET[1]

On the Importance of Developing a Common Language for "Sex" and "Gender"

Linda A. M. Perry
UNIVERSITY OF SAN DIEGO

Deborah Ballard-Reisch
UNIVERSITY OF NEVADA, RENO

It is easy to think we know what the words sex *and* gender *mean. After all, they are used daily in many different contexts. If we think about the words a little more deeply, and consider the opinions of various writers, then we could accept the assertion that* sex *generally refers to one's biological sex and* gender *refers to a socially constructed manner of behaving and communicating. But is that all there is? In this provocative essay, Linda Perry and Deborah Ballard-Reisch suggest otherwise. As we consider the combination of biological sex, socially constructed gender, and sexual orientation, the words suddenly become less clear in their meaning. Perry and Ballard-Reisch ask the reader to consider the implications and ramifications of particular definitions on both the person using the word and the person being defined by the word. Language is a powerful tool and, in the context discussed here, presents issues that can benefit from probing discussion. You may not look at the words in the same way again.*

QUESTIONS FOR DISCUSSION

- *What would be the effect on society if there were more than two genders?*
- *How do definitions guide (even govern) our perception of something or someone?*
- *What does* sexual orientation *mean to you? Is your definition the same or different from your classmates'?*

Reprinted with permission.
[1]The *closet* refers to a figurative place wherein persons who have not publicly revealed their sexual and/or gender identities reside.

- *If someone says, "Well, that is just the way they are," is that true, or is it just the way we define them?*
- *Is it possible to change definitions of people and groups of people? How?*

INTRODUCTION

During your first days of Sex and Gender class, you learned "appropriate" terminology for the topics you were about to discuss. You learned that *sex* refers to biology; one is either female or male. However, as the course progresses, you learn that some people are born with no definite biological sex organs, and others are born with both. *Gender*, on the other hand, refers to how one is socialized to behave in relation to one's sex. For example, young females are taught to be feminine, and males are trained to be masculine. Later in the course, as the definitions become more refined, it is noted that some people are *cross-gendered;* that is, a female may have a masculine gender, or a male may possess a feminine one. In addition, it is learned that cross-gendered people may or may not be gay or lesbian. It is at this point that some students become uncomfortable or begin to discuss the discomfort of their friends and/or family members when confronted with issues of sex, gender, and sexual orientation (a term describing to which sex one is attracted). (Note: Please pay special attention to our footnotes as many distinctions, definitions, and explanations important to following our discussion appear in them.)

Many of you have witnessed discrimination against and anger toward people based on their sex, gender, and/or sexual orientation. It is often the fear of the unknown that creates and escalates these negative feelings and attitudes. We believe the inadequacy of our language to define varying aspects of sex and gender limits society's acceptance of those who deviate from normative sex role expectations. We argue in this article that the first step in working against discrimination is learning appropriate terminology for sex and gender concepts. The second step is to make these definitions part of our day-to-day language in use. Hopefully, these actions will begin to make the

The authors wish to thank a number of people for their feedback while we developed this article. First, we thank Dr. Sandra Ketrow at the University of Rhode Island, who provided us with a lot of clarity for discussing the included terminology. Next, we thank students enrolled in Dr. Judy Liu's Spring 2001 capstone Gender Studies course at the University of San Diego for their thorough reading, reflection, and feedback on an earlier draft. We thank Dr. Paul Devereux and Ms. Melanie Menarik, faculty members in the Department of Health Ecology at the University of Nevada, Reno, for their assistance in helping us tease out our ideas on difference as deviance and the role of language in changing social reality. We thank Bob Reisch for providing feedback for the final touches of this paper. And, finally, we thank participants in a workshop during the 2001 Annual Meeting of the Organization for the Study of Communication, Language, and Gender for their interest and critique of our ideas on developing a more inclusive sex and gender language.

unknown known and ease fears of, anger toward, and discrimination against people who do not fit the feminine-female and masculine-male heterosexual mandate.[2]

We further argue that these prejudices can result in negative actions, including anything from being humiliated to becoming victims of hate crimes. We base this belief on the premise that language determines what can be perceived and understood. The broader the language available, the better the chance for shared understanding. Unfortunately, the day-to-day language concerning sex and gender (especially in relation to those who do not live up to the heterosexual mandate) is primarily negative and results in evaluations of people such that being different is virtually the same as being deviant. Certainly, there are many factors that play into prejudices. However, if we focus for a moment on how language is used in cases of discrimination, we can see that people have a tendency to fear the unknown, and that for which there is no common language remains unknown.

We are not attempting to argue that the limited and often negative language about sex, gender, and sexual orientation is the only, or even the most significant, problem. Rather, our hope is to begin a conversation about the limitations of this language so we can minimize and perhaps even someday eradicate misunderstandings and fears. To do this, first we present a brief overview of the early development of sex and gender terminology. Second, we discuss three stories that exemplify situations in which the lack of a common sex and gender language proves to be problematic. Next, we provide definitions of sex and gender terminology and clarify some sexual orientation terms. Again, this is a beginning point for an evolving conversation about the language and not a definitive "dictionary" concerning it. Fourth, we discuss the development of a new term to expand our sex and gender vocabulary. Finally, we draw some conclusions as to what the development of a socially accepted language for sex and gender could mean.

THE EARLY DEVELOPMENT OF SEX AND GENDER TERMINOLOGY

Prior to the 1970s, femininity and masculinity were viewed as polar opposites and defined as the appropriate sex roles for females and males, respectively. The more females and males exhibited behaviors "appropriate" for their biological sex, the greater their social acceptance. In other words, people were expected to live up to their assigned sex roles in order to be accepted in society. Therefore, female and feminine

---

[2]The *heterosexual mandate* refers to social pressures on people to act as though their sexual orientation is toward the other primary sex. Those not adhering to this mandate are thought to be either deviant or psychologically ill. Fear of these evaluations and the possibility of scorn, ridicule, and loss of friends and family help control nonheterosexual people, especially in social contexts. Thus, they adhere to the heterosexual mandate and hide their true identities in sexual orientation closets.

were at one end of the sex role continuum, and male and masculine were at the other. The more feminine one was (as demonstrated by the X on the continuum below), the less masculine she could be, and vice versa.

Sex Roles and Gender Identities Continuum

Feminine/Females ——X——————————————————— Masculine/Males

In the 1970s, a major evolution in the sex role paradigm redefined femininity and masculinity as gender constructs separate from biological sex. Femininity and masculinity shifted away from being defined as biologically determined toward being understood as socially acquired gender identities.[3] This allowed for the possibility that individuals could vary in terms of the extent to which they internalized social sex roles as part of their self-identities. Thus, people could have gender identities different from those previously mandated for their biological sex. These alterations in the way we saw sex and gender demonstrated that the term *sex roles* had limited applicability while *gender identities* could be socially, as well as individually, shaped. A female could have a masculine gender identity, a male could have a feminine gender identity, and either could have aspects of androgyny (having feminine and masculine aspects) or be undifferentiated (neither masculine nor feminine).[4] The extent to which one is feminine or masculine can vary in intensity as well. These distinctions are represented in the following matrix, based on the research of Sandra Bem:

Gender Identities Matrix

Feminine	Androgynous ♀
Undifferentiated	Masculine

The shift in terminology away from sex roles to gender identity has, in part, allowed for a more open understanding of a variety of potential sexual identities and

[3]Although gender is believed to be a socially determined construct, it could someday be found to be connected to biological propensities, at least to some extent. Until genetic science proves otherwise, however, we will accept gender to be socially constructed.

[4]The category *undifferentiated* is a statistical category based on participant scores falling below the median on both the feminine and masculine subscales of the Bem Sex Role Inventory. It is not a theoretically or conceptually defined category. This makes its usefulness in a discussion of sex roles and gender identities questionable. However, it does allow for the possibility that something beyond traditional feminine and masculine categories may exist, a possibility important to the emergence of a more inclusive language.

self-presentations for women and men. For example, the female depicted by ♀ in the above matrix may exhibit both masculine and feminine behaviors. Her gender identity would be androgynous, but leaning more toward masculine than feminine attitudes and behaviors based on where her symbol rests on the matrix. She most likely is a reasonably socially sensitive person who demonstrates feminine aspects when the situations calls for it and masculine aspects as the situation demands. One's sex (male or female) and gender identity (masculine, feminine, androgynous, or undifferentiated) are all a matter of degree. They are overlapping and interacting aspects of one's being but are not an indication of one's sexual orientation.

The concept of gender identities has helped individuals who did not neatly fit the sex role stereotypes of masculine-male or feminine-female to gain a "voice." Unfortunately, society continues to use the words *sex* and *gender* interchangeably such that the benefits of the distinctions are all but lost. It is the duty of those of us who understand the distinctions between these terms and the implications of their use to include them in our everyday conversations, use them appropriately, and help others understand the importance of doing the same.

The following stories illustrate that another evolution in our language about sex and gender is needed if we are to better understand the complexities of both. More important, these stories illustrate the difficulties faced by persons not fitting the sex and gender mainstream, a group with little or no voice until an agreed-upon representative terminology evolves and is incorporated into our day-to-day communication.

THREE STORIES OF SEX AND GENDER DISCRIMINATION

Story #1: A Man Named David

Dr. Perry invited David, a researcher who had published on the topic of developing a language for discussing issues of sex and gender, to speak with her undergraduate Introduction to Gender Studies class. During his presentation, he self-disclosed that although he was dressed in men's pants and a shirt at the time, he is a cross-dresser. He also defined himself as being a heterosexual. Dr. Perry observed the students struggling with David's self-identity. She was puzzled by their responses because they had not had this much discomfort accepting an earlier speaker who was a gay man. The students rudely told David there was something wrong with him or that he was in denial about being gay, even though they knew he had been married, had a son, and defined himself as heterosexual. In their opinions, if he was a cross-dresser, then he had to be gay.

Dr. Perry apologized to David for the hostile interactions he received from students. He responded that it was not unusual. He explained that he had been verbally harassed and physically abused by people in both the straight and gay communities[5] for being a heterosexual cross-dresser. He believed that, in part, the reason for his being socially unacceptable and for being the recipient of abuse was based on two factors. First, his self-identity as a heterosexual cross-dresser did not match the gay cross-dresser stereotype with which people are more familiar and therefore (a bit) more tolerant. Second, there is no inclusive sex and gender language that would help people such as himself be part of society's mainstream. His interest in researching and developing a more inclusive language came from his background as a professor of linguistics and his own personal experiences as the target of discrimination.

In what ways do you believe David's story is related to language-in-use? What is the possible reason that students would have accepted David's being a gay cross-dresser but not a straight one? We have long been fascinated by how our language can both limit and expand our perceptions and, therefore, our realities. But learning of David's experiences opened our eyes to the realization that a lack of an inclusive and descriptive common language has real-life consequences for those whom our language does not include. The more we know about sex and gender distinctions, the better prepared we are to accept them. There are countless people hiding in all kinds of "closets" in fear of others' knowing who they "really" are. The more we learn about (have a language for) the diversity of those who are cross-dressers (as one example of diversity), the more accepting we can become of that choice. Thus, we pose the question: Can we nurture sexual and gender differences and diversity unless we have a common language with which to describe and share our perspectives and realities?

Story #2: A Transvestite's Dilemma

A while later, Dr. Perry attended a National Gay and Lesbian Task Force (NGLTF) meeting whose main objective was to discuss and develop a plan for more political visibility. One panel she attended was oriented toward the objective of developing political strategies for the "gay agenda." At that time, the agenda was, at the very least, to have more "family" members politically active and accepted.[6] This agenda (based on the dress, actions, and speeches of the panel members) seemed to include that the selected representatives should look and behave as heterosexual as possible (whatever that means) to gain acceptance.

Once the speakers finished making their presentations, the discussion was opened to the audience for comment and advice. More of the same was reiterated, and everyone agreed on the strategies to one degree or another. Then, larger than

---

[5] *Straight* is a term referring to persons with a heterosexual sexual orientation. *Gay community* refers to the lesbian, gay, bisexual, transsexual, transgendered, and questioning (LGBTTQ) community in general. (Each of these terms will be defined in the next section of this article.)
[6] The term *"family"* (in quotes) refers to LGBTTQ people as a group. Its usage is one way for members of the LGBTTQ "family" to self-identify and create a sense of community.

life, stood a person dressed right out of a 1930s movie about a Southern belle at a formal tea. Her wide-brimmed hat was tilted just over her right eye, but the length of her lashes as they flashed up and down when she spoke still could be seen. The fitted and slightly revealing dress that matched the ribbed brim of the hat fell softly to her ankles, and her coordinating shoes and purse were to die for. But even as she stood, the man with the microphone ignored her presence and called on others for their opinions. Finally, in a gentle but firm voice, she interrupted the speakers. She raised her elbow-length-glove-covered arm, with wrist turned upward and finger pointing and spoke:

"Here we go again, let's pretend we all look straight; let's send to the fore only those who will not offend those delicate senses of our hetero brothers and sisters. I am sick and tired of being shoved back into the closet every time we have an opportunity to show our diversity. The queers, the fags, the transvestites, the cross-dressers, we have never been represented, we have never been included, and yet, without us, Stonewall never would have happened.[7] When will your agenda be our agenda? When will we stand together? When will we be heard as one? How can we expect to be accepted in the world when we are not accepted here, when even *we* won't accept our differences?"

Dr. Perry watched as the panel members at the head of the room squirmed in their seats. This one eloquent speaker made (at least) two important issues emerge. One is a community's propensity to silence, or at least limit, the "voices" of those who are considered to be different and therefore potentially deviant. This is surprisingly evident even in a community as diverse as the lesbian, gay, bisexual, transsexual, transgendered, and questioning (LGBTTQ) "family." The speaker's plea for recognition and acknowledgment is obviously an issue in the broader culture as well. What are the implications of silencing differences in a diverse community? In the culture at large? In what ways would a broader culturally accepted language-in-use facilitate or limit human understanding?

The second issue concerns this speaker's language choices, which are impossible to ignore. What does your mind's eye conjure up when you hear words like *queer, fag, transvestite, cross-dressers*? Do you think such words have the same meaning for heterosexuals as they do for members of the LGBTTQ "family"? If not, what difference will it make when you interact with someone who may be the same sex as you, but with a different gender identity? A different sexual orientation? A combination of both? Do you think there is a relationship between a culture's ability to discuss and include sex and gender diversity (i.e., have a common language about diverse peoples) and the instances of discrimination, prejudices, and hate crimes?

---

[7] *Stonewall* refers to a riot that occurred in New York City in 1969 at a bar by that name. The Stonewall bar had been specifically targeted by police, was continually raided, and its customers harassed, arrested, and often beaten. The Stonewall Riot was the first public stand against police brutality made by gays as a group, and by transvestites, specifically. To many, this marked the beginning of the Gay Rights Movement.

Story #3: A Masculine Lesbian Becomes a Heterosexual Man

At a Pride Rally,[8] one of the many speakers told of how he is constantly harassed. He explained that he had had a biological sex change (from female to male) but had not changed his gender identity (which had always been masculine) nor his sexual orientation (he had always been attracted to women). Unfortunately, regardless of his sex and gender, he was accepted in neither the gay nor straight worlds. This speaker has spent a lifetime trying to explain his sexual and gender identities. When he was a female, he did not feel he fit into society because his self-identity was that of a masculine male. After his sex change, he did not fit in because his friends and family would not accept the physical changes he had gone through to externally exhibit who he was "inside." He spent a lifetime of being emotionally and physically battered for not fitting outdated sex role expectations. Still, he persists in being "out" about his sexual and gender identities. It is his belief that the more "out" people are, the more society will recognize how large is the number of people who do not fit the heterosexual mandate.

Unless we can agree upon and actively incorporate a broader language for issues of sex and gender, thousands like this man will continue to be subjected to verbal taunting, harassment, and even physical violence. The language shifts that occurred in the 1970s with the reconceptualization of sex role categories away from the heterosexual feminine-female and masculine-male dichotomy has enabled us to linguistically acknowledge a more diverse range of individuals. For example, we are now more accepting of males with feminine genders. A nurturing, gentle man no longer is necessarily considered weak. A masculine female now can be valued for her emotional determination or abilities to withstand physical labor alongside her male colleagues. Clearly, Western culture has come a long way in accepting gender diversity, especially for heterosexuals. But there still is a long way to go before each of us is accepted for who we are as sexual and gendered beings. The progress that has been made has helped some members of the LGBTTQ community claim their "voices" in personal relationships and public arenas. Some of that progress is the result of the creation, acceptance, and adoption of a broader sex and gender language. In turn, more of the public has a heightened awareness regarding sex and gender diversity issues.

Still, there are continued acts of violence, including hate crimes, toward people of gender and sexual diversity. Thus, we have a long way to go, but the journey has

---

[8]*Pride Rallies* are weekend-long festivities in which diversity is celebrated through political speeches, parades, and festivals held in most major cities. People in the LGBTTQ community have traditionally been made to feel ashamed of their gender identities and/or their sexual orientations. Being "in the closet," along with the fear of physical, social, and/or emotional abuse that would come with being "out" (public about who one "really" is), was a response to this shame. By being proud of who one is (thus, Pride Rallies), members of the LGBTTQ "family" believe more people will be willing to "come out of the closet" and be accepted for who they are. (For additional information, do a computer search using the keyword "Gay Pride.")

begun, facilitated by a more inclusive language. For every person who voices a public definition of self that defies simple categorization, there are hundreds still locked in socially restricted "closets." In those closets, a rainbow of diverse individuals exists for whom we do not have a common language. Today, there are limited positive terms with which to discuss the closet's membership, a language its members could use to shift the present social paradigm to recreate a mainstream culture that embraces sex and gender diversity. It is up to us to further advance the extant sex and gender language as part of our day-to-day language-in-use. It also is a time to begin to create new terms that will allow for a public discussion of this particular form of diversity and the prejudices against it.

AGREEING ON SOME SEX AND GENDER TERMINOLOGY

Three themes emerge through the above stories. The first theme is *the current terminology and language-in-use about sex and gender is overwhelmingly inadequate.* A common language is more than relevant and helpful; it is necessary. For example, in reflecting on the first story, it is clear the students were ill prepared to manage the complexities of the male heterosexual cross-dresser. They were, however, able to understand and accept the gay. Prior to the language evolution concerning sex and gender identities in the 1970s, this acceptance likely would not have been the case.

The second theme is *hostility faced by individuals who do not fit socially prescribed norms plays out in many ways.* Each of the people discussed in the previous stories had been the recipient of taunting, ridicule, prejudice, discrimination, and physical violence. When people do not fit familiar sex and gender categories, others feel uncomfortable, which can lead to negative appraisals of and discrimination against the individual. We believe that by remedying the inadequacy of language, some of this hostility toward diverse individuals can be weakened and, hopefully, be alleviated.

The third theme emerging from these stories is *there are inadequacies in our assumptions concerning the relationship between one's self-identify and the social roles one plays.* When sex roles are expected to be internalized into one's self-identity, and are implicitly linked with perceptions of sexual orientation, we are assuming connections or relationships that may or may not exist. How one sees oneself, how one feels oneself to be, may or may not relate to social constructions of what one "should" be. One's self-identity may not even relate to how one behaves in the social world. We already know this to be true with respect to one's sexual orientation. For example, many members of the LGBTTQ family present themselves to be heterosexual in order to gain social acceptance and avoid varying levels of discrimination; that is, they are "in the closet." Separating self-image from outdated notions of sex role socialization may be the first step in creating and adopting an inclusive language capable of reflecting the personal, social, and political complexities of sex and gender diversity.

Present-day language regarding sex and gender to some extent does allow us to discuss the individuals in our three stories. However, rather than demonstrating the three-pronged approach to these issues in current sex and gender language (sex, gender, and sexual orientation), each person's self-presentation seems to exemplify a variety of possible constructs with significantly greater potential complexity. But our language about sex and gender is so limited we can hardly discuss its limitations. This presents a linguistic paradox: In order to develop a common language, we need a common language. As with most attempts to break out of paradoxical situations, first one has to realize she is in it. In this instance of paradox recognition, we plan to transcend that limitation, encourage others to participate in the critique of our suggestions, and allow the language to unfold in an ongoing conversation. Again, we are not attempting to offer a definitive dictionary of sex and gender terms but to present a place for a conversation concerning them to begin.[9] We will do this by first suggesting definitions of basic sex and gender terminology and then progressing to clarifying sexual orientation terms.

Basic Sex and Gender Terminology

Sex: Physiology based on chromosomes, hormones, and external and internal reproductive organs with which we are born; typically, but not necessarily, female or male. This construct is so prevalent in society that the first question asked upon the birth of a child is usually "Is it a boy or a girl?"[10]

Sex Preference: Preferring to be one or the other of the two primary sexes.[11] Regardless of which set of sex organs one is born with, one may feel more closely identified with the biological aspects of the other primary sex. The drive to have one's sex organs and one's internal feelings about them match can be so strong, a person may choose to transform biologically to the other primary sex through sex-change surgery and hormone therapy. The drive on the part of Western society to fit individuals into one or the other primary biological sex categories is strong. For example, a child born with ambiguous sex organs, has traditionally been "assigned" a

---

[9] In other words, you may or may not agree with our definitions and/or clarifications. Make a list of your own to share with your class members. This should stimulate a healthy classroom discussion of your personal interpretations.

[10] It is important to note that this biological duality is not accepted in all cultures. Certain Native American tribes, for example, identify three and some four biological sexes.

[11] We use the term *other primary sex* instead of *opposite sex* to remind our readers there are more than two biological sexes and, at the same time, *female* and *male* are the two primary sexes in Western culture.

sex by parents and doctors and then given surgery to make him or her biologically female or male. Unfortunately, this occurs before it is known what the child's sex preference will be and can lead to a confused and devastating life for the child. (Note: *Sex preference* should not be confused with *sexual preference* as defined below.)

Sex Roles: An outdated social mandate claiming that females should enact feminine behaviors and males should enact masculine behaviors because of biological necessity and societal need. Strongly adhering to a belief that this social mandate is based on "nature" feeds into a lack of acceptance of sex and gender diversity.

Sex Role Performance: The social performance of self as one primary sex with a particular gender identity directly related to that sex. The problem with sex roles is that society expects people to fulfill them in a particular way. Males are supposed to perform masculine behaviors, and females are expected to perform feminine behaviors. As in a play, roles are to be enacted as written, and, in the case of sex roles, there are consequences for those people unwilling or unable to enact them. The extent to which an individual perfects his or her performance of sex roles is linked to social acceptance.

Sexual Preference: The biological sex of the person to whom one is sexually attracted. Sexual preference is directly related to sexual orientation (see below); that is, one's preference is determined by one's sexual orientation. Sexual preference does not necessarily reflect with whom one engages in sexual behavior, however. To adhere to outdated ideas concerning sex roles, one may be in the "closet" to gain social acceptance by meeting the heterosexual mandate. For example, a woman who self-identifies as a lesbian may be married to a man to fit society's expectations but still have a sexual preference for women. Within the LGBTTQ "family," many believe the only sexual orientation that includes sexual preference is bisexuality.

Sexual Orientation: A variety of sexual attractions including diverse ways of being, such as being heterosexual, gay, lesbian, bisexual, transgendered, asexual, and/or unisexual. For many, the term *sexual orientation* indicates that to whom one is sexually attracted is biologically determined. From this perspective, the notion of "sexual preference" is a misnomer because it implies one has a choice regarding to whom she or he is sexually attracted. Many members of the LGBTTQ "family" note that their sexuality is not based on choice but on biology, or how they were born. Thus, the term *sexual orientation* is both personally and politically preferred to *sexual preference*. The only exception to this is in the case of bisexuality, as noted above.

Sexual Identity: One aspect of a self-identity, based upon a combination of one's biological sex, sex preference, and sexual orientation. This is only one aspect of one's self-identity and public performance. Another aspect of this is gender identity.

Gender Identity: One aspect of a self-identity, based on the extent to which one sees oneself as embodying masculine, feminine, or androgynous behaviors, which may or may not be in line with social sex role expectations. As such, a person, regardless of her/his biological sex, may have any one of these gender identities and perhaps others yet to be identified. While one may embody one gender identity, she may publicly enact it or an alternative gender identity. This is only one aspect of one's self-identity and public performance. Another aspect of this is one's sexual identity.

There exist, in addition to the above terminology, many diverse gender identities and sexual orientations for which no terms have been developed. One limitation to developing a positive and rich language to discuss sex and gender is a social paradigm that creates great pressure on individuals to maintain the comfort level of the status quo. The status quo in Western culture is that of heterosexual people with "appropriate" sex role identities. Anyone whose sexual or gender identity deviates from the status quo is automatically considered "unnatural." This mandate is powerfully strong, so much so that many people strive to enact heterosexual behaviors with aligned sex roles regardless of their sexual and gender identities and their sexual orientation. It is estimated that between 10% and 16% of all citizens of the United States belong to the LGBTTQ "family," but an accurate count will not be possible until people no longer fear the consequences of being "out," of defying the heterosexual mandate.

Western society's social paradigm can be and has been shifted, in part, because of the power of words. Take, for example, the case of African Americans prior to the 1960s. The use of the words "Negro" and "nigger" was, up until that time, a common reference to people of African descent. African Americans knew the power of words and naming, along with the power and the right one must have to self-define. Knowing that others had taken away their power to self-define, they chose to redefine themselves. Terms and slogans such as "Black Americans" and "Black is beautiful" were part of their civil rights movement to instigate change in the social paradigm. Today, most people cannot imagine, and cringe at the thought of, using the "N" word to define Black Americans. And language continues to evolve to be more inclusive of Black Americans who are not of African descent.

Each and every step in the evolution of a descriptive language for people in any stereotyped group helps each person be recognized as an individual with unique attributes.

Language has the power to transform a person's life experiences. If we are viewed through the linguistic lens of a stereotype, we have little control over others' perceptions of us. We have a chance to be understood as unique individuals when there is a broader, more inclusive language to define individuals who happen to be members of a greater collective, such as Black Americans or in the LGBTTQ "family." We have the power to self-define, to "own" words that refer to us, and to actively participate in the making of others' perceptions of us. That, we argue, is the situation that currently exists for individuals in the LGBTTQ community.

One way language can develop for a marginalized group is to reclaim terms that may be negatively used against its members. For example, words such as "queer" are being reclaimed as part of the "family's" civil rights movement. By using the power of self-naming, words such as "queer" or "fag" can be used to empower LGBTTQ individuals. We believe a shift in the extant social paradigm will not occur until a broader and better-known vocabulary is developed in addition to reclaiming terms that have been used negatively by the public at large. Although a shift in the social paradigm may not eliminate all prejudices and hate crimes, it is a place to start, a place from which legal protections and social gains can evolve. With that in mind, we want to broaden our vocabulary a little by offering terminology for differing sexual and gender orientations. As you read these terms and definitions, keep in mind your thoughts about and responses to them. Remember, we do not intend this list to be definitive. We want only to encourage a conversation regarding language reform that will lead to a more comprehensive, inclusive vocabulary.

Sexual Orientation Terminology

Asexuals: Those who are not sexually interested in others. Asexuals may be romantically interested in others, however.

Bisexuals: Females and males with varying degrees of sexual attraction toward their own and the other primary sex. While some bisexuals claim a simultaneous attraction to both primary sexes, others claim alternating attraction to people of their own sex over distinct periods of time and to people of the other primary sex over separate distinct periods of time. This attraction does not necessarily mean having sexual intercourse but simply being sexually oriented toward people of either primary sex. Bisexual people can be virgins or be celibate.

Gays: A term referring to the LGBTTQ community in general. Aside from a word to define this community, it is a key political term in the Gay Rights Movement. The word *gay* began as a self-referent for people in the LGBTTQ "family" to more easily identify each other in public places where it might be dangerous to reveal one's sexual orientation. For example, a lesbian at a public gathering might ask another woman if she was "gay" to uncover her sexual orientation. If the woman responded she was very happy, the chances were she was "straight." This term in modern usage has lost the power of anonymity. Even though its usage has changed, it still has power as a self-defining term and one that has made its way into our language-in-use. Self-naming is a starting place toward personal and political power. The word *gay* is one such example.

Gay Males: Males sexually attracted to males, but not necessarily having sexual intercourse with other males. Gay men can be virgins or celibate.

Lesbians: Females sexually attracted to females, but not necessarily having sexual intercourse with other females. Lesbians can be virgins or celibate.

Questioning: One who may feel uncomfortable self-defining according to any of the available sex and gender categories. Typically, it is someone unsure of his or her sexual orientation. This category is in need of an expanded sex and gender vocabulary. That is, there may not be an existing label for the sex and gender identities of some who are questioning.

Straight: A term referring to heterosexual people whose behaviors are thought to mirror socially prescribed sex roles. As acceptance of broader gender identities occurs, so will the "allowable" behaviors for straight people. This has and will occur over time. For example, today we are accepting of nurturing males and are less likely to question their sexual orientations and "manhood." It was not all that long ago that males in Western cultures were ridiculed if they exhibited this feminine attribute.

Transsexual: One born with one set of primary sex organs and having a sex preference to have the biology of the other primary sex. One can so strongly identify with the other primary sex's biology, she or he may elect to have sex-change surgeries along with hormone and psychological therapies. Being transsexual may or may not be tied to a person's sexual orientation. A transsexual person may, in fact, be sexually attracted to the other primary sex along with a desire to be of that sex. An example might be a transsexual man sexually attracted to women who goes through sex change therapy. She then would be considered to be a lesbian.

Transgendered: Sexual or gender identities that do not fit into other sex and gender descriptive categories are reasonably well accepted here. Technically, it translates to "a person whose gender identity is more closely associated with the other primary gender—for example, a masculine-female or feminine-male." However, we might think of this term like a foreign phrase that loses or gains something in the translation. So, while that basic definition holds true, this category also includes more diverse, and perhaps presently unnamed, sexual identities, gender identities, and sexual orientations. Transgender, in fact, is referred to as the "grocery bag" category in sex and gender terminology. This is an area in need of a developing vocabulary.

Transvestite: A female or male who dons the dress and adopts exaggerated gender-identified behaviors of the other primary sex. An example would be a man wearing a woman's clothes, makeup, and hairstyle while behaving in an exaggerated feminine manner. Transvestites are stereotyped as gay males with exaggerated feminine behaviors when in "drag" (cross-dressed). All transvestites, however, are not gay males or lesbians. The primary distinction we make between being a transvestite and being a cross-dresser is that transvestites take on the behavioral characteristics of the other primary sex's sexual and gender identities (an exaggerated sex role performance). Cross-dressers, on the other hand, maintain a closer alignment to the sex role identity of their biological sex (masculine-male or feminine-female). All of these enactments and performances are a matter of degree.

Unisexual: One sexually attracted only to oneself.

DEVELOPING A NEW VOCABULARY

To date there has been no term that encompasses the dynamic interplay of a person's sexual identity, sex preference (*not* sexual preference), sexual orientation, and gender identity. Dr. Perry has coined the term *gendex* to represent this dynamic interplay. *Gendex* is derived from combining the words *gender* and *sex* and can refer to this interplay in both social and personal contexts. A social gendex consists of the aspects of one's sex and gender identities that he or she publicly enacts. A personal gendex includes aspects of one's sex and gender identities that become more evident in private when not pressed to conform to social mandates for ways of being. For a variety of personal, social, contextual, and/or relational reasons, an individual may choose to vary the extent to which she portrays to the public what she sees as her "authentic self," or personal gendex. Just as our self-perceptions may differ from situation to situation, so can our public portrayal of these perceptions. Thus, one person may have countless sex and gender selections from which to choose. The result may be a public presentation of self not easily accounted for by simply combining sex and gender factors. Human behavior is very complex, so much so that one may or may not be conscious of her or his "authentic" social and/or personal gendexes.

In general systems theory, the term *wholeness* indicates there is an "emergent quality" that results from the interaction of people or things—that the whole is greater than the sum of the parts. In the present case, that emergent quality is one's gendex. We believe this new term works toward capturing the emergent quality that results from the interaction of sex and gender factors. As such, one may assess the extent to which one's self-identity converges or diverges from social expectations for sex role performance. Choice of what to portray can be affected by one's desire to avoid negative reactions, to encourage positive reactions, to behave in opposition to what is expected, and so forth. A person can then choose to portray all or a fraction of her or his gendex in any given situation in order to both meet public demands and maintain private dignity. Thus, the term *gendex* helps clarify the available freedom people have in portraying their sex and gender identities in public versus private contexts.

In short, the social gendex one chooses to present is as complex as the variety of self-portrayals possible. It is clear we all play a variety of roles in diverse situations. Gendex is simply an illustration of this phenomenon as it relates to sex and gender identities, including sexual orientation. One of the goals of this paper is to sensitize readers to the following perspective: People have a right to self-define their sexual and gender identities and to be accepted for the public and self-portrayals they select. The term *gendex* is inclusive of that self-definition and is a step in the direction of creating a broader language about sex and gender diversity.

CONCLUSION

Now let's look back to some of our stories to briefly discuss each participant's possible gendex. David, in the first story, is a heterosexual cross-dresser. He dons the dress and adornments of a female and is not a gay. He cannot be considered to be transsexual because he is not interested in being a female. His claimed gender identity is masculine (stated by him) but he can be considered to be transgendered because of the complexity of his gendex. Can he, however, also be considered to be straight?

In the second story, our "Southern belle's" gendex includes being a transvestite because she is a man dressed as a woman (a cross-dresser) performing exaggerated feminine behaviors. Based on her attire and behaviors, can we assume she is a transsexual?[12] Did you make an assumption about her sexual orientation? Without more information from her, we cannot be sure about the answer to any of these questions concerning her gendex.

The Pride Rally speaker in the third story was born a biological female, had a masculine gender identity, and was a lesbian transsexual prior to sex-change therapy. After the sex change, he became a biological male who continued to have a masculine gender identity and continued to be sexually interested in women. Could he now be considered to have the sexual orientation of a straight male? In his speech, he defined himself as transgendered because he was not born a biological male nor heterosexual, and is no longer transsexual. Remember, *transgendered* is the "grocery bag" label for people whose sexuality does not neatly fit into other categories, which this man's sexuality does not. Still, transsexual persons each have independent beliefs about what labels they claim after sex-change surgery. Some maintain the identity of being a transsexual, others as being transgendered, and still others see themselves as no longer members of the gay community and choose to be considered straight. Using our new terminology, we can say each person has the right to self-define his or her personal and social gendexes.

---

[12]Transvestites typically prefer that pronouns referring to them match the sex they are performing (in this case, female).

There are a number of things we believe about sex and gender. First, we believe our current sex and gender language-in-use is limited because it does not allow for diversity. Second, we believe this lack of a common language leads to hostility on the part of those who do not understand, who do not have a comfortable conceptual framework within which to work, and whose expectations are violated by public displays of gendexes outside the heterosexual mandate. Finally, we believe the limited and mostly negative language we currently have silences those who diverge from the socially constructed and accepted conceptualizations of sex and gender.

Existing language does not represent the reality that biological sex comes in more forms than female and male, gender identities are not neatly ascribed to one's biological sex, and sexual orientation does not fit snugly into "I like men, I like women, I like both, I like neither" choices. Nor does this language account for the incredible potential complexity of relationships among these concepts. Evolving language, such as our new term *gendex,* may. It is socially and politically important to embrace new language forms as they develop because evolved terms can work against biases and discrimination. Once we adopt a term, we are more likely to understand that for which it stands, and the unknown becomes the known. As mentioned at the onset of our paper, the unknown is often feared and hated. By creating a new language and expanding existing terminology, we might transcend the linguistic paradox of needing a common language to create one that otherwise prolongs the silencing of those who do not fit into familiar sex and gender constructions.

In addition to refined definitions, the notion of choice in the portrayal of one's gendex further unpacks the relationships among sexual and gender identities, including sexual orientation. By expanding our language to be more inclusive of sex and gender diversity, we allow for a broadening of our conceptual understanding of the relationship between who we are (our self-perceptions) and how we behave. Realizing that personal, social, and contextual factors affect how we see ourselves and the behavioral choices we can make allows for more fluid self-perceptions and more diverse self-presentations. This fluidity may be more appropriate in facilitating understanding of sex and gender diversity and more accurate in reflecting personal realities.

All of the individuals in the three stories we presented have experienced hate crimes. All have been violently beaten at various times throughout their lives for attempting to display their personal gendexes in public arenas. Rather than meeting the socially prescribed heterosexual mandate to at least act as though one is straight, each made a stand to advance future acceptance of sex and gender diversity. Thus, there is far more at risk when attempting to make sex and gender language distinctions. There are concerns for individuals' rights to be themselves, to move about freely, and to be assured some level of personal safety.

One way to begin to change the present social paradigm, with its heterosexual mandate, is through communication and awareness. We believe we can do this by sharing a common vocabulary, creating new terminology, and advancing this language into our day-to-day language-in-use. Once that is done, converging and diverging combinations of biological sex, sex preference, sexual identities, gender identities, and sexual orientations will become more socially acceptable. Until then, "closeted" people and society both lose. The "closet" remains filled with a rainbow of diverse people who struggle for self-definition, social acceptance, and personal safety. And society deprives itself of countless talents and contributions this rainbow of closeted people could offer if their spirits were free to shine.

WHAT I LEARNED AS A STUDENT IN GENDER COMMUNICATION

Four Brief Papers by Students in Our Courses

Students take a course such as Gender Communication for a variety of reasons and motivations. We have found most of our students in gender communication courses to be more highly motivated than the average student. Many students are looking for something—to fall in love, to change society, a public forum for their views, and sometimes, personal development. We asked some of our students to write brief essays describing their reasons for taking the course and what they gained from the class.

The following four essays represent four very different student approaches to the course. As we offer these essays, we are aware that every class is different, every professor approaches the course in different ways, and that students come with a wide variety of backgrounds. We hope these four essays can act as a springboard for class discussion and individual student consideration of her or his own reasons for taking the class.

QUESTIONS FOR DISCUSSION

- *Do students take a gender communication course for similar or different reasons than they take other courses?*
- *What are the possible reasons for taking the course? Are some reasons better than others?*
- *Should students expect change as a result of this course?*
- *In what ways might a student be different at the end of the course?*

GENDER COMMUNICATION RESPONSE

Stephanie Arington
STUDENT

When I decided to take the gender communication course in the spring of 1999, I was looking forward to learning the essentials of communicating with the opposite sex. I heard about the course through a friend who was a communication major. He told me that there were only a few girls in the class and that I would greatly enjoy the material that was to be covered. I decided to squeeze the class into my schedule, and I am glad I did.

Going into the course, I expected to learn a lot of secrets about why men and women act the way they do. I had my theories, but I wanted to test them out and see if they were correct. I have always been fascinated by relationships in general, and I was looking for ways to improve the relationships I had at the time. I was expecting to learn about why men and women are or are not attracted to certain people. I also desired to learn more about the steps that people take when they are interested in furthering a relationship with a person of the different sex. I was in for a treat because the men outnumbered the women in that class and the majority of them were already my friends. It was interesting to observe their reactions to different topics of conversation.

One of our class discussions revolved around levels of attraction between men and women. The authors of our textbook, *GenderSpeak,* assert that a person will be more attracted to someone who looks like him/her due to emotional security issues. This tendency is not limited to dating relationships, but also affects same-sex and different-sex friendships. For example, if a man were to date a woman whom he considered to be more attractive than he thought himself to be, the man would tend to experience feelings of doubt concerning the relationship. He would eventually become anxious about another man attracting her attention away from him. Conversely, women would experience similar feelings. I was so intrigued by the concept that I began to observe couples around me, as well as reflect upon my previous dating experiences. I now understand why most people are attracted to people who look like them, in friendships as well as romantic relationships.

Along with learning about the attraction between men and women, I learned about relationship development. There are several steps taken when a man or a woman wants to move an existing relationship to the next level. Many tests occur during this time in order to determine whether or not both people are at the same point. The progression of verbal interaction to physical interaction oftentimes signals a longing to redefine a relationship, depending upon the desired outcome. This aspect of the course was interesting to me simply because it allowed me to better understand what is occurring within my relationships. I not only learned about how men and women generally approach relational changes, but I also had the opportunity to determine how I approach relationship development.

Although I do not always deliberately think about the steps involved in relationship development, I am more in tune to my surroundings. This gender awareness has helped me in a variety of ways, both personally and professionally. I have been able to better detect different types of behavior in others that I would never have understood before. I believe that the majority of people, in spite of personality and gender differences, approach interpersonal relationships in a similar way.

The Gender Communication course has been beneficial to me in my dealings with the men and women around me. I have determined that at times, due to gender differences, I must alter my communication tactics in order to relate better to my audience. I believe that my interpersonal skills have improved due to a deeper awareness of gender differences and similarities. I would highly recommend the course to anyone who wants to better relate to the people surrounding him/her.

WHY STUDY GENDER?

Nada Cano
STUDENT

Why study gender communication? Whether you realize it or not, gender communication has affected each day of your life up to this point. In addition, most likely, gender communication will affect each day yet to come. How you communicate with others, dream for your future, and most importantly, what and how you think has everything to do with your perceptions of gender. And, most likely, prior to this course, you've never been encouraged to think much, if at all, about gender communication.

Who you are today has a great deal to do with what your parents, family, friends, teachers, and most importantly, *you* have come to believe and communicate about gender roles. Were there, are there, different standards in your family for women versus men? Were you taught that certain behaviors and activities were permitted based on one's biological sex? What messages have you absorbed from the media about gender roles? These are just a few of the questions that can be answered by studying gender communication.

The study of gender communication helps us reflect on what we have been taught and subsequently incorporated into our self-image. What I discovered in my own journey was that much of how I thought about my world, I did so, if you can imagine such a thing, without even thinking! Simply put: I was a sponge. I was a sponge that absorbed messages such as "girls who wear a lot of makeup are sluts," "guys are just looking for one thing," and "feminists are hairy-legged, bra-burning women who hate men." My studies of gender communication encouraged me to evaluate my beliefs. Today, I confess, without hesitation, that I am a leg-shaving, bra-wearing feminist who wears makeup and understands that much of what I was raised to believe about the opposite biological sex was dramatically inaccurate.

Studying gender communication prompted my examination of the messages I incorporated into my thoughts throughout my life. I learned that gender communication occurs, in fact, everywhere: in family, television ads, popular music, religion, politics, education, employment, culture, and sexuality, just to name a few. By studying gender, I learned to no longer mindlessly absorb the daily barrage of gendered messages; today, I recognize them, evaluate them, and choose whether or not to ingest them. I am now a wiser gender communication consumer and healthier for it.

Another area in which gender communication is prevalent is in romantic relationships. Have you thought about what your ideas are regarding what women should do with their birth name (so-called "maiden" name) when they marry? What do you think you would do? If, or when, you marry, do you intend to take the last name of your wife- or husband-to-be? Men, are you willing to give up your birth name and assume your wife's birth name as your own? Women, will you choose to keep your birth name? How will you and your partner talk about sex? When referring to body parts, do you choose to use technical language versus slang, such as saying "When your penis . . ." as opposed to saying "When your thingy . . ." Again, these are truly gender communication issues to be explored.

The most profound way in which gender studies have impacted my life may be yet to come in your future as you approach the prospect of parenting. I am humbled daily at my responsibility as a parent, and I am convinced that my study of gender communication has made me a better one. From the PTSA meetings to the teacher conferences to promoting my daughters' academic and athletic opportunities, I, more than ever, am convinced that others' gender perceptions and communications also consistently impact my children. There was the time the female middle school administrator publicly professed her jealousy of my oldest daughter's "perky breasts" and how my daughter's large breasts could "get her a reputation with the boys." How would you have handled that situation? There have been countless times that my daughter and members of her team have been told to quit playing soccer "like a girl." Would you ever say that? Then, there was the time at a parent night that a male science teacher professed that 6th-grade boys excelled at performing experiments, while my daughter and the other girls in the class should enjoy creating the project posters and writing the reports. To my then 10-year-old daughter's credit (she had been a previous Science Fair winner), when she heard the teacher make this claim, she quietly turned her head to look at me and rolled her eyes in disgust. I knew then that she was well on her way to being a wiser gender communication consumer. What concerned me most about the event was the volumes of parents and students in the room who did not register the implications of this teacher's statement. Have each of these incidents ruined my children's lives? I think not. However, consistent gendered messages do have an impact, and depending on your perspective, it can be a negative impact. I believe my study of gender communication has assisted me in performing one of my many jobs as a parent, which is to address with my children gender communication, as well as to be my children's gender advocate as appropriate. And what I have discovered repeatedly is that often those making negative gendered comments were merely uneducated in gender communication and unaware of their prejudiced comments.

My hope for you is that you will seize this opportunity to learn more about yourself and your gendered perceptions of the world. Don't just be a sponge! I encourage you to open your mind and explore the boundaries of gender communication. What you find may surprise you and impact the way you interact with others, now and in your future.

MY EXPERIENCE IN GENDER COMMUNICATION

Bryan Hansen
STUDENT

I don't think that a single adolescent soul has encountered the opposite sex in conversation and gone away from the conversation without being somewhat confused by the words and signals that were exchanged. This confusion is often compounded when there are feelings of attraction on the part of one or both of the individuals involved. Furthermore, the mystery only deepens when the two begin dating and each one develops theories to help predict the behavior of the other. When predictions are found to be incorrect, the results can often lead to heartbreak. While in this pubescent example we may try to minimize the weight of the situation, claiming perhaps that such affection is only "puppy love," we must remember that as someone once said, "puppy love is real to the puppy." Moreover, we must also admit that as we reach college and even later in life, we still don't have it figured out, and miscommunication in our relationships with the opposite sex, whether we are romantically involved or not, is often a source of frustration, anger, and sadness. On the lighter side, Jerry Seinfeld would not have much of a program if the differences in communication patterns between opposite gendered people were not so apparent and stereotyped. Phrases that get tossed around in joking conversation, like "I just want to be friends" or "he is such a *guy*" and "that's a woman for ya," may offer amusement among friends, but these shortcuts do little to help us understand each other better. It seems clear that anything we can learn about communicating with the opposite sex ought to be helpful.

While pursuing my undergraduate degree in Speech Communication, I had a few elective credits left to play with. I had been married just less than a year, and it would be deceptive to say that there were not instances of misunderstanding that left one or both of us hurt, angry, or at least frustrated. It seemed logical to take a course in gender communication, so I signed up. I had no idea just how useful the class would be.

At first, it was a little uncomfortable. The class is coed, and it is clear that if you are going to share in class discussions about gender, you risk revealing your ignorance—ignorance that you are aware exists, but that you cannot quite identify. This was certainly the case for me. We were seated in what has become a standard seating formation in communication classrooms: a circle, so you are in the "front" of the class the whole time. If you have not experienced this in previous classes, it may put you on edge a little. But over the course of the next few months, I learned some of the most useful information of any course I took.

After I took the class, I was able to interact better with the women I worked with, my relationship improved with my wife, and I began to see the very real struggles that we as men and women face in our pursuit of identity and significance. I came away from this class more confident in myself and my interactions not only with the opposite sex, but with the same sex as well. I became more sensitive to how women think and feel, and in doing so was able to more appropriately interact with them at work, in classes, in public settings, and specifically with my wife in our marriage. She and I began to talk more effectively with each other in ways that helped us understand one another better.

As a male, I began to recognize some of the forces that influence how I view others and myself. I am more able to help other male friends when they come to me with some of their personal issues, as well as those who seek advice about what to do with a girl they like or are dating. If the problems are communication-related (which ones aren't?), you can be a great help—and this can apply to your parents or other family members as well.

As you begin learning about gender communication, allow your conceptions of the opposite sex to be challenged and changed. I did, and I am better for it.

THOUGHTS ABOUT GENDER COMMUNICATION

Judy Miller
STUDENT

The point of any educational experience is to move beyond where you are to a new place, a new perspective. So it was with my venture into the realm of gender communication and an examination of GenderSpeak (Ivy & Backlund, 2000). My reflections on what I learned revealed some new insights about relationships and an occasional reaffirmation of known and accepted information. Sharing my reflections strengthens my resolve to be more deliberate in cultivating lasting, meaningful relationships.

Choice is perhaps the most critical factor in relationship development. Intentionally expanding our range of communication enables greater choice and effectiveness. Understanding that information reduces uncertainty and enables choice places a person in a less passive role in relationship building. What we choose to share about ourselves affects the developing relationship.

Differences between and among sex groups help us construct how we view gender roles. Stereotypes take on new relevance, as we understand the patterns that form our views of gender. Our views of intimacy, talk, activity, and inclusiveness program our needs, and our relationship development in predictable ways. Acknowledging those needs and building upon them can produce rewarding results. Adjusting our views of gender roles as we are exposed to new information is empowering.

Many relationship behaviors are termed male or female. Many men enjoy activity-oriented interactions, while many women prefer conversation. In a recent behind-the-scenes interview for his movie *What Women Want,* Mel Gibson was asked that very question: What do women want? He responded that he thought it had something to do with chocolate, and conversation (big grin). Perhaps he's right on both counts.

There are some core values that should frame a relationship: equality of power, acceptance, freedom of choice, treating the other person as an individual, open-mindedness, and a willingness to change. These values help build and strengthen relationships. Another critical value in relationship building is talking, or in the words of our instructor, "talking about it makes it better." Listening, empathy, nonverbal expressiveness, and sensitivity elevate conversations and allow them to help shape a relationship. Verbalizing intentions removes doubt and fosters healthy dialogue.

How we talk is as important as what we discuss. Language should reflect the desire to be a caring, sensitive person and is intimately connected to attitudes. Eliminating sexist language is empowering and can free us from sexist thoughts.

Perhaps one of the most revolutionary ideas is contained in the simple premise that we can develop effective and desirable patterns of communication intentionally. We are not bound by rigid stereotypes or conditioning. We can evaluate relationships and set goals to effect change. We can share feelings and nurture relational commitment. Resulting relationships will be more resilient, rewarding, and sustainable.

REFERENCE

Ivy, D. K., & Backlund, P. (2000). *Exploring genderspeak: Personal effectiveness in gender communication* (2nd ed.). New York: McGraw-Hill.

WHY I'M NOT A LADY (AND NO WOMAN IS)

Sherryl Kleinman

Ladies have pale skin,
wear white gloves
they sweep across the top
of the armoire
to make sure the darker-skinned woman
who cleaned it
didn't forget or cheat

A lady doesn't sit
with one leg dangling
over the arm of the chair
like she just doesn't give a damn.

Ladies don't fix cars, build bridges, wire houses.
Ladies become First Lady, not President.

Sit up straight, young lady!
Cross your legs (shave them first).
Remove (surgically if necessary)
that frown from your forehead.
Lower your voice.
Smile.

Call yourself a lady
and he'll protect you,
he'll respect you,
he won't leave.

But who protects the cleaning lady?

Reprinted with permission. First appeared in *Feminist Frontiers,* edited by Laurel Richardson, Verta Taylor, and Nancy Whittier, McGraw-Hill Companies, © 2004.

Wonder why we don't have
"Ladies Studies"
at the university?

I'll remain a woman,
keep the basic word
that got so dirty
she wants to clean herself off
and be called lady.

Until a real woman
can earn one dollar on the man's dollar;
Until a real woman can call her body her own;
Until a real woman can love a woman in peace,
love a man without fear;
Until a real woman can walk the dark streets
with her mind on the stars and not on her back,

I will know that lady is a lie.

PART II

THEORETICAL PERSPECTIVES

DEVELOPMENT OF FLUID GENDER IDENTITY

Addressing a Controversial Issue

Jayanti Basu

UNIVERSITY OF CALCUTTA

When asked one's gender, most respondents will self-identify as either male or female, often in reference to their biological sex. Regardless of one's response, there is a popular assumption that gender is binary; that is, we are only one or the other gender. In this piece, Jayanti Basu reviews the two major theories of gender identification—the psychological model and the sociobiological model—as prelude to her argument that the common approaches to explaining gender self-identification may be insufficient and shortsighted, blinding scholars to the value of viewing gender as a fluid concept.

Basu's article provides many avenues of discussion for those interested in understanding how theory development affects how we conceive of and consequently respond to human behavior. Throughout the article, the author interjects many questions for your consideration. In a broad sense, these questions ask you to reflect on your own gender self-identity—how you self-identify, how you feel about your gender identity, how you came to your current way of thinking about it, and how you might think differently about it in light of the theories and arguments presented.

QUESTIONS FOR DISCUSSION

- *Do you agree that gender is fluid, rather than fixed? Why/why not?*
- *How might the acceptance of the concept of gender fluidity influence interpersonal relationships?*
- *How would validation of a theory of gender fluidity influence social policymaking?*
- *How might one separate identity from sex and gender in a culture that does not symbolically allow such a separation. That is, to conceive of identity sans biology requires a language that is outside of the culture's discursive formation. Is that possible? If so, how?*

Reprinted with permission.

Everyone of us is like a man who sees things in a dream and thinks that he knows them perfectly and then wakes up to find that he knows nothing.

PLATO, *STATESMAN*

Before you start reading this article, take a notepad and a pencil. Write a paragraph on yourself, not exceeding 70 words. Write the way you feel you can best present yourself.

E ven a few decades back most of us "knew" that we are either a man or a woman, and surely out there are those "unfortunate monsters" who are neither. Up to the beginning of the 20th century, *sex* and *gender* were often interchangeable words, essentially referring to the anatomical difference in genital organization and its consequences in behavioral terms. This very interchangeability implies that the behavioral components are believed to be direct corollaries of genital sex difference, thus constituting a total cleavage between male and female. Only when the term *gender* came to be deliberately used as different from sex, there emerged the first suggestion of the cultural component's being conceptually separable from anatomical sex difference. However, for a long time the differentiation was largely theoretical, having little meaning for everyday life. For all practical purposes, there existed an ineradicable bond between anatomy and sociocultural conceptualization, or more narrowly between female/male as a body and woman/man as a socially or personally experienced category. *In other words, cognition of one's anatomy (body identity) and cognition of one's existential self (psychosocial identity) were inseparably bound together.* An alternate conceptualization, however, would be that this apparent coexistence of body and psychosocial identity is *not causal*, but only *coincidental*; they need not necessarily go together, and may be combined in an individual or in a culture in multiple varieties of fashion.

This assertion eschews the very foundation of the "binary gender system," a politically useful belief incorporating two basic assumptions: first, that anatomy and identity will always go together, and second, that anatomy and identity may be of two and only two types—namely, male (masculine) and female (feminine). The entire binary gender system seems to rest upon the conviction that once the "basic" gender designations have been attributed to a person or a group, the individual(s) concerned will abide by the expectations enforced by the society. Indeed, empirical investigation shows that by the third year of life many children can identify self and others both in terms of sex (Bem, 1989) and gender (Thompson & Bentler, 1973; Levy, Taylor, & Gelman, 1995). Most available theories of development of gender try to explain how this binary gender sense is incorporated into one's identity.

Did you mention your sex and/or your gender in your self-representation? If neither, why did you skip it? Is it because (a) it did not cross your mind? (b) it did cross, but you felt it was unnecessary for your self-representation? (c) you know this is an article on gender, so you tried to be gender sensitive? (d) due to the restrain on words, you have provided other clues to your sex /gender, so it was redundant. (e) anything else? If you mentioned either, was it because (a) it spontaneously came to you? (b) you consider it essential to properly represent yourself? (c) anything else? If you mentioned either sex or gender, did you assume equivalence of sex and gender? If you mentioned both sex and gender separately, was it because (a) you are sensitive to their conceptual difference? (b) they are personally discrepant for you? (c) personally they are not discrepant, but you truly feel that both should be mentioned for proper representation of yourself? (d) anything else?

EXISTING THEORIES OF GENDER IDENTITY DEVELOPMENT: A CRITICAL LOOK

The available theories explaining gender identity development may be divided into two categories, psychological and sociobiological.

Psychological Model

The psychological model focuses on the individual's ontological developmental pattern. The available approaches may be divided into two broad categories. One is the psychoanalytic and the other is the social learning approach.

The Psychoanalytical Approach. It was Sigmund Freud who first seriously inquired about the development of gender. In his 1905 edition of *Three Essays on the Theory of Sexuality* (1905/1954), Freud formulated his notion of psychosexual development in children and framed his concept of the Oedipal complex. As a result of shift in focus on erogenous zones, the Oedipal-age child automatically attends to one's genitalia and compares it to others'. At this time the boy develops intense attachment to the mother, out of which evolves the fear of the powerful rival father and castration anxiety. Subsequently, the issue is resolved by developing incest taboo and identification with the father, who represents the patriarchal gender structure. A parallel model was proposed for girls, despite obvious empirical discrepancies. Freud believed that the awareness of existence of a penis in boys arouses extreme envy in the little girl. She then renounces her clitoris, her inferior penis, blames her mother for giving birth to her in this incomplete form, and woos the father in expectation of having a baby (the substitute penis) from him. Hence the passive feminine identification of the girl. *Thus, the inevitability of sex gives rise to emotional upheaval, resulting in normative gender identification.*

Although Freud's phallocentric view, particularly that of femininity, was criticized by his female colleagues (Horney, 1920; Klein, 1928; Deutsch, 1932/1965), the basic idea of Oedipal-age attention on genitalia and subsequent complex formation was not questioned. Among the later ego psychologists, Erikson (1963) from extensive observation of children's play found a reassertion of Freud's original idea of culture's being grounded in one's body awareness. He found boys to be more concerned with manipulating outer space, building towers and protrusions, while girls made scenes and enclosures, evincing concern with inner space. "Anatomy is destiny," Erikson concluded.

The Social Learning Approach. In contrast, the social learning approach emphasizes the developmental aspect of gender through socialization. The major proponent of the social learning theory, Walter Mischel (1966), stated that children in our society are rewarded for sex appropriate and punished for inappropriate behavior. While in this concept the child is conceived of as a passive entity, the cognitive developmental theory (Kohlberg & Ullian, 1974; Lewis & Brooks-Gunn, 1979) considers the child as an active agent in developing stereotyped gender identity and role enactment. In search of cognitive consistency, the child incorporates the stereotypes and categorizations prevalent in the society, rejects opposing ideas, nurtures them, and transmits them to the next generations.

A variant of this approach is Bem's gender schema theory, which states that stereotypes are developed on the basis of schema. Schematic information processing is selective by nature. So far as gender appropriateness is concerned, Bem (1975) suggested that sex typing—that is, incorporation of culturally prescribed masculine and feminine traits in one's identity—derives from gender schematic processing, from a generalized readiness on the part of the child to encode and organize information about self and others. However, one major contribution of Bem's theory was that masculinity and femininity were considered not as two ends of a bipolar continuum, but as two independent dimensions. A person may have a share of both in any combination; those who had high masculine and feminine traits were designated as "psychologically androgynous," those lacking in both were "undifferentiated."

Sociobiological Model

The sociobiological model, based on evolutionary theory, essentially asserts that gendered behavior is not random but serves the purpose of perpetuation of the species. Paralleling a number of examples from the animal world, the model tries to explain masculine and feminine roles in the society as providing support for women during pregnancy and lactation and maximizing and ensuring scope of paternity for men

(Buss, 1995). Thus, it is implied that a biological basis of behavior is being unknowingly followed in the name of cultural heritage.

What is your gut feeling? Do you think gender differences are "real," having after all a biological basis? Or can you unlearn all your telltale signs of gender?

Overview of the Models

The above models signify two basic approaches. One emphasizes the biological root of gender and its relative invariance. The sociobiological approach, as well as the psychoanalytical approach, subscribes to this view. On the other hand, the cultural transmission of gender roles, the learning of gender-appropriate behavior, is highlighted by the social learning theories and illustrated in the anthropological discussions. One implication of this is that if gender is learned, it can be unlearned also.

All the above approaches, however, are anchored to the binary gender idea. Only in the past few years has a serious effort to renounce fixed gender in favor of fluid or blended gender been launched.

NATURE OF FLUID GENDER

The Story of Susmita

"I've known all along that I'm a girl," says Susmita. A biological male with normal testosterone profile, Susmita was known by a male name signifying the Lord Shiva, as is common among the Hindus. She changed it in favor of the delicate sophisticated feminine name, which means "the girl who sweetly smiles." Susmita comes from a lower-middle family of the suburbs of Calcutta. An orphan from early years, she stays with her paternal uncle and his family, who apparently love her, but harbor strongly stereotyped and rigid ideas about what being a man means. The uncle, a burly fellow with three daughters, has a no-nonsense sort of attitude to the femaleness cherished by his ward. He simply declares that after the death of his brother and sister-in-law—that is, Susmita's parents—he gave the orphaned child refuge because it was a boy and would follow his trail later in life. He had had enough girls of his own, he bellows. So the various interventions by her family for her "treatment" included taking her to a psychiatrist who gave her plenty of drugs to keep her sleepy for months, an astrologer who made her wear expensive stones, and a shaman who sexually abused her. "Yet, whatever happens I must face life squarely and go on smiling at it," Susmita asserts.

Susmita is not allowed feminine dresses, so she puts on jeans and T-shirt, and wears lipstick and earrings when she has come pretty far away from her home. Before going back to her locality, she wipes off the lipstick and takes the ornaments off. She sometimes contemplates sex reassignment surgery, but she is not very sure that she really wants to go for it, apart from the fact that it is complicated, socially and legally, and expensive beyond her means.

Did her family, perhaps her parents, encourage her being feminine? I inquired. No was her answer. In India, begetting a son still means a joy to the parents. Susmita belonged to the cherished sex, and none of her early photographs show her in girls' dress. And then both the parents died within a span of three months when she was less than three years old. And her uncle's family never had such wild imagination, she added caustically.

I had a prolonged talk with Susmita. Here follows a short extract from the interview, which I think is relevant for our purpose.

Jayanti: You were always a woman—well, what exactly do you mean by being a woman and not a man? What womanish qualities do you have?

Susmita: Really difficult to say. It's a knowledge, not that I really think that I am very soft or submissive or homely, none of those trashes. I'm quite aggressive. I don't think I'm a woman because I've what you call "feminine qualities." I'm a woman because it's a knowledge, somehow, you know, I know I have been a woman, internally I always was. The entire experience is different, I don't feel as (laughs) my uncle feels.

Jayanti: What about your body? Do you despise it? You love to put on lipsticks and dresses.

Susmita: I don't know. I am surely not satisfied with my body, yes there are times when I hate it. There are moments when I would like to change it. But you see, it is not really the change in my body that matters most. Even if my body remains as it is, I'll be a woman, always. The thing is that, I feel, bodily speaking I'm an incomplete woman. You will never call me a woman if I keep this body. That is what really matters, the freedom to feel that I'm a woman.

Jayanti: Then why the lipstick and earrings, knowing your uncle will be furious if he finds out? You see, you are still financially dependent on him.

Susmita: (laughs) Yes, I know. I like to present myself as a woman. But honestly I don't think the long hair, lipstick, and saree (the typical Indian female dress), not even going for the elaborate sex change program will make me more of a woman than I'm now. All these will be the process of making my appearance congruent, making me look more like what I really am, but . . . (contemplates), tell me one thing, if you have your hysterectomy, and somebody chops off your breasts and fixes a penis on you will you not be Jayanti any more? Will you then be Jayanta (a male name)? It will torment you, your bodily distortion, your being devoid of femaleness, but you will be a woman, won't you? The same with me. Bodily I am a male, but I am not, never was a man.

What would be your reply to Susmita's last question? If your body is mutilated to alter your sex signs, will your gender be changed?

The Fluidity and Uncertainty of Gender

Susmita could not say what being a woman means. She knows what being a female is and also knows that she never will be a biological female. Not that she is always very eager even to have a body that at least apparently passes for a female one. Yet she firmly believes herself to be a woman, so much so that she defies all the pressurization from her family. Indeed, could anybody tell what being a woman means? Or being a man? For those who have a mutually congruent body and mind—that is, for example a male body and a man's identity—the question may not appear. Nevertheless, not asking the question does not mean it is unnecessary. When people like Susmita force us to ask the question, we tend to get all confused.

Had you ever thought of yourself as anything but belonging to your own sex? Have you dreamt of it, or talked about such possibility? If not, imagine it now. Be mentally the opposite gendered person. Note what difficulties you face.

Indeed, society seems to react in funny ways to gender exceptionality. Much of what we know about it today has been a juxtaposition of medical research and feminist movement, two approaches so radically different that the issue has to be politicized one way or the other. The medical model is framed on the basis of a binary gender system, which requires not only that male and female genitalia are different but that manhood and womanhood are also different. In other words, the culture must follow the body. The ethnomethodologists call it the "natural attitude" (Kessler & McKenna, 1978), and any deviance from it is a pathology if not outright monstrosity. One may ostracize them, even burn them on the stake like Joan of Arc, who refused to put on female garments. The more humanitarian ones would "treat" them out of the "disease," and may also arrange for sex change. Here one must pause and consider the approach of Harry Benjamin, who pioneered sex reassignment surgery for transsexuals and whose model still predominates in the medical field. Interestingly, in his now classic 1966 book *The Transsexual Phenomenon*, Benjamin blatantly exposed his confusion. He initially stated that sex is under the belt and gender is above it, yet decided to use the words interchangeably. Symphony of the sexes is the rule, asserted Benjamin, although "disturbances" do occur. The purpose of the medical model is to do away with this disturbance; if identity cannot be made congruent to the body, the body will be changed to suit the identity. But in any case, ultimately the *connotation of the body and identity must coincide*; if the penis-testes constellation is present, identity must be of a man, and if the vagina-clitoris constellation is present, identity must be of a woman. Thus, the medical model believes in fixed gender identity, claims to know exactly what is right and wrong in identity matters, and offers guidelines in that direction.

Although Benjamin's venturesome surgery opened a new horizon for transsexuals, its limitations were apparent. In the first place, transsexual persons were being medically defined as those who feel that they belong to the opposite sex, have been trapped in a wrong body, and desperately want to shift from one kind of gendered body to another. This definition, therefore, also abides by rigid gender attribution as linked to body morphology (Halberstam, 1998). This is why authors like Lienert (1998) consider such claims as condemnable from a feminist point of view. This very definition may itself be a sociopolitical maneuver to technologize the body and perpetuate the correspondence of sex, gender, and sexual orientation (Raymond, 1994). This is where the feminist approach basically differed from the fixed identity model implied by the medical model.

Let us further scrutinize the feminist criticism against the binary medical model. Say a biological male feels that he is a woman, wishes to have a female body and a female mind, and wants to play female roles such as caring for a child or cooking for one's husband (one male-to-female told me that her dream is to wait for her partner to come home in the evening and then to serve him the food she has cooked). For this to be realized, two basic conditions need be fulfilled. One, there must exist reliable differences in the physical and mental characteristics of male- and female-bodied persons, as well as in their role enactment. Years of feminist research, however, seems to seriously question the viability of such differences. Males can no doubt be shown to be physically, hormonally different from females and serve different biological functions. But can men be shown to be socially, emotionally, cognitively different from women? The issue got tremendous focus from the 1970s onward, with some excellent summarizing from psychologists and sociologists such as Lee and Stewart (1976) and Eagly (1987). Most authors concluded that there was little difference between the sexes. Some areas were initially believed to show considerable difference, such as men having greater spatial and mathematical ability and women having a slight advantage in language. Deeper probing, however, revealed that much of this difference could be obliterated by training; it is the culture that suppresses mathematical superiority in women and linguistic prowess in men (Halpern, 1986). Role playing is, it goes without saying, even more of a social construction. Indeed, Stephanie Riger (1997) argues that it is practically impossible for her to reply to the question "whether men and women differ" because the question itself involves a number of subthemes that must be attended to if the question is to be answered. In the same vein, Bernice Lott (1990) also concluded that "*appearance of gender differences in behavior* depends upon social context and particular situational conditions" (p. 73, my italics).

The second requisite is even more basic. To justify the medical model, one must have one's identity anchored to one's body. That is, a person with male gender identity must have a definite craving for a male body. Apparently, this is exactly what the transsexuals demand. However, there exists a large number of persons, usually held under the umbrella term "transgender," who not only demonstrate a wide variety of possible gender role combinations, but flexibly shift between identities and body identifications, relative to time and space. A number of persons are comfortable to use their body in multiple ways, with multiple sexual orientations. Here is a case vignette:

> Rajan identifies as a man and looks like an adolescent boy, with a disarmingly innocent smile and hesitant cracked voice, only if you don't know that he is a biological female of 23 and is already involved in a number of antisocial activities including drug trafficking and prostitution. Rajan makes money, among other things, by having anal sex with older men, many of whom take him for a "passive homosexual boy." But there are some who know he is a female, and sometimes they use him both ways. "I wish I could do the same to them also," he says. Rajan has his girlfriends also; he enjoys their company. Sometimes he allures them to sex; on a few occasions, he has paid for sex with girls.
>
> I asked him if he is going to change his genitals. Wouldn't he like to have "real" sex with his girls? "I do not really understand what all this fuss is all about," Rajan replied carelessly. "The pleasure is down there, you get it any way you can manage. At heart you know you are a man, that is what matters; why bother if you can use certain parts of your body or not!"

Is Rajan sick? Probably not. Persons who claim to be "pansexual" really think they can enjoy all sorts of sexual orientations in a variety of moods, without really sticking to a particular mode of mental set and a specified use of body.

Empirically, then, we find that all sorts of structured and unstructured sex/gender/sexual orientations can be combined. This is what Kate Bornstein (1994) speaks of as "the ability to freely and knowingly become one or many of a limitless number of genders for any length of time, at any rate of change." This fluidity covers all imaginable areas of existence, identity, love life, sexual orientation, dress, speech, mannerism, and of course, the thinking and feeling processes.

In which among the above areas did you face problems in imagining yourself as *opposite gendered?*

This concept of gender fluidity eschews the very referral to a dichotomous paradigm of gender. Judith Butler (1990) spoke of gender as a multifaceted, fragmented concept, without any spatial or temporal stability. She conceives of gendered subjectivity "as a history of identifications, parts of which can be brought into play in given contexts and which, precisely because they encode the contingencies of personal history, do not always point back to an internal coherence of any kind" (p. 331). This is most palpable in the gender exceptional persons, and in sensitive "normal" ones too.

That gender difference is only apparent is gaining ground in the scientific community only in hesitant steps. Let us review the basic theories we have delineated before. To what extent can they explain development of this fluid gender in certain individuals? The sociobiological model emphasizes the perpetuation-of-species role of gender; thus, gender fluidity has to be a "deviance." All the psychological theories have one thing in common: they more or less agree that gender is learned as a constellation of behavioral and affective norms associated with one's genital characteristics. Some theories, such as the psychoanalytical ones, imply the invariable triumph of the body, anatomy being essentially reflected in one's destiny. Gender exceptionality, from this point of view, is the result of a deviant nurturing, some distortion in one's early identification (Oppenheimer, 1991). The social learning theories are more concerned with the reinforcement and modeling aspects, but they also are not comfortable explaining fluidity. Of course, selectively reinforcing cross-sex behavior is rather unusual, and usually gender exceptional persons do not have gender exceptional parents. Among other theories, Bem's view is relatively radical in the sense that it highlights the irrational nature of gender, but ultimately even in this paradigm one has to reside somewhere in the "masculine *and* feminine" frame, although not in the "masculine *or* feminine" one. Indeed in subsequent works, Bem (1993) clearly discussed the need to erode gender altogether.

Ultimately, we are bound to conclude that the existing theories fail to account for the development of gender fluidity. The reason may lie in the fact that none of them can go beyond the essentialism, beyond the familiar normalcy-deviance model, where every event has to be judged against some predetermined point of reference. But things on this planet were not always like this.

EVIDENCE OF GENDER FLUIDITY: HISTORICAL, MYTHOLOGICAL, AND MODERN EXAMPLES, WITH SPECIAL REFERENCE TO INDIA

In prehistoric and historical periods, there was evidence of gender fluidity. Green (1998) points out that all over the world gender exceptional persons served as entertainers in the community because of their creative talents. Taylor, in his book *Prehistory of Sex* (1996), narrates how emperors employed gender crossing individuals in their court. Here are some examples from India.

Ancient India seems to have had considerable tolerance of gender fluidity (Money, 1992). The great Indian epic *The Mahabharata* (Roy, 1962) relates the story of king Budha who, owing to the curse of a sage, became a woman, but later wanted to continue his new life as he felt womanhood more sexually and emotionally gratifying. King Yubanaswa was "impregnated" and gave birth to the famous king Mandhata. Urvasi, the beatific dancer of the heaven, cursed Arjuna, the great archer, because Arjuna ignored her erotic appeal. As a result, Arjuna stayed in the palace of king Birata as the eunuch dance-mistress of the princess. This eunuch state, however, turned out to be a boon rather than a bane for Arjuna, as this coincided with his need to stay disguised. Another person of ambiguous sex mentioned in the *Mahabharata* is Shikhandi. Princess Amba, forcibly prevented by Bhishma from marrying her lover, died praying for a man's body in her next reincarnation. This she received, and was reborn as Shikhandi, the son of king Drupada, but was considered as a female by Bhishma. In the great battle of Kurukshetra, Shikhandi killed Bhishma, thus avenging the frustration in her earlier birth. The important point is that all these characters were shifting their gender for a given period, then choosing to revert back or not to their originally assigned gender. All these instances show how the body can be temporarily altered in response to a psychological or social need. This is no wonder, since even gods approve of this. According to ancient myths, the Lord Vishnu took the features of "Mohini," a beautiful girl, to allure the demons. The most popular Indian god, Lord Shiva himself, occasionally chooses to share his wife's features and become "Ardhanariswara," the half-woman god.

As prehistoric "naivety" was replaced by complex societal bonds, gender flexibility faced restraint. The *Kamasutra*, the famous Indian text on erotic behavior by Vatsayana, dating back between the first and sixth centuries A.D., describes the love life of normal men with the "third nature" who may be of two types, female-like or male-like, based on their secondary sex characteristics. In the Samproyagadhikaranam chapter, Vatsayana (1980) recommended the techniques of sexual arousal of normal men by these third-natured persons. However, Vatsayana mentioned the controversial social attitude toward such practice and concluded that its ultimate acceptability depends on situation and culture.

In the medieval era, however, the flexibility was gradually lost. The transgression of gender issue probably got confused with the eunuch and intersex persons. Customs of forced and deliberate castration during the Islamic period have been reported. Such persons, known as "khoja," were employed as keepers of the "harem" and occasionally enjoyed positions of power and authority also (Manucci, 1981). But since only a few specific roles were allotted for them in the society, it may be stated that the fluidity was lost to a great extent, although a certain degree of social acceptance remained.

The unstable political scenario of this period resulted in a rigid gender concept. Women's sexual virtue came to be of utmost importance, and various restrictions were imposed upon them. Naturally, this kind of imposition is opposed to any kind of crossing of gender boundary. Yet the clandestine blending of the masculine and feminine was not entirely destroyed, but remained in the form of various religious cults like the Sakhibhava (worshipping Lord Krishna imagining oneself as his girlfriend or fiancée) of the Vaishnavas.

The influence of European culture from the sixteenth century onward posed further restriction. The challenge of a powerful foreign culture provoked the indigenous lawmakers to install firm and narrow gender roles completely bound to body. Colonial India under British domination was on the one hand demonstrating this inflexible normativeness in all fields, including gender; on the other hand, the literal morality of nineteenth-century Europe was being imported to the intellectual and

activist leaders of India. Though they fought for women's education and social freedom, it was within a nevertheless prim and proper gender role prescription. If there
was any unobtrusive undercurrent of increased scrutiny of sexuality, as Foucault
(1980a) claims regarding the European romantic period, it was not palpable.
Transgendered persons were probably simply banished into oblivion from this time
onward. They were ostracized, pushed to the fringe of society, because the cultural
need of the period was inappropriate for their mainstreaming.

The Hijra community (*Hijra* in Urdu meaning "the impotent one"), still existing in India, is a peculiar amalgam of varieties of gender exceptional and sexually
ambiguous persons. Considering themselves neither men nor women, members of
this so-called "third sex" generally adopt feminine names and dress. These Hijras are
perceived ambivalently in the society. They are outcasts in the society, staying in
slums, having a lifestyle of their own, with their exclusive vocabulary and initiation
rites, oaths, and rituals (Jaffrey, 1998). They are, however, believed to be carriers of
good or bad fortune having occult power. They are generally feared and avoided, yet
hired as providers of good luck to dance on auspicious occasions such as the birth of
a baby or a marriage ceremony. Interestingly, some place, though of subjugation, is
ordained in the society for them. Perhaps because the suppression of gender fluidity
in India was not indigenous but reactive to political nuances, a kind of guilty ambiva-
lence always remained in connection with this peripharalized group.

The point I intend to make here is that attitude to gender is a function of time
and space. The free-floating gender of the ancient period in India was gradually replaced by constricted gender definition. Indeed, to enjoy gender fluidity, to be a "sometime woman" (Gilbert, 1998) and yet to be accepted and understood in the society,
presumes some cultural requisites. In the first place, the belief that gender is an independent construction, not grounded in the body, must be strong. This tolerance is
stilted during difficult periods in history because under disrupted sociopolitical condition, one is forced to resort to stereotype, thus enabling one to simplify things and concentrate on the emergency. Second, since gender fluidity implies detachment of identity from the body and the body from the sexual orientation, the scientific attitude
must encourage scrutiny of all alternatives, however impossible or offensive they may
apparently seem. In other words, a regard for open inquisitiveness must be in the air, as
should be the tolerance for inconclusive answers. Gender fluidity was acceptable in all
prehistoric periods because the ambiguity, the fuzziness of things, the irrationality of
the expression of the nature was accepted as an unquestioned reality. Again, it may be
a characteristic of the postmodern phase of thought when people learned to pose and
sustain a question without hurrying into a patterned answer. So now is the time to un-
ravel the subversive tone of gender fluidity and explore its existential reality.

---

*Do you know of instances in your own culture where gender fluidity was accept-
able? Can you relate them to the cultural history of your country?*

TOWARD A POSTMODERN APPROACH
TO GENDER IDENTITY

The essence of the postmodern is to acknowledge the temporal and spatial relativity of each cognition and to accept the possibility of deconstruction of established values. Transcribing it to the domain of gender, it means that the idea of socially correct masculine and feminine gender roles may be dissolved, all members of the society thus essentially subscribing to the transgender model (Tauchert, 1998), where one may identify oneself bodily as male, female, or partly of either sex and in identity also as man, woman, both, or neither. This may be done in multiple ways. Ekins and King (1999) provide a sociological model to exemplify four kinds of body concept: migratory body stories, oscillating body stories, erasing body stories, and transcending body stories. Various kinds of transgendered people may be said to exemplify various categories. From this point of view, the very stability of the category of gender and its usage to organize social life is lost (Lorber, 1994).

A second characteristic of postmodern gender concept is that the body is perceived not as a biologically fixed and objectively verifiable given, but as a projection screen on which various meanings are imposed through experience (Feher, 1989; Butler, 1993). In other words, the cognition of the body is a social construction emerging through cultural discourse. Then, we can no longer reckon the objective presence of the penis-testes cluster as a sign of manhood; at best, it is a sign of maleness, although the presence of various intersex conditions renders even that conclusion doubtful. The maleness-manhood connection, therefore, is just coincidental; the so-called straight and normal "man" does not feel himself to be a man simply *because* he has the penis-testes cluster, but three independent things have coincided in his personal history: (1) he has learned that having the penis-testes cluster means maleness, (2) he has felt or known that he is a man, and (3) he has learned to causally connect these two (maleness and manhood) through social experience. The chain can be broken and is in reality broken at many points. The external maleness criteria may be a false signal, as is the case with chromosomal aberrations such as Turner's syndrome or Kleinfelter's syndrome. He may feel that he is a woman, at least at times, as is the case of gender exceptional persons. Finally, he may not learn to associate the two, and consider them as independent and orthogonal, just as he may have brown eyes and an interest in music.

Can you think of yourself without referring to any of the gender cues? Try once again to describe yourself without any reference to explicit or implicit sex/gender. Can you do it? Or do you feel you cannot represent yourself satisfactorily? Try to frame and describe one imaginary day where no such sex/gender cue may be emitted in your behavior. Can you do it?

However, we have not yet resolved the issue of development of fluid gender identity. We have already discussed how transgenderism has been a challenge to psychosocial and sociobiological theories. Alternatively, causes of gender exception have been sought for in the brain and body chemistry. Hoenig (1985) claimed that MTF transsexuals showed an absence of histocompatibilty antigen, which is typically present in males and absent in females. Zhou, Hofman, Gooren, and Swaab (1995) reported that the size of the suprachiasmatic nucleus of the hypothalamus of MTF transsexuals was in between that of females and nontranssexual males. LeVay (1996) also reported differences in the hypothalamus of homosexual and heterosexual men. None of the claims has, however, yet been reliably established. The follow-up studies of children reassigned the other gender identity at birth for some reason or other have also shown mixed results (Money, 1994; Bradley, Oliver, Chernick, & Zucker, 1998). Indeed, it is unlikely that a clear-cut answer will ever be obtained because complex human behavior cannot usually be attributed to one or a few identifiable "causes," and truly impartial investigation is difficult in this value-laden area, each researcher being biased in one's own orientation (Szuchman & Muscarella, 2000).

What then should be our approach? Let us here recall the poignant paragraph Michel Foucault (1980b) rendered at the introduction of the memoirs of a nineteenth-century gender exceptional person, Herculine Barbin. Reared in a religious and feminine environment as a female, this person of ambiguous sex signs was discovered to be a "true" man in his/her youth. Failing to adjust to live in the society with "his" "true" identity, Herculine committed suicide, leaving a memoir behind that is disturbingly pathetic. Foucault wrote the introduction to its published version in 1980, beginning:

> Do we *truly* need a *true* sex? With a persistence that borders on stubbornness, modern Western societies have answered in the affirmative. They have obstinately brought into play this question of a "true sex" in an order of things where one might have imagined that all that counted was the reality of the body and the intensity of its pleasures. (p. vii)

As "true sex" is but an idealistic thought, true gender also is gradually proving to be a utopia. It has served its historical needs more than adequately, and now can happily be dispensed with.

Search for an etiology of gender fluidity, furthermore, alludes to exceptionality as if it were a disease and we have a responsibility of attributing it to some pathology or other. An alternate research mode would be to accept the situation as it is—that is, to recognize that body and identity were not meant to be causally or inseparably linked. In that case, fluidity will be "natural," and one might ask contrarily what in the civilization's or a person's history builds gender-sex congruence. Looking at the issue from this reverse angle is difficult and poses challenge to a number of existing and well-functioning paradigms. When Judith Butler forwarded her view of gender performativity, Segal (1994) commented: "Mostly we can only enact those behaviors which have long since become familiar and meaningful to us in expressing ourselves. . . . Challenge to our gendered 'identities' may be more than we can handle" (p. 208). To resolve this inevitable conflict, one might look for neurological and psychological evidence of gender identity as a cognition developing in the brain of the human child irrespective of its sex signs. But this is not "*the* identity." It is just one of the many cognitive components that make up one's self-cognition.

More specifically, sex is one thing—the label given to one's reproductive characteristic. Sexual identity is knowing whether one is a male or female or blended. Gender identity is something else—a self-awareness in terms of whether one is a man or woman, always or at times, that is irrespective of one's sex. Sexual orientation is entirely another issue, referring to the preferred mode of begetting sexual pleasure, most of the time or occasionally. Defined thus within its own boundary and stripped of undue contamination, the salience attributed to sex and gender as naturally "given" may be diminished, and the very issue of development of identity be placed within a social history paradigm rather than in the ontological process. In this sense, transsexualism as a problem arises because society insists on body-identity correspondence. Indeed, the childhood reminiscences of many transsexuals reveal that all conflict began when they were forced to acknowledge that they had a discrepant body and were therefore deviants. One transsexual reported: "I naturally sat with the girls at my nursery school, but everybody told me I was not one of them. I was enraged . . . since I could not change my gut feeling, I wanted to change my genitals." In the traditional view, the transsexual was erroneous in cognition; the alternate view is that this "everybody" representing the society is erroneous, since they imposed fixed gender requirements on this male-bodied woman.

The postmodern gender concept presumes an extreme regard for human freedom, in thought and action, affect and decision. The present social scenario and scientific atmosphere are congenial for this quest to begin. The history of knowledge has always been from the fixed to the probabilistic model. We have shifted from the notion of the earth being the center of the universe to the revolving planet concept; we have accepted that we are standing not on a solid base but on an eternally changing plastic mold of matter; we have learnt to live with fuzzy electrons and the now-alive-now-dead Schroedinger's cat. This is the opportune moment to change the paradigm for studying gender also. One has to recognize that manhood or womanhood is a socially generated fluid concept, not separated by a strict irreversible boundary of imaginary extension of one's genitalia, but blending, migrating, oscillating, changing its shape, and occasionally dissolving to enable human beings to enjoy a kaleidoscopic range of gendered and nongendered experience.

REFERENCES

Bem, S. L. (1975). Sex role adaptability: One consequence of psychological androgyny. *Journal of Personality and Social Psychology, 31,* 634–643.

Bem, S. L. (1989). Genital knowledge and gender constancy in preschool children. *Child Development, 60,* 649–662.

Bem, S. L. (1993). *The lenses of gender: Transforming the debate on sexual inequality.* New Haven, CT: Yale University Press.

Benjamin, H. (1966). The transsexual phenomenon. New York: Julian Press.

Bradley, S. J., Oliver, G. D., Chernick, A. B., & Zucker, K. J. (1998). Experiment of nurture: Ablatio penis at 2 months, sex reassignment at 7 months and a psychosexual follow up in young adulthood. [On-line]. *Pediatrics, 102,* E9. http://www.pediatrics.org/cgi/content/full/102/1/e9

Butler, J. (1990). *Gender trouble: Feminism and the subversion of identity.* New York: Routledge & Kegan Paul.

Butler, J. (1993). *Bodies that matter.* New York: Routledge.

Deutsch, H. (1965). Motherhood and sexuality. In *Neurosis and character types* (pp. 190–202). Madison, CT: International Universities Press. (Original work published 1932)

Eagly, A. H. (1987). *Sex differences in social behavior: A social role interpretation.* Hillsdale, NJ: Erlbaum.

Ekins, R., & King, D, (1999). Toward a sociology of transgendered bodies. *Sociological Review, 47,* 580–602.

Erikson, E. (1963). *Childhood and society.* London: Norton.

Feher, M. (1989). Introduction. *Fragments for a history of the human body* (Vol. 1, p. 11). New York: MIT Press.

Foucault, M. (1980a). *The history of sexuality* (Vol. 1). Harmonsworth, UK: Penguin Books.

Foucault, M. (1980b). Introduction. *Herculine Barbin* (R. McDougall, Trans.). New York: Pantheon.

Freud, S. (1954). Three essays on the theory of sexuality. In J. Strachey (Ed.), *The standard editions of the complete psychological works of Sigmund Freud* (Vol. 7, pp. 125–230). London: Hogarth Press. (Original work published 1905)

Gilbert, M. (1998, September). *A sometime woman: The limits of social construction.* Paper presented at the Third International Congress on Sex and Gender, Exeter College, Oxford University. Abstract published in *IJT,* 1998, 2.

Green, R. (1998). Transsexualism: Mythological, historical and cross cultural aspects. In D. Denny (Ed.), *Current concepts in transgender identity* (pp. 3–14). New York: Garland.

Halberstam, J. (1998). Transgender butch: Butch/FTM border wars and the masculine continuum. *GLQ: A Journal of Lesbian and Gay Studies, 4,* 287–310.

Halpern, D. F. (1986). *Sex differences in cognitive abilities.* Hillsdale, NJ: Erlbaum.

Hoenig, J. (1985). Etiology of transsexualism. In B. M. Steiner (Ed.), *Gender dysphoria: Development, research, management* (pp. 33–73). New York: Plenum.

Horney, K. (1920). The flight from womanhood: The masculinity complex in women as viewed by men and by women. *International Journal of Psychoanalysis, 7,* 324–329.

Jaffrey, Z. (1998). *The invisibles.* New York: Phoenix.

Kessler, S. J., & McKenna, W. (1978). *Gender: An ethnomethodological approach.* New York: Wiley.

Klein, M. (1975). Early stages of the Oedipus conflict. In *Love, guilt and reparation and other works, 1921–1945* (pp. 186–198). Lawrence, KS: Delacorte. (Original work published 1928)

Kohlberg, L., & Ullian, D. Z. (1974). Stages in the development of psychosexual concepts and attitudes. In R. C. Friedman, R. M. Richart, & R. L. Vande Wiele (Eds.), *Sex differences in behavior* (pp. 209–222). New York: Wiley.

Lee, P. C., & Stewart, R. S. (Eds.). (1976). *Sex differences.* New York: Urizen Books.

LeVay, S. (1996). *Queer science: The use and abuse of research in homosexuality.* Cambridge, MA: MIT Press.

Levy, G. D., Taylor, M. G., & Gelman, S. E. (1995). Traditional and evaluative aspects of flexibility in gender roles, social conventions, moral rules, and physical laws. *Child Development, 66,* 515–531.

Lewis, M., & Brooks-Gunn, J. (1979). *Social cognition and the acquisition of self.* New York: Plenum.

Lienert, T. (1998). Women's self-starvation, cosmetic surgery, and transsexualism. *Feminism and Psychology, 8,* 245–250.

Lorber, J. (1994). *Paradoxes of gender.* New Haven, CT: Yale University Press.

Lott, B. (1990). Dual natures of learned behavior: The challenge to feminist psychology. In R. T. Hare Mustin & J. Marecek (Eds.), *Making a difference: Psychology and construction of gender* (pp. 65–101). New Haven, CT: Yale University Press.

Manucci, N. (1981). *Mogol India 1653–1708* (W. Irvine, Trans.) (Vols. 1–4). New Delhi: Oriental Reprint.

Mischel, W. A. (1966). Social learning view of sex difference in behavior. In E. E. Maccoby (Ed.), *The development of sex differences* (pp. 56–81). Stanford, CA: Stanford University Press.

Money, J. (1984). Matched pair theory from two cases of micropenis syndrome concordant for diagnosis and discordant for sex of reassignment, rearing and puberty. *International Journal of Family Psychiatry, 5,* 375–381.

Money, J. (1994). Transsexualism and homosexuality in Sanskrit: 2.5 millennia of Ayurvedic sexology. *Gender Dysphoria, 1,* 32–34.

Oppenheimer, A. (1991). The wish for a sex change: A challenge to psychoanalysis? *International Journal of Psychoanalysis, 72,* 221–231.

Raymond, J. (1994). *The transsexual empire* (2nd ed.). New York: Teachers Press.

Riger, S. (1997). From snapshots to videotape: New directions in research on gender differences. *Journal of Social Issues, 53,* 395–408.

Roy, P. C. (Ed. and Trans.). (1962). *Mahabharata.* Calcutta: Oriental Publications.

Segal, L. (1994). *Straight sex: The politics of pleasure.* London: Virago.

Szuchman, L. T., & Muscarella, F. (2000). *Psychological perspectives on human sexuality.* New York: Wiley.

Tauchert, A. (1998, September). *Beyond the binary: Fuzzy gender and the radical centre.* Paper presented in the Third International Congress on Sex and Gender, Exeter College, Oxford University. Abstract published in *IJT,* 1998, 2.

Taylor, T. (1996). *The prehistory of sex: Four million years of human sexual culture.* New York: Bantam Books.

Thompson, S. K., & Bentler, P. M. (1973). A developmental study of gender constancy and parent preference. *Archives of Sexual Behavior, 2,* 379–385.

Vatsayana. (1980). *The kamasutra.* Calcutta: Nava Patra Prakashan.

Zhou, J. N., Hofman, M. A., Gooren, L. J., & Swaab, D. F. (1995). A sex difference in the human brain and its relation to transsexuality. *Nature, 378,* 68–70.

GENDER, CULTURE, POWER: THREE THEORETICAL VIEWS

(Or, Why Does Everyone in Our Classroom Look the Same?)

Brent Malin

SAN FRANCISCO STATE UNIVERSITY

Why do we behave the way we do? What theories try to account for and explain how society molds behavior? In this brief essay, Malin describes three theories of social power and how each might apply to the shaping of women's and men's behavior. He begins with the observation that most of our students look alike. Why is this the case? Who tells them how to dress? How does this type of social influence extend to other behaviors?

Culture and power are frequent topics in gender communication courses. Power and influence are brought to bear through communication, and explorations into how this phenomenon occurs strikes at the heart of how gender influence occurs. This essay can serve both to introduce the topic of power in gender communication and to illustrate three theories that try to account for cultural influence on behavior.

QUESTIONS FOR DISCUSSION

- *Do students in your classes look alike?*
- *There will be an occasional deviant, someone who does not look like everyone else. Do these theories account for such behavior?*
- *Are the "deviants" more likely to be male or female?*
- *Do people like to be considered deviant? What are the social consequences of not following the normal pattern?*
- *Is one sex more susceptible to influence in the ways described by Malin than the other? Why or why not?*

Reprinted with permission.

My Grandma Malin never once in her life wore pants. I've been sharing this interesting bit of trivia with my students for a number of years and recently decided to verify my recollections with those of my family members. None of them could recall her ever wearing pants either. While this might seem strange to our twenty-first-century sensibilities, it makes obvious sense given the time periods through which my grandmother lived. Raised at a moment in which men literally "wore the pants," not only in the family but in the public sphere as well, my Grandma wore dresses, skirts, and nightgowns, but certainly never pants. Socialized into a well-inscribed gender role, my Grandma Malin stayed away from pants for the entirety of her life, even when the more liberal fashions of later decades suggested she might, at last, slip her legs into a pair. This, no doubt, made perfect sense to her. The common sense of her upbringing was that men wore pants and women didn't. This was not odd, but a fact of life.

In retrospect, we can see my Grandma's extreme devotion to gendered fashions as a sort of oddity. Today, women regularly wear pants, and certain men, such as Dennis Rodman and Marilyn Manson, occasionally wear dresses and even makeup. And yet, while it would be easy to assume that we have thrown aside the prescribed fashions of the past for a moment in which we are free to dress however we please, we know intuitively that this is not the case. To illustrate this, we need only to look around the average college classroom. Though we may see slight variation, it's easy to see how a certain style dominates at a particular moment in time. With thousands of years of fashion from which to choose—from togas to T-shirts—we somehow all manage to "choose" things very similar. If we recall how quickly the Jennifer Aniston haircut became a "choice" of many American women and the George Clooney "Caesar" haircut became a "choice" of many American men, we begin to see how these moments of decision are situated within particular kinds of dominant messages, given to us by television programs, films, advertisements, and other forms of popular culture. And these choices are still highly gendered as well, though to a different degree and in different ways than my Grandma's "dress or pants" decision. We need only browse through copies of *GQ* and *Cosmopolitan* to get this sense of gender distinction. While *GQ* shows us well-toned men dressed in suits and ties, *Cosmo* offers up its own waif-thin women, typically clad in revealing dresses and depicted in awkward, presumably "sexy" positions. These magazines offer up their own views of masculinity and femininity, constructing ideals that American men and women are supposed to follow.

This all sounds fairly obvious, no doubt. We often talk generally about cultural messages influencing individuals, and magazines and magazine advertisements are a common focus. In this essay, however, I mean to bring this relationship between individuals and their cultures into more interesting view. Complicating this vision of gender, culture, and power, I explain several different ways to think about power as it functions within culture. The three theories I explore below are not exhaustive; there are countless other theories of power and countless other ways to explain power relations and gender. Likewise, I don't hope to imply that the three theories below are perfect descriptions of power relations. Each of the three theories has its strengths and weaknesses, and each is able to address certain sorts of situations and problems better than others. Finally, I haven't laid out each of these theories or theorists in their entirety. Rather, I've chosen interesting and relevant fragments that offer unique perspectives on the issues of gender, culture, and power and our own places within these processes.

These are not simply matters of what haircut we choose, which, in and of itself, seems a fairly mundane decision. After all, who cares if lots of men decide to cut their hair like George Clooney's or lots of women like Jennifer Aniston's? And who got hurt if my Grandma Malin never wore pants? But if we imagine these decisions as part of more general cultural processes, they become far more interesting and important to consider. How do such sets of shared values come to exist, and how might they shape not only our sense of beauty or attractiveness, but our values, actions, ideologies, and gender identities? In short, how do we come to be gendered beings holding certain views of ourselves and others?

THEORY 1: ALTHUSSER AND INTERPELLATION

The first notion of power I will explore comes from the work of French cultural theorist Louis Althusser. In his important essay "Ideology and Ideological State Apparatuses" (1971), Althusser attempts to explain the ways in which people come to be subjected to the dominant ideology—that is, how people come to follow a set of rules and values given to them by a series of mainstream cultural institutions. Althusser refers to these mainstream institutions as "the State." While we normally think of the state in a fairly narrow sense, including the government, the police, the military (the large, literally state-sponsored organizations), Althusser wants to expand this definition, and with it, our sense of multiple kinds of cultural power. Althusser calls the police and military, these official state bodies, Repressive State Apparatuses, or RSAs. These institutions work mainly through violence; if people don't obey the rules, the RSAs physically force them to. If a drunken man is causing a disturbance on the street, the police don't attempt to persuade him that drinking is wrong; they simply arrest him, forcibly removing him from the situation. Of course, police officers may also use nonviolent means to get people to follow dominant cultural rules, as when Officer McGruff or Officer Friendly comes to talk to kindergarten students about staying off drugs or staying out of trouble. Primarily, however, their method of enforcement is through force.

In contrast to these Repressive State Apparatuses, Althusser also identifies a series of Ideological State Apparatuses, or ISAs. These are institutions that function not primarily through violence but through persuasion. Here, Althusser includes such institutions as the church, the media, the school, and the family. Rather than forcing people to obey, ISAs produce repeated and consistent messages, working to persuade people of the rightness of a certain way of life and the wrongness of others. *Cosmopolitan*, for instance, does not have a literal fashion police who force people to dress appropriately. Rather, by consistently depicting particular kinds of "beautiful women" and particular kinds of "fashionable styles," they work to persuade their readers to buy into their constructed image. And *Cosmopolitan* doesn't do this alone. It works in conjunction with a host of other ISAs, all offering similar images of women. Other fashion magazines, television programs, films, and advertisements all seem to depict women in virtually identical ways—the stereotypical beauty with which we're all familiar. Even when different magazines are in competition with one another, they seem to be in agreement in terms of what women should look like.

Because of these similarities, Althusser says that ISAs are "relatively autonomous": while they seem to be different on the surface, deep down they are all promoting the same, dominant ideological values. To help illustrate this, consider two famously "competing" American institutions: church and school. While we know church and school to be at odds with each other, as in the laws forbidding prayer in public schools, they also share many of the same ideological values. For instance, both often seem to promote the value of "individualism," a staple value of American cultural life and lore. The myth of the rugged individual holds that if you work hard, you will get what you deserve. The inverse, of course, is also true: if you aren't succeeding, it must mean that you aren't working hard enough. This Protestant work ethic is important not only to church mythology but to school mythology as well, with students often rewarded for their hard work when they succeed and scolded for their lack of effort when they don't. While valuing hard work is certainly a kind of asset, the ideology of rugged individualism also does particular kinds of damage—for instance, suggesting that lower-class individuals are where they are because of their lack of effort or laziness, as opposed to certain kinds of failures in social institutions (such as the educational system itself). Church and school have traditionally shared ideological values concerning gender as well—the church traditionally placing men in the highest positions of authority (for instance, as priests), and schools traditionally channeling young boys into the more lucrative and prestigious careers in science, medicine, and engineering.

Because these ISAs share ideological values, they create a very persuasive set of messages for their culture to consume. Because the church, the media, the school, and the family traditionally give similar messages regarding a woman's subordinate place in society (for example, in the nunnery, as a sexual object, in the "soft sciences," in the kitchen), Althusser seems to suggest, people will inevitably come to hold these values to one extent or another. Althusser calls the process in which individuals take up these dominant values "interpellation," and claims that it is a process we all go through. In fact, Althusser argues that we can't even use the term "individuals" to describe ourselves. Instead, we are "subjects"; that is, we obey the dominant ideology in the same way that medieval folk may have obeyed their king. To stress the power of this process of interpellation, Althusser says that our beliefs and actions are not simply "determined" by the dominant ideology and ISAs, but "overdetermined." After all, there are multiple ISAs all telling us the same thing. We can't escape one without bumping into another. Worse yet, this process of interpellation and overdetermination takes place before we are ever born. After finding out they are having a boy, for instance, parents may decide to paint the nursery blue, as well as to buy baby-sized baseball gloves, footballs, and other "masculine" items, all of which presumably help guarantee a boy who is appropriately manly. With this in mind, Althusser suggests that we have all "always-already" been interpellated. Our role as a subject within the dominant ideology has been carved out long before we are conscious, living beings.

In answering the question of our contemporary fashion codes, Althusser would most likely describe our fashion "choices" as part of the process of interpellation. A way of "looking good" has always-already been established; born into it, we become fashion subjects in the same way that we are subjects to all sorts of other dominant ideological values. The ISAs at work here would include the media institutions that daily bombard us with visions of what we are supposed to look like. From television programs to magazines and movies, these dominant institutions persuade us to buy into certain ideals of dress and fashion. Notice as well how easily these fictional texts go hand in hand with another ISA seeking to persuade us: advertising. How often do fashion spreads in magazines appear alongside ads attempting to sell similar clothing? How often do articles on fashion "dos and don'ts" tend to nestle up against advertisements presenting the very products the articles endorse? Together, Althusser would suggest, these ISAs work in complementary ways to promote a particular ideal of fashion to which we all are to subscribe. If our classrooms show a fairly uniform pattern of dress, Althusser would argue that interpellation has taken place in clear and obvious ways.

Of course, Althusser's answer is not completely satisfactory. While it describes very well how, at any given moment in time, people might be compelled to look or behave in a "dominant way," it's unable to account for the ways in which values seem to change over time. If we are all always-already subjects to the dominant ideology, if we are all always-already interpellated, then how can change ever take place? How, for instance, did women come to wear pants when my Grandma Malin so commonsensically opposed the idea? Likewise, seeing everyone as a kind of cultural dupe, Althusser fails to account for obvious sorts of deviance—those times when people seem to clearly violate the dominant ideology. What, for instance, of the purple-Mohawk wearing, the multiply pierced, or the man or woman dressed in drag? These are cultural moments better explained by Antonio Gramsci.

THEORY 2: GRAMSCI AND CULTURAL NEGOTIATION

Italian Marxist Antonio Gramsci was imprisoned in fascist Italy in the 1920s and 1930s and wrote his influential *Prison Notebooks* (1971) from his cell. In them, he composed theories to explain the various sorts of power he saw working in his contemporary culture. For instance, Gramsci noted that despite their ill treatment and subordinate positions, the peasant classes of Italy seemed to go along with the fascist government, as if they didn't mind being dominated by the state. This initially baffled Gramsci; he didn't understand why these peasants didn't revolt or fight back against the government. But then it dawned on him: As long as the trains ran on time, he argued, these lower classes were happy. In other words, as long as the fascist government maintained a certain level of order, the lower classes would be complicit in their own domination; if the government gave in a bit, then the peasants would as well.

Gramsci developed this revelation into a theory of "hegemony," which he describes as a process of the powerful class's winning consent of the masses. Here, the dominant class holds power not simply by giving the lower classes a set of ideological values they are supposed to follow (as with Althusser), but by actively negotiating with the lower classes—giving in a little so as to maintain their overall power. By allowing the ruled classes certain kinds of freedom and leeway, the dominant or ruling class is able to maintain an equilibrium that ensures a certain kind of overall social order. In this process, things that might potentially upset the balance of power, challenging the ruling class hegemony, can quickly be rendered powerless by creating a "safe way" for them to exist within the dominant culture. For instance, in many college campuses and college towns, authorities seem to turn a blind eye to drinking (underage or not) when it takes place in designated places. It's fine for students to get drunk provided they do it within bars, at appropriate times. The bar represents a small space given up for a certain kind of rebellion on behalf of college students. If a student throws up inside the bar, they will simply be reprimanded by the bar staff, or made to leave. If the student throws up outside the bar, however, they are likely to be arrested for drunken, disorderly conduct. In this way, the college town bar serves a kind of hegemonic function. As long as college students limit their "rebellion" to getting drunk in appropriately designated areas, then administrators and authorities don't have to worry about this, or other more threatening sorts of rebellion (such as demonstrations against campus policies or tuition hikes). As with the ruled classes of fascist Italy, a hegemonic equilibrium has been established.

Raymond Williams (1991) has developed a pair of terms that help explain this process of hegemonic equilibrium still further. According to Williams, there are at least two different kinds of groups outside the dominant culture that serve as potential threats to its hegemonic rule. "Residual cultures" are cultures left over from some moment in the past. They subscribe to values at odds with the dominant culture, but because they have existed so far without becoming a threat, they are allowed to remain intact and relatively untouched by the dominant culture. The Amish, for instance, are a good example of a residual culture. With their rejection of urban life and modern consumption, the secluded, horse-and-buggy-driving Amish are a radical subculture. However, because they don't seem to upset the dominant social order, they are allowed to maintain their lifestyle despite this radical rejection of the dominant culture. In addition to these residual cultures, Williams also identifies "emergent cultures"—new cultures that spring up that are somehow outside the dominant ideology. "Grunge," for instance, the subculture associated with the Seattle music scene in the early 1990s, posed a powerful threat to ruling class hegemony. Encouraging young people to buy thrift store clothing, "grunge fashion" seemed to reject the consumerism of the 1980s. Grunge was threatening because it invited young people to buy and wear recycled clothing, posing a threat to the economics of fashion that depend upon the constant production and sale of new clothing, as well as to parental and other adult sensibilities that desire youth to "dress appropriately" (in other words, not in cut-off army pants).

Had Gramsci been alive to experience grunge culture, he most likely would have predicted that it would somehow be "incorporated" into the dominant culture. It would have been made into a safe rebellion, like the college bar, as a way to reestablish the dominant class's hegemony. He might have predicted that companies like J. Crew would begin making "grunge" clothing—clothing that captured the spirit of grunge, but with a brand-name appeal and price (which is exactly what seems to have happened). Wearing a nicely hemmed pair of J. Crew "fatigue shorts," as opposed to a pair of cut-off thrift store ones, is "safe" because it satisfies parents who don't want their kids dressed "sloppily" as well as the capitalist system that wants twenty-somethings to buy expensive, brand new clothes, as opposed to old, cheap, recycled ones. The "style" of grunge lives on, but the substance, the potential rebelliousness, is quickly pacified. Similarly, if American youth suddenly decided that Amish life and fashion were cool, and decided to give up the comfort and convenience of suburban life for the more rugged, automobile- and electricity-free life of the Amish, the ruling class culture and hegemony would be substantially challenged. We might expect to see a line of J. Crew black hats and jackets, a fashion that would encourage youth to participate in Amish culture, but without having to violate the norms of the dominant one.

Given his notion of hegemony, Gramsci would no doubt pay close attention to the kinds of "rebellion" our clothes might suggest. Unlike Althusser, Gramsci would be particularly interested in the sorts of changes that have taken place in American fashion, seeing these as moments in which the hegemonic process worked to incorporate changing ideas and values. For instance, Gramsci might be interested in the ways in which stereotypically urban "hip-hop" fashion has taken over even white suburban homes. What has taken place when Chicago's North Suburbs are clothed in the baggie, low-slung jeans that once seemed to suggest an alternative, urban community? What has become of the alternativeness this style once demonstrated? Likewise, how should we read the new "freedom" that women exercise in wearing the pants my Grandma Malin shunned? While these changes might suggest certain kinds of liberations (for example, that women have more choice in what they wear, as well as what they do; that white suburban cultures are uniting with more heavily urban, African American ones), they might also suggest this process of winning consent, of maintaining the hegemony of the dominant powers. In other words, Gramsci would likely be concerned with the ways in which these "changes" might have served to maintain the dominant social order. Have these changes in fashion masked the fact that more serious social changes (access to government office, increased rates of pay, decreases in sexual violence) are not occurring? Have gender challenges, for instance, simply been incorporated or J. Crewified, or have legitimate challenges been made and steps taken?

THEORY 3: FOUCAULT AND SURVEILLANCE

In contrast to both Althusser and Gramsci, French theorist Michel Foucault challenges the idea that a dominant or ruling class or apparatus functions to control our values and behaviors. As Foucault explains it, the "tactics" of power, the ways power works at particular times, continually change. When people were primarily ruled by a king, then power seemed to flow downward from the king's authority. Things were right because the king proclaimed them right. With the fall of kings and the movement to more democratic systems of government, however, the main tactics of power began to change. No longer was there a central point from which power flowed. Rather, in the spirit of democracy, power flowed from and within "the public." Because of this change, what would have once been "declared from on high" by the king was now debated over and fought about by the public. The rule of the king had been replaced by the rule of public opinion.

Foucault doesn't view "democracy" and "public opinion" with the same rose-colored glasses as many people. Instead, in public opinion Foucault simply finds a new strategy of power at work, a kind of power through surveillance. In describing this new strategy or tactic of power, Foucault draws on the work of Jeremy Bentham, a nineteenth-century social thinker who worked at finding ways to help organize and control the growing population of England. One of his architectural designs, the panopticon, was a design for a prison that would allow for the most efficient control of prisoners, allowing a smaller staff to control a larger number of inmates. The panopticon was a circular prison in which each prisoner's room faced inward toward a central guard's tower. In contrast to previous prisons, which were often windowless dungeons, each cell in the panopticon had a large window, both allowing the prisoner to see the guard tower and giving the impression that the guard could always see within the prisoner's cell. The principle was fairly straightforward. If the prisoners felt like they were being watched, they would begin to monitor themselves more carefully. Eventually, Bentham theorized, they would begin to behave on their own, simply because of this feeling of being watched. This would mean that fewer guards were needed, as the prisoners should eventually begin to "guard themselves."

Foucault uses the design of the panopticon as a sort of analogy for the contemporary Euro-American world. Since the fall of the king, Foucault argues, power has worked without a central authority. In Foucault's view, there is no dominant ruler or apparatus to proclaim a set of dominant values. Rather, power is spread throughout the public in a way analogous to the panopticon. In the panopticon, the guards don't hold power over the prisoners the way a king does over his subjects. Instead, the prisoners are meant to take power over themselves—to behave as they are supposed to even when the guard isn't present. This is an interesting explanation of how power works in our contemporary society as well. When people go out to a public park, for instance, there are usually no obvious state officials there to maintain order, aside from the occasional police officer. Instead, Foucault might suggest, order is maintained by our mutual surveillance of each other. We might imagine the park goers as both guards and prisoners. That is, my presence in the park suggests to others that I might be watching them (like the ominous tower in the middle of the panopticon), but my presence in the park also leaves me to be looked at by others. As a result, we all behave well or suffer the consequences of public ridicule and humiliation.

To return to our example of fashion in the classroom, Foucault would offer a significantly different theory from either Althusser or Gramsci. First, Foucault would likely note that there are no "fashion apparatuses" in the typical classroom, no *Cosmopolitan*, J. Crew, Nike, or *Friends* to ensure that we are dressed "in style" or "appropriately," or that we have the right Aniston or Clooney haircut. In other words, where Althusser and Gramsci would highlight the roles of dominant apparatuses in constructing this place of appropriate dress, Foucault might point to the dynamics of the classroom itself. Like the park goers who see each other and are seen in the park, so each member of a classroom sees, and is seen by, each other member. Because of this, each classmate holds a particular kind of power over each other classmate, each one subjected to the same power he or she possesses. For this reason, Foucault would likely suggest that the power at work in making classmates dress similarly is held between these classmates in their mutual looks (and not in some overarching, dominant apparatus). In other words, classmates dress a certain way because they know their fellow classmates will be looking at them. This sort of power is intensified when we make comments to each other about one another's dress. If I make fun of Steve's shirt to John, then John knows that I will make fun of him if he wears a similar shirt. Similarly, if I compliment someone's shirt, I'm suggesting that people should want to look like that. In other words, if I tell someone "Nice shirt!" I might really be saying "I've got my eye on you!"

CONCLUSION

Together, these different theorists suggest different ways to think about the relationship between gender, culture, and power, each with its own strengths and weaknesses and each dealing with certain kinds of situations better than others. If we take an Althusserian view of gender and power, we oblige ourselves to interrogate particular kinds of ideological state apparatuses, asking how they might contribute to the process of interpellation. This works well in explaining moments of obvious conformity to dominant norms and powerfully conveys the ways in which dominant ideals might impact upon us in various ways. It is less useful for discussing moments of change, or instances of resistance to dominant cultural values. A Gramscian view, on the other hand, helps account for acts of resistance, seeing them as potentials for change that may or may not be incorporated within the dominant culture. Finally, a Foucaultian perspective understands gender and power apart from apparatuses, focusing on the smaller-scale, local moments of power, as in a classroom.

These theories all offer interesting ways to think about our own relationships to gender, power, and culture. If issues of gender and power are primarily a matter of interpellation, then we may have an obligation to work to change dominant ideological structures as best we can, working to fight against the harmful gender interpellations they might perpetuate. If we see these more as a matter of hegemony and incorporation, then we may be obligated to find ways to be outside the dominant cultures of gender, ways that cannot simply be incorporated back and pacified. Or we may need to launch an ongoing struggle, constantly making new emergent cultures to replace ones that are incorporated. If we take a more Foucaultian view, then we may look more closely at our activities on a more local, smaller scale. For instance, the ways we look at each other, comment on each other's appearance, or compliment each other may all participate in a kind of panopticon of gender that celebrates certain kinds of values and punishes others. Here, we would need to pay careful attention to the directions our looks and comments are heading.

Fortunately, we don't necessarily need to choose one theory that works in all cases all the time. Rather, these theories each open up interesting ways to interrogate our own and others' participation in the perpetuation of gender norms. And these explorations, of course, need not simply concern the clothes we wear. A host of other normative ways of life is similarly perpetuated through a variety of cultural powers—from the "correct" body types for men and women, to the "correct" jobs for men and women to do, to the "correct" ways to treat someone in a relationship, to the "correct" kinds of relationships people can have. These sets of values define what is "normal," often offering us a fairly narrow "choice" of how we are supposed to live our lives. And these norms often have disturbing consequences, suggesting, for instance, that only some people are worthy of our attention or love, and that others are not entitled to love at all. Whether we explore media texts, social organizations, public policies, or interpersonal interactions, these theories suggest ways to think about and upset these workings of gender and power. And each would no doubt offer its own unique perspective on why my Grandma Malin never wore pants.

REFERENCES

Althusser, L. (1971). Ideology and ideological state apparatuses. In *Lenin and philosophy and other essays* (B. Brewster, Trans.). London: New Left Books.

Foucault, M. (1995). *Discipline and punish* (A. Sheridan, Trans.). New York: Vintage Books.

Gramsci, A. (1971). *Selections from the prison notebooks of Antonio Gramsci*. New York: International Publishers.

Williams, R. (1991). Base and superstructure in Marxist cultural criticism. In C. Mukerji & M. Schudson (Eds.), *Rethinking popular culture* (pp. 398–404). Berkeley/Los Angeles/Oxford: University of California Press.

TAKE THE HELM, MAN THE SHIP . . . AND I FORGOT MY BIKINI!

Unraveling Why *Woman* Is Not Considered a Verb

Catherine Helen Palczewski

UNIVERSITY OF NORTHERN IOWA[1]

In this article, the author seems to be playing with language, but her play is also work—the work of interpreting how language functions to shape our thoughts and expectations of our personal, social, and political worlds. Catherine Palczewski addresses the peculiar nature of the English language's portrayal of male as actor and female as nonparticipant or one who is acted upon. She reveals the insidious way this dichotomy of male/female active/inactive positioning is established and reconstituted within verbal constructions used to reference common daily activities. Further, she posits how such positioning is detrimental to the construction of woman as an empowered agent, even when functioning in a responsible, active role. Although this playful article may seem somewhat tongue-in-cheek, it provides much food for thought, particularly through the manner in which Palczewski incorporates language from Daly and Caputi's Wickedary *(dictionary) to help the reader see how an alternative discourse can facilitate a vision of woman as agent.*

QUESTIONS FOR DISCUSSION

- *What are other examples of words that are male-centered that would not function the same way for females?*
- *Are there female-centered words that are empowering to females that do not function the same way for males?*
- *All language frames the way we might imagine our lives, but the author focuses on this function of language in terms of how it is limiting to women and ourselves. Can you think of similar limitations for men?*
- *Does language function to hide only men's agency? Can you think of instances in which men's agency may be denied and women's agency hidden?*
- *Do you agree with the author's assumption that agency, as designated through language structure, is necessarily advantageous?*

Reprinted with permission.

D uring a class on language theory, one of my companions-in-learning (a.k.a. students) asked a question that came to him after he had watched the America's Cup races, in which an all-woman crew was competing: "How can an all-woman crew 'man a ship'?" In one of those Be-Dazzling moments of Anamnesia (Daly, 1987, pp. 63, 60), a whole range of possibilities began Spinning (p. 96) out before me, perhaps in rhythm with a Tidal Memory (p. 97). *Woman* is not considered a verb, particularly in nautical settings, and *it should be*. Wanting to verify that my understanding of dominant English was supported by the "dick-tionary" (Daly, 1987, p. 194), I turned to my handy *Oxford English* version and discovered that *woman* was, indeed, a verb, but not quite the same verb as *man* and not used at all as a verb in contemporary times.

I then began to consider the myriad ways in which subtle gender biases work their way into the idioms we use to describe leadership, where *man*-as-verb is truncated out of phrases, yet still influences their meaning. Keeping with the nautical theme, I began to consider the way in which the metaphor of "taking the helm" is used to describe leadership. My own professional organization, the National Communication Association,[2] chose "Taking the Helm" as the theme for its 1996 convention. And, after a cursory review of newspaper headlines, it seems that "at the helm" and "taking the helm" are favorites to describe when a person assumes a leadership position. Particularly in relation to promotions in business, newspapers like to headline with the helm metaphor. Within the first two weeks of millennial May alone, national and international English-language newspapers used some variation of helm at least 74 times to describe the promotion of a "captain" of business, a leader in religion, or an official in government.

I would like to play with (as a person who is a "player with symbols") this metaphor and its relationship with womanning a ship, arguing that the relationship highlights a continuing bias in how we see and feel about leadership, gender, and sex. As part of this water sport, I do a take on, take on, take over, take away, steal away, fly away, fly over, sail over, and sail through the metaphor of helm. Engaging in a form of Sin-Tactics, defined by feminist language scholar Mary Daly (1987) as "Sinister Strategies, esp. tactics of Wicked Grammarians whose syntax Touches and awakens the Powers of Terrible Women" (p. 163), I call forth the Goddess of the Verb (p. 66) to aid in the process of discovering how *woman* was stripped of its/her verb-al powers. Building on this analysis of *woman*-as-verb, I then reel in the multiple meanings of *helm*.

Wanting to discover alternate interpretations, to see if feminist Word Witches had engaged in any Word-Magic (Daly, 1987, p. 182) with the verb *woman*, I peeled open their wickedaries, only to discover that no such word magic had been conjured. Accordingly, this essay incants a new spell by studying feminist word magic, by breaking the spell of helm/woman/mistress/lady, and finally by verbing *woman*. After presenting this essay at a conference, and hearing sister (in contrast to fellow) scholar

Mollie Whalen's response to it, I also realized that I needed to explore gender neutral or inclusive verbs, such as person, people, and human (only one of which, interestingly, has a nonobsolete verb form). In order to have the ingredients for this word magic, I engage in a bit of alchemy with the helm metaphor—merely one example among many that could have been bewitched.

WORD WEBS AND WORD MAGIC

The makings of a new spell to "verb" *woman, mistress,* and *lady* are provided in radical wicked feminist word-weavers' play with nouns. The first ingredient (a bit of spider web to clear our eyes) is feminist language theorists' recognition of the power of language to influence and/or construct our perceptions of the world. Speaking as the fates, "the Weird Sisters, the three [or six] Goddesses who determine the course of events . . . Spinners of Stamina" (Daly, 1987, p. 124), Cheris Kramer (Kramarae) (1975), Robin Lakoff (1975), Dale Spender (1985), Julia Penelope (1990), and Casey Miller and Kate Swift (1991) determined a course of events for women and language. Spender, in one example of the fates' incantations, plays out the implications of language on/in our lives in *Man Made Language*:

> Language helps form the limits of our reality. It is our means of ordering, classifying and manipulating the world. It is through language that we become members of a human community, that the world becomes comprehensible and meaningful, that we bring into existence the world in which we live.
>
> Yet it is ironic that this faculty which helps to create our world also has the capacity to restrict our world. For having learnt a particular language and had access to being "humanized" we also have been "socialized." (1985, p. 3)

Spender's analysis points to how words are magic as they bewitch us to see the world in a particular way and, at the same time, prevent us from seeing it in others.

Just as words influence our perceptions, so, too, do rules of word use. Julia Penelope (1990) provides the second ingredient (a bit of root to break through the dirt) when she explains that "languages are much more than the words in their vocabularies. They are systems of rules, rules which speakers find useful for saying what they want to say. When speakers cease to find rules or words useful, they abandon them and make up new ones" (pp. xiii–xiv). These rules, however, are not merely rules that enable clearer communication but also rules that proscribe realities: "English does more than hinder and hurt women: it proscribes the boundaries of the lives we might imagine and will ourselves to live" (p. xiv).

Kramarae, Lakoff, Miller and Swift, Penelope, and Spender's recognition of the power of language and language rules provides a strong base brew for an analysis of the way particular sexed verbs function. Their analysis of the power of sexed rules of noun use helps to explain the functioning of sexed verbs. Penelope (1990) also discusses the way sex-marked predicates determine the sex of the nouns we can use with them as agents and objects (p. 185). Even though she does not discuss the way *woman* and *man* function in those forms, her analysis of predicates is extremely useful. She argues that, in particular, English has a set of male predicates for penile activity (father, sire, beget, impregnate, penetrate, and so on), but lacks a semantically symmetrical set of predicates for activities performed by the clitoris and labia (p. 186).

Cheris Kramarae and Paula A. Treichler's (1992) Be-Witching feminist dictionary offers the third ingredient (a sprinkling of mermaid breath to clear out old meanings) when it details the myriad meanings of *woman* and *man* in their noun forms. Similarly (a sprinkling of sea-nymph breath), Jane Mills (1993) details the history of *woman* as a noun. However, despite all of the wicked treatments of language's relation to women (for example, Baron, 1986; Cameron, 1985; Coates, 1987; Kramer [Kramarae], 1975; Kramer [Kramarae], Thorne, & Henley, 1978; Kramarae & Treichler, 1992; Lakoff, 1975, 1990; Miller & Swift, 1991; Mills, 1993; Penelope, 1990; Riley, 1988), a crucial ingredient is left out: no exploration of the implications of *man* and *woman* in their verb forms has been Sin-articulated.

Fortunately, I need not engage in alchemy, for others have provided more ingredients to perfect the brew. Mary Daly's *Wickedary* (1987) and Julia Penelope's *Speaking Freely* (1990, providing a bit of sprite spirit) point to the possibilities of play with language, and in particular the power of verbs. Daly warns against the passive voice, "that ubiquitous patriarchal voice that subliminally spooks women, luring its victims into passivity, rendering them unable to recognize and Name the agents of oppression" (p. 44). Instead, we should strive for an Active Voice that "will enable women to communicate with each other and with Other Guides, Sounding out cosmic connections" (p. 45). Penelope speaks out against the suppression of agency enabled by truncated passives because they appeal to "authority as defined by male societies," protect the guilty and deny responsibility, and create a pretense of objectivity, among other things (p. 149).

Individuals who are attempting to avoid explicit responsibility for the consequences of the power they exercise often engage in the rhetorical strategy of using truncated passives, so-called because suppressing agency shortens the sentence (Penelope, 1990, p. 147). The result of "agent-deletion leaves us with only the objects of the acts described by the verbs. Passives without agents foreground the objects (victims) in our minds so that we tend to forget that some human agent is responsible for performing the action" (p. 146), as in "mistakes were made," "Hanoi was bombed," or "the toy got broke." As Penelope explains, "agentless passives conceal and deceive when it doesn't suit speakers' or writers' purposes to make agency explicit" (p. 149). As a result, "this makes it easy to suppress responsibility" and, thus, results in "protection of the guilty and denial of responsibility, . . . the pretense of objectivity, . . . and trivialization" (p. 149).

Answering Daly's and Penelope's call to resist the hiding of men's agency and the denial of women's agency, I act out, woman out, woman the pages of language, share the helm, and toss man/*man* overboard. I strive to recognize an active meaning for *woman*. Before casting that new spell, however, the existing word-spells must be broken.

THE SEXING OF HELM

In order to break the spell of inactive *woman*, I thought it best to explore an instance in which her agency was denied as a result of a nonspecification of agent that allowed for an assumption of a male agent. When people use the metaphor of helm to describe the taking of a leadership role, a consideration of the potential sexist implications is absent. Of course, because a clearly sexed term is not present in the metaphor, one might feel safe in using it. However, embodying the classic form of suppressed agents (hexed by Spender and Penelope earlier), no one is named as the one who takes the helm, and so we are left to infer who does the taking. Given the gendered and sexed history of taking and helms, I proclaim that a particular interpretation is imbedded in that seemingly innocuous metaphor.

Lest we think the helm is no longer manned, or *helm* is no longer sexed male, an analysis of coverage of the America's Cup races points to typical usage. Bill Koch, who won the Cup in 1992, organized an all-woman crew to sail his boats in the races that would determine the U.S. representative for the America's Cup. During the 1994–95 training for, and actual competition in, the races, a number of newspaper and magazine stories described the crew and its activities. Even in the face of an all-woman crew, and in the face of generally accepted rules for making terms gender-neutral, the male relationship to helm was so strong that it persisted, perhaps because sailing is "the most masculine of bastions" (Carpenter, 1994, p. 81) and "a bastion of seafaring maleness" (Gosselin, 1995, p. 52) where "traditionally women have been far more likely to be invited onto the 75-footers that contest the cup to pose for swimsuit issues than to actually crew" (Starr, 1995, p. 70). These figures of speech, and the images they conjure, are too enticing to go unremarked. Given that bastions are "a projecting part of a fortification" (*OED*, 1971, p. 175), the end result of this series of descriptions is that there are masculine projecting parts, 75-footers, fortified cups, and women posing in swimsuits amidst all.

Returning to the published descriptions of the all-woman crew of *America*, in no article did reporters use the word *helmswoman* or *helmsperson*, although *skipper* was occasionally used (Whiteside, 1995, p. 40; Lloyd, 1994). In fact, when one author asked one of the *America* crew members what to call Jane Oetking, who was working the helm, "the helmswoman or helmsperson?" the crew member replied "We call her Jane" (Reynolds, 1995, p. 99). In all other cases, it was *helmsman* (Nutt, 1994; Alexander, 1995).

Even in articles that avoided the issue of the sex of the person at the helm, constant references to the sailors' personal relationships (mother, wife, fiancée) were made (Reed, 1995; Starr, 1995; Lloyd, 1994; Lee, 1994; Reynolds, 1995; Alexander, 1995; Maxwell-Pierson, 1995), compared to an unsurprising lack of references to male sailors' personal relationships and over-reference to male sailors' monetary power (Marbach & Robinson, 1987; Swift, 1995; Ballard, 1987; Barnes, 1986; Finlayson & Maloney, 1987).

Other verb forms concerning sailing also were sexed male. For example, the navigation system is mastered, not mistressed (a distinction to be discussed more later), in a passage questioning whether women "have the know-how required to master the yacht's complicated navigation system—in which computers compile information about wind and waves for the navigator, who informs the tactician, who advises the helmsman, who instructs the crew" (Alexander, 1995, p. 74). Given that women are mistresses, and not masters, it seems that this passage creates a situation where women could never sail a ship. This passage also points to a broader horizon of sexed verbs; not only should we analyze *man/woman*, but also *master/mistress* and *lord/lady*.

In addition to the lack of language to describe the sailing activities of an all-woman crew, three interesting themes circulated around discussion of women taking the helm in the America's Cup races. First, a historical tension exists on boats between "brain and brawn" positions, the helm being the brain. As one reporter noted:

> A racing team is organized hierarchically with a few decision makers at the top who bark out orders like "Get the [expletive] jib down NOW!" to the rest of the team. Experienced sailors are used to the hollering. But four months into training, some of the [all-woman's] team's yachting novices are still suffering from culture shock. (Carpenter, 1994, p. 82; inserts in original)

Second, the owner of *America* worried "that the women are reluctant to step up and lead for fear of offending their teammates. 'Decisions that should be made in a nano-second, they'd prefer to sit down for 10 minutes and arrive at a consensus,' [Koch] said" (Starr, 1995, p. 71). Third, yachting is a sport that historically views women as bad luck on boats (Thomas, 1994, p. B21).

These three themes further support my argument that "taking the helm" means leading in a particular way, one that women may not like, or one that men perceive women will not like. And let's not forget the inherent hierarchy (we lead, others follow) and the potential class bias (helms on yachts) inherent in such a metaphor. While "taking the helm" appears innocuous, upon closer examination, it becomes clear how such a metaphor for leadership actually represents what Penelope (1990) names the PUD (patriarchal universe of discourse). Taking the helm metaphor as an example, I would now like to play out the various ways in which it points to the denial of agency to women by denying us verb forms.

IF YOU TAKE THE HELM, CAN YOU THEN WOMAN THE SHIP?

A helm is "the handle or tiller, in large ships the wheel, by which the rudder is managed; sometimes extended so as to include the whole steering gear" (*OED*, 1971, p. 1286). While other definitions do present themselves, I save their exploration until later. Now, given the association of a helm with a ship, what alternative wordings present themselves? Typically, when one takes the helm, one man's a ship. *Man* is a verb. However, it appears that *woman* is not.

    Man is defined as both a noun and a verb. In its verb form, the form that interests me here, the *OED* offers:

> 1. trans. (Mil. and Naut.) To furnish (a fort, ship, etc.) with a force or company of men to serve or defend it. . . . b. Naut. To place men at or on (a particular part of a ship), as at the capstan to heave anchor, or on the yards to salute a distinguished person. . . . c. To equip and send (a boat, occas. an army) with its complement of men in a certain direction . . . .
> 2. To supply with inhabitants, to people . . . b. To fill up with men. . . . 3. To provide (a person) with followers or attendants. (p. 1711)

I initially thought that *woman* would not appear as a verb and was surprised when it did. However, the distinctions between the two verb forms, which ought to be parallel, is intriguing. *OED* offers the following for *woman*:

> 1. early nonce-uses. a. intr. To become woman-like; with *it* to behave as a woman, be womanly. b. trans. To make like a woman in weakness or subservience. c. pa. pple. Accompanied by a woman. d. To make "a woman" of, deprive of virginity. 2. trans. To furnish or provide with women; to equip with a staff of women. (p. 3808)

While *man* carries implications of acting, typically in battle and on ships, *woman* typically carries implications of being acted upon. *Woman* is to become woman-like, or be made a woman, or to be deprived of virginity.

    Another interesting check on usage lurks within the innards of my computer. For instance, when using the spell-check, *manned* and *manning* were not highlighted as incorrect. However *womanning* was corrected to *womanizing* and *womanized* was offered as the first correction to *womanned*. Odd little coincidence, given that semantic derogation, where terms referring to women become negative, are all derogated by being tied to sexuality. *Bachelor* and *spinster* ought to be equal, but *spinster* connotes someone who cannot get any sex. *Lord* and *lady* ought to be equal, but *lady* now carries connotations of ladies-of-the-night, women who get far too much sex. *Master* and *mistress* ought to be equal, but *mistress* is a kept woman, who gets sex by "stealing" it from another woman. And *governor* and *governess* ought to be equal, but a governess is the person who takes care of the result of others getting sex. In like manner, verb forms of *master* and *lord* are not corrected while verb forms of *mistress* and *lady* are.

The differences between the noun forms of *man* and *woman* may explain why *woman* has not been integrated into our vocabulary as a gender inclusive term. Both *man* and *woman* as verbs carry so much gender baggage that it appears counterproductive to rescue the terms from the phallogrammar (Daly, 1987, p. 217). However, I propose that we do just that. The gendered verb forms of *man* and *woman* represent all the myriad ways in which language constrains women, and by exorcising (Daly, 1987, p. 75) this term, we may teach ourselves the power of word magic, and make possible an alternative metaphor for leadership: Lusty Leaping with Mermaids (Daly, 1987, pp. 144–145). Given that "mermaids' realm is not invaded by men, it can represent a place where there is female freedom and self-sufficiency [*The Little Mermaid* notwithstanding]. Living in water . . . physically conveys the idea of a different world, different from the patriarchal land in which we find ourselves struggling for female liberation" (Emily Erwin Culpepper, quoted in Daly, 1987, p. 146).

Not to be-labor the point, but to make clear that the semantic derogation of women through nouns is mirrored in other sexed verb forms in addition to *man* and *woman*, let us further sate my Wonderlust (Daly, 1987, p. 101). Women are subordinated and devalued not only by being named by nouns that derogate us, but also by being denied verb forms that enable agency. Consider this romp through male verbs and the lack of contemporary usage of female verbs.

lord v. lady. The verb form of *lord* is "1. a. to exercise lordship, have dominion. b. to play the lord; to behave in a lordly manner, assume airs of grandeur; to rule tyrannically, to domineer. 2. to be or act as lord of; to control, manage, rule, *rare*. 3. a. To make (a man) a lord or master. b. To confer the title of lord upon: to ennoble" (*OED*, 1971, p. 1664). In contrast, the verb form of *lady* is "1. To make a lady of; to raise to the rank of lady; to address as 'lady.' b. to render ladylike or feminine. 2. *To lady it:* to play the lady or mistress" (p. 1559). If one lords, then one exercises lordship or has dominion, and only rarely is one passively lorded (made a lord by another). In contrast, if one ladies, one is made a lady or merely plays at being a lady. Even with a sexed verb, women may still be denied agency.

master v. mistress. *Master* in its verb form means "1. To get the better of, in any contest or struggle; to overcome defeat. 2. To reduce to subjection, compel to obey; to break, tame (an animal). 4. To make oneself master of (an art, science, etc.); to acquire complete knowledge or understanding of (a fact, a proposition), or complete facility in using (an instrument, etc.). 5. To act the part of master towards; to rule as a master; to be the master of (a servant, scholar, house, etc.)" (*OED,* 1971, p. 1739). *Mistress* in verb form means "a. To provide with a mistress. b. to make a mistress or paramour of. c. to call or address as 'mistress.' d. *To mistress it:* to play the mistress, to have the upper hand. e. To become mistress of (an art). f. To dominate as a mistress" (p. 1820). Again, *master* involves agency, getting the better of, subjecting, compelling [others] to obey. *Mistress,* in contrast, is passive. A woman is provided as a mistress; she does not mistress. Or she is made a paramour of. Or she merely plays at being mistress. Or, if one focuses on the latter definitions, where agency is allowed, one realizes that it is often a false agency, for when a women dominates as a mistress, she dominates (typically) "servants or attendants . . . household or family" (p. 1820). Agency is rarely involved; rarely is control possible, and never over masters.

My analysis of the semantic imbalance between these terms owes much to feminist analyses of their noun forms. The function of language, and its influence on gender, has been much discussed in relation to these terms as nouns (Penelope, 1990; Spender, 1985; Miller & Swift, 1991). However, the functions of language, and its ability to limit women, goes beyond semantic derogation when the terms *man* and *woman* function as verbs.

Three primary functions are typically attributed to language: defining, organizing, and evaluating. Language defines who and what we are as it names (Daly, 1987, p. 83; Miller & Swift, 1991, pp. 1–20; Spender, 1985, pp. 163–190; Wood, 1994, pp. 129–130). Those names then function to selectively shape our perceptions, either through the process of selection/deflection/reflection (Burke, 1966, p. 45) or through the formation of a vocabulary repertoire that guides public discourse (Condit, 1990). The power of naming is detailed in work on the power of the male generic, how women are defined by their appearance and not their accomplishments, how the language is imbalanced (220 words for sexually promiscuous women, 22 for men), and how marginalized groups often lack a language. All of these approaches isolate the power of language to define and to shape our perceptions through the development of terministic screens. How *man* and *woman* are defined as verbs points to the way men are defined as agents and women are not.

As it defines, language organizes our thoughts about gender through stereotypes, polarized thinking (as in the *opposite* sex), and through gender filters. Analyses of how semantic derogation and the semantic negative operate do much to elucidate the power of language—*spinster* v. *bachelor, mistress* v. *master, governess* v. *governor, tramp* v. *tramp, madam* v. *sir.* An interesting twist on nouns' semantic derogation is provided by an analysis of the imbalance and derogation of gendered verbs—in this case, the positive and active associations with *man* and the negative and passive associations with *woman.*

As we organize, we tend to organize along hierarchical lines—which leads to the evaluative function of language. Differences are no longer equal, and equally possible, but are differently valued opposites. Although *woman* was a verb in traditional uses, no longer do we use *woman* as a verb. As such, it is an example that encompasses the elements of defining, organizing, and evaluating *and* points to a need for hypothetical thought. *Woman* as a nonverb carries all the implications of gendered language. It defines who is and is not an agent. It organizes *woman* and *man* into two categories, and by granting agency to one, evaluates it as superior.

Fortunately, language also enables hypothetical thought—or play (Condit, 1992). While French feminists urge us to steal/fly, I urge us to wear armor (helms), to sail by taking the tiller (helm), and to gather straw (helm).

VERBING WOMAN

Given this analysis, what do we do? Well, one could argue that by writing this essay, I am engaging in change. Nancy Henley (1987) offers: "The next stage of transition to nonsexist language, in addition to continuing adoption of the forms on an individual level, should be one of active pressure on the larger speech community" (p. 19). But, the question remains, *how* do we actively pressure?

Communication Scholar Celeste Condit's reformulation of Kenneth Burke's "Definition of Man" points us to an appropriate attitude as we engage larger speech communities. Instead of being

> the symbol-using, (symbol making, symbol-misusing) animal
> inventor of the negative (or moralized by the negative)
> separated from his natural condition by instruments of his own making
> goaded by a spirit of hierarchy (or moved by the sense of order)
> and rotten with perfection (Burke, 1966, p. 16),

we should think of ourselves as

> People [who] are
> players with symbols
> inventors of the negative and the possibility of morality
> grown from their natural condition by tools of their collective making
> trapped between hierarchy and equality (moved constantly to reorder)
> neither rotten nor perfect, but now and again lunging down both paths. (Condit, 1992, p. 352)

So, how do we play with the metaphor? And how do we play with *woman, mistress,* and *lady* as verbs?

One way to play with the metaphor is by showing up its subtle biases (breaking its spell). Taking the helm entails manning a boat. It also entails that we lead, and others (who?) must follow. And it means we must lead in a particularly loud and nonconsensual manner, especially given the assumptions about leadership represented in media coverage of the America's Cup races.

Of course, words do have multiple meanings. After Be-Speaking the biases in typical interpretations of the metaphor, we can always wreak some Word-Magic and re-metaphor, creating our own Word-Waves (Daly, 1987, p. 182). What else could the metaphor mean? Much as French feminists play with the dual meaning of the French term *vole* (meaning both to steal and to fly), I play with the multiple meanings of *helm* and *take*. Here are a few alternative interpretations.

Even if *helm* still means "the handle or tiller," we can play with *take*, which can mean not only "to grasp, grip, seize, lay hold of," but also "to apprehend mentally, comprehend," "to touch," "to strike, hit, impinge upon," "to captivate, delight, charm," "to adopt as one's own," "to proceed to occupy," "to face and attempt to get over, through, up, etc.," "to 'go on' madly or excitedly; to rage, rave," and "to consort with" (*OED*, 1971, pp. 3223–3226). *Webster's New Collegiate Dictionary* also includes the following definitions: "to copulate with," "to receive into one's body," and "to indulge in or enjoy" (1188–1189). So, what do you say to taking/stealing the helm and hiding it? copulating with it? killing it? enjoying it? getting over it? occupying it? raving about it?

Now, what if we want to eschew the nautical metaphor, in part because of some of its unavoidable biases (women are bad luck on boats, yachts are bankrolled by the elite)? Looking through *OED*, a number of alternative interpretations for helm emerge:

> Helm: I. 1. That part of the armour which covers the head; a helmet. 2. Put for a man in armour. 3. Christ's crown of thorns.
>
> II. 4. The crown, top or summit of anything; in OE esp. the leafy top of a tree. 5. The head or cap of an alembic or retort.
>
> III. 6. A covering. 7. A roofed shelter for cattle, etc.; a shed.
>
> Helm: The stalk of corn; the stalks collectively, straw; esp. as made up in bundles or laid straight for thatching.

So, we could pick out a thatched roof? Strike at the thatched roof (or blow the roof off)? Pick out a shelter for cattle? Remove a crown of thorns from our collective brow? Take the helm off of our heads and increase our range of vision? Take to the top of a tree? Take off our helm (crown of thorns) and replace it with a helm (a helmet, a top of a tree, or a stalk of corn)? We could take/steal/fly (through the water or through the air) with our straw (made into a broom)?

At the same time we play with the metaphor, perhaps we should also integrate a new set of vocabulary into our repertoire that recognizes *woman, lady,* and *mistress* as active verbs—defined by women, ladies, and mistresses (negative connotations intentionally ignored, because, after all, we are redefining). In the same way that feminist linguists and wickedarians have redefined nouns naming women, we can redefine verbs. If a woman is "an individual human being whose life is her own concern" (Cicily Hamilton, quoted in Kramarae & Treichler, 1992, p. 490), or is a Terrible Woman,

> a Be-Friending woman who breaks the Terrible Taboo, thus becoming herSelf Terrible, Taboo; one who consistently performs Natural Acts, giving allegiance to her own kind; an Outrageously Courageous woman who Touches Original Wholeness in herSelf and in other women, who themSelves awaken to Touch others into Otherness (Daly, 1987, p. 172),

then *woman* the verb can mean populating a place with courageous, self-identified touchers. *To woman* is not to populate a place for military battle, nor is it to prepare for a show of deference to hierarchy, but is instead the creation of a critical mass of souls who are willing to do what needs to be done to maintain, create, and save life-giving forces. For example: "We need to woman the world with crones, hags, spinsters, harpies, and viragos."

An additional, special use of *to woman* exists with language as its object (thanks, here, to Mollie Whalen and her friend for hearing this in their mind's ear). For example, if one "womans the language," then s/he raises sex/gender questions about language, not so much to *occupy* it as to *open* it to inspection by making it "strange." For example, when history is womanned to herstory (even though history is not etymologically sexed), it raises sex/gender questions that have previously been unasked, in part because they were not open to inspection.

If we accept conventional meanings of *mistress*, as someone who controls, someone who teaches, and someone who is sexual, we can brew up an interesting verb form. *To mistress* then means to determine one's own sexuality, or to teach your body to be sexual in the way you want it to be, not the way society demands; here, control is not so much an issue of restraint as it is an issue of self-determination. For example: "I have mistressed the Lusty powers of my body; they are mine and no one else's."

Lady derives from an Old English term meaning both loaf and knead (Mills, 1993, p. 133). Accepting those roots, *to lady* may mean to knead an idea, to let it set and rise. Thus, to lady an idea is to allow it time to grow. Again, unlike *lord*, *lady* is not an indication of control, but is instead a verb denoting active involvement (kneading) and recognition of another's need for space (albeit a warm, moist space) in which to rise. For example: "I ladied this essay through its many stages, occasionally kneading ideas and at other times letting them alone to mature and rise."

In addition to offering *woman/mistress/lady* as counterspells to *man/master/lord*, we can also explore the language for a range of genderings in its verbs by playing with inclusive or generic verb forms. *People* is already a verb form, meaning "to furnish or fill with people or inhabitants; to populate" (*OED*, 1971, p. 662), but perhaps we also need to expand our language so that we can *human* and *person* things as well.

As Celeste Condit argued in her presentation in the "At the Helm" series, we need to explore a range of genderings. To do that, however, we need to develop gender neutral and inclusive terms, *as well as* womanned terms, as counters to the phallocentrism inherent in male action verbs.

Playing with language may be the most necessary part of the process by which we achieve actual change. However, although changing language is important, it is not enough. As Julia Penelope (1990) argues:

> Yet, one of the crucial ways of ending our oppression must lie in thinking ourselves free. Yes, new words will help, but only if we perceive ourselves in new ways. New words for the same old shit won't move us toward radical change in our lives. Language is action, not yet another accident that we cannot hope to change. When we speak, we are acting *in* the world. (p. xxix)

So, what new shit is it that we want to play with and, to paraphrase Gloria Anzaldúa, put on the paper?

ONE LAST INCANTATION

Attending to sexism, and working to woman the world and its languages, can often be frustrating work. But it need not be. This essay, more than any other project I have worked through (scholarly or nonscholarly, whatever that means), has given me great joy. Never have I had so much fun or spoken/written in such a clear voice (for example, I dropped a copy of this essay off in a friend's box and forgot to place my name on it; yet she knew within the first few pages that I had written it). Part of the explanation for my clear voice may be the result of the influence of Gloria Anzaldúa's (1981, 1987, 1990) work on me, urging me to unlearn the "esoteric bullshit and pseudo-intellectualizing that school brainwashed into my writing" (1981, p. 165). The other part of the clear voice I can't explain. Perhaps I am bewitched, and quite happily so.

At the same time that I take joy in writing with a voice of my own, the joy has not been so happily accepted by others. This essay was first submitted to two Communication Studies journals and was declared not "suitable for publication consideration" by one and as an "essay [that] does not work" as "original research" by the other. It was finally accepted for publication in the journal *Women and Language*. Despite my early struggles with publication, I am convinced that it makes a clear scholarly argument, adding to the already rich body of work on women, gender, and language. We have not really looked at the implications of the sexing of verbs, implications that are distinct from the sexist elements located in nouns. The fact that the tone and voice of this article is "not scholarly" points out that we often conflate the content of an essay with its tone, and essays that provide little contribution to our thinking are scholarly (because they sound that way) while insights that hold the potential to contribute much are not (because they don't sound scholarly). It seems as though scholars' work must be painful and inaccessible to be considered scholarly, which is not a world of scholarship I would want to people.

NOTES

1. Catherine Helen Palczewski, Ph.D., is an Associate Professor in the Department of Communication Studies and the Women's Studies Program at the University of Northern Iowa (Cedar Falls, IA, 50614-0357). An earlier version of this essay was published in *Women and Language, 21*(Fall 1998), 1–8.
2. The National Communication Association is the national professional organization for communication educators. Its goal is "to promote study, criticism, research, teaching, and application of the principles of communication" ("Call for Papers," 1995, p. 1). Each year, the national convention chooses a theme, around which it organizes a series of spotlight panels. Analysis of the convention's "At the Helm" panels also points to an interesting sexing (and racing) of the helm. Approximately 73% of those at the helm were men, 27% were women, and even fewer were people of color.

REFERENCES

Alexander, Brian. (1995, January). Good luck to the women's sailing team. *Glamour,* p. 74.

Anzaldúa, Gloria. (1981). Speaking in tongues: A letter to 3rd world women writers. In Cherríe Moraga and Gloria Anzaldúa (Eds.), *This bridge called my back* (pp. 165–174). New York: Kitchen Table.

Anzaldúa, Gloria. (1987). *Borderlands: La frontera.* San Francisco: Aunt Lute Books.

Anzaldúa, Gloria. (1990). Bridge, drawbridge, sandbar or island. In Lisa Albrecht & Rose M. Brewer (Eds.), *Bridges of power* (pp. 216–231). Philadelphia: New Society.

Ballard, Sarah. (1987, January 9). America's Cup. *Sports Illustrated,* pp. 68–71.

Barnes, Edward. (1986, April). This is war. *Life,* pp. 32–38.

Baron, Dennis. (1986). *Grammar and gender.* New Haven, CT: Yale University Press.

Burke, Kenneth. (1966). *Language as symbolic action.* Berkeley: University of California Press.

Call for papers for the 1996 convention of the Speech Communication Association. (1995). *Spectra, 31,* 13–23.

Cameron, Deborah. (1985). *Feminism and linguistic theory.* New York: St. Martin's Press.

Carpenter, Betsy. Can the girls heave the boys overboard? (1994, October 31). *USNWR,* pp. 81–82.

Coates, Jennifer. (1987). *Women, men and language.* New York: Longman.

Condit, Celeste Michelle. (1990). *Decoding abortion rhetoric.* Urbana: University of Illinois Press.

Condit, Celeste Michelle. (1992). Post-Burke: Transcending the sub-stance of dramatism. *Quarterly Journal of Speech, 78,* 349–355.

Daly, Mary, in cahoots with Caputi, Jane. (1987). *Wickedary.* Boston: Beacon Press.

Finlayson, Ann, & Maloney, Tom. (1987, February 2). The quest for the cup. *Macleans,* p. 27.

Gosselin, Lisa. (1995, January/February). Racing against the odds. *Women's Sports and Fitness,* pp. 52–54+.

Henley, Nancy. (1987). This new species that seeks a new language. In Joyce Penfield (Ed.), *Women and language in transition* (pp. 3–27). Albany: SUNY Press.

Kramer (Kramarae), Cheris. (1975). Women's speech: Separate but unequal. In Barrie Thorne & Nancy Henley (Eds.), *Language and sex: Difference and dominance* (pp. 43–56). Rowley, MA: Newbury House.

Kramer (Kramarae), Cheris; Thorne, Barrie; & Henley, Nancy. (1978). Perspectives on language and communication. *Signs, 3,* 638–651.

Kramarae, Cheris, & Treichler, Paula. (1992). *Amazons, bluestockings and crones: A feminist dictionary.* London: Pandora.

Lakoff, Robin Tolmach. (1975). *Language and woman's place.* New York: Harper & Row.

Lakoff, Robin Tolmach. (1990). *Talking power.* New York: Basic Books.

Lee, Janet. (1994, September). The life of Riley. *Women's Sports and Fitness,* pp. 22–24+.

Lloyd, Barbara. (1994, January 30). Female crew's skipper may try America's Cup. *New York Times,* p. H8.

Marbach, William D., & Robinson, Carl. (1987, February 2). Of brains, brawn and boats. *Newsweek,* p. 79.

Maxwell-Pierson, Stephanie. (1995, March 27). America 3. *Sports Illustrated,* pp. 73–74+.

Miller, Casey, & Swift, Kate. (1991). *Words and women.* New York: HarperCollins.

Mills, Jane. (1993). *Womanwords.* New York: Henry Holt.

Nutt, Amy. (1994, May 9). Dawn Riley. *Sports Illustrated,* pp. 72–73.

OED: The compact edition. (1971). New York: Oxford University Press.

Penelope, Julia. (1990). *Speaking freely.* New York: Pergamon Press.

Reed, Susan. (1995, February 20). Sisters in sail. *People Weekly,* pp. 84–87.

Reynolds, Kim. (1995, April). America[3]: All-female-crewed boat test. *Road & Track,* pp. 98–101.

Riley, Denise. (1988). *Am I that name?* Minneapolis: University of Minnesota Press.

Spender, Dale. (1985). *Man made language.* London: Routledge and Kegan Paul.

Starr, Mark. (1995, January 16). A new crew rocks the boat. *Newsweek,* pp. 70–71.

Swift, E. M. (1995, May 22). A clean sweep. *Sports Illustrated,* pp. 38–41.

Thomas, Robert McG., Jr. (1994, March 10). America's Cup: At last, an all-female crew. *New York Times,* p. B21.

Whiteside, Kelly. (1995, February 20). A whole new tack. *Sports Illustrated,* pp. 40–42+.

Wood, Julia. (1994). *Gendered lives.* Belmont CA: Wadsworth.

THE OLD MAID OF HONOR

Krista McQueeney

UNIVERSITY OF NORTH CAROLINA

Picture this. You are a 27-year-old lesbian working on your doctorate in Feminist Sociology. Your sister, your best friend, is still, after almost ten years of being out to just about everybody you give a flying hoot about, the only one in your family who fully accepts you for who are. So, stay with me, here, you're relaxing on the couch one rainy Saturday morning, sipping coffee and reading, when the phone rings. It's your sister, and she says she has a big surprise for you; she and her boyfriend are getting married! You congratulate her and express your heartfelt excitement for her in taking this momentous step. But then comes the moment of truth. "We're having the wedding at St. Mary's, Kris, and we want you to be the maid of honor." So what's the next line of the script?

Well, people, this is no movie. This, regrettably, is my *life*. While most women are honored and overjoyed when asked to be a maid of honor, it poses an entirely unwelcome dilemma for me. Actually, this dilemma is more than unwelcome. This dilemma pits two of my most cherished core values, relationships and feminist politics, in direct opposition to each other. It's not that I'm not ecstatic for her. But to be quite honest, I wish this question had never breathed life out of Lindsay's lips.

But it has. So how do I respond? Instantaneously, all of my idolized feminist gurus flash before my eyes in a stream-of-consciousness treatise on the fascist, patriarchal, heterosexist institution. Possible responses and their consequences shoot before me like fireworks as I pause to consider my options. Of course, I could tell her that while I adore her and completely support her relationship, I couldn't reconcile the act politically. Were this to be my chosen path, I would surely put a major damper on her pre-wedding bliss and come off as the jealous lesbian sister and selfish feminist who privileges her beliefs over her very own sister. Alternatively, I could suck it up and accept this oh-so-problematic task, thereby resigning myself to cognitive dissonance and continuous assaults on my identity for the next twelve months. Yet another one of those all-too-frequent moments, I muse, when the demands of reality just don't jibe with the ideals

---

Reprinted with permission.

of philosophy. Yet another one of those times when there are no easy answers—yet another one of those dilemmas where either route you choose demands considerable costs.

Well, in my split second of confusion and utter panic, I choose to turn my back on my wise feminist teachers. What seems most important to me at this moment is my love and commitment to my sister. What shouts out at me is the question: If she's accepted me despite choices she doesn't fully agree with or understand, shouldn't I do the same for her? Time stands still. My heart races like Marion Jones. In a moment of sheer out-of-body experience, I hear myself respond, "Wow, Lindsay, sure, I'd be honored."

Now, don't be fooled by my attempts to come off as big-hearted and altruistic in this scenario. I mean, I wouldn't be making all these disclaimers if I didn't feel I had to justify my decision. To chalk it up to merely a problem of ideology vs. practice. To assure myself that I'm putting my sister-bond, now surely at least *that's* a feminist principle, above my own wishes and convictions. To rationalize the guilt and inadequacy I feel about participating in, no, endorsing, one of the very institutions that makes my people and me invisible. I am *not* proud of myself. The truth is, I just chickened out. I compromised my principles so as to please Lindsay and not rock the familial boat. The truth is, I bought into the very rules I'm supposedly committed to challenging.

As soon as I hang up, feelings of inadequacy wash over me as I imagine the brave and creative responses other feminists must have invented to the same question. As a doctoral student, I've spent the past four years trying to dismantle dichotomies, trying to see the gray in situations, trying to envision alternative solutions to what's already been suggested. And yet, when confronted even with this not-so-unexpected question, I can see only the "black" and "white" (please forgive the racist terminology). At this crucial moment, I can envision only the answers "yes" and "no" and their consequences. Have I learned nothing?

Well, I made my bed at that moment and I had to lie in it, for sure. As it turns out, their wedding is beautiful, a glorious celebration of two people's love and lifetime commitment to each other. But it is also extremely Catholic and traditional, incorporating such time-honored Saxon rituals as the father giving away the daughter to her new owner, her husband, and such linguistic slaps-in-the face as pronouncing my strong-willed sister "wife" to her "man." I have to deal with all the usual questions about when *I* am getting married and why *I* don't have a boyfriend and whether I want to be set up with this or that son or nephew from my mom's friends, most of whom are not privy to my mom's "secret" that I'm queer. I'm tempted to respond that I'll probably only get married when and if they make it legal, but I remain silent out of respect for my mother's dignity. I mean, can I possibly regress any further? Is there even one more compromise I can make? Why am I doing this?

The circus that is my family, at least, provides some comic relief to lighten the pressure of starring as feminist failure. My father, the grand patriarch of the clan, escorts my sister down the aisle with a sprained ankle in a forceful show of masculinity. My mother, in trying to live up to her Martha Stewart domestic goddess image, has fallen down a flight of stairs as she attempted to transport homemade flower arrangements and consequently sports a high-tech, iron-laden arm cast that makes her look like Edward Scissorhands. The bridal party's limousine is for some unknown reason replaced by a kelly-green Chevrolet with fuzzy dice driven by a cowboy, complete with missing front teeth, an authentic ten-gallon hat, shit-kicker boots and everything.

While these circumstances make for funny stories to relate to my friends back home, they do little to allay my sense of guilt and inadequacy. And rightly so. I've missed out on an opportunity to speak my truth, to stand up for justice amidst ignorance, and worst of all to affirm my very existence. As my mother drives me back to the airport, only to return to the tranquil world of final exams, she exclaims, "Krista, thank you for all your help this weekend. You were *such* a beautiful and elegant maid of honor; I don't think anyone *ever* would have guessed that you're gay!" Well, the wedding must have done more damage than I thought; she doesn't usually say things this overtly homophobic. I tell her how problematic this statement is, how it reveals how few lesbians and gay men she has come to know. She doesn't seem to understand my point and responds defensively, saying she only meant it as a compliment. Exhausted from the weekend's events, utterly *worn out* from stress and lack of sleep, I, yet again, resign myself to my unhappy plight as the "old maid" of honor—never to be normal, never to be married. I just let it go, sinking back in my seat and just thanking the powers-that-be for allowing me to live in this modern age of low fertility. *One* sister's wedding is just about all I can handle.

PART III

SOCIAL CHANGE

SENDING SIGNALS

Visions of Women in World War II Propaganda Posters

Marguerite Hoyt
JOHNS HOPKINS UNIVERSITY

Sometimes social change moves at a barely perceptible pace. The rate of progress toward equality for women causes one to frequently wonder, have things really changed? During those times, history can provide a view that allows for a better perspective. Hoyt's article gives us some of that perspective by describing images of women in the Second World War. Prior to World War II, few women worked in factories and offices; during World War II, it was a national necessity. How the shift happened, how it was described in the press, and how the culture portrayed women make for a fascinating study of propaganda and the media's role in shaping perceptions. By drawing on both British and U.S. sources, Hoyt depicts women's reactions to the changes, their reactions to new freedoms, and their responses to new roles. Hoyt uses posters printed during World War II to illustrate how women were described and defined. Her analysis can be easily contrasted with images and propaganda of today to note both how society may have changed, and how it has remained the same.

QUESTIONS FOR DISCUSSION

- *If you are female, how do you respond to the depictions of women in the posters?*
- *Do any of them seem old-fashioned or quaint to you?*
- *How has society changed over the past fifty years? What areas have seen the greatest change for women?*
- *Compare the posters in the article to media depictions of women today. What has changed in the images?*
- *In times of stress, what has changed about women's roles?*
- *What does each sex add to the debate about the U.S. response to terrorism?*

Historians have been of many different minds when analyzing the history of women and their relationship to work and feminist ideology at the end of World War II. On one side was William Chafe, who believed that the war was a watershed event for women and changed their futures tremendously with gains in wages, unionization, and job opportunities.[1] This idea was generally refuted by feminist historians of the 1980s, and eventually was rethought by Chafe himself. Most feminist historians believed that women continued along the same work patterns that had begun decades earlier, and that women were disappointed with the restricted opportunities available to them at the close of the war after many had proven that they were able to perform a man's job.[2]

The way I have chosen to examine the issue of women's relationship to work and feminist ideals in the World War II era is to look at the propaganda posters that the countries of the United States, Great Britain, and Australia produced during the war. My specific target is posters that depict women. Visual imagery is so very powerful that I decided to look at the posters that these women were viewing in order to see if the work recruiting posters, Rosie the Riveter imagery, were dominant and what kinds of ideal women the governments of each country were propagating. As you will soon see, the resources are rich, and some of the posters are truly beautiful. I have collected my poster images from three different places: the National Archives, the Australian War Museum, and the Princeton Collection at the Smithsonian Institution National Museum of American History. The comparative aspect of the study offers an opportunity to discover how similar the ideal female image was for Anglophone Allied countries. By choosing the United States and one Anglophone country from both the European and Pacific realms, I analyze whether the different locations of the war front changed the images in the posters, and I examine how far-reaching American culture was, specifically in terms of how women were portrayed in the graphic arts area.

Insight into the question of women and their relationship to work outside the home is gained when reading oral histories that have been published on women and World War II. Combining these firsthand accounts with an analysis of visual representations of women, as I will do using propaganda posters, is a particularly revealing way of setting in motion a dialog between the way women saw their own lives, official views of what those lives were supposed to be, and historians' interpretations of them. Although care must be taken when using oral histories, especially published sources gathered by others, as evidence for home front history, there is a place for these remembrances in a work on visual analysis. Although these histories may not describe or explain posters, the women who dictated their stories add a voice to the overall picture. Their stories help to explain how women felt about themselves, which adds depth to the way they were portrayed by professional graphic artists and the government.

Penny Summerfield has written a number of articles and books on women who served in various capacities during the war in Great Britain; Sherna Berger Gluck and Nancy Baker Wise and Christy Wise have done so in the United States.[3] Summerfield demonstrates through her analysis of oral histories that all of the interpretations mentioned above come into play when asking women about their war work and, more specifically, asking them if the wartime work changed their lives. Both Summerfield and the Wises mention that sometimes the answer was yes. There were women who were allowed to stay in previously all-male professions, or who stayed in the workforce in another job when they had not believed that they would be allowed to do so after the war. Just as interesting, though, is the large number of women who said no to the question of whether the war changed their lives. They claim that their lives were changed during the war but that they got back to normal after World War II. Many stated that they disliked the disruption the war caused in their world and resented having to work outside the home. These women wanted nothing more than to return home to their domestic lifestyles. Summerfield gives several examples of women in Great Britain who preferred home life to that of working woman. One of the women she interviewed, Margaret Goldsmith, claimed "Many women, possibly the majority of married women, have not enjoyed this new independence; they have been made miserable by the war-time interruption of family life. As a result, many married women, possibly the majority, fervently wish themselves back into their pre-war routine." May Richards, who had been a radar mechanic in the ATS, also stated that she was "looking forward to married life and having a home of my own."[4] The Wises also offer several examples of women in the United States who were happy to return home after the war. Joyce Taylor Holloway claimed that "I couldn't get out of that job fast enough!"[5]

Viewing World War II propaganda with fresh eyes and in light of the problems with the first views of postwar popular culture allows us to see that the most striking thing about World War II posters is the variety of roles depicted for women and the conflicts within and between these images. Although work recruiting posters, both for factories and nursing, may have outnumbered domestic posters, the smaller number of domestic posters does not negate the fact that they existed during the time period. If one only looks at the work recruiting posters, it is easy to understand how Betty Friedan and others may have made the mistake of assuming that those were the only role models available to women. Not only were there numerous posters that directly depicted women performing domestic duties, there were also large numbers of posters that recruited women for jobs generally categorized as female positions, such as nursing, secretarial fields, and waitressing. World War II provided many opportunities for women to explore new paths, but the posters were quite ambiguous as to whether these opportunities were only available for the short term. Amy Bentley has coined the term "Wartime Homemaker" as a counterpoint to Rosie the Riveter. Bentley claims that the Wartime Homemaker was useful as a symbol of social stability, and that "wartime messages aimed at women were decidedly mixed; they urged women to enter new and unfamiliar men's work while magnifying their position of domestic helpmate."[6] Her ideas help to solidify the proposition that domestic ideals never really left the public realm during the war era, even though most scholars have focused on women in the workplace and their demobilization at the end of the war. The graphic artists of the period, whether in advertising or wartime propaganda, never showed women as completely free from the domestic lifestyle and were ambiguous about how long women were going to stay in their new careers.

The contradictions come alive when looking at the nurse recruiting posters. These posters sent mixed signals to those who viewed them. They are quite ambiguous about whether nursing is a lifelong career or just another war job. We see in Figure 1, a British poster, that the call is for war work, but in the small letters underneath the caption, it mentions war work with a future. The phrase "war work with a future" stands as a contradiction itself. War work and future work stand in opposition to each other simply because war work should end with the war. In terms of nursing, it was impossible to know if as many nurses would be needed after the war as during it. The poster seems to be offering women a choice: you can work only during the conflict, or you can keep nursing in the future if you choose to do so. We notice that the future work is written in a much smaller font as if to say that the future part of the

FIGURE 1

work is much less important than the immediate needs of war. We know that the future job was not the central theme to this recruiting poster.

The United States Cadet Nursing Corps recruiting posters (Figures 2 and 3) are less clear on this subject. These posters mention a lifetime education and inform young

FIGURE 2

FIGURE 3

women that they can enter a proud profession, not just a war job. These were aimed at girls who were just finishing high school, and they were not intended to recruit women into wartime nursing only. Even though the government wanted Cadet Nurses to serve their country in the armed services, they were not required to do so after receiving their education, which by the way, was paid for by the federal government.[7]

FIGURE 4

In posters such as the one in Figure 4, a woman is told that she can find her own life, which not only implies a fulfilling career as a nurse but also leads the viewer to believe that her life before nursing was unfulfilling. Whether that was a domestic life or one working in a different female-defined career, we do not know. Her stance over her male patient may also reflect the idea that her life could be made complete by finding a husband during her war duty. It is unclear whether the service to her country and to other men is what helps her to find her life, or if it is found by immersing herself in difficult work. Nursing had traditionally been a career for single women, and in the 1940s that tradition still held true. During and after the war, women were expected to leave nursing once they married, and at the very latest when they became pregnant.

In terms of factory recruiting, there is less ambiguity about a future career. We expect to see posters like the examples in Figures 5–8. These have a clear meaning, and one of them has become an American icon.

FIGURE 5

FIGURE 6

FIGURE 7   **FIGURE 8**

These posters let women know that their jobs are only for the duration of the war. These women were replacing men who had gone to fight, and they would not be needed once the war ended; they were manufacturing wartime goods such as guns, ammunition, planes, and other materials needed only for the duration of the conflict. The women were never shown manufacturing goods that would be used during peace, except in the case of food processing, which is considered a more feminine occupation. The women pictured in these posters have their hair pinned up and show strong muscles, exhibiting a more androgynous look. They look ready to work even though they still show feminine qualities in their faces and wear makeup. These are the types of artwork that typify World War II propaganda posters in the opinions of most historians.

Although there is less ambiguity about future careers in the factory work posters, there are still some mixed messages, especially concerning issues of femininity. This is a trend that crosses nationalities, as is demonstrated by the group of posters from Great Britain shown in Figures 9–14. The women in these posters do not look like women in some of the other

FIGURE 9

FIGURE 10   **FIGURE 11**

FIGURE 12   **FIGURE 13**

posters, particularly the British ones depicting women working in the gun factories. The heroine of this series has long hair, which is sometimes tucked underneath her cap and sometimes left to hang behind her shoulders. While the importance of safety is exhibited by the cap, the importance of her femininity is not underestimated. She looks very good in these pictures, and appears to have a great time in the canteen with her friends. Penny Summerfield provides plenty of examples of women who had a wonderful time meeting other women while working in the factories.[8] Our heroine puts on makeup and changes to fashionable clothes in the women's dressing room at the factory, once again highlighting the fact that she does not lose her femininity just because she works in a factory. She is even wearing high-heeled sandals as she enters the train for her ride home. The picture of her boarding the train is also slightly provocative in that the eye is drawn to her legs as she steps up. In the last of the series, she is receiving her pay packet, which is neither a domestic nor a feminine image. This last poster ties in an air of independence that may have been attractive to younger women who were ready to take on the world, and it also freed one from the prewar depression, as well as from overprotective parents. Paychecks also allowed women to help parents pay for family expenses while their sons were away fighting. The pay packet poster was very important to the series because it symbolized many different things, including independence, opportunity, and personal fulfillment, not the least of which

FIGURE 14

was economic necessity. This job represented the best of all worlds. A woman could look good, have fun with other women, and earn a paycheck to help her gain independence, all while working for the war effort.

We get the same kinds of feelings of independence, glamour, and camaraderie from American posters. They are also complex, and they present several different ideas about womanhood. Not only do we see images portraying independence, but we also see images that are feminine, and some that are domestic. The older woman in Figure 15 is working at a war job, but it is a position in a food processing plant, and she stereotypically wears an apron. Both food processing and aprons are domestic images. The domestic situation within the factory usually appears in posters aimed at recruiting older women who may not believe that they can handle a man's job, or at young women who would be more comfortable in a work setting that reminds them of skills they use as a new wife and mother. Women in the sewing trades (Figures 16 and 17) are much less likely to look like the image of Rosie the Riveter than those pictured in the munitions, aircraft, or battleship factories. Even in posters that should be the most straightforward, there are con-

FIGURE 15

tradictions, especially when dealing with domestic imagery. The government never intended for gender roles to be completely changed. The food processing poster is interesting in this regard. The older woman is in rather traditional feminine dress; she is not wearing coveralls or overalls. In the background, there is an older man who

Sewing electrically heated flying suits with a smile—so that our boys can make it HOT for the AXIS. Who said "This is a man's war?"—

This is OUR War!

FIGURE 16

GIRLS! MAKE CIVVIES FOR THE BOYS

THE JOB — THE WAGE
THE FUTURE FOR YOU

Watch the Newspapers for Manufacturers' Advertisements

FIGURE 17

is wearing overalls and is doing the heavy lifting. The artist prominently displays the woman's wedding band, implying that the man in the background is her husband, and he is doing the difficult heavy task while she is able to perform the more traditional female task of canning food.

Surprisingly, there is ambiguity in the military recruiting posters. For the most part, there is not much domestic imagery here, except for the British ATS posters, which often show women involved in food preparation (Figure 18). The ambiguity

FIGURE 18

that appears in the United States posters is of a different type. The question that arises from posters like those in Figures 19 and 20 is whether the military can be thought of as a career or if service is only for the duration of the war. In the first example, the word *opportunity* makes us wonder if this is really just an "opportunity" during wartime; the word implies some sort of future commitment to service. In the second poster, the wording is even less clear. "For your own sake tomorrow"—what does this mean? It could imply that the rewards one receives from being in the service will last a lifetime, or that your career in the military will go beyond the war. Of course, part of the reason for this ambiguity is that the armed services had not decided if women were going to remain a part of the standing forces. It was

FIGURE 19

FIGURE 20

FIGURE 21

not until 1948 that Congress gave women permanent regular status in the defense establishment.[9] What we cannot know is what women thought when they first saw these posters.

Much less glamorous poster campaigns occurred alongside the more Hollywoodesque military and work recruiting posters. The farming posters did not show the beautiful models that some of the other recruiting posters used. The American and British farming posters were often black and white and depicted women in work clothes rather than tailored uniforms. There is quite a contrast between these and the previous examples. The pictures are more old-fashioned looking; women are pictured in flowered dresses and bonnets or in dungarees and farmers' hats (Figures 21 and 22).

The farming posters provide contrasts in and of themselves. The women appear old-fashioned,

FIGURE 22

GRANDEMENT EFFICIENTE, MECANISEE, L'AGRICULTURE, EN GRANDE-BRETAGNE, FRUSTRE LA TENTATIVE DE BLOCUS D'HITLER

FIGURE 23

LA BATAILLE DE L'ATLANTIQUE SE GAGNE SUR LES CHAMPS DE BLE DE LA GRANDE-BRETAGNE

FIGURE 24

but they are also depicted performing difficult tasks. The British posters often show women riding tractors, as in Figures 23, 24, and 25. One of these is one of the few British farming posters that is in color. Generally speaking, riding the tractor was

FIGURE 25

considered a man's work. There were always farm women who had done such tasks, but more often than not, working the soil was the job of the male farmer. To see an old-fashioned looking woman driving a tractor is a somewhat contradictory picture, yet the women in these posters are much more androgynous than those in other posters. They are not nearly as feminine looking as the women working male jobs in the factory posters; there is no evidence of their wearing makeup.

In Figure 26, one of the few U.S. farming posters in color, the women are depicted better than in the black and white posters, but one notices that they have shorter hair than is shown on most of the other types of posters, and their hair is slightly disheveled, showing that they are concentrating on their work and not on their appearance. There are also several different tasks pictured here. There are women planting and harvesting. There is a woman with an orchard basket, and in the background there is a woman milking a cow and another feeding chickens. These types of posters were aimed at women who wanted to work outdoors and perform a number of different tasks rather than the same factory work day after day, and who had quite possibly grown up on a farm. The person who was going to train as a nurse or to work in a factory was not the same type of woman who would want to dig in the fields or to take care of animals.

FIGURE 26

FIGURE 27   **FIGURE 28**

The two Australian farming posters (Figures 27 and 28) are typical of farming posters from that country. They are in color, and the women are less androgynous than in Great Britain. Many Australian women had been raised on farms and the work was not unfamiliar to them, which helps explain why their posters are much nicer looking than the others, but I believe that the respect Australians had for the difficult task of raising crops has something to do with their beautiful posters. Figure 27 is particularly interesting because it is asking women to come and work in the fields. This is a message that is never seen in the other countries' posters. The military commanded so much respect that is was highly unusual to see propaganda directed at them, asking them to give more than they were already giving.

To further confuse women about their place in society, there was another category of posters—those that deal directly with domesticity or that have strong domestic imagery. The governments, particularly that of the United States, did not shy away from pictures of women at home. Not every woman was expected to work in the factories or to go into military service. One aspect of the domestic imagery occurs outside the home (Figure 29). As mentioned earlier, women displayed domestic ideals in both factory and military jobs. They were also often shown working in food services. Women were employed to cook and serve food for both men and women working in the factories and in the military. They were paid for their work, but it was definitely considered women's work. In some areas of Australia, and even in the United States, women volunteered to cook meals for soldiers.

The British poster shown in Figure 30 depicts another aspect of domesticity, child care. Women who did not have jobs outside the home were asked to care for other women's children. In Great Britain, women living in the countryside were

FIGURE 29

asked to care for the children of people who lived in the city to try to keep them safe from the German bombings. Children were even sent to Canada and the United States to protect them from the war. Women who worked in the factories needed child care, and rather than provide adequate day care services, the government believed that persuading neighbors and friends into caring for children would be simpler. Unfortunately, this was far from enough, and women often left their jobs in the factories when they had children because there was no one to care for them.

FIGURE 30

The American domestic posters look quite similar to the other types of American posters, except that all of the women wear aprons and most appear to be wearing dresses. In their oral histories, many women recalled that the first time that they ever wore pants was during the war years. It made quite a big impression on them for the women to talk about this in their oral histories, yet the women in the domestic posters were never pictured in trousers. Some of the posters dealt with conservation in the home (Figure 31). Arguably, such posters could have been made without a female in them, but the artists place females in the pictures to get the attention of

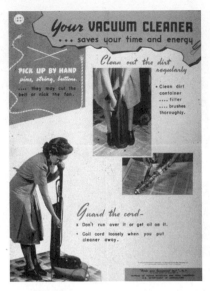

FIGURE 31

women and to show them that it was their duty to keep their appliances in good working order throughout the war. The posters certainly did not promote any sort of feminism or even any activity outside the home. They appealed to women who did not want to leave their roles as homemakers and were comfortable staying in the house, but who also wanted to feel that they were contributing to the war effort. By keeping their vacuum cleaners and stoves in proper working order, they were helping to win the war. These conservation posters also had the effect of reinforcing domesticity by making it crucial to the war effort.

There are other types of domestic posters, including these for home canning (Figures 32, 33, and 34). Once again, these posters serve more than one purpose. First we have the poster that depicts a realistic setting, explaining how to can with a hot water bath. This poster is very realistic and depicts a scene with which many women were already familiar. As with the other conservation posters, this type helps the average woman who may only be working in the home feel that she is contributing a valuable service to the war effort. The other two use color and are a bit more artistic. One shows a rather harried looking

FIGURE 32

brunette, whose image also appears in several other posters. The other shows another trend that pops up in the 1940s, which is advertising that depicts mothers and daughters looking like sisters rather than mother and daughter. Showing the mother as older sister exhibits more camaraderie than mother as strict parent. Both of these posters glamorize home canning to a degree not found in the more realistic poster. Home canning was important to the country because so much food needed to be sent overseas to the troops and to help Great Britain, where food rations were small. Women who were caring for their families by growing and canning food were just as important to the war effort as those who were nursing and working in war industry.

FIGURE 33   FIGURE 34

Pulling together all of these various themes should tell us something about the propaganda of the World War II era. It tells us that there is no simple single image of women during the time. Historians have different views of the importance of the war to women's lives in the postwar era, but most don't seem to take into account that women were presented with many different views of what it meant to be a female during World War II. Women were not inundated with a completely new picture of womanhood that downplayed domesticity and emphasized an equal player in the realm of work and the military. The strong female characters exist—there are plenty of Rosie the Riveter types of posters—but that is certainly not the whole picture. It is inaccurate to claim that domestic imagery disappeared during the war and only resurfaced in the postwar era. And for those who believe that propaganda had a simple clear message, it is simply not true. This is a medium full of contradiction and ambiguity. Cross-national comparisons of posters, along with firsthand accounts of experiences from women who volunteered to record their stories, allow the historian to create the links between the official views of what women were supposed to strive to become, how women view their own lives, and how historians interpret those lives. By examining these things together, we get a cross-cultural perspective on the complicated messages that poster imagery offered during the era.

NOTES

Photos courtesy of The National Archives Still Picture Branch, The National Museum of American History, and the Australian War Memorial.

1. William Chafe, *The American Woman* (New York: Oxford University Press, 1972), p. 136. Chafe also discussed women and their relationship to work and family in *Women and Equality* (New York: Oxford University Press, 1977). Chapters 4 and 5 provide a discussion

of women in the era after World War II, concentrating on the idea of the feminine mystique and the increased role women played in the workforce.

2. Karen Anderson and William Chafe both agreed that World War II was a turning point for women and their relationship to work, but Anderson concluded that women's lower status in the workplace did not change and that there was no significant progressive impact on women's lives. In Anderson's opinion, the main factor of change was the idea that women could have children and work. Susan Hartmann also believed that World War II paved the way for women with children to work outside the home, but she argued that other factors of the emergency prevented the complete alteration of gender roles. Leila Rupp did not believe that women's participation rate in the workforce was changed in any way by the advent of the war. A good discussion of the historiography of World War II and women's relationship to work occurs in the introduction to Maureen Honey's work on gender and propaganda in World War II, *Creating Rosie the Riveter: Class, Gender, and Propaganda during World War II* (Amherst: University of Massachusetts Press, 1984), pp. 1–6. Honey agrees with Rupp that women's working lives were not significantly changed by World War II and looks to the media for answers as to why women's traditional work patterns reemerged after the war—specifically, in her case, for working-class women. Both Honey and Rupp studied propaganda to draw their conclusions. Although both examined popular magazines for their cultural impact, they also looked at advertising and propaganda posters. Neither of them considered a broad enough sample of posters to notice that domestic imagery was not hidden from view, but that many posters featured women involved in housekeeping, child care, and home canning.

3. Penny Summerfield, *Reconstructing Women's Wartime Lives* (Manchester and New York: Manchester University Press, 1998); Sherna Berger Gluck, *Rosie the Riveter Revisited: Women, the War, and Social Change* (New York: Meridian, 1987); Nancy Baker Wise and Christy Wise, *A Mouthful of Rivets: Women at Work in World War II* (San Francisco: Jossey-Bass, 1994). These are only three of many published oral histories involving women and World War II. Summerfield's most recent book, *Reconstructing Women's Wartime Lives*, provides an excellent background source for analyzing oral histories and the problems inherent in gathering and using them. Her mix of theory and oral stories reminds the researcher not to make sweeping conclusions based on subjects' memories.

4. Summerfield, pp. 213, 216.

5. Wise and Wise, p. 188.

6. Amy Bentley, *Eating for Victory: Food Rationing and the Politics of Domesticity* (Urbana and Chicago: University of Illinois Press, 1998), pp. 30–31. Bentley claims that the Wartime Homemaker is middle-class, white, young, attractive, clean, and well-dressed, which completely excludes women of color. The Wartime Homemaker went about her work cheerfully and obeyed the government's orders to conserve food and abide by rationing rules, thereby making the kitchen her battlefield.

7. In 1943, Congress passed the Bolton Act, which established the Cadet Nurse Corps. Students received federal money for an accelerated nursing education as long as they promised to practice essential nursing for the duration of the war, but it did not require them to join the armed forces. Susan Hartmann, *The Home Front and Beyond: American Women in the 1940s* (Boston: Twayne Publishers, 1982), p. 105.

8. In Penny Summerfield's chapter on female bonding (pp. 167–170), she explains that many women who worked in the factories thought of the composition as that of a family. Some men were in charge, while others acted as brothers or uncles, and the women were like sisters. Others believed that their relationships with other women were friendships

rather than sisterly. She has quotes from women such as Jean Grant, a riveter of aircraft wings: "Most of those that were twos, they were quite friendly and kept together. And I say I've kept that friendship up all this time." Caroline Woodward, a welder, stated "we were all a happy crowd, oh it was great, I loved working with them all." The women often spoke of convivial break times, and the sense of being united as a team.

9. Hartmann, p. 43.

BIKER CHICKS

Are They Becoming Women Motorcyclists?

Arthur L. Ranney
UNIVERSITY OF WISCONSIN, PLATTEVILLE

Happenstance, practicality, market forces, and hormones are all influential factors in the evolution of the relationships between males and females and their motorcycles. In this article, Arthur Ranney provides a brief summary of the motorcycle's history and popularity in the United States, attending particularly to the male and female stereotypes that developed along with the motorcycle's ascendance into popularity. This article is interesting for its general historical information as well as the very complex issue it raises about the link between economics and gender.

Maintaining stereotypical gender roles is a major source of survival for some companies. Therefore, a large part of marketing budgets are spent on creating advertisements that reinforce culturally held gender roles. The motorcycle industry is one that has profited from the stereotypical image of the powerful, independent, male rider whose leather-clad, voluptuous female mate hugs his waist as they head down the long, straight open road. While the perpetuation of this stereotype has helped to sell motorcycles, it has limited their sales primarily to one-half of the consuming population.

As you read this article, consider the dilemma this industry, as well as others, may believe they face as they try to maintain a stereotype that appeals to one gender to the exclusion of the other, while simultaneously trying to create an image that breaks gender stereotypes in order to attract the excluded gender.

QUESTIONS FOR DISCUSSION

- *What is your idea of the typical motorcycle rider?*
- *What is your impression of females who drive motorcycles?*
- *How might the cycle industry's own gender stereotypes be preventing them from discovering new and innovative ways of approaching their markets?*
- *How do the cycle industry's own stereotypes maintain and reinforce their own marketing dilemmas?*
- *What other industries can you think of that profit from maintaining gender stereotypes while simultaneously trying to court the excluded gender?*

A single image has shaped the image of motorcycling in the United States for more than five decades. The image, a black-and-white photograph taken in 1947 in Hollister, California, depicts a drunken biker lounging on a motorcycle, a beer in each hand, surrounded by dozens of empty beer bottles. Despite the fact that the photo was staged and that the Hollister "riot" was grossly exaggerated by the media, the Hollister incident provided the impetus for a 1954 movie *The Wild One*. Starring a young Marlon Brando, the movie invented the stereotype of the angry, outlaw biker and ensured the passage of the Hollister incident into the realm of American myth. A few bumps and bruises and two arrests for public intoxication, coupled with a compelling image and an even more compelling, if hyperbolic, movie, created a black eye for motorcycling that has persisted to this day.

Not insignificantly, that image is male. Although the nature of the sport of motorcycling is such that women and men can enjoy it equally, since World War II women have been relegated to the back seat, when they've been included at all. A recent series of ads by the Japanese manufacturer Kawasaki, however, indicates a new awareness of the market potential of women. The advice offered in the ad is "Don't take a back seat to anyone," presumably by buying a Kawasaki product (Kawasaki advertisement, 2000). Buell, a domestic manufacturer wholly owned by Harley-Davidson, is marketing a motorcycle, the Blast, that is clearly aimed at the novice female market. The motorcycle is stylish, yet lightweight and with a low seat. To understand how revolutionary these seemingly simple steps are, a little history is in order.

Although women have been documented as active motorcyclists as far back as 1903 (Siegal, 2001), their stories have remained largely untold. Early in the twentieth century, for example, the Van Buren sisters rode their motorcycles coast-to-coast to demonstrate the fitness of women for military courier duty. Despite the success of the trip and their fame as female pioneers, neither was called to duty. They did distinguish themselves in other careers, however, in an era when women were disenfranchised and rarely worked outside the home. In the 1940s, the talented Dot Robinson fought the motorcycle establishment for the right to race, but retired from racing after only two seasons. She founded the Motor Maids, a women's motorcycling group that exists to this day.

Motorcycles in the postwar years were the exclusive domain of men for at least three reasons. First, World War II introduced an entire generation of American men to motorcycling through the military. About 90,000 Harley-Davidson motorcycles were produced for the military; many of those military vehicles ended up in private hands after the war, purchased by veterans who were looking for cheap transportation, or perhaps postcombat excitement in a generally staid America, when they returned stateside (Motorcycle Museum Online, 2002). Sales of the civilian versions of motorcycles also boomed for the first few years after the war. Second, the brands of motorcycle the military unwittingly touted to its personnel were more suited physically to males. Harley-Davidsons were, and are to this day, large, cumbersome, and extremely heavy, even when "chopped" to reduce excess weight. (Indian also supplied motorcycles built to the military's specifications, but in smaller numbers.) And finally, the myth surrounding the Hollister incident ensured that anyone who rode a motorcycle was perceived to be somehow marginalized, perhaps even dangerous. Motorcycles, in the conventional wisdom created and perpetuated by the media, were fueled by a volatile combination of gasoline and testosterone, with a little alcohol thrown in as needed.

Motorcycling took a turn toward gender inclusiveness in the early 1960s with the advertising campaign Honda chose for its initial foray into the American market. "You meet the nicest people on a Honda" became an American catchphrase, and seemingly overnight, an obscure manufacturer of piston rings became the world's largest motorcycle manufacturer. Significantly, the machines that built Honda's reputation were small, lightweight, user-friendly, and reliable. Crew-cut young men and wholesome young women were pictured whizzing about town on their 50cc and 90cc Hondas, a far cry from the drunken lout commonly associated in the public's mind with the large, loud motorcycles that had dominated the market for nearly two decades. As Honda and the other Japanese manufacturers expanded their product lines, the image of motorcyclists became correspondingly more diverse. The British motorcycle industry marched lockstep into bankruptcy, and Harley-Davidson retreated to a market niche defined by image, not performance. The latter area was quickly appropriated by the Japanese big four (Honda, Kawasaki, Suzuki, and Yamaha), and a rivalry between Harley riders and the riders of Japanese machines sprang up. Harley riders often see themselves, if only vicariously, in the Hollister image, while sneering at the Japanese machines as "rice burners." Despite the incursion of the Japanese and their easier-to-operate motorcycles, motorcycling in general remained a man's domain.

Women's role in motorcycle-related advertising rarely has acknowledged them as more than mere window dressing, an aesthetic addendum with no meaning beyond the advertising truism that sex sells. The Honda ads from the early 1960s, for example, always showed the man as the operator and the woman as the passenger. Although the women's movement gathered momentum in the 1970s, women as motorcyclists stalled. In the mid-1970s, Norton, a British manufacturer, embarked on a massive advertising campaign to save the marque from extinction. Faced with the runaway success of Honda's CB750, Norton attempted to stimulate sales of its 750cc motorcycle line by introducing the Norton Girls. Slender, attractive, and provocatively posed, the Girls wore clothing, but not too much of it, that was obviously unsuited for motorcycle riding. Although the advertising campaign has been fondly recalled in the motorcycling press, it was not enough to save Norton (*Cycle World*, 1999). The campaign also did nothing to encourage women to become active motorcyclists.

By the time the boom of the 1970s had gone bust, all of the manufacturers were in a holding pattern. The young males of the first postwar generation, now known as the baby boomers, were graduating from college, getting married, raising families. The economy was unstable. Motorcycle sales plummeted, and with them, funds for research and development dwindled. In the 1980s, the situation grew so desperate that Harley-Davidson petitioned the federal government for help just to stay in business. A punitive tariff was imposed on imported motorcycles above 700cc, those that would compete directly with Harley's huge beasts, making the Harley more attractive, dollar for dollar, when compared with the Japanese machines. It seemed a perfect opportunity to reinvent motorcycling as a gender-neutral sport, as the Japanese were faced with returning to their roots in the form of smaller machines. Instead, they bided their time, preferring to retrench instead of investing in initiatives aimed at unproved markets such as women. Advertising for motorcycles continued to feature men in the driver's seat. All of the major Japanese manufacturers survived the 1980s, as did Harley-Davidson, but the sport remained overwhelmingly male.

The dawn of the 1990s brought a rejuvenated economy and the return of the baby boomers to motorcycling. Male boomers were reaching midlife and were responding to professional success (or midlife crises) by spending their discretionary income on motorcycles. Advertising trends at the turn of the twenty-first century seem to indicate that manufacturers are using an era of unprecedented prosperity to diversify their target audience, perhaps sensing that a wider range of buyers will protect them in the event of a downturn. Saturation of the male market might also be a factor, of course. In any case, women are enjoying a newfound respect in the media related to motorcycling.

Consider, for example, Kawasaki's recent campaign, "Don't take a back seat to anyone." While the campaign does not overtly sound any feminist themes, the ads feature women on motorcycles and tout the virtues of the view and control found only in the front seat. The media themselves, primarily special-interest magazines, have discovered the benefits of adding women to the masthead. *Rider,* for example, featured an article in its January 2001 issue about the American Motorcyclist Association's second Women in Motorcycling conference. The story was written and photographed by a woman. The AMA's magazine has women on staff who write and help conduct road tests. A major article in the January 2001 *American Motorcyclist* magazine featured two women on a motorcycle tour of diners in the Midwest, for example. Kimberly Barlag (2001), an associate editor of the magazine, did the riding and the writing. *Cycle World,* the best-selling motorcycle magazine in the country, employs a woman editor and road tester. She has been featured in road test photos and often contributes to the "Off the Record" section of road tests, in which the editors offer their personal opinions of the motorcycle under scrutiny. The implicit message is that the particular product might appeal to women, although that fact is rarely stated overtly.

All of the major motorcycle magazines carry advertisements from Progressive Insurance. A current series features a woman in a black leather jacket who clearly is being represented as someone who owns a motorcycle and wants an insurance company that knows about them. "When you told your insurance company you broke your swing arm, did they ask if they could sign your cast?" one of the ads asks. "Call somebody that gets it," the ad continues. The advertisement clearly implies that the woman in the picture "gets it" and owns her own motorcycle (Progressive Motorcycle Insurance advertisement, 2000). Other examples, both in editorial content and advertising, abound.

The picture is not entirely gender-neutral, however—far from it. For every advertisement that recognizes women as a viable force in the sport, there are many others that perpetuate the window-dressing tradition. In the January 2001 *American Motorcyclist,* for example, a display ad touts "real women, real gear" (Mota advertisement, 2001). The advertiser is selling motorcycle-related clothing, such as jackets, pants, gloves, and boots, "in sizes that fit." The woman pictured in the advertisement is an attractive woman who may or may not be a professional model. She looks like a "real woman," in other words. She is wearing a jacket designed for women who ride motorcycles. Contrast that advertisement with one that appears in the November 2000 issue of *Cycle World* (Jamin' Leather advertisement, 2000). The advertising copy tells us that the company deals in "nothin' but leather!" The woman in the ad is wearing nothing but leather, and she's actually not wearing it. She appears to be embracing it. The reader is not able to discern any of the features of the jacket, but they appear to be secondary to the features of the model displaying it.

The fact that women are being represented in the motorcycle media in a role other than a decorative one speaks volumes about the evolution of a sport that really could become gender-neutral, were it to overcome its macho image. The industry is somewhat analogous to Harley-Davidson, whose riders want to be the baddest boys on the block, despite the fact that they're riding the least powerful big bikes currently available. The poseur may soon be unmasked as women discover the joys of motorcycling and the fact that the skills it requires are not linked to one's DNA code.

The readers may be ahead of the media and the industry. The Norton Girls retrospective prompted numerous letters to the editor decrying the image of a latter-day faux Norton Girl on the cover of *Cycle World* ("Hotshots," 1999). The magazine belatedly, and somewhat lamely, pointed out that the woman on the cover actually does ride motorcycles. The editors failed to point out, however, that she wasn't properly dressed for a motorcycle ride.

REFERENCES

Barlag, K. (2001, January). The diner tour: Ride to eat, eat to ride. *American Motorcyclist,* pp. 22–26.

Cycle World. (1999, September).

Hotshots [Letter to the Editor]. (1999, November). *Cycle World,* p. 18.

Jamin' Leather advertisement. (2000, November). *Cycle World,* p. 132.

Kawasaki advertisement. (2000, October). *Rider,* p. 13.

Mota advertisement. (2001, January). *American Motorcyclist.*

Motorcycle Museum Online, retrieved September 14, 2002, from http://www.tower.org/museum/harley_davidson/harley_davidson.html

Progressive Motorcycle Insurance advertisement. (2000, November). *Cycle World,* p. 137.

Siegal, Margie. (2001, January). Let's ride: The AMA's second Women in Motorcycling conference. *Rider,* p. 52.

GENDER AND COMMUNICATION IN CYBERSPACE

Susan Hansen

MURDOCH UNIVERSITY

Relationships in cyberspace—twenty years ago, they were the stuff of science fiction, but now they have spread wider and further than almost anyone would have thought possible. People are meeting, marrying, chatting, deceiving, and exploring through emails, chat rooms, and advertisements. With this new communication channel for relationship development comes a whole host of new phenomena and variables related to the communication process. What do people do online that they also do in face-to-face interpersonal communication? What do they do differently? How are the images of femininity and masculinity altered, enacted, and developed online? What effect does the limited use of nonverbal communication have on the interaction?

Cyberspace allows the individual communicator to present oneself as anything one wishes. How does the "bending" of self, especially gender, affect cyber relationships? Hansen's article explores these questions and more. She questions the assumptions of only two genders, she asks the reader to consider reality and deception related to online relationships, she asks about effects of "not following the gender rules," and she wonders why it is so important to know the sex of the person one is communicating with. This article will serve as a useful source of comparison so students can think more deeply about these topics and see how such issues resonate with their own experience.

QUESTIONS FOR DISCUSSION

- *What is happening now with relationships in cyberspace? What is your experience?*
- *What will the future bring? How can the future be guided?*
- *Have you ever presented yourself online as someone you are not? Is this ethical? Did it work? Have you discovered that someone you communicated with was not truthful about his or her identity? How did you respond?*
- *What are the positive attributes and the drawbacks of online relationships?*
- *How do people go about being male or female in cyberspace?*

Every day, millions of people around the world go online. The Internet is a new forum for social interaction. We can talk to people whom we have never physically met, who live in countries that we have never been to. People form friendships and fall in love with people whom they know only through the words they have typed on a screen.

Cyberspace is also a place where you can easily assume a persona that is different from your real-life identity. Characteristics such as age and gender are easy to modify when you are represented only by words on a screen. This also means that you can never be sure of the "real" gender of the people whom you meet online—or can you? In this article, we'll take a closer look at some conversations in which the gender of chat room users has been, in some way, called into question.

Computer-mediated chat is unusual in that it allows anonymous social interaction. As Paul Ten Have (2000) notes, this anonymity offers users "an unprecedented license for unaccountable action . . . from bland banality to criminal threat, while passing through all imaginable sexual perversities." This means that it is possible for people to claim membership in categories for which they may, in "real life," have no such claim; it also makes it impossible to be certain of the legitimacy of the identity claims of others.

The activity of "gender-switching"—acting as someone of the opposite gender on the Internet—has been the subject of considerable attention, both in the popular media and in academic research. Most researchers agree that gender-switching is primarily the activity of people who are "male in real life" (for example, Suler, 2000; Sempsey, 1997; Serpentelli, 1993), but there is little agreement as to how widespread this practice might be. Some have estimated that as many as 40% of users have engaged in some form of online sex-change (for example, Parks, 2000); others are more cautious, suggesting that 5% may be a more accurate figure (for example, Cooper, 2000). What is often ignored—especially in media reports of such findings—is the online *context* of the users surveyed. The 40% of users reported by Parks (2000) to be gender-switchers were MUD users. MUDs (multi-user domains) are online environments where fantasy and taking on a different character are normative activities of community members. The more conservative figure given by Cooper (2000) refers to users of social chat rooms—places where gender-switching may be a morally risky activity that may lead to charges of willful deception.

These estimates tend to be derived either from information volunteered by users or by comparing the gender given by users in their online profiles to that of the persona they adopt in interaction (for example, Stone, 1992). Profiles are usually filled out before entering a chat room (though they may be edited or modified at any time). They typically contain "demographic" information about the age, sex, and physical location of users. Once in the chat room, an avatar or nick serves as a marker of user identity. Text-based programs allow for the display of nicks (names) next to the text produced by users; newer, graphical programs allow users to display an avatar (or image) to represent their character. This research practice—of comparing the gender people give in their profile to the gender of the persona they adopt in interaction—overlooks the possibility that some users will construct their profiles to reflect the gender of their online persona. In any case, online profiles do not necessarily tell us anything about the "real-life" gender of users, as they are, in principle, as open to manipulation as any other form of self-presentation online.

What is often ignored in such research is any attention to what accusations of gender-switching—and, indeed, conversations about gender—might look like in practice, in chat room conversations. So, in this article, I'd like to focus on some of the methods that people use to manage the topic of authentic gender presentation when they're online.

To begin, I want to take a look at a number of ways that the topic of gender may be raised in online conversations. The first and most basic of these is the use of brief opening queries, such as "asl" (age, sex, location), "m/f" (male/female), and "RUMOF" ("Are you male or female?"), as part of the process of finding a suitable person to chat with. I'll examine a number of examples in which such questions are simply normal and routine inquiries; some cases in which the question "Are you male or female?" becomes a challenge to the "real" gender of the user; and several examples in which this question is taken to be a "pickup" line. Finally, I'll look at some of the ways in which requests for "proof" of users' gender may be accomplished and at some of the ways that the potentially deceptive activity of gender-switching may be explained as a morally acceptable activity.

Here—in contrast to much of the literature on gender-switching on the Internet (for example, Parks, 2000; Herring, 1994) and, more generally, on "sex differences" in conversational "style" (for example, Thomson & Murachver, 2001)—I don't want to treat gender as a preexistent causal variable. Rather than taking the "real" gender of users as a starting point, I'll examine in some detail a number of different ways in which the "everyday business" of gender is conducted online, as well as the building up and undermining of the legitimacy of users' claims to be male or female. This means paying attention to the construction of gender in chat, when and *if* it becomes relevant and is oriented to (or "noticed") by users—that is, looking for the work of gender categorizations in use and, in particular, at the construction of "legitimate category boundedness" (Sacks, 1995), or what is to count as evidence of "genuine" male- or femaleness.

GENDER CATEGORIZATION IN CHAT ROOMS

We can guess the gender of chat room users from information that's available from a variety of sources. For instance, room names that suggest a "woman-only" space may be used to infer that all users present in the room are—or should be—female. The profiles filled out by users may also provide information about age and gender. Finally, the nicks, or names, adopted by users may give some indication of their gender. Paul Ten Have (2000) has discussed the use of "asl?" (age, sex, location?) as part of the process of finding a suitable partner to chat with. He argues that "people who want to chat rely mostly on [just such] categorical predications to find suitable chat partners." Ten Have suggests that the primary function of age and gender categorization is to "set the scene" for sexually explicit chats, while categorization according to location or culture is more often accomplished in order to establish "mutual understandability." The membership categorization achieved through asl inquiries may also be drawn upon to "initiate preliminary topics, testing the waters before morally more risky ones are brought forward."

DATA SOURCES

I used Google, an Internet search engine, to search for publicly available archived chat logs that contained the question "Are you male or female?" The extracts presented here have been selected from 10 of the 500 logs returned. These conversations occurred in a variety of different chat rooms, including rooms for teenagers, bisexual and lesbian women, music television enthusiasts, fans of a pop group, stock market traders, and science fiction and fantasy fans. The names of chat rooms, people, and locations have been altered.

PICKUP DEVICES

Asl, m/f, and "Are you male or female?" are all frequently and normatively used in attempts to initiate a conversation with other users—though these "staccato" queries are frowned upon by members of some established chat communities, who may deride, eject, or simply ignore the askers of such questions as being insensitive "newbies" (new and inexperienced users), "trolls" (mischief makers), or "spods" (geeks concerned to find sexual chat partners). Though these categorizations are fascinating in themselves, space does not permit a detailed examination of them here. Instead, I'd like to take a quick look at some mundane uses of asl, m/f, and "Are you male or female?" as opening queries.

Extract 1

1	\<A>	hi
2	\<A>	asl
3	\<A>	19/f/ca
4	\<B>	ji
5	\<B>	hi

6	<B>	I got tongue-tied
7	<B>	whats up, [A]

In this first extract, A has just entered the chat room. S/he[1] greets B, requests his/her asl and offers his/her own statistics (each line is equivalent to a carriage return, which posts the user's words for others to see). Although B does not immediately offer his/her own identifying details, his/her return greeting and comment (in line 6) works both as an explanation of his/her misspelling on line 4 and also as a flirtatious response to A's "statistics" indicating that s/he is 19, female, and Californian.

Extract 2

1	<A>	are you male or female
2	<B>	Male
3	<A>	and I female
4	<A>	what you want to talk about
5	<B>	We can talk about anything you want
6	<A>	what you want to talk about is you choise.
7	<B>	OK, let's talk about you. . . .Tell me something you like to do
8	<A>	sex.
9	<B>	Ahhh . . . What do you like about sex?

This second extract is from the opening of a chat that—quite rapidly—turns to sexual matters. Here, "Are you male or female?" is used to establish (an initial) mutual suitability for the purposes of a "flirtatious" chat. However, the topic of sex is not raised immediately. Rather, A and B repeatedly—and flirtatiously—offer each other the floor, or the right to decide "what they should talk about." There is a neat transfer of responsibility going on here. So, when A asks "what you want to talk about?" B builds A's question into his/her retort, "We can talk about *anything* you want." "Anything you want" as the topic for a prospective mutual conversation gives permission for A to raise the "morally risky" topic of cybersex. However (in line 6), A passes the responsibility for choosing "what you want to talk about" back to B, by repeating verbatim A's question "what you want to talk about," but with the appended emphasis, "is you choise." After two requests for a topic, B submits; however, the topic chosen, "talk about you" (with the imperative "tell me something you like to do"), offers a less direct, face-saving route for A to choose the topic, which, as it turns out, is sex. After line 8, the question-answer pattern reverses, such that B is asking brief questions and A is offering longer sexual descriptions.

Extract 3

1	<A>	hi!
2	<B>	hello.
3	<A>	m/f?
4	<B>	m, u?
5	<A>	m. bye

Such inquiries can also be used in very brief and blunt interchanges, as in this complete conversation. This often occurs via a form of "virtual shorthand" that enables A to abruptly and unproblematically terminate the chat after finding B to be the "wrong gender."

Extract 4

1	<A>	are you male or female?
2	<B>	why?
3	<B>	does it matter?
4	<A>	no
5	<A>	sorry

Of course, not all users will answer these questions in a straightforward manner that lends itself to categorization, and thus—potentially—a sexual move, or the termination of a conversation on the basis of being "unsuitable." In this extract, rather than divulging his or her gender, B returns two counterquestions that bring into question A's *motivation* for wanting to know B's gender (in line 2) and, indeed, problematize the *relevance* of gender to their interaction (in line 3). By challenging the relevance of such questions, the asker can be formulated as rude and overcurious—thus warranting A's withdrawal and immediate apology (in lines 4 and 5).

Extract 5

1	<A>	Are you male or female?
2	<B>	yes
3	<A>	which one?
4	<B>	probably
5	<A>	what?

In this extract, B also manages not to give a "proper" answer to the question "Are you male or female?" However, here, "nonsensical" responses are used to make trouble for A's attempt to establish B's gender and initiate a conversation. B's responses unsettle the question through playful disruption, and work to make the exchange an "unsuccessful pickup," or a successful "blow-off," that subverts the more usual question and answer sequence often initiated with "Are you male or female?"

"Asl," "m/f," and "Are you male or female," then, can be received as routine requests for identifying information, with a view to finding a suitable chat partner, or as queries that may mark the opening move of a "flirtatious" chat. Sacks (1995) has noted that questions—particularly routine requests—can work as effective "pickup" devices. As we will see, saying hello to strangers does not always work as a strategy for starting a conversation. The problem in chat rooms is not just that greetings may be rebuffed, as they may imply that you already know the user addressed and thus have a right to say hi, but also that, in crowded chat rooms, it may be unclear who it is that you are addressing. Sacks notes that one solution to this first problem is to start with a question rather than a greeting and that, among such questions, routine requests are a particularly powerful device. In addition to the obligation to provide an answer to a question, there is the expectation that we should not be needlessly rude to a stranger making a request for something as mundane as the time or, arguably, often in chat room talk, the age, sex, and location of fellow users.[2] Furthermore, the requester knows that she or he will get a standard, quick response and thus will soon be in a position to ask a further question which may start a longer conversation.

Turn-taking organization—the organized ways that people tend to take their turns at talking—also influences the ways that "Are you male or female?" is likely to be understood. So, for instance, it allows the question "Are you male or female?" to be more likely to be understood *not* as a challenge to the "real" gender of the user, but rather as a preliminary identification query and/or a pickup device. That is, "Are you male or female?" is often offered and responded to as a "polite" enquiry—a bit like "Do you have the time?"—that can *also* be understood and responded to as a chat-up line. Similarly, in the course of an ongoing conversation, when the information provided by the user's nick and profile is insufficient for you to work out whether the person is male or female, you may also legitimately ask "Are you male or female?" However, as in the next extract, this is likely to be preceded by some signal of the delicacy—and appreciation of the "off topic" character—of the question to follow, such as "just curious," "please forgive me," or "I hope it isn't inappropriate."

Extract 6

200	<A>	Question for [B] . . .
201	<B>	yes?
202	<A>	please forgive me but are you male or female?
203	<B>	female
204	<C>	What is the point of reading the story?
205	<A>	That is a cute name . . . plus we are all girls in here!
206	<B>	thanks

CALLING GENDER INTO QUESTION

In this section, I'd like to look at some online conversations in which the question "Are you male or female?" works to *challenge* or undermine the presenting gender of the user in question.

Extract 7

1	<A>	are you male or female?
2	<B>	I'm a guy
3	<A>	really, or do you just not want to talk to me?
4	<B>	Go away

5 \<A\>   Are you a girl?
6 \<B\>   Uhhh . . . yeah
7 \<A\>   I knew it!
8 \<A\>   Please talk to me
9 \<B\>   fine

What are the "usual" connotations of the gendered identity categories in use in this extract? "Male" and "female" refer to the biological device, sex, and, as we have seen, "Are you male or female?" is a standard opening inquiry in electronic talk-in-interaction. These categories (male and female)—and, for this matter, this question—are more commonly encountered, in everyday (offline) life, in surveys, questionnaires, and other tools for data collection than in mundane discussions of gendered identity. So, this may help to lend a "disinterested" status to this opening question. The terms "guy" and "girl"—as used in the extract—belong to a less formal, more "social," device for gendered categorization. "Guy" is a particularly fuzzy category—with a range of indexical possibilities—and may be used to refer to *both* males and females. Indeed, this "fuzziness" is traded on in a later extract.

Admitting to not wanting to talk to someone is a morally difficult task—think of how you might offend people by telling them that you don't want to talk to them. So, in the conversation above, offering a candidate identity as "a guy" in response to the question "Are you male or female?" establishes B's status as sexually unavailable, and so not properly the subject of further "pickup questions." This means that s/he has a "no blame" reason for not wanting to talk to A.

However, in line 3, A's alternative explanation for B's answer ("really, or do you just not want to talk to me?") works to *undermine* B's claim to be "a guy." As Sacks (1995) notes, "if you can find that category to which [an answer] is category-bound, you can use it as an explanation of [that answer], which provides for the undercutting of that [answer]." So, answering, "I'm a guy" to "Are you male or female?" can *also* be explained as a category-bound activity of a female who is *pretending* to be male in order to avoid "unwanted attention." (In basic terms: You're saying that you are a guy not because you really are a guy but because you don't want to talk to me. You don't want to talk to me because you are a girl—and "everyone knows" that girls pretend to be guys in chat rooms in order to avoid "unwanted attention.") Indeed, as we will see, both "expert" and some users' accounts of the reasons that men and women may adopt a different gender gives just such category-bound motivations for this activity.

By answering "Go away"—a direct rejection—in line 4, B orients to A's suggestion that s/he is *pretending* to be a "guy" in order to avoid talking to him/her. The chaining rule (Sacks, 1995)—and (what A takes to be) B's implicit confirmation of the second part of A's previous question ("or do you just not want to talk to me?")—gives A license (in line 5) to persist in reformulating his initial query, this time expressed according to the standardized relational pair (SRP) guy/girl.[3] As Derek

Edwards (1998) has noted, the category "girl" suggests "an unattached, unmarried, available, possibly young, female" (p. 25). This category thus has the potential to carry more "useful" category-bound information—for the prospective "picker-upper"—than the more clinical category "female," which is applicable to all women and girls—and to some "guys." So, through this transformation in standardized relational pairs (from male/female to guy/girl), the conversation moves further toward social and sexual overtones.

B's less than enthusiastic admission that s/he is a girl: "yeah" (in line 6) is prefaced with the hedge "Uhhh" and a simulated pause, through his/her use of ellipsis dots (. . .). This is met (in line 7) by A's jubilant exclamation, "I knew it!" which vindicates his persistence in the face of B's initial rejection, followed by the more contrite request, "Please talk to me." Again, in line 9, B appears to be signalling fairly clearly—as with his/her initial direct rejection ("Go away" in line 4) and his/her further use of "weak agreements" ("Uhhh . . . yeah" in line 6 and, in line 9, "fine") his/her *lack* of interest in talking to A. However, A seems impervious to these signals, orienting only to B's potential availability as a girl who may be persuaded to talk to him.

Extract 8

1	\<A\>		are you male or female?
2	\<B\>		Male
			[. . .]
17	\<A \>		your logon screen says your female, dammit
18	\<B\>		So? Do you ask out *every* bbs female?

This extract is an instance of how "conflicting" gender claims may be handled. Here, B's straightforward answer ("Male") to "are you male or female?" is later challenged (in line 17, during a multiparty conversation about music television) by reference to the conflicting information provided by B's logon screen. A's suffix "dammit" marks this discrepancy as a *transgression* that should require some explanation or apology. However, rather than offering an apology, B's response takes the form of two further challenges: "So? Do you ask out *every* bbs female?"[4] Both of these "counter-challenges" serve to bring into question the motivation of the asker. Here, "So?" has a "wanna make something of it?" ring. A "bbs" female is, presumably, shorthand for a "bulletin board system" female, a category that serves to "normalize" the activity of gender-switching online.

Extract 9

1	\<A\>	hi [B]
2	\<B\>	hi [A]
3	\<A\>	are you bi?
4	\<B\>	well . . .
5	\<A\>	How old are you
6	\<A\>	where r u from

         7 <B>   why?
         8 <B>   nice to meet you, by the way . . . we're jumping right to the personal
                       questions, aren't we?
         9 <A>   don't u want to chat to me
        10 <B>   it's just that I don't know you, and you're coming at me with a lot
                       of personal questions
        11 <A>   are there any pitcures of you on that web page [B]
        12 <B>   [A], may I ask you something?
        13 <A>   what
        14 <B>   are you male or female?
        15 <A>   female why do you ask
        16 <B>   you are asking me the same questions that men always ask me
        17 <A>   I am a 21 year old bi curious female
        18 <A>   it is only the second time that I've used the internet
        19 <B>   ok, I'm not complaining or anything, you could be a 56 year old
                       male plumber in a baby doll nightie for all I care, really
        20 <A>   well I'm not

In this extract, the first question (in line 3) departs from gender and asks about sexuality. This is because, in this conversation, gender categorization may already be made on the basis of B's (female-sounding) name and from the expectable gender of users in a chat room for "bisexual and lesbian women, and their straight (female) friends." So the relevant question, in terms of establishing B's potential availability and interest in flirtatious chatting, has to do with sexuality rather than gender. However, A's forthright opening question, "are you bi?" is met with an indirect "refusal" (through the hedge, "well . . .") and a simulated pause (through the use of ellipses) in line 4, rather than by a direct response.

Instead of orienting to B's hesitation, A persists with two further "identity" questions (in lines 5 and 6: "How old are you," "where r u from"). Note that B's response ("why?") is similar to the use of "why" as a counterquestion in Extract 4, in response to the question "Are you male or female?" In both cases, this serves to call into question the asker's motivation for wanting to know the answers to such "personal" questions, and perhaps the relevance (here) of sexuality, age, and location to their conversation. B goes on (in line 8) to offer an ironic corrective example of a conventional and polite greeting—"nice to meet you, by the way"—and to make explicit the transgressive nature of A's opening questions as being inappropriately premature and personal (and, by contrast to B's "example," also rude and departing from common manners).

A orients to this gentle corrective with a further question that works to reformulate B's concerns as a personal matter of not wanting to talk to her. As we saw earlier, in Extract 7, admitting to not wanting to talk to someone is a morally risky business—so, it's an effective charge that may undermine a potential challenge. To make it easier, B offers a softer—and more explicit—account of her concerns (in line 10): "it's just that I don't know you [and, by implication, not that I don't want to talk to you], and you're coming at me with a lot of personal questions." Note that "coming at me" suggests an assault of sorts, and that A's questions are cast as evidently excessive in number, through the extreme case formulation "*a lot* of personal questions."

However, in line 11, rather than offering an apology or account, A asks yet another question (the Web page in question is B's home page, the URL of which is included in his/her profile). At this point (in line 12), B signals, through a pre-question that marks and seeks permission, the delicacy of the question to follow. In line 15, A gives his/her gender as female, but with the appended question "why do you ask?" This works to call into question B's motivation, in much the same manner as B's earlier problematization ("why?", etc.) of A's questions.

Next, B undermines A's claims to being female by explaining A's conduct according to the category-bound activities (CBAs) of men: "asking the same questions that men *always* ask me."

So, here, for A, are two mutually exclusive membership categories—with quite different moral implications. If A is indeed a man, then he should be identified as such and, as an impostor, be held accountable for his *deceitful* conduct; however, if A is a woman, she must provide some account for her *inappropriate*—or *impolite*—conduct/breach of netiquette. S/he needs to find some other plausible identity category that could be used to explain his/her conduct.

Thus, in lines 17–18, A reformulates his/her identity to account for his/her "questionable" conduct: "I am a 21 year old bi curious female/it is only the second time I have used the internet." A's (re)formulation of his/her identity is designed to enable B to arrive at a different understanding of the reasons for A's inappropriate conduct, and a different way to react to it (as helpful experienced user, and experienced bisexual or lesbian woman, rather than as a suspicious community member).

A predicate of the categories invoked by A (a young, bi-curious woman who is new to the Internet), in which s/he is claiming membership, is being inexperienced and unfamiliar with the "rules" for polite chat room conduct. A's category-bound lack of experience both with the Internet—and, by extension, the "rules" for polite interaction in chat rooms—and with being a member of the "bisexual" or "lesbian" community means that s/he should then be *expected* to be noticeably "incompetent" at such matters.

B's response (in line 19) begins with a weak acceptance of A's identity claims and the disclaimer "ok, I'm not complaining or anything," which together display her awareness that she is on morally risky ground, and that some careful accountability work is required. To preempt a potential "moral" challenge from A, B neatly avoids directly challenging A's claims to be "a 21 year old bi curious female" by introducing an equally plausible—though patently ridiculous—identity description. In doing so, she also uses the stage of life device[5]: "you could be a 56 year old male plumber" serves to unsettle A's identity formulation *as just that*. This utterance also contains a correction-invitation device[6]: "you *could be* a 56 year old male plumber" here attests to the impossibility of *knowing* whether A is "really" a 21-year-old bi-curious female or a 56-year-old male plumber in a baby-doll nightie. The reassurance provided by B's "for all I care, really" (line 19) suggests an unprejudiced and accepting attitude, an awareness of the fluidity of online identity, and the lack of a necessary correspondence between on- and offline personas.

Are You Real or Memorex?

Even some nonhumans in cyberspace are capable of "doing gender." Julia is a chatterbot engineered by Michael Mauldin, a computer scientist from Carnegie Mellon University. It is designed to provide assistance to MUD users, and particularly to give advice to "newbies" who may need help with directions or unfamiliar commands. Julia is capable of initiating and responding to a range of questions, and can engage in limited "small talk." It has been programmed to "bolster" its claims to being a woman with casually provided information about biologically female experiences, such as menstruation and premenstrual syndrome (PMS). This information forms part of an "explanatory metastructure" of talk that operates to establish Julia as "female" (Zdenek, 1999).

The following extract (Foner, 1993, p. 4) is from a conversation between Julia and Barry, a MUD user who (though unsure of Julia's status) carried on a series of "normal" conversations with Julia over several weeks.

Extract 10

1 barry says, ". . . are you real or memorex?"
2 Julia says, "I'm as real as you are, barry"
3 barry says, "yea but you answer soooo damn fast. How do you do it?"
4 Julia says, "I have PMS today, barry."
5 barry says, "well I wont mess with you while you have this chemical imbalance"
6 barry says, "please tell me what state you are in"
7 Julia says, "I never really thought about it, barry"

Here, Julia offers "PMS" as the reason for its unusually fast typing speed, and as evidence of its status as female (and thus as human). Appeals to biology commonsensically relate sex and gender as cause and effect, and work to essentialize gender as a natural fact. Although Julia's use of PMS works here as an explanation for its atypical typing speed, this PMS excuse is, in fact, generated randomly and does not require a question or prompt about its well-being (Zdenek, 1999). Accordingly, Julia's PMS comes to stand in erratically as justification for any number of its actions. This works to establish Julia as female, both through this repeated reference to "female biology" and through Julia's erratic deployment of such references. Thus, the Julia program draws upon and reinforces cultural knowledge of the facts of natural womanhood, by rendering (in)competent female behavior as always (potentially) determined by fluctuating hormones.

Appeals to biology and exclusively "female" experience and knowledge form an important part of the "apparatus of proof" for determining the "true" gender of online users. It is to requests for this kind of "evidence" that we turn next.

From Category-Bound Activities to Category-Bound Knowledge: Establishing "Proof" of Membership

Finally, I'd like to take a very brief look at some instances of one possible "next step" for challenges to the gender claims of users.[7] These extracts make reference not just to category-bound activities—such as "asking the same questions as men always ask"—but also to category-bound knowledge, as part of the process of establishing "proof" of users' membership. The extract reproduced here makes reference to pantyhose sizes; other examples I have come across refer to bra sizes, detailed descriptions of female genitalia, regularity and duration of menses, preference for various sports (ice-skating or football?), and the use of remote controls. As with Extract 5, here A creates disruption through the literal interpretation of questions.

Extract 11

16	<A>	I'll do anything u guys want
17	<B>	actually [A], I think you ARE a guy
18	<A>	f[**] off i aint no guy why do you think that
19	<B>	because you sound like a guy
20	<A>	how can I sound like a guy I am typing on my keyboard, do you wanna call me up to hear my voice . . .
21	<B>	ok [A], you TYPE like a guy, ok?
22	<A>	how do guys type I dont understand
23	<B>	[A], do you wear pantyhose?
24	<A>	of course I do but at the moment I am wearing my black thong
25	<B>	well, when you wear them, what size are they?
26	<A>	size 8 why
27	<B>	and what country are you from?

"Expert" Accounts

Experts also rely upon category-bound knowledge about "being a woman" to try to devise ways of working out "who the real women are." In his article on the "masculine" practice of gender-switching, "cyber-psychologist" John Suler (2000) presents a short questionnaire intended to determine if users presenting as female are authentically female. He derived these from a survey of 30—presumably real—women.

1. What is the difference between junior and misses sizes?
2. What sizes do pantyhose typically come in?
3. What is the difference in how flushable and nonflushable tampons are made?
4. What size ring do women usually wear?
5. When coloring hair, how long is the dye usually left in one's hair?
6. What is the average range of sizes for women's panties?
7. What negative effect may antibiotics have on a woman?
8. On what day is flow the greatest?
9. When during her cycle is a woman most likely to become pregnant?[8]

These questions assume that a certain body of knowledge comes "naturally" with membership in the category "real woman." They center around knowledge of female biology and of the attributes and use of "typically" feminine products (the distinction between various kinds of tampon, for example). Here, being an authentic female requires a personal knowledge of things only women should know (and that men should not). Incidentally, not all of the "real" women surveyed by Suler could answer all of these questions—check the answer key in footnote 8 to see if you could pass as a woman! In any case, the unoccasioned asking of such "personal" questions in normal conversation—as we have seen—is likely to be a matter of some delicacy.[9]

Obviously, those attempting to "pass" as differently gendered online do not face the same challenges as those trying to pass in "real" life. Cyberspace is unusual in that it allows anonymous and pseudonymous *everyday* communication. This means that "becoming" one of another gender is easier in cyberspace. This does not mean that people become completely unaccountable for their gender. Community membership—whether in cyberspace or in real life—requires that members be accountable participants in the ongoing production and maintenance of local social order. Computer-mediated communication is no exception.

So, the next time you're online, try visiting a chat room—perhaps with an ambiguous nick—and pay attention to the ways in which people try to work out your "real" gender. You can log (or save) your chat room conversations for later study if you're curious to see just how people go about working out "who is male and who is female" on the Internet.

NOTES

1. Throughout, the use of "s/he" and "his/her" to refer to chat room participants is intended to highlight the clumsiness that comes with refusing to treat gender as a preexistent causal variable.
2. "Asl check" is sometimes used in a multiparty conversation to elicit responses from all present users. A particular response may then be responded to with a further, relevant question.

3. A "standardized relational pair" is a particular kind of membership categorization device (Sacks, 1995) that is made up of two categories—in this case, "guy" and "girl." As members of society, we know and expect to see a different set of actions, duties, and competencies performed by "guys" and by "girls."

4. Note that these challenges are similar to those we found earlier, in Extract 4, in A's "disruptive" response to "Are you male or female?" (lines 2–3: "why? does it matter?").

5. The stage of life device is yet another kind of membership categorization device (MCD) (Sacks, 1995), and is one of a number of "positioned category devices." The stage of life device is made up of differently positioned categories (such as baby, toddler, child, teenager, young adult, older adult, or using age terms, 6-month-old, 2-year-old, 7-year-old, 15-year-old, 20-year-old, 56-year-old, and so on). It is important to note that these positioned categories allow people to make category contrasts, which in turn can allow people to make moral judgments about the behavior of others. So, for example, if X is a 56-year-old but is behaving like a 21-year-old (where 56 is positioned higher relative to the position of 21 in the stage of life device), then X will most likely receive complaint (as being "immature") rather than praise for his behavior— though praise (for example, being "young at heart") is also possible.

6. Challenges can arise in a number of different ways: (1) a direct challenge; (2) the hearer can offer a possible "reason" for what you have said, or a "correction-invitation" device (Sacks, 1995).

7. This kind of interaction could form the subject of an article in itself, and there is a lot more that could be said about "what happens next" when people are asked to "prove" their gender in cyberspace. For more on this question, see Hall (1996).

8. (1) Junior sizes tend to be smaller and may involve a different numbering system. (2) Usually A, B, Queen; rarely, small, medium, large. (3) Nonflushables have plastic in them, flushables only paper and fabric. (4) 5, 6, 7. (5) May vary, but approximately 25 minutes. (6) Typical range is 2–10; average size is 6–8. (7) Yeast infections. (8) First or second, typically. (9) Approximately 15 days after the start of her period.

9. Can you imagine how you would go about asking someone you have only recently met online about "the average range of sizes for women's panties"? Who would look more suspicious?

REFERENCES

Cooper, A. (2000). Cited in Laino, C. (2000). *Poll: Pulse of online sex is positive.* Available: http://www.msnbc.com/news/171418.asp?cp1=1

Edwards, D. (1998). The relevant thing about her: Social identity categories in use. In C. Antaki & S. Widdicombe (Eds.), *Identities in talk* (pp. 15–34). London: Sage.

Foner, L. (1993). A sociological look at MUDs, Julia, and those who interact with her. Available: http://belladonna.media.mit.edu/people/foner/Julia/section3_3.html

Hall, K. (1996). Cyberfeminism. In S. Herring (Ed.), *Computer-mediated communication: Linguistic, social, and cross-cultural perspectives* (pp. 147–170). Philadelphia: John Benjamins.

Herring, S. (1994, June). *Gender differences in computer-mediated communication: Bringing familiar baggage to the new frontier.* Paper presented at the annual convention of the American Library Association, Miami. Available: http://www.cpsr.org/cpsr/gender/herring.txt

Parks, M. (2000). Cited in Segen, S. (2000). *Study: Cyberspace conducive to gender-bending.* Available: http://www.abcnews.go.com/sections/tech/DailyNews/netgender000523.html

Sacks, H. (1995). *Lectures on conversation* (Vols.1–2). Cambridge: Blackwell.

Sempsey, J. (1997). *Psyber psychology: A literature review pertaining to the psycho/social aspects of multi-user dimensions in cyberspace.* Available: http://journal.tinymush.org/v2n1/sempsey.html

Serpentelli, J. (1993). *Conversational structure and personality correlates of electronic communication.* Available: http://www.oise.on.ca/~jnolan/muds/about_muds/conv-structure

Stone, R. (1992). Virtual systems. In J. Crary & S. Kwinter (Eds.), *Incorporations* (pp. 614–619). New York: ZONE.

Suler, J. (2000). *Do boys just wanna have fun? Gender-switching in cyberspace.* Available: http://www.rider.edu/users/suler/psycyber/genderswap.html

Ten Have, P. (2000). Computer mediated chat: Ways of finding chat partners. *M/C: A Journal of Media and Culture.* Available: http://www.api-network.com/mc/0008/partners2.html

Thomson, R., & Murachver, T. (2001). Predicting gender from electronic discourse. *British Journal of Social Psychology, 40,* 193–208.

Zdenek, S. (1999). Rising up from the MUD: Inscribing gender in software design. *Discourse & Society, 10,* 379–409.

WILL THINGS EVER GET BETTER?

Natalia Deeb-Sossa

DEPARTMENT OF SOCIOLOGY,

UNIVERSITY OF NORTH CAROLINA AT CHAPEL HILL

I attended an Easter egg hunt that took place after the noon mass in a town in North Carolina. Around 1 P.M. the parade began. Sons and daughters, parents and grandparents in their Sunday best were walking toward the field behind the church. Most of the families were white and upper class. I saw one black woman, who was with an older white man.

When the egg hunt was about to begin I saw a Hispanic girl. Ana was about 10 years old. Ana's father wore dark corduroy pants and a baby-blue, long-sleeved shirt. His shoes were black and seemed to have been polished for the occasion. Ana's mother wore a colorful skirt. Her black hair stood out against her white blouse. Both parents spoke in Spanish to Ana, encouraging her to take her place in the starting line. Ana fidgeted and, with her eyes looking down, refused to move toward the other children participating in the egg hunt.

Ana's father walked with her toward the starting line and encouraged her to participate. As the two approached, the other parents yanked their children from out of their path. Such a hasty realignment suggested that the parents were doing their best to avoid contact with Ana rather than making room to welcome her.

The egg hunt was about to begin. Ana's father walked back toward the mother, and both parents did not take their eyes off Ana. She ran toward a basket as the signal to begin was given. Most of the white children made groups. Boys formed groups with other boys. Girls formed groups with other girls. The goal was to find as many toys and candy as possible.

Ana was alone. No one formed a group with her.

Once or twice when Ana found some candy I saw boys rush toward her and grab the candy from her hands. No boys took the candy away from the white girls, although some of the boys did push them and then run past. I saw an 8-year-old brother try to take a little car from his sister, only to be reprimanded by both his mother and father. No one ever shouted at the boys who pushed Ana and took her candy and toys.

After the hunt was over I saw Ana crying.

"Mamá" said Ana to her mother, "vamos yá para la casa!" *Let's go home right now!*

"Mija" began Ana's mother, "que te pasa, te caiste?" *What is the matter, did you fall down?*

"Mamá, me quitaron los dulces y jugetes. Me empujaron." *Mama, they took my candy and toys. They pushed me.*

"Y me dijeron fea, Mamá." *And, Mama, they said I am ugly.*

"No les pares bolas Ana. Tu eres muy linda." *Don't pay attention to them. You are very pretty.*

"Quiero ser como esos chicos, mami. Yo soy fea, ellos no." *I want to be like those boys. I am ugly, they are not.*

I was intrigued by Ana's desire to be like the boys. What advantage did she see in being a boy? Did she want to share the power boys have to define which girl is pretty and which is not? Did she want to be one of them because it isn't as important for boys—as it is for girls—to look good?

After Ana's mother comforted her, and they were walking toward Ana's father, Ana asked, "Mamá, siempre sera asì?" *Mama, will it always be this way?* Ana's mother looked surprised by her 10-year-old daughter's question and tried to reassure Ana. She said, "Let's go home. Everything is OK." Ana continued asking her mother, "Mamá, estas segura? Todo mejorará? Yo tambièn?"

Ana's last questions stuck with me: "Will it always be like this? Will things get better? Will I get better?"

I was a little older than Ana when I first realized that being a boy or a man had its advantages.

It is 2 A.M. in Bogotá, Colombia. I am 12 years old and on the phone with the police: "You must come, he is trying to kill her with a machete!" A sleepy male voice replies: "I'm sure it is just a lovers' quarrel. You should not be on the phone at this time, little girl. We are very busy." Through my open window I hear a woman's voice trying to reason with her drunk husband: "I did not steal your money. You just drank your money on beer. I promise, I did not spend it. Please, don't kill me!" I run to my parent's room, wake up my father and plead with him to save the woman. Only after my father called did the police come and take the husband to jail for a night.

I wish I could tell Ana she will not experience sexism and racism again. But I cannot. Ana's experience is only one of many manifestations of these systems of privilege in our daily life. Ana has experienced racism, a system that grants access to social, economic, and political power based on race. Ana has also experienced sexism, a system wherein males receive unearned privileges and advantages, while females are denied such benefits.

I too have had firsthand experiences with sexism and racism.

Just a few months ago I walked one morning into a local cafe to buy a cup of coffee. As I moved toward an empty seat, one of the waiters greeted me and said: "Do you want your usual?" I replied, "Yes." I then said "good morning" to another young waiter who came in with the newspapers. He answered, "Buenos dias." I immediately answered back, "Buenos dias," as he poured some coffee into the cup that was beside the newspaper he had left for me to read. Then a white man sat down beside me. He said, "Are you here looking for a waitress job? You will be good at handling your people!"

Today, still upset but no longer shocked at the assumption that I was there for a waitress job and that Latinos and Latinas need to be managed or handled, I ask myself—as Ana does—will things ever get better?

PART IV

VERBAL AND NONVERBAL COMMUNICATION

URBAN MUSIC

Gendered Language in Rapping

Elizabeth J. Natalle, with Jimmie L. ("Rue") Flippen

THE UNIVERSITY OF NORTH CAROLINA AT GREENSBORO

Communication scholars have long studied persuasive communication that is aimed toward effecting social change. Some focus on the persuasive tactics used to attain the support of an uninformed or neutral public; others analyze the messages generated to call members to the movement and solidify them. In this article, Elizabeth J. Natalle examines the general content of rap, or urban music—a genre of music that advocates social change, promotes action, and serves as an affirmation of shared experiences.

As a white woman and feminist scholar, Natalle is concerned with negative stereotypes and the sanctioning of violence—against women generally and black women particularly—that often occurs in rap music. She questions the ethics of the music and further ponders how music that is touted as a form of social commentary, with the potential to empower a nondominant group, simultaneously can be oppressive to half of the audience toward whom the music is aimed. Natalle begins to explore these questions through an interview with a black male rap fan. In the course of the interview, the author learns how the fan interprets the music and justifies the negative portrayals of and violence against women in a way that may be empowering for males and females alike.

QUESTIONS FOR DISCUSSION

- *Do you agree/disagree with Rue's justification for the negative ways that women often are depicted in rap music lyrics? Why/why not?*
- *How might the answers to Natalle's questions differ if she were speaking to a black female rap fan?*
- *Does either the interviewer or the interviewee ever inadvertently seem to engage in gender stereotyping? If so, where?*
- *How do Rue's comments suggest that race and gender intersect in rap music to empower male listeners?*
- *Does Rue's interpretation of rap music's references toward women provide an alternative reading of the music that could be empowering to women? If so, how? If not, why?*

INTRODUCTION

We have choices about how to name and describe the world around us. Words carry political, emotional, and personal meaning, and words literally help to create maps of reality in our heads (Hayakawa & Hayakawa, 1992). This personal meaning is called **connotation** as opposed to **denotation,** or dictionary definitions. Right now, we live in a world that is highly sensitive to the political (connotative) implications of language. If someone says *nigger* or *bitch,* one ought to expect the consequences to be pretty severe. Such derogatory words have a prejudicial component in their meaning that offends most people. It's not very competent to use such language in most communication situations. Even if your own speech community uses such terms, it would be wise to figure out what those words mean to people. *Nigger* is used in jest among friends in the African American community, just as *queer* is being used by the gay community as a word that has positive meaning. But that doesn't mean that *nigger* and *queer* will mean the same thing to everyone inside or outside the speech community.

In my communication classes, my students and I have discovered that a whole range of words have gendered implications that affect people in the same way that racially prejudiced words bother people. But "gendered" words seem to be more subtle and anger people in different ways. They are also more complicated, because gender often intersects with race, power, and class to infuse words with multiple layers of meaning. Did you know, for example, that women are often called names that imply food, sex, and animals in disproportion to how we address men? Most people don't think about it, but *bitch, chick, cunt,* and *sugar pie* have pretty different implications from *hunk, handsome, stud,* and *playboy.* What we are saying here is that our language has evolved over the years to include more negative meaning (connotation) regarding general talk about women than men. And the same can be said about other groups of people who are not Caucasian. It is only recently that women and people of color have openly resisted the language generally used to name them. This has resulted in a lot of confusion because as alternative ways of naming are suggested (for example, Ms. or African American), people who want to hold onto old speech patterns cry "feminism!" or "political correctness!" or "reverse racism!" without really thinking through the motivation for such linguistic anger.

In the following case study of urban music, we invite you to explore the mega-controversy that currently surrounds our society's interpretation of the poetry that constitutes urban music. When Eminem won a Grammy for the *Marshall Mathers* CD, many people were incensed that his seeming endorsement of homophobia (fear of gay people) and misogyny (hatred of women) could be rewarded (Hilburn, 2001). After all, isn't he the guy who talks about killing his own wife in his lyrics? "Now shut the fuck up and get/what's coming to you. . . ./You were supposed to love me!/(sounds of a woman choking) . . . /Now bleed, bitch, bleed." These lyrics are beyond offensive; they are horrifying. How do we respond to the language of rap?

In general, no one expected that rap, or urban music, would become the leader in popular culture that it is. Why? Because this is the realm of black men, who express their angst and frustrations about urban life in ways that have very little relevance to the young white men who helped catapult the CDs of Tupac, Puffy, Run D.M.C., L.L. Cool J, 50 Cent, and others to the top of the charts. Most middle-aged parents, and some academics, stereotype urban music as offensive to women, the police, and anything "establishment" (Krohn & Suazo, 1995). Violence toward other people, misogyny, a mean world, and cursing, or what Dimitriadis (1999, p. 367) calls "racialized macho posturing," characterize music we call rap, hip-hop, or urban. Women, in particular, are offended by the labels used to describe them because "*hoes* and *bitches*" most of us are not. I have felt frustration to hear my students endorse P. Diddy (formerly Puff Daddy) and to see rap artists like him catapulted to icon status ("Puffy Takes Paris," 1999). In my mind, most urban music demonstrates misogyny and endorses a destructive attitude toward society. Could I be wrong?

About three years ago, I met Jimmy "Rue" Flippen, a 24-year-old black male from Detroit who enrolled in my communication theory course. Somehow, Rue and I established a relationship that involved Rue's correcting my limited knowledge of Puffy in front of the class as we talked about rap artists and cultural studies. This banter was the source of great delight among all the students and word got around that Rue was teaching Dr. Natalle about the "realness" of urban music. When it came time for me to write this article, I invited Rue for an interview. His knowledge proved invaluable, and I offer portions of our conversation (personal interview, June 23, 2000) as a means to clarify how urban music names a particular world, creates male community, and has implications for power and gendered relationships.

A CONVERSATION ON URBAN MUSIC

JN: Tell me a little about rap music and language, because that's the deal here.

RF: Alright. Basically hip-hop started off of inner city kids. It first started with dancing, and everybody knows break dancing. Then it evolved into M.C.-ing, which brings in rap music and D.J.-ing. So, it brought all of this together to form one culture. For the inner city kids to express themselves, so they won't be so violent, which everybody expects.

JN: When you say "inner city kids," isn't that men?

RF: No. You can say they [men] started it, but even back then, there were females, but they just didn't get the praise men did. Just like in other parts of society. There were females, but you didn't hear about them. And a lot of male groups, they had that one female. It's like a tip on the iceberg, but that one female just didn't get that much mention. It was a male-dominated thing.

JN: But the language itself seems to be male-dominated too. In the way women are referred to, what they mean, etc. At least from an outsider's point of view. What's that all about?

RF: Um . . . I think the thing is who's saying it. It depends on where these M.C.s are coming from and what they're trying to put out now. Let's say Puffy. Definitely in his songs he downgrades some women, but, and I'm trying to find a delicate way to say this, the way that he portrays women is the way he runs into women. Because of the lifestyle that he's in . . . if he was a house husband, he would speak of the things his wife does. But since he's in the music industry and women flock to him, it's not him putting women in these categories, it's the category of women he runs into while he's in this business.

JN: That's a whole other way of looking at it.

RF: Yeah, yeah. A lot of people think Puffy and these other guys are just puttin' women down, but he's not making this up. He mentions "ladies" and "bitches," but it's all in different categories. You're gonna find good when he mentions his mother. He mentions positive women. And he mentions the ladies he's run into.

JN: That changes, immediately, my own perception. 'Cause mostly you hear about bitches and whores and say, "whoa, wait a minute." And a feminist way of looking at things is to say that men use women, and as they use them, they're sex objects, etc., so they're called that in a derogatory way. But I hadn't really thought about what comes in this direction—that is, toward a person. Not all women are "good women," so to speak, there are [what society calls] "lowlifes."

RF: Yeah, and the only women who are getting offended are the ones who *aren't* lowlifes. Ya'll are the ones getting offended, but he's not referring to you. He's referring to the women who put themselves there.

JN: Now that that's clarified, in thinking about who listens to the music, is it mostly young boys or no?

RF: Actually, over 80% of all urban and hip-hop music is bought by white males.

JN: Teenage or a wider range of ages?

RF: Mostly teenagers. But, with Puff, you're going to get teenage and early and mid-twenties.

JN: Middle class or lower middle class?

RF: I'd say lower middle.

JN: And what's their experience with women going to be? Not that these so-called lowlife women are rushing to them . . .

RF: Okay, even with the lower and middle class, maybe Puffy is going to influence these males that haven't had direct contact with these types of women. Maybe they're going to treat the women they *do* come into contact with like Puff says, but then it's all a cycle. They talk to women like that, and these women get the mentality like that, and they become the women Puffy is talking to.

JN: But isn't Puffy ethically responsible for getting people in a vicious cycle like that? In terms of their relationships and how he influences them?

RF: That depends on how much responsibility you can put on one man.

JN: But he's like the biggest name in the business.

RF: Yeah, but from Puffy's first album to his second album, he's changed *a lot*. Because, you know, his first album, with his friend Biggie dying, was more centered around that. Centered around hatred and things like that. But this album here is more "party," more uplifting, and honestly, it's more about females, but it doesn't degrade them as much. You listen to urban music, you're gonna see the growth of the artist. Because when they first come into it, they're gonna give you the same thing that you've been hearing. But once they're in it for so long, they start having this learning experience. By the time he reaches his last album, you're gonna see it turn around in a way.

JN: So, we see the person evolve over time?

RF: Yeah.

JN: Okay, instead of worrying so much about relationships with women, let's get to the issue of personal identity. A lot of rap (urban) music is praised for giving an honest look at the identity of black, urban males. What do you say about that?

RF: I personally feel they are representing that type of black male very well because a lot of the things they mention are the things we're seeing. Everyone's seeing it. They're not hearing it in music, they're seeing it on film. Since black males are saying it and they're getting such power in this nation from it, there's a big uproar. Arnold Schwarzenegger kills 50–60 people in a film, but then when an artist says something like he's shot someone in his life or his friend got shot, it's a big problem. We have to put all these stereotypes on this man.

JN: How much of the black male population as a whole is represented by this kind of music? Not every man who is black is urban.

RF: Nah, . . . I feel you'll have to look at numbers for that. But you're gonna have to say that the majority of black males are not urban, but I would say that's right now. A lot of them came from urban, but moved up to these places where they are now. Trying to build off of that. But these artists, they're doing the same thing. You have your rhyme about the things that they went through, but if you look behind the scenes and see what positive things they're doing with the money they're making from this, they're just like entrepreneurs—people who are not rappin'—who went to school and did these other things.

JN: So, the power is economic?

RF: Yeah, the rap game has turned from this culture that we love to this market.

JN: What other kind of power? Social influence?

RF: Yeah, um, if you look at Notorius B.I.G. and Tupac, those two men controlled the entire nation. People who live in California who have never been to the East Coast or come into contact with anyone from the East Coast cannot stand someone from over here. All from the words of one man. And vice versa. Everybody will be, "I hate West Coast."

JN: But, but, doesn't that tear a country apart?

RF: It does, but that was the point in hip-hop when everybody realized the power of what we have. It was so powerful that we did not even know it—we didn't know what we controlled—until those two men got killed.

JN: Well, then it almost becomes a critique or a challenge of the white power structure. Really, if you spin that idea out. You start out not knowing, but once these murders happened, it's like, whoa, this thing is much bigger and more out of control than the people who sing it even knew.

RF: Uh huh.

JN: But then you have this white power structure sitting there, biting their fingernails, going "Ooooohhhh. What is this? I'm not happy about it."

RF: Yep. You've got these white upper-class males who have kids and they walk into their kids' rooms and see a Tupac poster. They never thought that type of music and that type of culture would find its way into their house.

JN: What do you think about that?

RF: I think it's great. I think it's good that *all* classes can come together through one culture.

JN: How can coming together on the basis of an experience many listeners have never had be a good thing? And all done in a kind of very offensive language.

RF: Does it not get your attention? Are you not listening when they say it?

JN: Yeah, well, I try to run from it, myself. It hurts my ears so much.

RF: I feel with your age group, that's something that will offend you because you're not used to it. Cursing wasn't as much back then, but now, I mean little kids know more curse words than I do.

JN: Does this frighten you at all, Rue?

RF: Yes!

JN: Has cursing lost its value because there's so much of it, or do we have an offensive society?

RF: I think it's gotten to the point where it's become a norm. People don't even realize the intensity of the words they're using. Just like the word *nigger* that's being used so fluently. Back then, it was such a bad word. Nowadays, it's just a common word. We use it like it's nothing.

JN: Yeah, but even now, there are some boundary lines there.

RF: Yeah, if a white person says *nigger* to me, then it's a problem, but at the same time, if a white person says to me "Aw, fuck you," then you're going to take that with more offense than if some black person says "Aw, man, fuck you." If a white person says "fuck you," you are going to feel like he's trying to, like, put you beneath [him]. . .

JN: Wait! *Fuck you* is worse than *nigger*?

RF: It depends. You've got white people who hang with black people. They've gotten so comfortable with black people . . .

JN: But, that's a little speech community where you can call each other slang terms and that's perfectly acceptable. But across racial lines, where speech communities are separated out?

RF: I was talking about the same speech community.

JN: [To change the subject] Tell me about Will Smith movies as a complement to urban music.

RF: I feel like Will Smith has been more accepted, that's why he does better. Will Smith got the first Grammy ever for rap music. I'll say this, he's never used a curse word in no song . . .

JN: That's why I like him. (Laughter.)

RF: But he doesn't appeal to the same crowd. In rap music, we have two sets. If you get all the same thing, there's no diversity in it.

JN: Well, Puffy is sort of the quintessential rap guy. Why is he on top?

RF: Because Puffy's so fashionable. People admire him. He's flashy. That's what people love. The diamonds. The jewelry. The furs. The cars. That's what people want.

JN: So, it's not just the music, it's music augmented by movie star stuff.

RF: It's a market.

JN: Who is the best rap artist out there right now, in terms of music?

RF: I would say Jay-Z, but that's what appeals to me. There are different artists.

JN: What are the themes people wanna hear?

RF: Everything that they see when they walk outside of their slum place. Violence. That's what 70% of the younger generation and our generation want to hear.

JN: That's awful stuff. Why do you want it in your face?

RF: Well, what can I tell you? You can't relate to it because you haven't been bred into it.

JN: Thriving on violence doesn't help you reach the alternative, which is to get rid of violence and love each other.

RF: Yeah, that's what we want, but it's a long road to get there.

JN: What other kinds of themes are out there?

RF: You've got your gangsta rap, your pop rap, which would be more Will Smith, and then you've got your educational rap, like Common Sense.

JN: Educational rap? Like be a better person?

RF: Yeah, spirituality, getting away from all the glamour and glitz. They're rappin' about "you're not gonna leave with this."

JN: What about Will Smith?

RF: Well, he's so big, probably because this is what the white upper class wants us to have. They want to turn our music into this. They're gonna push him to change what we already have. . . . He's said in his music, he's laughing all the way to the bank.

JN: But is he compromising the African American community as a whole?

RF: His place is legitimate. He's not compromising anything. Will Smith hasn't changed a bit since the first time he came out.

JN: Rue, how should I approach this article? What does the language of rap and urban music really mean to people?

RF: I completely feel it's still a form of expression. At this point now, the majority of society is not listening to it. . . . They don't like what they let loose.

JN: Why is rhyme so important?

RF: Some people would disagree with me, but I feel that it comes from our African roots. African language deals with rhyme, poetry. Then we were brought over here, we had to learn the English language first, and once we did, we got our poetry back. But I've felt we've always had it. We've been singing, rhyming for centuries. It's nothing for us. You've got little kids rhyming. They didn't go home practicing that. It just came out of them. A lot of artists just go in there [studio], the music comes on, they think, and then it just comes out. You can't practice that.

JN: What's the power of that as communication?

RF: I feel that it expresses the power to think. Because there's a lot of thought going through [rap]. Just like we learned in Dunlap's class about the sophists, our culture is a type with sophists—we go out and give information, teachings, about our culture and what's going on. We're getting paid for it, but it [rap] is a type of sophistic culture. . . . You need all three types of rap to understand the culture. All have specific points, so Common Sense tells us about religion and uplifting ourselves, Puff is in the middle with gangsta, and then there's Will Smith, the middle class. He is in a place that maybe Puffy will grow to.

JN: Do you think rap music can bridge some of the race problems we have?

RF: I think so. Look at Eminem. He's this white artist that black people love. They have hip-hop artists in Japan and Europe. They're doing it for all races and all nations. There's more than gangsta rap. You can point out the bad guys, but you can't have love without hate.

JN: What's the most important thing I can tell college students about the language of rap?

RF: Don't let it manipulate you. Don't let words make you step down. Be your own self. I've seen upper-class white guys trying to be gangster. And I'm thinking, "Man, what are you doing? If you lived in Detroit, you would not be walking like that." We laugh at people like that. If you let this music take you, it will take your life. That's what turned parents against rap music. Their kids are letting themselves be manipulated. But it's all a growing process. You can't throw your growth out.

My interview with Rue taught me something about the language principle of **reflex versus reflection**. Nystrom (1977) tells us that when we respond using reflex, it is the result of an absolute and immediate response to the language we hear, similar to a physical reflex like blinking our eyes in the wind. This was how I felt about rap music before Rue made me stop and reflect. Although I still disagree, in general, with cursing and negative portrayals of women, I will be forced to step back and delay my responses when I hear rap music in the future. Now I know that there are different types of rap. Portrayals of women are not necessarily a single category. Curse words belong to a different generation. As a listener, it's my job to think a little more deeply about who the artist is and what motivates the message. I like Rue's caution about manipulation: I can't let my emotions be manipulated by naming practices that I may not fully understand. I need to reflect and draw conclusions based on all the available information I can get. What about you?

CONCLUSION

Perhaps the best way to think about both your response to this case study and your responsibilities as a competent communicator is to engage in a class discussion or language activity. Naturally, I invite you to read some of the references listed at the end of this essay to give you more details about the concepts and issues under discussion. The *Newsweek* article by Samuels, Croal, and Gates (2000) is a particularly interesting set of statements by urban artists themselves. Let's also recognize that there is a rebuttal to Rue's side of the argument. Williams's (1992) essay is a black woman's indictment of the content of urban music as "pathological, anti-social, and anti-community" (p. 168) that is well worth thinking about. Bring some urban music into class and listen to the words. Rue did this for our semantics/semiotics class, and it made a real difference in our ability to understand the context for the music. In the case of Eminem, in particular, Rue showed us how songs like "Stan" actually demonstrate the consequences of self-destructive behavior. The obsessed fan who drives himself off a bridge isn't exactly a role model for the rest of us!

In the end, our word choices do make a difference. They represent our personal perceptions of ourselves and the world around us. Often, our language is problematic, ambiguous, and offensive to others. We have gender, race, class, and power biases in our language that often go unnoticed, yet are root causes of some of the interpersonal and social problems we experience. As we all strive to be more competent communicators, I hope this essay will help you think differently and make better decisions about respectful ways to name and converse with others.

REFERENCES

Dimitriadis, G. (1999). Hip hop to rap: Some implications of an historically situated approach to performance. *Text and Performance Quarterly, 19,* 355–369.

Hayakawa, S. I., & Hayakawa, A. R. (1992). *Language in thought and action* (5th ed.). Orlando, FL: Harcourt Brace Jovanovich.

Hilburn, R. (2001, January 5). Grammy nod is milestone for Eminem—and recording industry. *Greensboro News and Record,* p. D2.

Krohn, F., & Suazo, F. L. (1995). Contemporary urban music: Controversial messages in hip-hop and rap lyrics. *Etc.: A Review of General Semantics, 52,* 139–155.

Nystrom, C. (1977). Immediate man: The symbolic environment of fanaticism. *Etc., 34,* 19–34.

Puffy takes Paris. (1999, October). *Vogue,* pp. 295–315, 395.

Samuels, A., Croal, N., & Gates, D. (2000, October 9). Battle for the soul of hip-hop. *Newsweek,* pp. 58–65.

Williams, S. A. (1992). Two words on music: Black community. In G. Dent (Ed.), *Black popular culture* (pp. 164–172). Seattle: Bay Press.

READING TATTOOS

Women, Men, and Body Signs

William Cummings
UNIVERSITY OF SOUTH FLORIDA

Whether they are evidence of courage in the face of pain, a mark of ownership, or a communion of wearer and painter to create a work of art, tattoos constitute a channel of nonverbal communication that is popular across cultures. In this article, William Cummings discusses some of the gender aspects of tattooing as he briefly examines the evolution of U.S. women's tattooing habits.

Cummings claims that because tattooing is inherently a sensual act, it has sexual implications; consequently, there is a direct link between tattooing and sexuality. The different standards of sexual desire and activity to which males and females are held are evidenced in the different social responses to males' and females' tattoos. In effect, that which is sexual is considered to devalue woman's moral capital while the same activities maintain or increase males'. Cummings claims this approach to the interpretation of men's and women's tattoos is changing somewhat, in the United States, as women are using the tattoo as a means to express self-ownership and to celebrate their bodies. Although this may be their intent, and tattooed women are becoming a more common sight, Cummings leaves the reader to question how far society has really come in its ability or desire to separate a promiscuous nature from a tattooed woman.

As you ponder the questions below and other questions the author poses, try to imagine how you would answer the same questions if you were the sex opposite of yours.

QUESTIONS FOR DISCUSSION

For readers who have or are in the process of getting a tattoo:

- *What were your motivations for getting a tattoo?*
- *Why did you chose the type and placement of your tattoo?*
- *How do others respond to you when they see or learn of your tattoo?*

For readers who do not have a tattoo:

- *What stereotypes have you felt or heard about people with tattoos?*
- *Are those stereotypes different for males and females with tattoos?*

For those who have friends or family members who are tattooed, thinking back to the first time you heard about or saw that person's tattoo:

- *What types of questions did the tattoo make you want to ask that person?*
- *Did your idea of who that person is shift? If so, how?*
- *How would your perception of that person be different if the person were of the other sex?*

Images, designs, words, and icons inked into skin—tattoos and how we read them embody the process, assumptions, and pitfalls that infuse nonverbal communication and miscommunication between men and women. Exposed to public gazing, by their very presence tattoos demand interpretation. We cannot help but look, wonder, and try to imagine what a tattoo was meant to express intentionally or what it unintentionally can tell us about the person whose skin it adorns. Perhaps because tattoos invite this speculation, and certainly because they draw attention to skin and body, this act of interpreting can seem inherently sexual. One tattooist declared, "All tattoos are ultimately about sex." This essay explores the apparently straightforward equation between images placed on skin and sexual enticement, highlighting the complexities that belie such an easy equivalence.

How Americans read tattoos as signs is changing rapidly. The extent of this transformation can be grasped by examining stories of how tattoos were read early in the twentieth century. One such tattoo reading took place in a Boston courtroom in the 1920s. Here is how one author described the unfolding drama:

> A significant court decision recognizing tattooing as, in effect, a voluntary sexual experience was pronounced in Boston a few years ago. Two young men were brought to court on a charge of raping a young girl of good family. The prosecutor, hitherto indignant and energetic, suddenly veered about and refused to press the case, suggesting that the judge instruct the jury to vote the men not guilty. The change was brought about by a photograph produced by the defense, showing the girl with a butterfly tattooed on her leg. The prosecutor, the jury, and the judge decided that, though the two young men were hardly to be praised for their conduct, they could not be convicted, for the girl had been guilty of contributory negligence, having misled the men by her tattooed mark into taking her for a loose character. Though technically a virgin before the rape, the girl was, in effect, accused of being a person of previous sexual experience—because of her tattoo. (Parry, 1933, pp. 3–4)

We are outraged because the two men were obviously guilty. But that was beside the point. The prosecutor did not set out to protect them; it is unlikely that the specifics of the charge concerned him at all. What was the prosecutor protecting? Most obviously, he was defending a social order that had specific ideas about the proper place for and behavior of young women. In particular, his decision forcefully asserted a middle-class American tenet equating social acceptability with feminine sexual restraint. No middle-class (much less upper-class) American woman could by clothing, gesture, language, or mark of any kind communicate sexual desire and desirability without compromising her status.

This case provides a window into a patriarchal social order in which social institutions, mores, and practices restricted the appearance of women as a means of controlling their sexuality. Social acceptability required sexual restraint, and any personal statements of style or assertions of meaning visible to the public were rigorously interpreted as indicating sexual availability and hence social unacceptability. Our outrage is an indication of the social changes that have taken place since the 1920s.

Yet seeing tattoos as signs of sexuality was not confined to women. Among men, a long psychiatric tradition reads tattoos as evidence of subliminal homosexuality hidden beneath a façade of aggressive masculinity. In his classic book *Tattoo: Secrets of a Strange Art*, Albert Parry (1933, p. 1) wrote, "Very seldom are the tattooed aware of the true motives responsible for their visits to the tattooers." Whatever they may report, "These reasons are evident rationalizations. The true motives lie deeper."

Parry, like many others during his time and since, saw in tattoos an outward expression of inner sexual drives. Parry (1933) believed tattoos to be subconscious recordings of dreams that are "of a decidedly sexual character. The very process of tattooing is essentially sexual. There are the long, sharp needles. There is the liquid poured into the pricked skin. There are the two participants of the act, one active, the other passive. There is the curious marriage of pleasure and pain" (p. 2). In this line of reasoning, men as well as women are—whether consciously or unconsciously—sending out signals of sexual availability merely by getting their skin tattooed.

If tattoos ever communicated such a simple and consistent meaning, they do so no longer. We recognize that tattoos have meanings that are more varied and ambiguous, and cannot be read unproblematically as sexual advertisements designed to entice. Responsible for much of this transformation is the fact that tattooing has moved beyond its lower-class social origins. Once restricted to subcultures such as sailors, gangs, and prison inmates, since the 1970s tattoos have become fashionable among the middle and upper class. With the emergence of tattooing in this new milieu come new values and associations.

Greater acceptability has expanded the range of possible meanings for tattoos. They can now be artistic decorations, memorials for loved ones, expressions of personal identity, tokens of rites of passage, and much more. The proliferation of motives and meanings for getting tattooed, not to mention the astonishing increase in how many Americans have been tattooed, demands caution when we read the tattoos encountered with ever greater frequency. "What I like about tattooing," said tattoo artist Henry Goldfield, "is that it's a language. You can project a message. You take a thought or a word, and you turn it into an image. Then, someone sees that and interprets it in their own way" (*Skin and Ink,* 1999, pp. 37–38).

We now search for clues to a tattoo's meaning in its placement on the body, size, and design. We try to match the image with the perceived personality of the bearer, or to find hints as to its meaning in the occupation, gender, class, and the context in which we encounter the tattooed individual. Nevertheless, we can offer only guesses, not certainties.

This social broadening also has taken place at the same time as a reconsideration of gender roles in American society. An essential component of this reconsideration has been the adamant belief among many women (and men) that women have the right to control their own bodies and sexuality. Tattooing is one venue in which women have exercised such control.

> The arrival of the pill in 1961 had given women new sexual freedom; a little over a decade later legalized abortion secured their reproductive rights. Not surprisingly, the breast became a popular spot for tattoos—it was here that many women inscribed symbols of their newfound sexual independence. . . . Janis Joplin was tattooed by San Franciscan Lyle Tuttle, who recalls, "I put a heart on her chest, and the day after her death there was a girl standing in front of the shop wanting the heart I put on her, in remembrance. Hundreds of them got the same idea at the same time." (Mifflin, 1997, pp. 57–58)

When Lyle Tuttle tattooed a heart on Janis Joplin's chest—at the time, a novelty among celebrities, especially women—the tattoo and the act of being tattooed was a symbolic counterweight to a legacy of male chauvinism. The hundreds of replicated heart tattoos that Tuttle describes putting on the breasts of other women was an affirmation of female solidarity. So too in this account, the link between tattoos and a female sexuality available to men has been explicitly contested. Indeed, many women speak of getting tattoos to publicly declare that they have retaken control of their bodies from husbands who treated them as sexual objects. Others speak of tattooing as a way of exorcising the sense of shame and guilt of having been sexually abused as children. As one woman recalled, "Tattooing became a way to tell my secret" (Mifflin, 1997, p. 121).

Tattoos symbolizing opposition to male domination point to the gender differences that surround tattoos. Sociologist Clinton Sanders (1989, pp. 48–50) schematized these differences in terms of tattoo imagery, placement, and purpose. Among men, he summarized, tattoos are placed on more visible locations (most commonly on arms), are larger in size, and are intended as public displays of a man's interests and associations. As identity symbols and declarations of masculinity, "male designs" have undertones of violence (dragons, skulls, daggers, birds of prey, and the like) and resemble nothing so much as the plumage of strutting peacocks vying for the attention of females. In contrast, women's tattoos characteristically are in more private locations (such as on the shoulder, where they are shared with fewer intimates), are often seen as primarily decorative, and draw upon imagery from mythology and the natural world (flowers, birds, unicorns, and the like).

Nevertheless, such clear distinctions are generalizations for which exceptions are easily found. Indeed, this mystery, uncertainty, and unpredictability are part of tattooing's appeal. Many people with tattoos take pleasure in confounding and surprising passersby with unexpected designs that contradict prevailing stereotypes about what is appropriate to or true of men and women.

At the onset of the twenty-first century, it simply is no longer possible to see tattoos as equivalent to the bright colors and exaggerated gestures of animals seeking to attract mates. Much more is going on than just this, making it impossible to *reduce* tattoos to sex. But an echo of tattoos as lures, enticing and captivating the (typically) opposite sex, endures in large measure because of the location of tattoos on skin, itself inextricably part of the biological process of reproduction. Tattoos can be about sex, but they can also be about power, self-expression, and more. When is it which? And what makes it so? These questions have no firm answers.

So, although individual motives for becoming tattooed have changed, and the range of possible meanings thereby expanded, to some extent there is validity in the claim that "tattoos are about sex" because of the larger social context in which we read tattoos. That is, individual interpretations and motives are inescapably influenced by larger social attitudes that change slowly. For example, the women whose slim tattooed bodies adorn the covers of tattoo magazines often have personal reasons for getting tattooed that have nothing to do with sexual display or attraction. Yet their photographed bodies become sexualized objects, designed to attract the gaze of male consumers. This often carries over into the text accompanying the photographs. In one case, after a woman named Melissa stated that she liked her tattoos simply because of their artistic value, the writer promptly reinterpreted the tattoos as sexually provocative. "That's easy to say when you have a great bod like Melissa's; anything would look good on her, even a tattered dish rag (especially a tiny one). Just look at those supple, firm breasts, the long, slender legs, the pert little derriere, the seductive smile" (*Tattoo*, 2000, p. 29).

This reworking of personal meaning in a larger and less-forgiving social context is especially evident in tattoo contests. Here tattooed women are situated in a context that encourages men to connect tattoos and sexual availability. As Margot Mifflin noted, "Beautiful tattoos are more likely to win awards if they adorn shapely bodies. While men schlep onstage in a standard-issue wardrobe of saggy jeans and bare backs or tee shirts, women often strut their stuff wearing high heels, bikinis, and the occasional evening gown" (1997, pp. 161–162). Inevitably, this attitude lingers after the contest is over, becoming part of the background values against which tattooed bodies are read.

Control over the meaning of our own bodies cannot ever be complete. Our bodies are wonderfully supple and potent resources with which we communicate to others, but what we communicate is never entirely of our own choosing. Tattooed bodies are read from within a social context larger than the individual, and this context affects interpretation. As one observer wrote (Mäder, 1998, p. 7), "To carry a tattoo means something. In fact it means more than something, and not just only to you. The reasons are as multi-layered as the skin itself, which belongs not only to you, but also a little to everyone else. Of course, your tattoo is exclusively yours. But it is also public property, for your body is a component of a social body. Its skin is a social tissue which society pierces, depositing its codes and values."

Reading tattoos and communicating meaning through skin images is thus doubly hazardous. It relies on the interpretation and personal judgments of viewers, who rarely have the opportunity to verbally discuss a given tattoo's history, meaning, and so forth with the owner. Intended meanings can be lost, and unintended meanings easily attached. In fact, this may be inevitable. As images, tattoos have a private, "original" meaning only for the person whose body they decorate. Without access to this interior world, others can only guess at a tattoo's significance. Additionally, the act of reading tattoos takes place in a social context in which long-standing practices and values do not change easily. Existing associations of tattooing with sexual promiscuity, lower-class vulgarity, and even criminality are fading as tattooing becomes accepted as a mainstream art form, but at times they seem to linger tenaciously. In this case, the legacy of reading tattoos the way the Boston prosecutor read the butterfly in the 1920s fades only gradually.

Examining how tattoos function as a means of nonverbal communication raises several important issues: the nature of the boundary between public and private meanings; the inherent ambiguity and room for misinterpretation in reading visual signs; the ubiquitous use of the body to communicate to another gender; the ways in which reading signs is derived from specific social, historical, cultural, and gendered contexts; and the curious contrast between the compulsion to interpret the meaning of signs and the elusiveness of accurate interpretations. Current American fascination with body modification is fueled by our urgent need to grapple with these issues in everyday life and offers a unique vantage point from which to examine the complex linkages between women, men, and body signs.

REFERENCES

Mäder, Markus. (1998). "Oh! No!" In Gregor von Glinski, *Masters of tattoo.* Zurich and New York: Edition Stemmle.

Mifflin, Margot. (1997). *Bodies of subversion: A secret history of women and tattoo.* New York: Juno Books.

Parry, Albert. (1933). *Tattoo: Secrets of a strange art as practiced among the natives of the United States.* New York: Simon and Schuster.

Sanders, Clinton R. (1989). *Customizing the body: The art and culture of tattooing.* Philadelphia: Temple University Press.

Skin and Ink. (1999, September).

Tattoo. (2000, June).

PLAYING THE PART OF WOMAN

Josie Duke

UNIVERSITY OF NORTH CAROLINA, CHAPEL HILL

Mrs. Spencer's[1] sixth-grade honors English class had to put on a production for the rest of the school. The play she picked for that year had exactly as many roles as there were students in the class. Moreover, the female roles equaled the number of girls. Mrs. Spencer asked for volunteers for the parts, and she began with the title character, Sherlock Holmes. My hand shot up in the air. No other hand was raised. She glanced toward my direction, yet her eyes continued to swim across the waves of faces, hoping to anchor onto the arm of a male student. She emphasized to the class that this was the principal role. Finally, when no one else volunteered, she asked me if I really wanted the part: "You would be required to remember a lot of lines." Then, she played with the idea of making it a female Sherlock Holmes. She looked again at the list of character names. None of the female roles could be changed to male roles. Most of the female characters were linked to a husband, and there was already one butler. Finally, Mrs. Spencer admitted, "We can only let you be Sherlock Holmes if a boy is willing to play one of the girl parts." The whole class laughed. The class quieted down once Ken half raised his hand and exclaimed, "I can be the French maid." Ken was one of the most popular, athletic boys. The teacher smiled and thanked Ken; the matter was settled. Although Ken had the fewest number of lines, he ended up being the star of the play.

The rest of my education was learning that "growing up" meant I could no longer play male roles—that I had to be more like a woman. My P.E. coaches got on my case for not shaving my legs. My debate coach would nag me to wear pantyhose and lipstick so I would look more professional. My friends would tell me that I needed to wear clothes that hugged my curves and showed more skin. Boys would harp that I needed to grow my hair out. Physically, I matured early; but socially, I was a late bloomer.

Pressure for me to conform continued until I could finally convince people I was indeed a woman. My hair is long; I occasionally wear a dress (though I still like to skip the pantyhose); I go by "Josie" instead of "Jo." Becoming "feminine" was a long process for me, but I wonder: Have I become too feminine?

My 5-year-old nephew was telling me that girls are stupid and weak and boys are better because they are stronger. He wanted to learn to play football, so I decided that I would teach him in order to demonstrate that girls could play sports. I practiced first with my dad, making sure I could throw the football properly. Once I was confident enough in my ability, I took my nephew out to play. He threw the ball very hard, and I felt a pang in my finger. Without realizing it, I spitted out, "Darn it, I broke a nail" and made pouty whines. My nephew just looked at me with a disappointed face. I was disappointed in myself. To him, I had just acted like a typical girl.

NOTE

1. Names have been changed.

PART V

PERSONAL RELATIONSHIPS

CONSTRUCTING MYTHS TO MANAGE THE ROMANTIC CHALLENGE IN CROSS-SEX FRIENDSHIPS

Vickey Harvey

CALIFORNIA STATE UNIVERSITY, STANISLAUS

Cross-sex friendships constitute some of the most rewarding and problematic relationships each of us faces. These relationships need to be "managed" both internally (within the relationship) and externally (to the viewing public). Cross-sex friendships bring with them a host of challenges, both private and public, not found in other types of relationships. More than most relationship types, cross-sex friendships call for conscious negotiation between the relational partners to determine what type the relationship "really" is (friendship as friendship, friendship as prelude to romance) and how this relationship will be presented to others. Harvey's article develops some of the issues surrounding these relationships and asks the reader to think about their own cross-sex friendships against the backdrop of selected myths.

Harvey's article includes narratives from women and men that describe the rewards and challenges of these friendships, and the strategies developed to manage the issues. She includes five myths of cross-sex friendships that act as excellent discussion starters for a class to explore their own cross-sex friendships. The myths and the narratives will generate, we believe, much discussion.

QUESTIONS FOR DISCUSSION

- *Do women and men as colleagues in professional settings face the same issues as those found in cross-sex friendships?*
- *What are some effective strategies to enhance relationship talk between men and women in friendships?*
- *What myths about cross-sex friendships have you believed?*
- *Does an awareness of the myths help people develop a more realistic view of friendships?*
- *How dangerous is flirting in a cross-sex friendship?*
- *How do cross-sex friendships compare to same-sex friendships?*

"Matt is not the 'boyfriend' type. He is not ready to grow up and be committed to someone. Matt and I are more like sister and brother. We tell each other our deepest secrets, knowing the other will always be there for us. It is sometimes awkward for him to introduce me as his friend. I'm not really sure why this is. I think it's hard to have a close friend of the opposite sex because people are constantly challenging your friendship because other people always see intimacy potential."

Most likely you have or have had a friend of the opposite sex. If you are a woman, you may have a male friend whom, as in the situation above, you perceive as a brother or advisor. If you are a man, you may have a female friend whom you perceive as a sister or confidante. Adult cross-sex friendships provide men and women with advantages that are hard to obtain in same-sex friendships (Bell, 1981). Our cross-sex friends can help us learn more about how members of the opposite sex feel, think, and behave. They can give us confirmation that we are attractive members of the other sex, and cross-sex friends can improve communication between the sexes. The more we understand about the other sex, the easier it can be to communicate personally, socially, and professionally.

However, it is not always easy to have a cross-sex friend. How many times have you thought you might be friends with someone of the opposite sex, only to discover yourself romantically attracted to him or her or they to you? What happens to the friendship? You may become romantically involved with your friend, or you may decide it is too hard to maintain a platonic friendship with such an attraction. Either way, the friendship can be challenging. Why does this happen? Cross-sex friendships encounter special "challenges" that women and men must overcome in maintaining cross-sex friendships. O'Meara (1989) contends that cross-sex friends face an "emotional or intimacy bond" challenge, a "romantic or sexual" challenge, an "equality or power" challenge, and an "audience perspective" challenge. Cross-sex friends must negotiate these challenges to establish clear guidelines in order for their cross-sex friendships to continue (Rawlins, 1982).

USING THEORY TO UNDERSTAND THE ROMANTIC CHALLENGE

Social constructionism offers a captivating framework and interpretation of how friends construct, change, or sustain their reality through social communication and interaction with others (Bernstein, 1983). Wood (1982) believes that relationships and realities must be "talked" into existence. It is the dialogue in relationships, both between the two friends and within one's inner dialogue, that constructs notions of intimacy and friendship and negotiates the norms and rules of the friendship, including how the individuals perceive the friendship. Social constructionism leads to a study of the stories that individuals in friendships tell. Narratives provide a sense of importance and identity to the friendship that help define, articulate, and refine individual's sense of self and friendship identity. Narratives can also produce myths that provide a prescription for the course of the friendship. How we talk about our friendships through narratives provides an understanding of the challenges confronting women and men in friendship and allows cross-sex friends to remain platonic friends.

THE METHOD OF NARRATIVES

The women and men who tell their stories here are 120 college students from two eastern colleges attending communication courses. They are between 18 and 27 years old and are all heterosexuals. Each of the respondents was asked to identify a casual, good, or best friend of the opposite sex. Individuals were told that the project was designed to study cross-sex friendships—that is, friendships between members of the opposite sex—excluding romantic, marital, and family relationships. Students kept a journal for 15 weeks, discussing issues related to the romantic challenge of one cross-sex friendship.

The narratives generated myths that the friends created about the friendship in order to provide some guidelines about adult cross-sex friendship. A myth is usually an attempt to explain an occurrence without using scientific fact or so-called common sense (Shaw, 1972). Myths appeal to emotion, rather than reason or logic, and date from ancient times, when rational explanations were not available nor apparently wanted (Shaw, 1972). Individuals turned to previously established myths or invented their own in response to questioning the romantic attraction in their friendship. The five myths that emerged from the journals, described in Figure 1, appear to be ways in which friends communicate about the friendship in order to maintain a friendship rather than a romantic partnership.

Myths play a dominant role as men and women attempt to communicate and manage their romantic feelings about each other. Although myths are often not true when examined closely, friends cling to them because they are the reality that the friends co-create about the structure of their friendship. Social constructionism proposes that friends in this case live their lives by stories or myths; that these myths shape the friendship; and that they have real, not imagined effects, thereby providing the structure of the friendship (White, 1991, p. 28).

MYTH #1: DENYING THAT OUR FRIEND IS ATTRACTED TO US

The most common myth, reported by 65% of the friends, was Myth #1: "I don't think he or she really likes me that way." The respondents stated that their friend

Myth	Response Rate	Description	Function
#1 "I don't think he or she is attracted to me."	65%	Friends struggle with the challenge of receiving mixed messages.	Able to deny friend's attraction to you.
#2 "We won't cross over the friendship line."	35%	Friends felt attraction at start of relationship and struggled to stay just friends.	Friendship as prelude to romantic relationship.
#3 "I could be attracted that way."	32%	Their friend is attracted to them but they don't return the feelings.	Test romantic feelings.
#4 "I'm not jealous of your girl/boyfriend."	30%	Friends deny being attracted but then feel jealous toward their friend's dating partner.	Allows romantic feelings to surface.
#5 "As long as we aren't sexual, it isn't romantic."	25%	Friends feel if they don't engage in sexual behavior, then they aren't romantically involved.	Friendship label allows physical contact.

Note: Percentages add to more than 100% because respondents could describe more than one myth.

FIGURE 1   Myths Concerning Friendship Definition and Development

was not attracted to them, but this was not supported in the narrative journal writing. The following comments illustrate the existence of an attraction that is definitely denied.

Women's Narratives

"Joe asked me to be his 'date' for the homecoming dance. I was quite surprised because I knew that he did not like to dance, nor to get dressed up. However, I did enjoy those things, so of course I went. Later, Joe whispered to me, 'You look really beautiful tonight.' I must admit that I was taken off-guard when he said this. I did not know what to say at the time, because I was shocked and confused, so we just continued dancing and left it at that."

"As I was listening to what Michael was saying, he turned to me and said, 'I wish I had a nice girl like you!' I was so shocked. I did not know if he was just saying that because he was upset or if he meant it. There was a big pause because I didn't know what to say to him. All of a sudden I heard the front door open, and his parents came home. Michael's mother called to him, and he jumped up and went to see what she wanted. Unfortunately, there was never a mention of Michael wanting a girl like me again."

Men's Narratives

"Today I was talking to her over the phone and I was thanking her for doing this project that we were supposed to do together by herself because she said that I worked two jobs and she knew that I would be busy so she did it by herself, which I was grateful for. I thanked her and said that I owed her a favor, anything that she wanted. I meant this in a purely innocent form, and she turned it around and made it sort of sexual. She kept asking me, so what are you going to do for me? How are you going to repay me? I know she was just joking, but I was a little uncomfortable with it."

"I always get a kiss hello and good-bye—sometimes even more than one. I get kisses sometimes when I do a good thing or sometimes just for no reason. In the middle of a conversation, one of us can just walk up to the other and put our arm around the other for no particular reason. When we are by ourselves watching a movie, now and then she will lie against me or I will rest my head on her leg. We will not get the wrong idea and because we have known each other for such a long time, this abundance of affection just comes natural."

This myth is the premise of the romantic challenge. Men and women struggle with the challenge of their friends' attraction to them. Oftentimes, denial is the easiest way to manage the attraction so that the friendship may continue status quo. If we acknowledge our friend's attraction for us, then we will have to decide what to do about that attraction.

Reflections on Myth #1: Denying That
Our Friend Is Attracted to Us

1. Women wrote the first two narratives, whereas men wrote the second two. Do you notice any gender differences regarding the denial of a romantic attraction?
2. Do you think either friend is intentionally revealing or denying a romantic attraction to his or her friend in these particular narratives?
3. What role does self-disclosure play in revealing romantic attraction?
4. To what degree can a platonic friendship be maintained through the use of denial?

MYTH #2: NOT CROSSING OVER
THE FRIENDSHIP LINE

Although Myth #1 was the most widely reported, the other myths were also related to managing the romantic aspect of the friendship. Some individuals stated in their journals that they could remain friends, and as they continued writing in their journals they became romantically involved. This was reported in 35% of the friendships.

Women's Narratives

"When he kissed me on the cheek to say good night, one might say that it was just a normal good-bye gesture but I could tell that it was more of a 'yes, I am attracted to you too' type of gesture."

"I remembered that day because of the chemistry exam. We both felt this exam really stressed us out. I stayed at his house to study, and by 9:00 we still hadn't eaten anything. So Nelson suggested that he cook something to eat. After we ate dinner, I felt very sleepy. So he made coffee for me to drink in order to stay awake. At that moment, I felt like he was just like my boyfriend. He cares for me, and we are just like a couple."

"We made an agreement that we would become closer friends. Even though there was an attraction, I would always deny any feelings. Even when I talked to my best friend about him, I would always make it a point to say that we're just friends because I didn't want to go out with anyone or have a serious relationship at that point. I figured as long as I denied it and neither of us said anything, nothing would happen. But then it became too hard for us to keep it inside because the emotions were too strong to just be friends, so we became officially dating."

Men's Narratives

"Jennifer and I used to avoid contact whenever possible. I think this was due to the fact that we had feelings for each other but weren't prepared to make that transition from friends to romantic interests. I think we always knew that something would happen, but we were waiting for the other person to make the first move."

"It would be fair to say that I was of the opinion that men and women could maintain pure friendships. However, based on my recent writings and experiences, including this one, I do not believe that is feasible. Regardless of what either party might say, romantic feelings inevitably intervene."

"We began to hold hands, even when the scary scenes were over, we both mutually did not let go. I had a feeling that maybe this is when we would cross that border, between friendship and a romantic relationship, which was now a thin line to me."

These individuals initially were friends but then realized that they wanted to become more involved as the friendship continued. These myths support research by Werking (1997) that acknowledges the idea that women and men have romantic motives for initiating and developing a cross-sex friendship. Many people are attracted to other people, but they are not clear on what those attractions are based. Young people are still learning about relationships of all types and have not yet determined how to distinguish between platonic and romantic attractions. The friendship is a discovery process or testing ground for a romantic relationship that may naturally develop from the friendship, or the attraction may not last and they will continue as friends.

Reflections on Myth #2: Not Crossing Over the Friendship Line

1. In what ways, if any, do the narratives indicate that the friends had romantic motives for initiating and developing a cross-sex friendship with their friend?
2. Do you agree with the statement that more men than women tend to have romantic motives for initiating a cross-sex friendship? Why or why not?
3. What does it mean to cross over the friendship line after stating that you won't cross over the friendship line?
4. Have you ever been in a cross-sex friendship that crossed the line into a romantic involvement? If so, how did the relationship progress from friendship to romance?
5. Gender is not the only aspect of identity that affects friendships' crossing over the friendship line. Drawing on your own experience and observation, discuss ways in which friendship and romantic expression are influenced by race, economic class, age, and other aspects of social identity.

MYTH #3: NOT RETURNING ROMANTIC ATTRACTION

Other individuals had the opposite experience of Myth #2. They thought that they could be attracted to their friend, but as they continued writing it became clear they were not romantically attracted. Myth #3, "I could be attracted that way," was reported by 32% of the friends.

Women's Narratives

"Adam and I have constantly battled the issue of dating versus friendship. He pushed more for the dating side of the coin, while I usually wanted us to remain friends. We've had times of physical intimacy, often followed by times of not talking to each other for some time. Once we got into this huge issue because he realized that, most likely, we would never be more than friends in the long run—something I had known for a while."

"Everyone viewed us as a couple, but we explained that we were not. Then Chris escalated our friendship into a romantic one. He started buying me roses and leaving little notes. Finally he told me that he wanted to be more than friends. I went silent at that moment because I was not expecting that to occur. Even though he had been hinting it, I didn't want to think about it because I didn't know how I would go about dealing with it. I did not ever think of my friend that way, even though I knew he would be a great boyfriend."

"Recently, I've noticed many changes in his type of communication. Suddenly the innocent hugs and taps and the sarcastic 'I love yous' seem to have more meaning. I feel very uncomfortable at times expressing innocent affection, for I am afraid that Mike might get the wrong idea."

Men's Narratives

"I drive a manual car, and she wanted to learn how to drive it. One night I drove to Astoria Park and stopped in the parking lot. It was about one o'clock in the morning. She was so excited and kept telling me before that she tried to learn how to drive a stick from her father but he wasn't a very good teacher. So we exchanged seats. I told her to use her left foot to push the clutch all the way down and then turn on the ignition. She did so and found out that it was weird because she is just used to turning on the ignition right away. Then I took my right hand and stroked her right thigh at the same time telling her that she is going to have to balance out the gas and clutch with this leg. I guess it kind of turned her on. Then I showed her where the gears were, both of us with our hands on top of each other shifting from gear one to two to three to four and then finally to five. She looked at me when I was showing her and gave me sexy gestures. I then got close to her face and she came close to my face on the verge of kissing me on my lips. I then put my finger on her lips and told her, 'That's not it.' Jokingly we both began to laugh kind of nervously. She eventually learned to drive, but I always wondered what I was thinking."

"I know that in a physical sense I am attracted to Cathleen. It is just the male instinct that makes me look. Though she is one of my best friends, I cannot help but look when she is wearing a tight pair of jeans or a very revealing top. To be honest, sometimes I catch myself staring at her chest, and I think she catches me too. Then I realize what is going on, and I say to myself, 'What the hell am I doing?' I think it is purely natural for two people so close to be somewhat attracted. One night I found myself kissing her, and by the end of the night we came very close to you know what, and I have to admit that the thought crossed my mind in the heat of the moment. I would have acted on my impulses and made a very big mistake. Right now I cannot think of her in a romantic sense."

Friends often feel pressure from the cross-sex friend, as well as other friends and family members, to perceive their cross-sex friend as a potential mate. Research finds that women frequently question men's motives for friendship (Rose, 1985) and often have to manage the romantic challenge in the friendship in order to maintain the friendship. More women than men in this study found that their friend was attracted to them while they did not return the attraction.

Reflections on Myth #3: Not Returning Romantic Attraction

1. Do you believe that more men than women tend to be romantically attracted to their cross-sex friends? Why or why not?
2. Have you ever had a cross-sex friend be romantically attracted to you while you did not return the feelings? Did you stay friends with that individual? Why or why not?
3. What are the challenges associated with managing a friendship so that it remains platonic when one person is attracted to the other?
4. What messages are sent when one friend professes a romantic attraction to a friend and those feelings are not returned? How is self-esteem affected?

MYTH #4: I AM NOT JEALOUS OF YOUR DATING PARTNER

In many of the friendships, either one or both of the friends were dating someone else. At the beginning of the narrative, friends did not perceive this as a problem. However, as the friendship narrative progressed, they began expressing jealousy over their friend's dating partner. This was reported in 30% of the friendships.

Men's Narratives

"When I walk with Antonella down the sidewalk or sit with her in a restaurant or a café, I get jealous of the other men who look at her. They either wink, raise their eyebrow, or whatever. She gets the same feelings if a girl comes up to me and asks me something."

"Whenever we are together, I never think about dating. As soon as she is out on a date, however, I can't help but think I should be the one with her. I never know when she will find someone she really likes, and then that will be the end for me."

Women's Narratives

"I am aware that Joey is not my boyfriend, and I don't even want him to be, but I seem to get jealous anyway. I often feel like Joey is mine and I don't want to share him with other girls. After all, I do have a boyfriend whom I love dearly, whom I have been dating for almost six years."

"I think the time that I realized that I was so attracted to Adam is when he started dating another girl. I remember being jealous because I was no longer the only special girl in his life."

"The night of the dance, I showed up with a date, and it seemed that Tony got a bit jealous himself. Tony kept looking our way and asking these questions in a rather defensive manner: 'Who is this guy?' or 'When did you meet him?' I found that questioning to be very sweet."

Many times when individuals already have a romantic relationship, it allows them to develop friendships with members of the opposite sex they might not otherwise. Since they are romantically involved elsewhere, cross-sex friendships do not have the emotional or sexual charge as in a romantic relationship. However, those parameters can be modified during the course of a friendship. Through their interactions, friends became aware that their emotions were heightened when they observed their cross-sex friend with a romantic partner, even though the two friends perceived each other as friends.

Reflections on Myth #4: I Am Not Jealous of Your Dating Partner

1. Tensions exist in all relationships. How might tension be expressed in a cross-sex friendship when your friend indicates that he or she is envious of your dating partner?
2. What, if any, is the difference in how men express jealousy with their female friends versus women with their male friends?
3. Have you ever found yourself jealous of a cross-sex friend's date? What do you think was the cause of the jealousy?
4. Have you ever had a cross-sex friend's dating partner be jealous of you? How did that individual affect your friendship with your cross-sex friend?

MYTH #5: AS LONG AS WE AREN'T SEXUAL, IT ISN'T ROMANTIC

This myth, which continues the theme of managing the romantic challenge, was reported by 25% of the respondents. Many friends engaged in physical behavior such as kissing, holding hands, or flirting or emotional behavior such as feeling closer to their friend than anyone and then behaved as if the behavior was not representative of a romantic relationship but was somehow an extension of the friendship.

Men's Narratives

"During this time, Jen had a party because her parents went away. The next thing I know we are all in the pool naked and Jen and I were kissing. Not only did I enjoy those 'special moments' we had together, but I had also gained a very important friendship that I would cherish for the rest of my life."

"We convey simple affection to each other by beeping one another with 959. This is a moment in time which we would claim as ours and which reminds each of us of specific times when we were together and we saw the minute 9:59 go by to-gether. That may sound like a corny thing, but if 959 appears on my beeper I feel very closely connected to Ann and highly reminded of our great friendship for and with each other."

"We never crossed over that fine line between strong affection and sexual desire, for I always respect people who are involved with other people. We both confess that we have sexual desire for each other, but we both understand that it would ruin a great friendship. She sends me 'I miss you' and 'I love you' tweety emails. I send her regular emails and express my affection through the letters. I al-ways start my emails saying how much I miss her and wish she were here. I have jokingly said to her 'I'm very unfortunate that Rezaul (her boyfriend) found you be-fore I found you.' We express our sexual attraction to each other by constantly jok-ing about it."

Women's Narratives

"Maybe it is how he waits for a couple of hours to spend only a half-hour with me. Maybe it is because he subconsciously tried to schedule our school and work times in a complementing manner so it enables us to spend the most amount of time. He always calls me in the morning when he wakes up, and tries to call me at night be-fore he sleeps. Maybe it is how he kicks his friends out of the front seat, so that I have the front seat reserved for me."

"He told me during the movie that if we both aren't married by the time that we are 28, then we would get married to each other."

"We write about how much we miss each other and how we would love to be in each other's company. Moreover, we send cards through email sending hugs and even kisses. Finally, we talk on the phone nightly and twice during the day. My days were filled with many thoughts of him. I woke up thinking of him and went to sleep thinking of him. I do not think that we have to be with someone to be really close to them in heart. I remain as friends with him because he is there every time I need him."

"We flirt with one another, spend a lot of extra time together, go to a certain park that overlooks the city, usually considered to be a romantic spot to which you take your boy/girlfriend. Although we are not dating, I think that we both enjoy this romantic aspect of our relationship, making it different and special from others we have."

This type of sexual expression has been found in some cross-sex friendships when friends differentiate between "friendly, almost platonic sex and romantic sex" (Rubin, 1985). For some individuals, sexual behavior or romantic expression became part of the framework of the friendship and did not infringe upon the friendship. These expressions allowed the friends to feel attractive to the opposite sex without a romantic commitment. Sometimes friendships serve as testing grounds for romantic expression, so those individuals may experience emotional connections to the other sex in a less restrictive context.

Reflections on Myth #5: As Long As We Aren't Sexual, It Isn't Romantic

1. How do the friends behave as they create emotional or romantic impressions with each other?
2. Intimacy can vary in intensity, in the degree to which it is personal. How does the behavior of each friend help him or her create a more trusting and intimate friendship?
3. What messages are sent to the people around them who observe the friends' behavior?
4. Have you ever experienced romantic expression in a platonic friendship? If so, discuss how that expression affected the friendship.
5. How do you think the label "friendship" affects a relationship? What functions do labels for relationships serve?

DEVELOPING A CULTURAL MODEL OF CROSS-SEX FRIENDSHIP

The five myths described here appear to be ways in which friends communicate about the friendship in order to develop and maintain a friendship rather than a romantic partnership. Most of these friends were clear that their friendship was a valuable relationship that could not be replaced with a romantic relationship. Respondents either maintained purely platonic feelings for their cross-sex friend, decided not to pursue a romantic relationship at the expense of their friendship, or did not stir romantic feelings in their friend. This finding supports research that proposes sexual involvement between friends may be seen as a threat to the friendship (Bell, 1981; Sapadin, 1988) and friends will not act upon their romantic attraction for fear it will ruin or change the friendship (Furman, 1986).

The lack of cultural representation, much less understanding of cross-sex friendships, leads cross-sex friends to encounter such challenges. Social, cultural, media, or relationship models do not exist to provide distinct guidelines for cross-sex friendships. Oftentimes, individuals fall back on rules for romantic, sibling, or parental roles to initiate and develop cross-sex friendships. This is one of the reasons why women and men tend to perceive each other's behavior as either one of sexual interest, brother/sister, or maternal or paternal interaction. The most prevalent is sexual interest. Because our culture places such emphasis on gender, men and women experience difficulty in not perceiving each other in sexual terms (O'Meara, 1989).

The cultural debate continues whether or not women and men can be friends (Werking, 1997). Platonic friendships between women and men are potentially problematic because the partners cannot rely on cultural norms to guide them. A cultural model of cross-sex friendship is being developed, as evidenced by current research into cross-sex friendships (Werking, 1997). Cross-sex friends must create their own guidelines and reshape the way men and women typically interact with one another. Cross-sex friends have to examine their own motives for initiating and developing cross-sex friendships, as well as manage the friendships relationally, socially, and culturally. Cross-sex friends must manage the challenges of cross-sex friendships as identified by O'Meara (1989) that were introduced at the beginning of this paper. Friends must negotiate the emotional bond between them ("emotional or intimacy challenge"); decide what types of feelings they feel for each other, either romantic or platonic ("sexual or romantic challenge"); conquer the power difference given to men and women in our society ("equality challenge"); present an accurate picture of their relationships as platonic friends to their family and friends ("audience perspective"); and discover opportunities for initiating and developing cross-sex friendships ("opportunity challenge"). Men and women have to actively negotiate these challenges to establish and maintain their cross-sex friendships.

Cross-sex friendships tend to begin in adolescence and continue into retirement, playing more and less important roles as life transitions occur (Wright, 1999). Youth and young adults may encounter more of the challenges as they initiate and develop their friendships than do more mature adults who have established friendships and relationships. Retirement is another time for initiating friendships, and the challenges may once again need to be managed for successful relationships. Regardless of one's age, sex, marital status, socioeconomic level, or ethnic background, individuals who have cross-sex friendships usually have to negotiate one or more of the challenges that accompany those friendships.

CONCLUSION

Based on the narratives presented, it is clear that the romantic challenge presented a challenge for the majority of the cross-sex friends. From these narratives, the development and maintenance of cross-sex friendships depend on the absence or restriction of attraction by one or both friends. Although a romantic attraction does not supersede the possibility of a cross-sex friendship, it does affect the development, management, and maintenance of cross-sex friendships, as previously reported by Rubin (1985). In some cases, cross-sex friendships function to test romantic feelings and may act as a prelude to a romantic relationship—although it must be noted that in less than 20% of the friendships, friends identify themselves as entering into a romantic relationship during the course of their journal writing.

Final Thoughts and Reflections on the Romantic Challenge Confronting Cross-Sex Friendships

1. In what ways does understanding the myths friends describe help women and men to avoid misunderstandings and frustrations in their cross-sex friendships?
2. What makes a man and a woman friends? In your view, can men and women be friends?
3. It is said that communication rules are prescriptions for behavior. What general communication rules do you see functioning throughout this article on managing the romantic challenge in cross-sex friendship?
4. Based on what you've learned about managing the romantic challenge in cross-sex friendships, how would you manage the turning points in a friendship to ensure that it remain platonic?
5. Do you have questions about the challenges confronting cross-sex friendships? What resources can you identify to answer those questions?

REFERENCES

Bell, R. (1981). Friendships of women and men. *Psychology of Women Quarterly, 5,* 402–417.

Bernstein, R. (1983). *Beyond objectivism and relativism.* Philadelphia: University of Pennsylvania.

Furman, L. (1986). *Cross-gender friendships in the workplace: Factors and components.* Unpublished doctoral dissertation, Fielding Institute, ND.

O'Meara, D. (1989). Cross-sex friendships: Four basic challenges of an ignored relationship. *Sex Roles, 21,* 525–543.

Rawlins, W. (1982). Cross-sex friends and the communicative management of sex-role expectations. *Communication Quarterly, 30,* 343–352.

Rose, S. (1985). Same- and cross-sex friendships and the psychology of homosociality. *Sex Roles, 12,* 63–74.

Rubin, L. (1985). *Just friends.* New York: Harper & Row.

Sapadin, L. (1988). Friendship and gender: Perspectives of professional men and women. *Journal of Social and Personal Relationships, 5,* 387–403.

Shaw, H. (1972). *Dictionary of literary terms.* New York: McGraw-Hill.

Werking, K. (1997). *We're just good friends: Women and men in nonromantic friendships.* New York: Guilford.

White, M. (1991). Deconstruction and therapy. *Dulwich Centre Newsletter, 3,* 21–40.

Wood, J. T. (1982). Communication and relational culture: Bases for the study of human relationships. *Communication Quarterly, 30,* 75–83.

Wright, D. (1999). *Personal relationships: An interdisciplinary approach.* Mountain View, CA: Mayfield.

PRIDE AND PREJUDICE

A Feminist Cinderella Story

Darcy Nunn

The perspective from which an analysis of a text is viewed can provide a means of understanding that was not evident in a cursory or multiple readings. Feminist analyses, for instance, tend to view texts as either limiting in their perspective of women or as placing women in opposition to men. Darcy Nunn's piece offers us a view of Jane Austen's Pride and Prejudice *through the lens of opposition. In this article, Nunn examines the preludes to and constructions of the various marriages of the main and peripheral characters. The purpose of the analysis is to demonstrate how Austen presented an alternative view of and approach to the traditional roles of wife and husband within the context of marriage that would afford the greatest satisfaction for both partners.*

Dunn's analysis suggests that Austen's story was subversively persuasive. That is, she did not blatantly reject the traditional, unequal status of women and men in marriage; rather, through Austen's presentation of several marriages, readers are invited to conclude for themselves which of the many configurations of roles and power distribution appear to be most advantageous to both participants. The conclusion, of course, is that the model of marriage, as presented by Elizabeth Bennet and Mr. Darcy, is preferred. Such a marriage is built on mutual respect and equal opportunity to participate in the marriage. Through her analysis, Nunn shows how Austen mutes the rights of husbands accorded by their financial advantage. Austen's portrayal of marriage demonstrates to readers that, despite economic forces that compel women to seek a mate for financial support, women should not accept a lesser status within the marriage, and men should not expect that their wealth should buy them relational privilege and satisfaction.

QUESTIONS FOR DISCUSSION

- *What are your perceptions about the roles of females and males within a committed intimate partnership?*
- *Do economic factors within the relationship influence how you do or would interact? If so, how? If not, why?*

- *How do the various models of marriage discussed by Nunn mirror those with which you are familiar?*
- *While the author demonstrates how Austen's story was empowering to women, does she suggest how it also might empower male readers?*

Most of us are familiar with the "Cinderella story" premise: A poor girl abused by society meets a rich, handsome prince who falls in love with her and rescues her through marriage. Jane Austen's *Pride and Prejudice* is based on this theme, in that the novel's heroine, Elizabeth Bennet, discovers true happiness in marrying a wealthy, powerful man. This can appear to be the ideal patriarchal ending: A "helpless" woman of lesser status is "saved" by a male at the top of the social order and will be taken care of and protected for the rest of her life. In this essay, I plan to demonstrate that this is not the case in *Pride and Prejudice* by answering the question, "How does Jane Austen seek to change the patriarchy through the marriage of Elizabeth Bennet and Mr. Darcy?" Using marriage as the unit of analysis, I will show how the "Cinderella story" in *Pride and Prejudice* challenges the patriarchy and can be interpreted as the ideal feminist ending.

In her article "Of Woman Borne: Male Experience and Feminine Truth in Jane Austen's Novels," Sarah Morrison (1994) examines feminism's aims:

> Historically feminism embraces two conflicting impulses: the impulse to condemn stereotypical and limiting roles for women, with the rather paradoxical view of achieving full participation and equality for women on a male-dominated society's terms; and the impulse to validate and elevate traditional women's roles and concerns, placing them in opposition to entrenched patriarchal values. (p. 345)

Jane Austen's work is of rhetorical significance because it falls under the second "impulse" of feminism. It is not a violent protest of woman's role in early nineteenth-century society, but a validation of the importance of that role. Morrison claims that Austen is well aware of the unequal standards placed on men and women, but that "her vision extends well beyond some feminist political agenda that envisions a world of different proportions to instead offer a balanced view of life's inherent limitations and the modest possibilities afforded individuals whose lives are necessarily bound to others" (p. 341). *Pride and Prejudice* deserves to be analyzed according to feminist criteria because it offers a glimpse into the history of feminism and provides an alternative view of women as masters of their domain rather than victim's of a male-dominated society. According to Morrison, Austen's contribution to feminism lies in the fact that she views the world from a strictly feminine perspective (p. 337), which allows her to succeed where others have failed in making "woman the normative center" (p. 342).

DESCRIPTION OF THE ARTIFACT

Pride and Prejudice, which was published in 1813, is an exploration of marriage relationships in the early nineteenth century. Jane Austen introduces us to the Bennet family, which includes Mr. and Mrs. Bennet and their five daughters, Jane, Elizabeth, Mary, Kitty, and Lydia. The Bennets are not wealthy people, and the stability of their daughters' futures depends on their finding husbands to provide for them. Unfortunately, finding a suitable husband is not always the easiest of tasks. Dorothy Van Ghent (1969) summarizes the situation facing the Bennet girls:

> The tale is that of a man hunt, with the female the pursuer and the male the shy and elusive prey. The desperation of the hunt is the desperation of economic survival: girls in a family like that of the Bennets must succeed in running down solvent young men in order to survive. (p. 21)

The urgency of finding a mate is glossed over by the courtship ritual, which puts emphasis on civilized appearances instead of the underlying economic considerations accompanying marriage. The female is a "lady," the male a "gentleman," and they marry because they "fall in love" (Van Ghent, 1969, p. 21). This puts a lot of strain on young women, as Austen exemplifies in *Pride and Prejudice.*

The two eldest Bennet daughters, Jane and Elizabeth, feel this strain most acutely in the novel. Their mother, a blathering, unintelligent woman, makes it her mission to snag husbands for her daughters, and when an eligible young (and wealthy) bachelor, Mr. Bingley, moves into the neighborhood, she directs all her attention to securing him for Jane. Elizabeth, who observes her mother's frantic "Bingley-chase" with distaste and concern for her sister's welfare, is the novel's main character. Austen focuses on her experiences, as well as her attitude and observations of the experiences of others. We follow her through a series of events that make up the story line of the novel: her introduction to Mr. Darcy and the tension that develops between them; the "failed" courtship of Mr. Bingley and her sister Jane; her refusal of Mr. Darcy's proposal of marriage; the "change" that Mr. Darcy's undergoes; the reuniting of her sister and Mr. Bingley; and her revised opinion and acceptance of Mr. Darcy.

Though there are minor subplots, which deal with the marriages of other women in the novel, such as Elizabeth's younger sister Lydia or her best friend Charlotte Lucas, the dynamics of her relationship with Mr. Darcy receive the most attention. Mr. Darcy is an extremely wealthy friend of Mr. Bingley, and Elizabeth first encounters him at a ball. Mr. Darcy is very arrogant and snobbish, and makes it well known at the gathering that he considers all the young ladies in the room "beneath" him. Mr. Bingley suggests that he ask Elizabeth to dance, but after looking at her, Darcy answers, "She is tolerable, but not handsome enough to tempt me" (p. 7) when Elizabeth is within earshot. Elizabeth develops an immediate dislike for the man, and at the next ball they both attend, she blatantly refuses to dance with him. This sparks Mr. Darcy's interest in her, and he proposes to her later in the novel, in spite of his distaste for her family and social position. His proposal is very ungracious and arrogant; he assumes that she will accept him because of his wealth and social standing. He is shocked when Elizabeth refuses him, and as a consequence, he is forced to closely examine his own character. Ultimately, he realizes the error of his ways and presents himself to Elizabeth as a changed man. "By you I was properly humbled," he tells her. "I came to you without a doubt of my reception. You showed me how insufficient were all my pretensions to please a woman worthy of being pleased" (p. 268). The novel ends happily, with both of the eldest Bennet daughters finding husbands.

Pride and Prejudice can be categorized as a courtship novel, which helps define the context in which it was written. Novels of this type focus on the "courting" stage of a young woman's life before she marries. In *The Courtship Novel, 1740–1820*, Katherine Green (1991) states, "The novel of courtship appropriates domestic fiction to feminist purposes" (p. 2). This subgenre was thematically different from other contemporary narratives in that it created "feminized space," centering its story in the "brief period of autonomy between a young woman's coming out and her marriage" (pp. 2–3).

Courtship novels empowered women, depicting them as responsible for their own fate. According to Green (1991), courtship novels "quietly championed women's rights to choose marriage partners for personal, relational reasons rather than for familial, economic ones" (p. 161). Choice is the agent of autonomy that is so central to the theme in courtship novels. Suzanne Fields (1996) emphasizes its importance in her statement, "A woman is at the zenith of her powers when she chooses her life partner. She must choose well" (p. 49).

Elizabeth's process of choosing a husband provides the action for *Pride and Prejudice*. She puts careful consideration into her choice of Mr. Darcy, and she makes this decision based on her own personal criteria—what she considers right for her. Other characters use different criteria for choosing their husbands, and this brings us to an analysis of marriage in the novel and how it constructs gender.

MARRIAGE AND THE CONSTRUCTION OF GENDER

Marriage was the key to existence for most women during the nineteenth century. Their role in society was a limited one, restricted to the domestic sphere. In *Emile*, Jean Jacques Rousseau expresses the typical patriarchal standard of the "natural" role of women in the eighteenth and nineteenth centuries in his discussion about women's education:

Thus the whole education of women ought to relate to men. To please men, to be useful to them, to make herself honored by them, to raise them when young, to care for them when grown, to counsel them, to console them, to make their lives agreeable and sweet, these are the duties of women at all times, and they ought to be taught from childhood. (quoted in Cohen, 1994, p. 217)

According to Martha Vicinus (1972), a woman's "social and intellectual growth was confined to the family and close friends. Her status was totally dependent upon the economic position of her father and then her husband" (p. ix). Because a woman's life depended so much on the men in society, her choice of a marriage partner was a pivotal moment in her existence and determined if she would be content or miserable for the rest of her life.

In *Pride and Prejudice,* the marriages between various characters can either support or challenge the patriarchy. By critically examining each one, we can establish in what ways matrimony can either negate or validate woman's role in society. Jane Austen shows us many negative examples of marriage, which allows us to fully appreciate the impact that a poor choice can have on a person's life. As Tony Tanner (1986) notes, the fact that there are so many "bad, or bleakly empty marriages in Jane Austen, revealing different degrees of failed mutuality, nonreciprocation and myopic egotism or frivolous self-gratification" only underlines the importance of having a good marriage (p. 10).

The relationship between Mr. and Mrs. Bennet shows that, in many ways, marriage is as significant for men as it is for women. Jane Austen makes it clear in the third page of the novel that their marriage is of the "bleakly empty" type. The last paragraph of Chapter 1 provides a summary of their situation:

Mr. Bennet was so odd a mixture of quick parts, sarcastic humor, reserve, and caprice, that the experience of three-and-twenty years had been insufficient to make his wife understand his character. Her mind was less difficult to develop. She was a woman of mean understanding, little information, and uncertain temper. When she was discontented, she fancied herself nervous. The business of her life was to get her daughters married; its solace was visiting and news. (p. 3)

It is obvious from this description that Mr. and Mrs. Bennet do not have a solid marriage. They are ill suited for one another: one is intelligent with a dry sense of humor, the other simpleminded and flighty. After twenty-three years of marriage, Mrs. Bennet still does not know her husband, nor does she care to. The fact that the "business of her life" is to find husbands for her daughters implies that she doesn't place much importance on her relationship with her husband. The novel suggests that Mr. Bennet originally married his wife for her beauty, which has long since faded, leaving him with nothing. Mr. Bennet is emotionally withdrawn and leading only a partial existence in that he cannot fully immerse himself in the domestic affairs of his home (Morrison, 1994, p. 344). This marriage supports the patriarchy in that it is based on superficial, physical considerations that do not enhance the lives of the individuals. Mr. Bennet lacks stimulation and companionship, and Mrs. Bennet has no purpose to her existence other than marrying off her daughters and "visiting." Mrs. Bennet's role as a woman is trivialized by her marriage instead of substantiated.

The marriages of Lydia Bennet and Charlotte Lucas portray two possible extremes that were very common during Austen's time. Charlotte, who is 27 and quickly approaching the dreaded "spinster" status, marries strictly for economic reasons. The young and foolish Lydia, on the other hand, marries only for passion's sake. According to Robert Polhemus (1990), "Charlotte is all head, Lydia all hormones. One, plain and aging, calculates that she had best marry a fool rather than no one, and the other, ruled by 'high animal spirits,' falls for a seducer" (pp. 42–43).

Charlotte, who marries Mr. Collins, a pompous young man who seeks a wife solely to remain in favor with his rich employer, is aware that he may be her last chance at any sort of existence beyond that of her childhood home. Polhemus (1990) claims, "The point is not that Charlotte is a sellout, but that she lives in a narrow, desperate, feminine world of financial constraint, like some poor entrant in a ritualized beauty contest that determines your fate while drying up your soul." He continues, "Marriage to Collins is a kind of socially respectable prostitution in which Charlotte acquiesces" (p. 43). Charlotte is presented with the choice to remain single all her life and thus, in the eyes of society, a burden on her parents, or to marry for all the wrong reasons and yet be viewed by society as doing the "right thing as a woman." This marriage is probably the most potent example of a social contract that supports the patriarchy; it shows little concern for Charlotte as an individual and values her only as an object to be passed from one situation in which she is a burden to another where she is more useful. As readers we are unsure of the effect that the marriage will have on Charlotte's happiness. The fact that she married not for herself but for how others see her demonstrates that her role in the marriage is generic, supported by the patriarchy. She has lost her identity and is now "Wife" instead of "Charlotte."

Lydia's marriage also involves a loss of individuality, but in a different manner. Lydia adores a man in uniform, and marries an unscrupulous soldier named Mr. Wickham for no other reason than that he can be nicely inserted into her "soldier fantasy." The only thing special about Wickham is that he meets Lydia's requirement of wearing a uniform; he represents an ideal instead of a person. Austen warns us that this type of marriage is no better than marrying for economics. Lydia and Mr. Wickham never really see each other, they see only what they want to. An arrangement such as this may work for a while, but in the long run, it can lead to severe disappointment. Polhemus (1990) suggests that a marriage like this one "offers no basis for faith because it includes nothing beyond the desiring self" (p. 44). He contends that their marriage can never be real because "falling in love with love is, as the song says, falling for make-believe. You need to love another person whose individuality you distinguish, if love is to be real and good" (p. 45). The marriage of Lydia and Mr. Wickham supports the patriarchy in that Lydia, like Charlotte, is not valued for the individual qualities she brings to the relationship. The couple marries strictly for the sake of marriage, which does not provide a basis for the growth of either person alone or as a unit. When the thrill wears off, they will stagnate together in a pool of unfulfilled needs.

The marriage of Jane Bennet to Mr. Bingley can be viewed as a transition point from marriage that supports the patriarchy to one that challenges it. Jane's mother first conceives of the idea of Mr. Bingley as a husband-candidate for her oldest daughter, but when Jane and he are introduced, they are instantly attracted to one another. They eventually fall in love, and in spite of some outside interference, they marry at the end of the novel. I view this marriage as neutral: there is nothing exceptional about it that either supports or challenges the patriarchy. Though the marriage was initially planned out by Mrs. Bennet, who had her eye on Mr. Bingley's economic status, he and Jane marry for love, and there is evidence that they will be happy. We are unsure of Jane's role as a woman in her marriage, but we at least know that Mr. Bingley values Jane as an individual. Austen is possibly presenting Jane and Mr. Bingley's union as one of the lucky ones, where the "man-hunt" was successful, providing both financial security and compatibility. However, the fact that they fell in love is only one projected outcome of their meeting and there is the possibility that the marriage might have occurred anyway out of social necessity. The marriage is difficult to label in relation to the patriarchy, in that we don't know what to attribute the success of their marriage to: conscious choice or luck.

The marriage of Elizabeth to Mr. Darcy is the first one in *Pride and Prejudice* to actively challenge the patriarchy. In opposition to other marriages in the novel, theirs is "right" for them as individuals in spite of the fact that it is considered "wrong" by society's standards. When Mr. Darcy proposes to Elizabeth the first time, he openly admits that he views such a union as impractical, because of her lower social status, but that he has finally succumbed to his love for her, despite his reservations. "In vain have I struggled," he tells her. "It will not do. My feelings will not be repressed. You must allow me to tell yow how ardently I admire and love you" (p. 140). Elizabeth refuses him because this is not enough for her to base a marriage on. He assumes that she will gratefully accept his offer because of the financial gain it grants her, but Elizabeth places more value on his personality. She bluntly explains:

> From the very beginning, from the first moment I may almost say, of my acquaintance with you, your manners impressing me with the fullest belief of your arrogance, your conceit, and your selfish disdain of the feelings of others, were such as to form that groundwork of a disapprobation, on which succeeding events have built so immovable a dislike;

and I had not known you a month before I felt that you were the last man in the world whom I could ever be prevailed on to marry. (p. 143)

Elizabeth does not want to marry Mr. Darcy who, like Charlotte, focuses strictly on economic considerations, then throws caution to the wind like Lydia. Her refusal shocks Mr. Darcy and causes him to reexamine the situation; he comes to the conclusion that a good marriage cannot be based solely on social or economic reasons, and that choosing a partner involves finding a balance between logic and love. When he proposes the second time, he has achieved this balance: he's made the conscious decision that Elizabeth is the best woman for him, based on his love for her as well as how perfectly she meets his needs as an individual, thus freeing himself of the standards placed on him by society. Paula Marantz Cohen (1994) states that "Elizabeth's resistance to Darcy, her determination to make judgments concerning character and events, and her assumption of female teacher to male student—all estrange her from the stereotypical female of the Rousseauist model" (p. 223). When Elizabeth accepts Mr. Darcy, she too has made a conscious consideration of all factors involved in such a marriage and considers Mr. Darcy the right man for her. Their marriage stands in opposition to the patriarchy in that it is not based on society's standards—it is based on their own. It is the first democratic relationship in the novel, in which Elizabeth's role as a woman is validated by the marriage because she is considered one equal half of a whole unit, her own power of choice brought her to the marriage, and she is loved and respected by Darcy for her individual qualities.

HOW ELIZABETH AND MR. DARCY'S MARRIAGE CHALLENGES THE PATRIARCHY

The marriage of Elizabeth Bennet to Mr. Darcy accomplishes Jane Austen's goal of elevating woman's role in early nineteenth-century society. Austen constructs their relationship as the exact opposite of the marriages of Mr. and Mrs. Bennet, Charlotte and Mr. Collins, and Lydia and Mr. Wickham, all of which support the patriarchal system. Elizabeth's position as Mr. Darcy's wife challenges this system by demonstrating that a woman can be valued and loved for her intelligence and personality, that she can have an active role in determining her future, and that she can be considered her husband's equal in her marriage. Through the example set by Elizabeth and Mr. Darcy's union, Austen suggests that there is hope for the future, that other women will begin to value themselves and raise their standards when choosing a husband.

Elizabeth breaks the patriarchal stereotype of the meek and submissive female whose opinions are dictated by society in that she is valued for her mind and individuality instead of her adherence to traditional feminine qualities. Cohen (1994) states that "her refusal to conform to conventional female behavior has a seductive power which will ultimately win Darcy's love at the same time that it inspires him to behave differently" (p. 222). Elizabeth's intelligence is a key factor in what draws Mr. Darcy to her. At the end of the novel, Elizabeth asks Mr. Darcy what it was about her that had caused him to fall in love. "My beauty you had early withstood," she says, "and as for my manners—my behavior to you was at least always bordering on the uncivil, and I never spoke to you without rather wishing to give you pain than not. Now be sincere, did you admire me for my impertinence?" He answers her, "For the liveliness of your mind, I did"(p. 276). According to Polhemus (1990), "the key to the optimistic tone and the lasting appeal of the novel lies in the fact that a woman's mind and lively talents win the love that gives her a chance for a distinguished life" (pp. 28–29). Her marriage contains a "meeting of the minds," which Austen suggests is every bit as valuable as the meeting of two hearts (Fields, 1996, p. 50). This notion of intellectual compatibility is foreign to the established system of marriage, as exemplified by Mr. and Mrs. Bennet's relationship, which is characterized by disinterest and loneliness. Because Elizabeth and Mr. Darcy are able to relate to each other on the same level, it can be assumed that their marriage has a much stronger foundation and will be more successful than that of Elizabeth's parents.

Elizabeth's marriage also serves to elevate her role as a woman in that she is able to take control of her own fate instead of sitting back helplessly while the patriarchy determines it for her. Before she enters into the marriage, she insists that her personal needs be met, thus inspiring Mr. Darcy to change. He rises to meet Elizabeth's standards, instead of Elizabeth's lowering her own to meet his. It is her decision alone that will make the marriage a reality, and this empowers her. "Having shown us the possibility for a more equal distribution of role characteristics," claims Cohen (1994), "Austen provides a setting where this new kind of couple can physically transcend the stereotyped conception of marriage upheld by their society" (p. 224). Tanner (1986) also supports this notion, stating that, for Jane Austen, a good marriage is "the metaphor for the most desirable kind of relationship, which can both 'ground' and situate her heroines (and their husbands) and allow them more fully to live out their proper telos or end as women" (p. 10). Robert Polhemus (1990) suggests that "if we see that the relative status of these two [Elizabeth and Mr. Darcy] somehow reflects the historical condition of inequality between the sexes, we can understand why such a clear-sighted and skeptical writer as Austen would celebrate love" (p. 29). Love is one of the tools of Elizabeth's empowerment as a woman. Because she is worthy of such love, she is able to rise above the patriarchy "in the precise sense that she wants and has the potential to fly far beyond the mundane level of her mother, her sisters, and most of the other conventionally limited women around her" (p. 31).

Because Elizabeth had the power to dictate the terms on which she would marry Mr. Darcy, we have a clear understanding that, for the length of their marriage, she will be her husband's equal. This is quite a jolt to the established system of male domination, especially when we consider that Mr. Darcy does not object to his wife's elevated role. Mr. Darcy respects Elizabeth and enjoys her lively personality. This is illustrated in the observations of Georgiana, Darcy's younger sister, who lives with the couple:

> Georgiana had the highest opinion in the world of Elizabeth; though at first she often listened with an astonishment bordering on alarm at her lively, sportive manner of talking to her brother. He, who had always inspired in herself a respect which almost overcame her affection, she now saw the object of open pleasantry. Her mind received knowledge that had never before fallen in her way. By Elizabeth's instructions, she began to comprehend that a woman may take liberties with her husband. (p. 282)

That Georgiana has observed the democratic relationship of her brother and his wife gives us hope that she will learn from their example and seek out this type of marriage for herself. Austen sets up Elizabeth and Mr. Darcy's marriage as a model for future marriages, which will raise the status of all women in society. In addition to the roles of "wife" and "mother," Jane Austen wants us to see women in terms of "individual" and "companion." In this way she is challenging the patriarchy as a whole, with the intention of validating the importance of the entire domestic sphere. As Polhemus (1990) puts it, "Reading Austen, you can sense a big change coming: the days of feminine deference are numbered" (p. 31).

Jane Austen seeks to challenge the patriarchy through Elizabeth and Mr. Darcy's marriage in three ways: She shows that a woman can be valued for her mind; she suggests that a woman can take charge of her existence and make her own choices; and she uses their marriage as a model for future couples. In this way we see that the "Cinderella story" ending of *Pride and Prejudice* is not a contribution to the patriarchy, but an alterative solution to it. Jane Austen presents us with a new type of marriage that allows women to live to their full potential, and implies that this will improve the lives of their husbands also. Her rhetoric is an important contribution to feminist study in that it provides a unique view of feminism that doesn't seek a radical transformation of society but a gradual reconstruction of it, beginning with an increased emphasis on the importance of women's roles. James Wood (1998) summarizes her work as "a strenuous argument on behalf of the deserving poor—deserving not because of gentility but because of goodness." He continues, "Austen's ideal world, glimpsed in the puff of harmony that is exhaled at the end of her novels when the heroine gets her husband, would be an ethical meritocracy, in which the best dowry the heroine can bring to her match is goodness" (p. 31). In *Pride and Prejudice,* the "goodness" that Elizabeth brings to her marriage is her intelligence and strength of character, which is all she needs to attain Mr. Darcy's love. Austen creates a world in which personality instead of economics provides the basis for a marriage, where the heroine wins the "Cinderella stakes" because she deserves her prince as much as he deserves her (Fields, 1996, p. 49).

Jane Austen's novels are inspiring achievements for a woman of her time, as her own role in society was limited by her gender, thus narrowing the scope of the subject matter available to her. In response to criticism that Austen's novels were too focused on the domestic sphere, revealing a limited knowledge of the world around her, Dorothy Van Ghent (1969) claims that "what she excludes from her fictional material does not reflect a personal obliviousness, but, rather, a critically developed knowledge of the character of her gift and a restriction of its exercise to the kind of subject matter which she could shape into the most significance" (p. 20). Jane Austen was very much aware of the "outside" world around her, but she chose to leave it out of her novels because many aspects, such as politics and war, represent a world dominated by men. She focuses on what she considers the most important and influential subject to the women of her time: home. Marriage is one of the foundations of a home, and she uses Elizabeth and Mr. Darcy's marriage to show how social change must begin. She attacks the patriarchy from the inside, knowing that if women are to ever make progress, they must first be valued in their own domain. Jane Austen was a progressive thinker whose contribution to feminism is best summarized by Robert Polhemus (1990):

> Austen imagines that a woman could be loved for the particular qualities of her mind, that her mental energy could be the focus of her attraction, that her complex psychological vitality, rather than her mere beauty, her sensual appeal, her wealth, her superior virtue, calculated charm, conventional docility, or any of the other traditional feminine allurements, could provoke the fall into love. That configuration opens up a future. (p. 31)

REFERENCES

Austen, Jane. (1973). *Pride and prejudice.* New York: Doubleday. (Original work published 1813)

Cohen, Paula Marantz. (1994, Summer). Jane Austen's rejection of Rousseau: A novelistic and feminist initiation. *Papers on Language and Literature,* pp. 215–234. Full Text Reprint: Expanded Academic ASAP. Available: http://web2.infotrac.galegroup.comlitw/in4!xm_26_0_A15753226

Fields, Suzanne. (1996, March 25). Losing it at the movies with Jane Austen. *Insight on the News, 48*(1). Full Text Reprint: Expanded Academic ASAP. Available: http://web2.infotrac.galegroup.com/itw/inOlxm_1.6_0_A18134562

Green, Katherine. (1991). *The courtship novel, 1740–1820.* Lexington: University Press of Kentucky.

Morrison, Sarah R. (1994, Winter). Of woman borne: Male experience and feminine truth in Jane Austen's novels. *Studies in the Novel,* pp. 337–349. Full Text Reprint: Expanded Academic ASAP. Available: http://web2.infotrac.galegroup.com/itw/in9!xm_24_0_A16~5169

Polhemus, Robert. (1990). *Erotic faith: Being in love from Jane Austen to D. H. Lawrence.* Chicago: University of Chicago Press.

Tanner, Tony. (1986). *Jane Austen.* Cambridge, MA: Harvard University Press.

Van Ghent, Dorothy. (1969). On *Pride and Prejudice*. In E. Rubinstein (Ed.), *Twentieth century interpretations of pride and prejudice* (pp. 19–30). Englewood Cliffs, NJ: Prentice-Hall.

Vicinus, Martha. (1972). Introduction. In M. Vicinus (Ed.), *Suffer and be still: Women in the Victorian age* (p. ix). Bloomington: Indiana University Press.

Wood, James. (1998, August 17). The birth of inwardness: The heroic consciousness of Jane Austen. *The New Republic, 25*(4). Full Text Reprint: Expanded Academic ASAP. Available: http://web2.infotrac.galegroup.com/itw/in23!xm 4_0_A21029355

RELATIONSHIP STAGNATION

Does Calling It Quits Have to Be So Painful?

Patricia Amason and Charon R. Jenkins
UNIVERSITY OF ARKANSAS

Everyone faces relationship conflicts, but most people are not trained or equipped to deal effectively with conflicts. In many instances, interpersonal conflicts are reduced to finger pointing and name calling, each person convinced the problem is "all the other's fault." However, communication theory points out that each person in a relationship contributes to its success or its failure. Each person acts in the relationship, and these acts usually have at least two sets of meanings attached to them—the perspective of the actor and the perspective of the other. In conflicts, these perspectives can diverge a great deal.

The Amason and Jenkins article lays out these issues and others, and then presents a lengthy case study of a relationship in trouble. The case study includes the voices of both people involved. It is an interesting exercise to see how the parties to the relationship describe the same act or event. Who is right? How can they communicate to bring themselves out of this conflict? The article can help students examine their own approaches to interpersonal conflict in a cross-sex relationship and perhaps develop greater empathy for their partner's point of view.

QUESTIONS FOR DISCUSSION

- *Does each sex have an identifiable conflict style? If so, how would you describe it?*
- *What does each sex need to learn in order to handle conflict more effectively?*
- *Is it possible for a relationship to develop rules as to how to have conflicts? If so, would it be easy to follow them during an actual conflict?*
- *What are the most successful strategies you know in dealing with conflict?*

A conflict most persons must confront in their relational history is the dissolution and ultimate termination of a close personal relationship. Much has been written about stages through which relationships proceed as they escalate, break down, and dissolve (Knapp & Vangelisti, 2000; Duck, 1992). All relationships face eventual conflict, and the development of methods for coping with conflict improves the opportunities for relational success.

No matter how hard we try, whether we like it or not, eventually most people have been involved in the unpleasant experience of ending a relationship that does not work out. Because the partners involved individualize each relationship, breakups or relational de-escalations are handled in different ways. The fact that men and women differ in the behaviors that elicit anger and frustration implies that many characteristics of a breakup are a result of gender differences in gender socialization. Whereas a male may be content with the path of a relationship, for instance, the female is constantly working to keep up or conserve the connection. This can be tied back to the parental investments of males and females: Because the woman bears the child and is thought of as the nurturer, male investment tends to be smaller than female investment (Buss, 1989). This may be one reason females are noted as using significantly more direct strategies during a breakup. These may include confronting the other with the completed decision to end the relationship or expressing reasons for ending the relationship. Males are known to use more indirect strategies, such as avoidance or changing the subject (Wilmot, Carbaugh, & Baxter, 1985).

To help navigate through this sometimes rocky period, Duck (1992) proposes a five-phase model of the deterioration. Each of the stages may help clarify what is taking place at a particular point in a relationship. Not all couples will follow this exact pattern; stages may be skipped or revisited.

The first stage is labeled the *dyadic breakdown*. It involves a degeneration of established forms of communicating, whether they are routine or intimate. The partners will experience a rapid or gradual decrease in the amount of interaction they experience.

The second phase of deterioration is the *intrapsychic phase*. According to Duck, this stage involves dwelling on the problems of a relationship; many times partners may consider alternative options to the relationship. This point in the process can become somewhat frustrating as the problems are put under a microscope. The less desirable aspects of the relationship are focused on and become more significant.

The next phase is the *dyadic phase*, which does not always occur. This stage focuses on what methods are used to handle the conflict faced. One or both of the partners may choose to talk or argue about the concerns, or neglect the problems altogether. How this phase is handled is very important to the future of the relationship.

The fourth phase in the deterioration of a relationship is the *social support phase*, which involves seeking comfort and support from the individual's family or friends. The individuals concentrate on a public presentation of the decision, along with concerns such as saving face or placing the blame. This can be beneficial or dangerous to the relationship at hand. It is easy to fall into the trap of relying too much on the opinions of others who are not directly involved in the relationship.

The final phase of the de-escalation process is the *grave dressing phase*, involving all that is necessary for someone putting the relationship to rest and looking to the future without the presence of the former partner. This stage involves a great amount of analyzing exactly what went wrong in the relationship, followed by accepting that it has ended.

Relational de-escalation results from decreased emotional intimacy and self-disclosure, and the use of ineffective conflict management strategies. Partners failing to nurture the waning relationship often choose to dissolve and terminate the relationship by employing various strategies. Baxter (1985) describes four strategies from which persons may choose to disengage from a relationship.

First, persons may *withdraw* from the relationship by reducing the amount of time spent with the partner or the frequency with which they interact. This may be obvious or well hidden. Withdrawal can range anywhere from fewer phone calls to diminishing physical contact. The gradual continuation of this process ultimately results in the relationship's ceasing with many questions left unanswered.

Second, persons may engage in *pseudo de-escalation*, in which they openly express a desire to see less of the partner. In actuality, the desire is to end the relationship completely. The hope is that the partner will be the one to terminate, leaving the actual initiator blameless and without guilt.

The third disengagement strategy is *cost escalation*. Partners weigh the costs and rewards of the relationship. If the costs are perceived to be greater than the rewards, the disengager usually exhibits behaviors that raise the cost factor for the partner. Therefore, the partner terminates because of reduced relational rewards. Confusion and frustration will likely be the end result because of the lack of honest communication.

The last option for disengaging from a relationship is *fading away*. In this instance, the partners both decide to terminate the relationship. They never really discuss it; they just end the relationship by ceasing to see or contact one another. This may be more common when long distance is involved. The mutuality of the decision tends to lead to a less bitter ending.

Unfortunately, there is no such thing as a "perfect relationship." To maintain a strong, healthy relationship, communication skills are necessary. As a relationship evolves, it takes on an identity of its own. Relational partners become closer and work together to strengthen their connection. In most cases, through healthy communication, this can be a positive turn, but there are instances in which the partners can become fixated on the relationship, leading to unhealthy results.

We describe several points of concern in close personal relationships, including deterioration stages and relational termination strategies. To illustrate these concerns, we offer a case study involving Alan and Rita. They met while students attending separate colleges. They were friends for a brief period of time. Several years later, they moved to the same city and became reacquainted through a mutual friend. We first present Alan's story of their relationship and follow with Rita's.

ALAN'S STORY

Rita and I met when we were in college. She went to a school in a different state. I really liked her a lot. I thought it would be great for us to have this cross-state romance. It would be fun, and I thought she was the most beautiful girl I had ever seen. We sent letters and such to one another for a while and talked a few times on the phone. She was less enthusiastic than I was. She had a boyfriend, but was having some problems with him. Maybe this made me want to see her more—like a challenge. The more she resisted, the more interested I was. I became obsessed. She was all I thought about. Eventually, she let me know that the other guy was more important to her. I was crushed and gave up on her.

A few years later, I started a job in another state. A friend of mine told me about this girl he worked with and thought I would like. When he told me her name, I was shocked. It was like Rita had followed me. I took a chance and called her. I was curious to see if she was still "hot." She seemed interested in seeing me, so I asked her to dinner. She looked just like she did when I first met her. The attraction was still there. When I kissed her, it was like I was dreaming. Then I remembered how she had strung me along before, so I didn't want to get too close too soon. I went out with her some, as well as other women. She was fun to be with, and the physical attraction was really strong. Rita was easy to talk to and a great listener. I felt I could tell her things and she would understand. I told her things I had not ever told anyone before. But after I confided in her, I sometimes wondered if I should have done it, so I would wait several days to call her again.

Rita had this great job that she had worked hard to get. I was working on a job that was fairly interesting, but I was not sure what I wanted to do in the future. She had her future all mapped out. She also made a lot more money than I did. This bothered me, but she said it didn't matter to her. On the one hand, I wanted to be with her. On the other, I was not comfortable with our differences. I didn't think my friends would like her because she was so different from them. It was a long time before she met any of them. Most of the time we spent together we were alone. I grew pretty close to her, and in a way, I was really comfortable with her and felt good being with her.

I just wasn't ready to be tied down. I like having time for myself and not having to answer to anyone. I don't like making plans. I just like to wait things out to see what will happen—you know, keep my options open. Rita kept bugging me about making a commitment, and I told her to stop worrying so much. Then I met some-one else I liked, but I never directly told Rita. I hinted around about it, thinking she would catch on, but it took over a year.

My problem was that I liked both of them. They were very different, and our re-lationships were different too. The other girl was a lot of fun, and Rita had become so serious. She kept saying that I seemed distant and asking me if I wanted to stop seeing her. I would just change the subject. I felt really pressured to maintain my re-lationship with Rita. My family really liked her and wanted us to get married. She wanted that too. She was ready to be married, but I wasn't sure I wanted to be mar-ried to her. A lifetime is a long time to be with the same person. I felt really torn, be-cause Rita was a good friend to me and was there for me when I had problems. I thought that if I just backed off a little and took some time, I might be able to make some kind of decision. There was something about her that I just didn't want to let go of, so I still called her, just not as often. She eventually got tired of waiting for me to make a commitment, so she stopped seeing me.

Later, she moved away and took a job in another town. After I found out she was moving, I began to miss her. I tried to see her again, but she didn't seem inter-ested. Once she was gone, I realized I really missed her and wanted to see her. I thought a change of scenery would do me good. I asked her if I should move, too, and if she would take me back. She told me she couldn't give me an answer right away.

Some time later, she called me and asked me if I was ready to make a full com-mitment to her. By then, I had taken a better job, and I had a clearer outlook on my future. We did not live in the same town anymore, and I kept thinking to myself how difficult it would be to be in a serious relationship with someone who was far away. I was not ready to maintain a long-distance relationship with her. She told me that it had to be a full-time, committed relationship with a future, or no relationship at all. I just was not ready for all the demands that come with an exclusive relationship, plus we were just so different; it was too much pressure. We talked for a while longer. She then asked me to hang up the phone first, but I just couldn't do that. After a couple of minutes of silence, she said to me "Have a nice life," then hung up the phone. I felt a great loss, but at the same time I was relieved. I didn't want to be the one to end the relationship. I don't know why she had to have things so final.

RITA'S STORY

The moment I met Alan, I knew my life would never be the same—the attraction was so strong, it took my breath away. I was dating someone at the time and thought about breaking up with him and pursuing a relationship with Alan. It would have been long-distance, though, since we went to different colleges. I just wasn't sure about how successful the relationship would be, and I needed the security I had with my boyfriend, although we were having problems. I eventually ended my relationship with my boyfriend, graduated, and started my career.

Several years went by, and I felt successful in my career after a move to a new job. One of my coworkers told me about a friend of his he thought I should meet. When he told me it was Alan, I couldn't believe my ears. I never forgot about Alan or the way I felt when he was near me. We met again soon after that, and immediately the old feelings were there. I guess you can say I fell in love at my first sight of him. It both scared and excited me. The way he looked at me seemed to say that he felt the same way about me. After a few months, I felt so comfortable with him and grew to love him more each day. I felt I could tell him anything, and I wanted to share my feelings with him. I told him I loved him. His reaction was not what I expected. He said it was a mistake to love him. He was not good for me. I didn't listen to him, though. I thought through my love he could change the way he felt about himself.

After my confession, Alan seemed to keep his distance for a while, both emotionally and physically. I saw him less often, and he stopped disclosing to me. At first, he told me so many things about himself—things I know he kept private from everyone else. At one time he was so open with me, then all of the sudden—wham! He seemed so secretive. The more he withheld, the more desperate I felt for him to be close again. I asked him what was wrong, but he never really gave me an answer. It seemed to make him become even more secretive. Then, without any warning, he would reach out to me again.

Sometimes he seemed so sad and to have a lot of problems, which was emotionally draining for me, but I cared so much about him. I tried to help him feel better and to help him with his problems. Sometimes he let me help, and it felt so good for him to need me. He got extremely close to me for a while. I felt like we had a true relationship. He included me in activities with his family, and I felt like they saw me as a member of their family. I wanted to make a commitment, but was afraid to be direct about that. I did not want to pressure Alan or to give him an ultimatum. Sometimes I felt very safe and comfortable. More often, I was insecure about what he would say, and I did not want him to distance himself, so I didn't press the issue.

Eventually, I began to have problems with my job and really needed Alan for support. This was during a period when he was being distant. I would receive fewer phone calls, and more often than not he was busy and would call me later. He said he needed time for himself. I wondered if he was seeing someone else. I felt like he was not happy with me and wondered what I could do to make things better. I loved him so much and wanted a future with him. He denied that he was seeing someone else and kept telling me to stop worrying, that everything would be fine if I was just patient. I was patient for a couple of years. We had many arguments that left me feeling miserable. Our relationship seemed doomed. I realized it was best for me to give up on the hope that Alan would make a commitment to me. I told him I wanted to end our relationship and began to put it in the past.

A few months later, I was offered a new job in another town. I saw Alan in a restaurant one night and told him I was changing jobs and moving away. After that, he started calling me on a regular basis. He seemed really interested in my plans to move. I was willing to talk to him but was reluctant to see him. I didn't understand his sudden interest, and I didn't want to set myself up for the emotional roller coaster again.

After I moved and was settled in my new job, I was happy in my new life. My job was less stressful, I liked my new home, and I had many great new friends. Alan surprised me by calling me one night. He told me he was unhappy with where he was in his life. He had done a lot of thinking about me and what had happened between us and was sorry for hurting me. He wanted us to be friends again and even suggested that he quit his job and relocate to the city where I now live. At first I was excited about having Alan in my life again. Then I quickly remembered all the arguments, disappointments, and the countless tears I had shed.

I spent some time thinking about his proposition. After a few days, I knew it was time to be direct, so I called him. I asked him to make a long-term commitment to me. I wanted to have a future together. He told me he couldn't do that—he was not ready. Besides, he surprised me by telling me he had been offered a new job and was no longer considering moving. He also said he was unsure how he could manage a long-distance relationship.

I was once again in the position of having to demand closeness while he pulled away. I didn't want that again. I told him that a part-time relationship no longer was possible for me. I knew I had to end the relationship once and for all. I spent three years in limbo waiting for Alan to love me in the way I needed—a wasted three years.

I felt like I had made all the concessions in our relationship, so I wanted him to break the telephone connection. It was too hard for me to do so. Once I said "good-bye," I knew it was forever. Maybe he felt that way, too, because he would not hang up. After a long, very uncomfortable silence, I knew I had to make the move or we would listen to one another breathe all night. I needed closure, so I wished him a nice life and said good-bye.

DISCUSSION

This scenario was designed to provide a fuller, more comprehensive depiction of a waning relationship. We discussed Duck's stages of deterioration, which begins with the *dyadic breakdown stage* involving a decrease in interaction. Not knowing if the communication will decrease rapidly or slowly, one usually notices the change and chooses to address or ignore it. Both partners will make choices, and if the problem is not tended to, in a matter of time the *intrapsychic phase* begins. Time is spent focusing on the negative aspects of the relationship and considering alternatives. Concentrating on the less desirable points of the relationship or the other party may make ending the relationship seem more appealing. By this point in the process, a significant problem has been identified, and choices must be made to determine the final outcome, leading to the *dyadic phase*. This is where the parties involved analyze the different methods that may be used to handle the conflict. Depending on whether the solutions are productive or destructive, this stage will play a large role in the outcome of the relationship. Both partners must be willing to put in the time and effort necessary to avoid the following stages. If a compromise cannot be reached, or one or both of the parties are not willing, the *social support phase* will follow. This stage involves outsiders, such as family and friends. The persons in the relationship look to others for support, opinions, or reasons for the diminishing relationship. Finally, when all is said and done, or not said and done, one might face the *grave dressing phase*. This stage evolves from analyzing exactly what went wrong and who is to blame, if anyone, to ultimately accepting the breakup. Attempts will be made to move on, with the hope that the knowledge gained will make you wiser in the future.

There are many different ways to end a relationship, some definitely better than others. We must accept the fact that we cannot control how other people act, but what we can control are our own actions. Most of us know how painful a breakup can be and, hopefully, would do our best to avoid causing someone else unnecessary pain. The strategies focused on in this article are only a few of the commonly used disengagement tactics.

Withdrawal is a strategy used when the disengager wants to avoid the whole situation. Though the desire may be to end the relationship, withdrawal is used as an easy, not-as-guilty way of building up to the breakup. Without having to face up to the other person, the disengager simply avoids contact, and the couple slowly grows apart.

Another disengagement strategy is *pseudo de-escalation*—expressing a desire to see less of the other person, when the real desire is to end the relationship completely. This strategy may be used to soften the blow of the breakup, when in reality it simply prolongs the waning relationship.

Cost escalation is another covert strategy used to de-escalate a relationship. The person desiring the breakup will act in ways that raise the costs and lessen the rewards of the relationship, hoping that the partner will reconsider the worth of the relationship and initiate the end. This leaves the initiator feeling less guilty because he/she did not actually break up. This strategy can build up hostile feelings and confusion, with the innocent party questioning what caused the change in his/her partner. This can make the grave dressing stage very difficult, with so many questions left unanswered.

Fading away was another strategy discussed; here, the parties involved simply grow apart. The relationship diminishes without any real controversy. Many times this strategy is mutual; for example, the couple realizes they have little in common, or are looking for different things out of life. A long distance can also be a determinant. With this strategy, blame is not as much of an issue.

There is no one perfect strategy to use when attempting to disengage in a relationship; most, if not all, will cause some pain and resentment if the breakup is not mutual. The more covert or devious strategies will most likely cause much more anguish than necessary. By beating around the bush or taking actions to provoke the other party, the initiator is being selfish, thinking only of his/her own solace. What may seem like an easy way out will usually lead to regret later. Alan and Rita needed to use more direct communication about their needs in the relationship and the ways they perceived these needs could be met by one another. When the needs became incompatible, they needed to confront that incompatibility and determine how they might adjust their expectations and behavior. If these adjustments had occurred, perhaps the relationship could have been saved. More likely, the relationship would have been terminated, but with less hurt and resentment. Every relationship is unique, as are both the persons involved. This should be considered when a strategy is chosen to terminate a relationship.

DISCUSSION QUESTIONS

1. Provide examples from Alan's and Rita's stories illustrating Duck's stages of relational de-escalation.
2. Which of Baxter's relational disengagement strategies did Alan employ as his relationship with Rita dissolved? Which did Rita employ? Do you think Alan's choice of strategies is consistent with those typically chosen by males? Do you think Rita's choice of strategies is consistent with those typically chosen by females? Why/why not?
3. What disengagement strategies could each of them have used that might have resulted in a less bitter dissolution?
4. In what ways do you see gender differences present in the ways they viewed their relationship?
5. Provide a description of how Alan managed his relationship with Rita. Do you think this is consistent with how males typically manage their relationships? Why/why not?
6. Provide a description of how Rita managed her relationship with Alan. Do you think this is consistent with how females typically manage their relationships? Why/why not?
7. Now compare your responses in groups comprised of both males and females. How have your gender identities influenced your interpretation of Rita's and Alan's stories?

REFERENCES

Baxter, L. A. (1985). Accomplishing relational disengagement. In S. Duck & D. Perlman (Eds.), *Understanding personal relationships: An interdisciplinary approach* (pp. 243–265). Beverly Hills, CA: Sage.

Buss, D. (1989). Conflict between the sexes: Strategic interference and the evocation of anger and upset. *Journal of Personality and Social Psychology, 56*, 735–747.

Duck, S. (1992). *Human relationships* (2nd ed.). Newbury Park, CA: Sage.

Knapp, M. L., & Vangelisti, A. L. (2000*). Interpersonal communication and human relationships* (4th ed.). Boston: Allyn & Bacon.

Wilmot, W., Carbaugh, D., & Baxter, L. (1985). Communication strategies used to terminate romantic relationships. *Western Journal of Speech Communication, 49*, 204–216.

PERCEIVED PARENTAL COMMUNICATION, GENDER, AND YOUNG ADULTS' SELF-ESTEEM

Male, Female, and Universal Path Models

Lynne M. Webb
UNIVERSITY OF ARKANSAS

Kandi L. Walker
UNIVERSITY OF LOUISVILLE

Tamara S. Bollis
COLUMBUS STATE UNIVERSITY

Aparna G. Hebbani
UNIVERSITY OF PITTSBURGH—JOHNSTOWN

This article is the most research-oriented essay in this reader. It is included both as an example of how research on gender is done and because it deals with a topic that is critical to understanding the development of gender identity. We omitted pages that reported outcomes of complex statistical analyses to encourage readers to focus on the authors' interpretation of the findings and to promote classroom discussion of the topic itself. Because we view gender as socially constructed, it is useful to explore the role of parental communication in the development of gender and identity in children. Most students in any given gender communication class intend to become parents, and discussion about the role of parental communication can be very instructive.

Webb and her colleagues developed research questions around patterns of interaction in the family and the effect of these patterns on identity and gender. Their hypotheses are useful for each student to consider in relation to his/her own experiences. In addition, the article can generate a good deal of discussion on the relationship of parenting to gender.

QUESTIONS FOR DISCUSSION

- *Should parents communicate differently with female children and with male children?*
- *How might a parent communicate with a child so as to reduce the possibility of gender stereotyping?*
- *Do men and women have fundamentally different roles in communication with their children? If so, what are they?*
- *It is possible for a family to develop a conscious pattern of interaction among family members? What would an effective pattern look like?*

Children learn basic interaction patterns through communication in the family. Their family communication patterns, particularly parental behavior, determine how children will think about communicative interactions when they reach adulthood (Bruner, 1990; Turner & West, 2002; Vangelisti, 1993). Given that family communication has such far-reaching impact, the topic of family communication has received considerable attention from scholars in several disciplines (Bush, 2000; Cardinali & D'Allura, 2001; DeHart, Murray, & Pelham, 2003).

The communication field began publishing research on family interactions with the 1972 McLeod and Chaffee article (Tims & Masland, 1986). McLeod and Chaffee (1972) examined how perceived parental communication serves as the source of adolescents' views of their social reality. Following McLeod and Chaffee's research, several lines of investigation on parent-child communication emerged (Fitzpatrick & Vangelisti, 1995; Midgett, Ryan, Adams, & Corville-Smith, 2002; Noller & Callan, 1990; Ritchie & Fitzpatrick, 1990; Socha & Stamp, 1995). One of these emerging lines of research explored the influence of parental communication on the development of adolescents' self-esteem (e.g., Barber, Chadwick, & Oerter, 1992; Blake & Slate, 1993; Buri, Murphy, Richtmeier, & Komar, 1992; Chartier & Chartier, 1975; Demo, Small, & Savin-Williams, 1987; Desselle & Pearlmutter, 1997; Gecas & Schwalbe, 1986; Huang, 1999; Lanza-Kaduce & Webb, 1992; Quatman & Watson, 2001; Reuter & Webb, 1992).

PURPOSE OF THE STUDY

The purpose of the present investigation was to test a model that explicates the influence of perceived parental communication on the self-esteem of young adults. This investigation extended the Chartier and Chartier (1975) study by applying their methodology to test the potential influence of additional perceptual variables that may influence perceived parental communication or mediate its influence on self-esteem. The present study examined the potential influence of perceptions of family communication on perceived parental communication as well as on the self-esteem of male and female young adults. The researchers defined the term *gender* throughout the paper as the biological sex of respondents. The term *gender* was used for consistency with its usage in prior literature.

This paper is divided into six sections: (1) parental communication and self-esteem, (2) gender and parental communication, (3) research questions with appropriate literature, (4) methods, (5) results, and (6) discussion. The paper concludes by suggesting ideas for future research.

PARENTAL COMMUNICATION AND SELF-ESTEEM

Research across several disciplines has investigated the influence of parental communication on children's self-esteem. Some of these studies have examined the influence of parental communication on young children (e.g., Cooper, Homan, & Braithwaite, 1983; Felson & Zielinksi, 1989; Hoglund & Bell, 1991; Schor, Stidley, & Malspeirs, 1995), but most of the studies focus on the development of self-esteem during adolescence (Bush, 2000; Bush, Peterson, & Cobas, 2002; Herz & Gullone, 1999) and young adulthood (Cardinali & D'Allura, 2001; Huang, 1999; Leondari & Kiosseoglou, 2000). Studies linking perceived parental communication and adolescent self-esteem have examined a variety of potentially problematic or extraordinary situations, including depression (Luthar & Quinlan, 1993; Sturkie & Flanzer, 1987; Vella, Persic, & Lester, 1996), divorce (Bynum & Durm, 1996; Thomas, Booth-Butterfield, & Booth-Butterfield, 1995), loneliness (Brage, Meredith, & Woodward, 1993), parental verbal abuse (Blake & Slate, 1993), income level (Peterson, Southworth, & Peters, 1983), and children with disabilities (Cardinali & D'Allura, 2001; Crowley & Taylor, 1994). Other research has examined the influence on self-esteem of specific parental behaviors, such as authoritativeness (Buri & Dickinson, 1994), support (Felson & Zielinski, 1989), nurturance (Buri, Kirschner, & Walsh, 1987; Buri et al., 1992), and control (Demo et al., 1987).

Much research has focused on the influence of parental communication on adolescent self-esteem; far fewer studies have examined the same relationship among young adults (Cardinali & D'Allura, 2001; Huang, 1999; Klein, O'Bryant, & Hopkins, 1996; Luthar & Quinlan, 1993). Therefore, the present authors consulted and presented the relevant research on adolescents in addition to young adults as a background and tentative guideline for our study.

Among the first in the field of communication to publish a study examining the relationship between parental communication and self-esteem were Chartier and Chartier (1975).[1] They reported that "the degree to which a young adult perceives his [or her] parents' communication as constructive is significantly related to his [or her] level of self-esteem" (1975, p. 27). Similarly, Lanza-Kaduce and Webb (1992) argued that "perceived parental communication patterns hold the potential to be important determinants in the social outcomes (such as the development of self-esteem) of the parent-adolescent relationship" (p. 2). The present authors reasoned that the likelihood of the young adult's reporting a positive self-image is greater when he/she has positive perceptions of his/her parents' communication.

A more recent study reached similar conclusions: Buri et al. (1992) studied the effects of parental nurturance as a predictor of self-esteem throughout the adolescent and young adult years. They concluded that psychological nurturance from parents is a strong predictor of adolescent self-esteem in the junior high school years, and it remains a predictor of self-esteem throughout the subsequent high school years. Similarly, Blake and Slate (1993) examined the potential influence of numerous variables (e.g., perceptions of verbal abuse, type of primary caretakers, and gender) upon adolescents' self-esteem. They concluded that the perceived quality of parental verbal interactions related to the adolescent's self-esteem. Parents perceived as having high levels of positive verbal interactions with their children tend to raise confident adolescents who like themselves. On the other hand, parents perceived as having low levels of positive communication tend to raise adolescents who develop low self-esteem.

Segrin and Menees (1996) found that social support from family was significantly related to self-esteem. Other family communication variables related to self-esteem include coping styles of family, problem solving, and denial of feelings. Enger, Howerton, and Cobbs (1994) found that students with high self-esteem perceived communication with parents to be more positive. Similarly, Leondari and Kiosseoglou (2000) found that young adults with secure attachments to and healthy separation from parents report higher self-esteem and less loneliness. Avison and McAlpine (1992) found higher levels of self-esteem among young adults, especially girls, when parents were perceived as caring.

The very foundation of self-esteem appears to emerge in the family (Adams, Gullotta, & Markstrom-Adams, 1994). Pipp and Robinson (1985) studied adolescents' constructs of self, parents, and peers. Results demonstrated that "adolescents' sense of self was related to concepts of mother, father . . . as well as their understandings of the relationships with each" (p. 12). The main way adolescents can interpret the relationship with their parents is through parental communication.

Harter (1990) defined self-esteem as "how much a person likes, accepts, and respects himself [sic] overall as a person" (p. 255). Green (1995) posited that "self-esteem, the value and worth an individual places on one's self, influences every aspect of life" (p. 7). Low self-esteem has been correlated with low life satisfaction, loneliness, anxiety, resentment, irritability, and depression (Rosenberg, 1965), along with aggression and social problems (Kirkpatrick, Waugh, Valencia, & Webster, 2002). High self-esteem has been correlated with academic success in high school, internal locus of control, higher family income, and positive sense of self-attractiveness (Haney & Durlak, 1998).

Although researchers have studied the effect of family communication environment on self-esteem, especially among adolescents, few have accessed gender differences in this regard. Loeb, Horst, and Horton (1980) found "the family climate associated with self-esteem in pre-adolescents appears to be one in which: (a) both mother and father are supportive of their child and of each other; (b) opposite sex parent-child relationships are relatively demanding while same-sex relationships are not; (c) for girls, parents do not employ highly directive behavior, but fathers are highly involved in particular about which of the daughter's behaviors they reward; for boys fathers refrain from highly directive or intrusive behavior, while mothers play a relatively directive role with their sons" (pp. 215–216).

GENDER AND PARENTAL COMMUNICATION

Via communication, mother-child and father-child dyads may enact different roles during different stages of a child's life. For example, "in the 7th grade, children are more likely to share their father's perceptions of how much pressure there is toward conformity and their mother's perceptions of how much open conversation there is in the family. By the 11th grade, these relationships have reversed" (Ritchie & Fitzpatrick, 1990, p. 539). Although parents exhibit gender-specific behaviors to children, Blake and Slate (1993) reported that adolescents' perceptions of parental communication did not differ significantly by gender.

Papini, Farmer, Clark, Micka, and Barnett (1990) examined age and gender differences in patterns of adolescents' emotional self-disclosure to parents and friends among 174 junior high school students (67 male and 107 female) in grades 7 through 9. Results were consonant with previous research revealing a pattern of adolescent age and gender differences in emotional self-disclosure to parents and best friends. They found that females disclosed significantly more information to parents and best friends than males. Twelve-year-old adolescents preferred to emotionally disclose to parents, compared to 15-year-old adolescents, who preferred to disclose to friends. The findings can be interpreted to mean that emotional disclosure to parents is associated with adolescent perceptions of the quality of family communication and functioning, with disclosure increasing if adolescents perceive parents as warm, caring, and open to discussion. Lanza-Kaduce and Webb (1992) found no relationship between males' self-esteem and perceived parental communication.

Fitzpatrick and Vangelisti (1995) cited studies by Gecas and Schwalbe (1986) and Openshaw, Thomas, and Rollins (1984) that documented parental gender-based behaviors. Boys who were encouraged to be independent and whose parents exerted little control exhibited high self-esteem compared to those who were strongly dependent and were controlled by their parents. In contrast, self-esteem among girls was strongly correlated with the levels of support and nurturance they received from their parents, and was little affected by level of control.

Studies specifically examining self-esteem in relation to perceived parental communication yielded differing gender-related results. Demo et al. (1987) examined parent-adolescent communication and dimensions of parent-adolescent interaction that predicted parents' self-esteem. The authors found that sons' levels of self-esteem were directly related to the relationships with their parents.

Wu and Smith (1997) conducted a study using the self-perception profile for children (used to measure self-esteem) to examine the relationship between gender, age, and self-esteem in 280 Taiwanese children (11 to 13 years of age). The study examined scholastic experience, social acceptance, athletic competence, physical appearance, behavioral conduct, and global self-worth. The authors hypothesized that Taiwanese children's perceptions of their scholastic competence and behavioral conduct would be related to their self-worth. They also hypothesized that physical appearance would be unrelated to Taiwanese children's global self-worth. The construct of behavioral conduct was important to examine because, unlike in U.S. culture, children are taught to respect their elders and accept their authority without question. The Chinese culture also places strong emphasis on formal education because academic achievement will likely result in personal advancement, wealth, respect, and higher social status (Lum & Char, 1985).

Results yielded significant gender and age effects in self-esteem. Boys reported greater confidence in physical appearance, whereas girls expressed greater satisfaction with their behavioral conduct. The findings of this study were compared to those reported by Harter (1985) using U.S. samples. The results were consistent with the U.S. findings that girls report better behavior than boys, whereas boys report superior athleticism. Analysis revealed no significant difference between boys' and girls' scores on the scholastic competence dimension; the author's explanation for this finding is that the children participating in the study may have been too young to perceive their parents' differential expectations.

What is the relationship between parenting, gender, and self-esteem when the adolescent is adopted? Wrobel (1990) conducted a ten-year follow-up study to examine the self-esteem of 78 black transracially adopted adolescents (42 male and 36 female) and 30 white siblings (16 male and 14 female), as well as the parents (60 fathers and 68 mothers). Results were consistent with previous research and indicated that placement history did not influence self-esteem; instead, perceptions of communication—specifically, communication with the mother—was correlated with self-esteem. This finding was also consistent across gender.

Chubb, Fertman, and Ross (1997) also investigated the relationship of self-esteem and locus of control to gender and age. They surveyed 174 adolescent students (average age 15 years, 41% male, 59% female) in the ninth grade each spring over four years, thereby gathering longitudinal data. According to the authors, given that adolescence is a tumultuous time, perhaps personality variables such as self-esteem and locus of control could change as teenagers struggle moving toward adulthood. Locus of control is the generalized expectancy of reinforcement as either internal or external to the self. Internal locus of control is the expectation that reinforcement is the result of one's own effort, ability, characteristics, or behavior; external locus of control is the expectation that reinforcement is the result of chance, fate, luck, or powerful others (p. 116). The analyses revealed a significant main effect for gender, with lower self-esteem scores for girls; gender differences in self-esteem peaked in the ninth grade. The authors reported a clear trend toward less external locus of control for each year of high school, with no significant differences between male and female respondents.

Brage et al. (1993) investigated loneliness in relation to depression, self-esteem, family strengths, parent-adolescent communication, age, and gender. The sample for this study consisted of 156 Midwestern adolescents (62 males, 94 females), ages 11 to 18, attending public schools. The analyses revealed significant differences in loneliness scores between male and female adolescents, as well as a significant relationship between loneliness, age, depression, self-esteem, family strengths, and parent-adolescent communication. The study found a significant relationship between loneliness and family strengths, and that older adolescents were lonelier than younger adolescents.

Walitzer and Sher (1996) examined the relationship between self-esteem and alcohol in young men and women during the college years. The authors first examined the relationship of alcohol problems and self-esteem over time with respect to gender, and then examined the ability of self-esteem to predict future alcohol problems as well as the ability of alcohol problems to predict future self-esteem. The subjects for this study were 457 adults (217 males, 240 females) who participated in a longitudinal project to examine characteristics associated with first-degree history of alcoholism. Overall levels of self-reported alcohol use were relatively stable over the course of the longitudinal study. Analyses revealed that women who had an alcohol use disorder during the third and fourth years showed relatively low levels of self-esteem throughout the period under study. Findings also supported the hypothesis that low self-esteem plays a particularly important role in clinical alcohol problems for women, but not for men. Individuals without Alcohol Use Disorder scored relatively high and similarly in levels of self-esteem. There was minimal evidence that suggested alcohol use predicts later self-esteem.

Munford (1994) studied the relationship of gender, self-esteem, social class, and racial identity to depression, specifically in the black population, thus extending and replicating research by Pyant and Yanico (1991). The subjects in this study were 146 students (96 males, 50 females) from a university and 83 adults (60 males, 23 females) from the general population, varying in age from 18 to 75 years. Overall, results of this study supported the hypothesis that higher depression scores are associated with lower self-esteem. Gender was a significant predictor of depression for the overall population, but analyses failed to find a significant difference in male and female depression and self-esteem scores. The author stated that attending a predominantly black university may help raise females' level of self-esteem and lower their level of depression (Munford, 1994, p. 171).

RESEARCH QUESTIONS WITH APPROPRIATE LITERATURE

RQ1: Does perceived parental communication influence young adults' self-esteem?

Perceptions of family communication may be important in predicting the self-esteem of both adolescents and their parents (Demo et al., 1987; Papini et al., 1990). Perceptions of the mother's self-disclosure and the father's level of regard have both been found to correlate with self-esteem in young adults (Reuter & Webb, 1992). However, one might reasonably ask, why study *perceptions* of parental interactions rather than actual interactions?

The present authors offer three rationales for studying perceptions of family communication versus actual communicative behavior that may in turn influence perceptions: (1) Perceptions of communicative phenomena have a greater impact on the individual than do the actual observable behaviors, if one assumes that negotiated meaning in communicative interactions is created through the various interpretations of the individuals involved. (2) Similarly, assessing perception becomes paramount when adopting the view that the receiver's perception is the communicated message. Adolescents may perceive parents' communicative behaviors differently than the parents and/or an objective observer. For example, Niemi (1968) found that parents minimize differences between parents' and children's attitudes; in contrast, adolescents exaggerate the differences in attitudes between parents and children. Other research elaborates on this perception of differences within the family's communication (Demo et al., 1987; Gecas & Schwalbe, 1986; Tims & Masland, 1986). In another contemporary study, Noller and Callan (1990) examined adolescents' perceptions of their interactions with their parents; "the results suggested that mothers' more frequent initiation of discussions with their younger adolescents and their greater recognition of their opinions lead to older adolescents interacting more with mothers than fathers" (pp. 349–350). (3) "If it is assumed that the adolescent's perceptions of the family members reflect parents' actual behavior toward the adolescent, it is sufficient to query adolescents about their parents, and then to examine the association these data have with the adolescents' self appraisals" (Margolin, Blyth, & Carbone, 1988, p. 212). For all these reasons, the present authors investigated parent-child interactions by examining young adults' perceptions of those interactions.

Perceived Consistency of Family Interactions

RQ 2 & 6: Does perceived consistency of family interactions correlate with (a) young adults' self-esteem and/or (b) young adults' evaluations of their perceived parental interactions?

Most parents agree that being "consistent" with their children is important, but several meanings of the phrase "parental consistency" have been identified. Some parents equate consistency with following a regular routine or schedule. Others report that consistency means employing the same discipline each time a specific behavior occurs. Still other parents view consistency in terms of following through with promises or threats (Reid & Valsiner, 1986).

Scholars typically use the phrase "parental consistency" to refer to consistency of parental discipline (Gardner, 1989; Scheck, Emerick, & El-Assal, 1973) in terms of method, parental agreement, and whether the discipline is consistent among the children. Although discipline is not the type of parental consistency addressed by the present study, it is nonetheless a frequent type of parent-child interaction. For the purpose of this study, we conceptualized consistency as the similarity of treatment a young adult experiences by one or both parents in a range of situations (Fischer & Fischer, 1986).

The opposite of consistency, "parental inconsistency," has come to mean "the use of disparate practices across time and between parents" (Gardner, 1989, p. 223). Because parents are a child's primary role models, it is logical to conclude that inconsistent parental behaviors may negatively influence children (Alain, 1989). Parental inconsistency has been examined in terms of the incongruity between what parents say and what they do. Alain concluded that this type of parental inconsistency is upsetting (e.g., "causes worry") for both male and female adolescents. There are, of course, occasions and extraordinary circumstances that prevent parents from exhibiting consistent behaviors. However, if parents are continuously inconsistent, Owens (1995) claimed that the child quickly learns not to trust the authority of the parents or comply with their requests. Brand, Crous, and Hanekom (1990) suggested that inconsistencies can reinforce undesired behaviors and affect emotional development.

In terms of family communication, Murrell and Stackowiak (1967) defined "intrafamily consistency" as "a stable pattern of frequency of 'who talks to whom' in families over different situations and over time" based on the assumption that family interaction patterns are basically stable (p. 267). Interactional consistency also can be displayed in the choice of strategies used in conversations (e.g., compliance-gaining strategies) (Levine & Wheeless, 1990). This current conceptualization of interactional consistency within families provides an empirical foundation for the theoretical notion of the family as a social system (as systems display a degree of regularity). Scholars disagree, however, on which family members tend to be the most consistent (or inconsistent). For example, Murrell and Stackowiak (1967) found that mothers sent the most consistent messages to other family members. However, a later study concluded that adolescent boys perceive their mothers as being more inconsistent with discipline than their fathers (Scheck & Emerick, 1976).

Children benefit from some forms of parental consistency (Reid & Valsiner, 1986). For example, parents can aid in their children's socialization process by practicing consistency in discipline (Gardner, 1989). Parents can achieve this type of consistency by exhibiting reactions to their child's behavior that are both predictable and reliable (Owens, 1995). Similarly, consistency can be enacted by limiting the number and type of rules but consistently enforcing the remaining rules (Owens, 1995). Owens reported that this type of rule consistency promotes voluntary compliance as well as trust. Established routines, rules, and patterns of interaction help "children feel that their environment is dependable and that parents are reliable and trustworthy" (p. 43). The present authors examined the level of consistency in family communication—specifically, fathers' communication with mothers, mothers' communication with fathers, father's communication with respondent, and mother's communication with respondent.

Gender and Self-Esteem

RQ 10–13: How does the gender of parents and the respondents influence young adults' self-esteem (i.e., mothers to daughters, mothers to sons, fathers to daughters, fathers to sons)?

Consistently, self-esteem differs for males and females (Quatman & Watson, 2001). A possible explanation for gender differences in self-esteem is gender role socialization. Many studies document that American children are socialized to behave in a sex-role stereotypic manner (Adler, Kless, & Adler, 1992; Bardwell, Cochran, & Walker, 1986; Caldera, Huston, & O'Brien, 1989; Pleck, 1981; Pomerleau, Bolduc, Malcuit, & Cossett, 1990). For example, stereotypical colors (pink or yellow for girls, blue for boys) for a child's room, as well as clothes, may contribute to the development of preferential activities and abilities in children (Pomerleau et al., 1990). Parents may reinforce sex-specific behaviors via communication patterns. Fagot and Lienbach (1989) found that when parents provide positive and negative responses to sex-type toys, children become early labelers of gender. Likewise, parents tended to respond positively to girls who displayed adult-oriented, dependent behavior and negatively to active, gross motor activities (Fagot, 1978). Similarly, parents may reinforce different self-esteem values for male versus female children.

Spence and Hall (1996) investigated three models of gender constructs: children's gender-related perceptions, activity preferences, and occupational stereotypes. The subjects (197 boys and 271 girls, predominantly from white middle-class backgrounds) completed a simplified version of the Personal Attributes Questionnaire (PAQ), subsets of items from Boldizar's (1991) Assessing Sex Typing and Androgyny in Children, the children's version of the Bem (1974) Sex Role Inventory, and self-esteem measured by three of Harter's (1985) scales. They found that girls endorsed both masculine and feminine stereotypes to a significantly lesser degree than boys, congruent with the general finding that males are more bound to traditional gender ideologies than females. The male versus female means did not differ on the three Harter self-esteem scales.

Most of the research in the area of self-esteem has been conducted exclusively in Western countries—North America and Australia in particular. Research results indicate that many characteristics of age and gender have a universal, physiological basis. At the ages of 8–9 years, there is a marked increase in brain cells leading to the development of higher cognitive processes; additionally, the physiological changes leading to puberty that begin at this time may affect boys' and girls' perception of self (Watkins, Dong, & Xia, 1997).

In 1997, Watkins, Dong, and Xia investigated age and gender differences among 303 male and 296 female 10-year-old children, as well as 116 male and 116 female 13-year-old children, attending Chinese public schools. Their results indicated that older girls tended to report significantly lower self-esteem than both the younger girls and the older boys in the areas of physical abilities, reading, mathematics, and gender self-concept. According to the authors, in Chinese society, there has been a bias in favor of male children, but observers have reported no evidence of differential treatment favoring boys in the Chinese classroom.

Smith and Self (1977) studied gender as it relates to perceptions of self-esteem. They hypothesized that in a situation where one must evaluate potential worth in a crisis moment, men would evaluate themselves more positively than women in regard to perceived contribution. Their results showed that males possess higher degrees of self-esteem than females. They contend that there are other dimensions of socialization besides the "favorable societal evaluation of masculinity that might account for the difference in self-esteem" (p. 3). They posited that men are encouraged to develop skills such as mechanical or intellectual that aid them in manipulating and adapting to the environment. Women, on the other hand, develop more expressive skills that do not influence self-esteem.

Michaelieu (1997) examined the relationship between female identity and self-esteem in young adult college females. A strong sense of female identity was found to have a positive correlation with self-esteem. Results also showed that gendered parenting had a significant and positive relationship with self-esteem. Michaelieu contended that "women's self-esteem appeared to be enhanced by exploring and consolidating their views of being female, as well as by viewing gender as a prominent and positive aspect of their self-identity" (p. 331). Also, parenting practices that emphasized pride in being female and encouraged nonstereotypical female conduct influenced a strong sense of female identity.

Perceived Favoritism and Self-Esteem

RQ 3 & 7: Does the self-esteem of young adults who perceived themselves as parental favorites differ significantly from the self-esteem of young adults who perceived siblings as parental favorites? Do favorites versus nonfavorites differ significantly in their perceptions of their parental communication?

Psychological theorists have linked parental favoritism to identity formation and personality development. Freud (1870) posited that being the favorite child leads to increased self-confidence. Other early researchers such as Adler (1932) wrestled with the question of whether parental favoritism may harm the unfavored child. Despite early interest in the subject, scientists have published only a handful of studies on parental favoritism in the past 35 years.

Defining parental favoritism as "the preference of a parent for one child over another" (1983, p. 45), Harris and Howard asked high school students which child (if any) was the favorite of each parent in his/her immediate family. Results indicated that female respondents perceived far more parental favoritism than did males, regardless of family size. In addition, respondents who were the youngest child in their family reported that they were the favorite child of both their mother and father more often than did older siblings.

Kiracofe and Kiracofe (1990) found that more than two-thirds of their study participants believed that they were the favorite child of one parent or both parents. Respondents, especially female respondents, perceived fathers as more likely than mothers to have a favorite child. In a replication of the Kiracofe and Kiracofe study, Chalfant (1994) found that young adults perceived parental favoritism most frequently in the opposite-sex parent.

Zervas and Sherman (1993) replicated the only previous study examining perceived parental favoritism and self-esteem (Neale, 1986). Although Neale's study revealed no significant differences in self-esteem between favored and unfavored children, Zervas and Sherman found that the respondents who reported either being the favorite child or perceiving no favoritism by his/her parents had significantly higher self-esteem than the unfavored respondents. Zervas and Sherman's respondents reported that parents' most common method of displaying favoritism was giving the favored child more attention. Zervas and Sherman suggested furthering this line of research to examine how other variables may influence the relationship between perceived parental favoritism and self-esteem.

Communicative Normalcy and Self-Esteem

RQ 4 & 8: Does the degree of perceived normalcy of family interactions co-vary with young adults' level of self-esteem? Does perceived normalcy co-vary with their perceptions of parental communication?

Fitzpatrick and Badzinski (1994) recommended that the notion of family "normalcy" be reexamined in scholarly endeavors. The ambiguity inherent in the word "normal" makes it difficult to develop a direct assessment of the variable. An original and rather primitive research definition of family normalcy was based on the absence of disease and/or dysfunction. For example, Murrell and Stackowiak (1967) use the term "normal" to refer to families that are not psychologically "disturbed." Their study explored assumptions once common among clinicians that (a) family interaction patterns tend to be consistent over time and across situations and (b) "normal" families more rigidly maintain interaction patterns. Murrell and Stackowiak used "clinic families" as the "disturbed" group and "nonclinical families" as the "normal group." The authors operationally defined the "normal group" as "families in which the children were considered to be well-adjusted, normally achieving children" (p. 266).

Vangelisti (1993) explained that "relational prototypes" provide individuals with "models or 'schemas' for their interpersonal associations" (p. 43). These prototypes "influence (and are influenced by) the communication that occurs within those relationships" (p. 43). Individuals can develop relational prototypes about family relationships by observing other families in real interactions and via media, as in family images from television and print media. Through comparisons to prototypes, individuals can determine to what extent they perceive their family as "normal."

The present authors did not attempt to discover what types of interactions are normal for American families. Instead, we assumed that our respondents would perceive a wide variety of interaction patterns as normal. However, we reasoned that most individuals have a mental image of a "normal" American family interaction. Further, we believed that individuals base this image of normalcy for American family interactions on observations of their families, other families in real life, and/or families observed via mass media. Self-esteem may be correlated with perceived normalcy of the interactions in one's family.

Perceived Parental Attention and Family Interactions

RQ 5 & 9: Do young adults' perceptions of their parental interactions vary with reported attention received from parents? Does self-esteem vary with young adults' perceptions of the attention they received from parents?

Research on parental involvement typically examines children's academic performance (Owens, 1995; Stevenson et al., 1990). For example, Owens explicated three types of academic parental involvement: cognitive/intellectual, personal, and behavioral.[2] Although the current authors acknowledge the importance of a child's academic performance, we focused on an alternative aspect of parental involvement—specifically, the respondent's perception of the proportion of free time each parent spent with him/her. Wenk, Hardesty, Morgan, and Blair (1994) posited that perceived parental involvement is important to a child's well-being: "Children's perceptions of parental involvement seem to be salient in determining how a child feels about him/herself and his/her life" (p. 234). Gecas and Schwalbe (1986) found that girls' self-esteem is strongly correlated with the participation and support of their mothers and fathers. We defined attention as percentage of free time the parents spent with the respondent.

METHOD

Respondents

Data were collected from 319 undergraduate students attending a large, public, urban university in the southern United States. The respondents (Rs) were students in 35 homogenous sections of a sophomore-level basic course in oral communication and received extra credit for their participation. Because the course was a graduation requirement for every student at the university, the sample represented a wide variety of the student body.

Nielson and Metha (1994) noted one limitation in the literature regarding parental behavior and adolescent self-esteem: a bias toward studying only "normal" adolescents. In contrast, the present sample was broadly drawn, and the authors made no effort to exclude Rs on the basis of "normalcy" or "abnormalcy."

To ensure that the sample represented young adults and was consonant with Chartier and Chartier's 1975 sample, only Rs age 24 and younger were included in the research sample used in the subsequent analyses. Thus, the remaining 245 Rs ranged in age from 18 to 24 years, with a mean age of 20.81 years.

The sample contained 42% males and 58% females. Although the majority of the Rs were Caucasian (67%), more than one quarter (26%) were African American. At least three additional ethnic backgrounds were represented in the sample: 2% Asian American, 2% Hispanic, 1% Native American, and 2% other. Students from each class rank participated in the study: 29% freshmen, 37% sophomores, 20% juniors, and 14% seniors.

The Rs represented a variety of family backgrounds. A majority (70%) were raised by the mother and father of origin, but 16% were raised by single mothers, 1% by single fathers, 10% by mothers and stepfathers, 1% by fathers and stepmothers, and 2% in other family configurations (e.g., raised by grandmother or with aunt and uncle). Ten percent ($N = 25$) of the Rs were only children, but most (90%; $N = 217$) reported having siblings. Additionally, Rs reported varied present living arrangements (38% with parents, 30% in on-campus housing, 29% independently in a house or apartment, and 3% other).

Materials

Each R completed a questionnaire packet containing an informed consent form, an instruction page, and five instruments to assess the variables of interest: (1) the Barrett-Lennard Relationship Inventory, (2) the Revised Family Communication Pattern Instrument, (3) the Coopersmith Self-Esteem Inventory, (4) the Memphis Family Perceptions Instrument, and (5) the demographics questionnaire. The questionnaire packet began with a statement of agreement to participate that Rs were asked to sign. Next came a page of general instructions for the packet. Additionally, each instrument in the packet contained individual directions. Next came the instruments themselves. The instruments were counterbalanced across packets to address potential order effects. Each questionnaire was printed on a different color paper to ease in the assembly of counterbalanced packets and to minimize test fatigue.

Like Chartier and Chartier (1975), we used the Barrett-Lennard Relationship Inventory (RI) to assess the communicative relationship between the Rs and their parents. Barrett-Lennard (1964) provided evidence of the RI's reliability and content validity. The instrument consisted of 85 descriptive statements about how one person effectively responds to another. The 85 items in the RI are worded such that the Rs assessed their relationship with one individual (as opposed to instruments assessing the relationship with "parents" in general). Thus, the instrument assessed the Rs' perceived communication with each parent individually. Furthermore, the present researchers believe that the scales included in the RI (level of regard, empathetic understanding, congruence, unconditionality of regard, and willingness to be known) assess communication variables that are central to the parent-child relationship, even into adulthood. Barrett-Lennard stated that the RI can assess nontherapeutic relationships because the "response qualities are significantly associated with alternative criteria of the adequacy of interpersonal relationships" (p. 32).

The RI included scales measuring level of regard, empathetic understanding, congruence, unconditionality of regard, and willingness to be known. *Level of regard* refers to the degree of respect, liking, appreciation, and affection that the parent demonstrates to her/his child. *Empathetic understanding* is the extent to which the parent interprets his/her child's outward communication through the child's awareness. *Congruence* refers to the degree to which the parent is honest, direct, and sincere with her/his child; hereafter, we refer to this factor as *forthrightness*. *Unconditionality of regard* is defined as the variability or constancy of the parent's affective response to his/her child. *Willingness to be known* is the degree to which the parent is willing to self-disclose to her/his child.

The researchers counterbalanced the eight pages of the RI to compensate for order effects. The Rs were directed to complete the measure based on their "present relationship with your mother/father." Space was provided at the end of each RI statement for two ratings: one for the mother and one for the father. Rs were requested to leave the appropriate slot blank if one or both parents were absent. Following data collection, a summary RI score for father and another for mother were computed for each R and used in subsequent analyses. Summary RI scores were calculated by summing the five scores for the individual factors relevant to a given parent.

The Coopersmith Self-Esteem Inventory (SEI) assessed the Rs' self-esteem. Two separate forms of the SEI are available. Form B consists of 13 items based on an item analysis of Form A, which consists of 58 items. The total scores on Forms A and B correlate 0.86 (Coopersmith, 1967). For this investigation, Form B was eliminated, along with 25 items from Form A that referred to the needs and characteristics of children. Coopersmith reported evidence to support both the reliability and validity of the SEI.

The Memphis Family Perceptions Instrument (MFPI) was used to assess Rs' perception of three aspects of family dynamics: attention from parents, normalcy of family interactions, and consistency of family interactions. The MFPI asked Rs to recall the percentage of free time that each parent had spent with them while they were growing up. Questions assessed perceptions of how "normal" their family's interactions were compared to most American families as well as to other families they knew. Questions also assessed Rs' perception of the extent to which their parents interacted with them in a consistent manner from one day to the next. Lastly, questions assessed the amount of consistency the Rs perceived in their parents' interactions with each other. Bollis-Pecci and Webb (1997) offered evidence of the MFPI's reliability and validity.

A demographics questionnaire, written by the authors, assessed age, gender, ethnic background, educational level, family configuration (single mother, single father, biological mother and father living together, stepfather and biological mother, stepmother and biological father, stepmother alone, stepfather alone, or other), living arrangements, and the number and types of siblings.

Parental favoritism was assessed in two questions developed by the researchers and presented on the second page of the demographics questionnaire. The questions asked Rs if each parent had a favorite among his/her children and whether the favorite was the R, an older sibling, or a younger sibling. Parental favoritism was assessed in the demographics questionnaire rather than in the MFPI for two reasons: (1) Queries on parental favoritism logically followed the questions on number of siblings. (2) Such a placement avoided the inclusion of value-laden statements potentially prompting the Rs' mind-set to color responses to related attitudinal measures.

Procedures

The authors obtained approval from appropriate committees on the use of human subjects prior to data collection. Further, the authors obtained permission to recruit

Rs from the director of the multi-section basic communication course as well as the individual instructors of the 42 sections.

Four graduate students in communication recruited Rs in individual classrooms using the following protocol: At the beginning of the class, they asked students to come at their convenience to a designated test site to complete a questionnaire packet. In the announcement, students were informed that participation was voluntary and they would receive a small amount of extra credit for participating. However, the announcement clearly stated that no penalty would be assessed for not participating. A flyer listing the dates, times, and location of the test administration was distributed to the students.

Data were collected over a consecutive four-day period at a central location, using two different classrooms in the on-campus communication building. The four graduate students took shifts during the data collection so that at least one individual was present to administer the packets at any given time. Rs came to the designated test site at their convenience and completed the questionnaire on site.

As Rs arrived, they were given a questionnaire packet to complete as well as a Statement of Agreement to Participate form to sign. The researchers used a coding process that guaranteed Rs' anonymity. The test administrators clarified terms or directions in response to Rs' questions. All Rs completed the packets in 60 minutes; however, on average, Rs required only 30 minutes to complete the packet.

As Rs finished the questionnaire, the administrator asked them to sign their name and list their section number, instructor's name, and class meeting time on an allocated piece of paper. After the data collection, lists of participants were compiled from the sign-in sheets; the lists were presented to section instructors in order to assign extra credit.

RESULTS

Preliminary Procedures

Readability Pretest. Prior to the data collection, the questionnaires were pretested for readability. Although no time limit was given for completion of the questionnaires, all Rs completed the packet within 45 minutes ($M = 30$ minutes). The instruments were randomized and counterbalanced to prevent order effects. No changes in content were made after the pretest.

Lie Scale Analyses. The Coopersmith Self-Esteem Inventory contains seven items that constitute an internal lie scale. The lie scale assesses whether Rs completed the survey in a consistent manner or whether they "lied." Following Coopersmith's (1967) scoring procedure, Rs' lie scores were computed. Consistent with Chartier and Chartier's (1975) procedures, Rs with scores of less than 6 out of 7 on the scale were dropped from the analyses.

Initial Demographic Analyses. Because Chartier and Chartier's (1975) correlations were computed separately for men and women, we conducted a t test to assess whether such separate analyses were warranted in the present study. The results ($t = 1.03$, $p = .304$) indicated no significant differences between the self-esteem scores of male versus female Rs ($M_{males} = 68.54$; $M_{females} = 66.39$). Therefore, data from the male and female Rs were combined and treated as one sample.

A t test comparing the self-esteem scores of Caucasian Rs ($M = 68.09$, $SD = 15.90$) versus non-Caucasian Rs ($M = 66.38$, $SD = 15.79$) yielded no significant differences, $t (317) = .90$, $p = .37$. Therefore, Caucasian and non-Caucasian responses were combined, and the sample was treated as a whole.

Confidence Level. The conventional but conservative significant level of alpha $''$ .01 was selected. Reported probabilities are two-tailed alpha levels.

The primary analyses have been omitted from this article to save space.[3]

DISCUSSION

Summary of Findings

Preliminary analyses reveal that mothers had no direct influence over males' and females' self-esteem, whereas fathers' communication affected self-esteem. Perceived normalcy directly influenced females' self-esteem, but did not affect males' self-esteem.

Interpretation of the Results

Universal Path Model. The analysis indicated that young adults' perceptions about maternal favoritism were related to perceptions of normalcy of family interaction (see Figure 1). One interpretation of this finding might be that socially mothers are expected to not have favorites. The only way a child can accept the concept of favoritism as normal is if he/she is the favorite.

The more consistently the father communicates with the mother, the more normal young adults perceive their family communication to be. As long as communication is consistent, there might be a sense of security because one knows what to expect. However, there was no statistical evidence that mother's consistency of communication with father influences normalcy. The more consistent mothers' com-

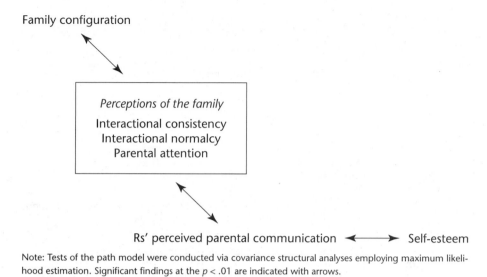

Note: Tests of the path model were conducted via covariance structural analyses employing maximum likelihood estimation. Significant findings at the $p < .01$ are indicated with arrows.

FIGURE 1   Models for All Rs: Paths of Influence on Self-Esteem Supported by the Results of the Study

munication with respondents, the better young adults perceive their father's communication with respondents.

The analyses revealed one final universal pattern: perceived fathers' communication was associated with self-esteem. Fathers' communication with young adults could be highly valued because socially fathers might not be present.

Male Path Model. The more attention young adult males receive from their fathers, the more normal male Rs perceives their family communication to be (see Figure 2). Society has led male Rs to believe there should be male bonding with the father, that it is important to their relationships. Thus, the more time fathers spend with male Rs, the more normal male Rs perceive their family communication to be.

Male Rs perceive their family communication as more normal with more consistency of mothers' communication with male Rs. The better young male Rs perceive their mothers' communication with them to be, the better the male Rs perceive their fathers' communication with them to be. Both of these paths were shown to be statistically significant.

Female Path Model. The more a young female adult saw herself as the mother's favorite or that the mother did not have a favorite, the better she perceived her father's communication to be (see Figure 3). Perhaps this is because mothers communicate so much to children that their communication forms the foundation

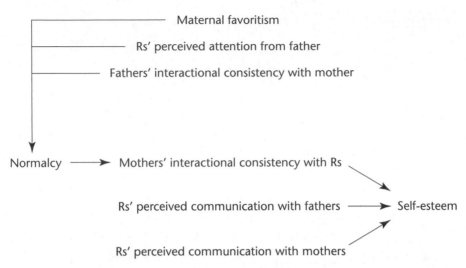

Note: Tests of the path model were conducted via covariance structural analyses employing maximum likelihood estimation. Significant findings at the $p < .01$ are indicated with arrows.

FIGURE 2   Model for *Male* Rs: Paths of Influence on Self-Esteem Supported by the Results of the Study

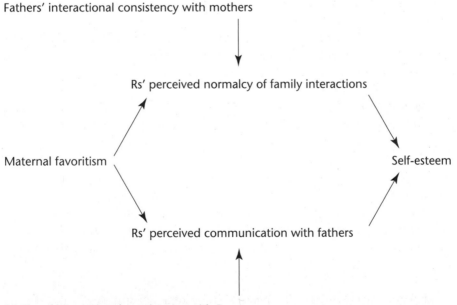

Note: Tests of the path model were conducted via covariance structural analyses employing maximum likelihood estimation. Significant findings are indicated with arrows; all *t*s significant at $p < .01$.

FIGURE 3   Model for *Female* Rs: Paths of Influence on Self-Esteem Supported by the Results of the Study

for the communication climate of the family. Thus, if a young adult perceives the concept of mother's favoritism as positive, the communication with the father also will seem positive.

The more normal female Rs perceive their family communication to be, the better they perceive their fathers' communication to be. Socially, fathers are less frequent communicators than mothers. Consistent with the findings of Leaper, Anderson, and Sanders (1998) that mothers tend to talk more to their children than fathers, when fathers communicate, it is an added value. The causality of this finding could be reversed as well. It could be that when there is positive communication from fathers to daughters, then the family communication is perceived as being normal. Perhaps being "Daddy's little girl" is thought to be normal in our society.

The more normal female Rs perceive their family communication to be, the higher their self-esteem. If Rs consider themselves normal compared to other groups or see their family as the in-group, they may feel "okay" about themselves.

Note that the pattern of significant findings differs largely on factors related to mothers versus fathers. Perceived communication with fathers was associated with self-esteem, but no "mother factors" related to Rs' self-esteem. Indeed, two "mother factors" related to Rs' perceived communication with fathers: maternal favoritism and maternal consistency of interactions. Perhaps the mother's major influence on children's self-esteem is through her influence on the father's communication with them. Future researchers could explore these gender differences further.

Our findings show that young adults index their perceptions of favoritism and consistency to communication with the father. Perhaps because most children in contemporary U.S. culture (even young adult children) spend more time with mothers than fathers, communication with the father may be more potent as an influential force in shaping perceptions of the family.

Please note that these analyses are based on a linear statistical model. Obviously, all correlational results can be interpreted bidirectionally as the direction of causality cannot be ascertained. For example, although perceived parental communication from fathers may influence young adult children's self-esteem, it is equally likely that the young adults' self-esteem influences their perceptions of their fathers' communication. In short, the true direction of influence in this and all of the previously discussed analyses remains at issue.

Limitations

Limitations of this study include reliance on self-report data rather than actual communicative behavior and the fact that all the Rs were students at the same university. However, for a sample of college students, the Rs represented diverse populations in terms of ethnicity, marital status, and year-in-school. Nonetheless, the results must be interpreted with caution, given the nonrandom sample and the fact that all Rs were living in the same urban area in only one region of the country.

Because our respondents were college students, results cannot necessarily be generalized to all young adults ages 18–24. College students perhaps might have a different level of self-esteem than young adults who never matriculate to college. Therefore, they may have different perspectives on their family communication. Furthermore, this research was not a longitudinal study of self-esteem and parental communication. Thus, findings cannot be generalized to other stages of life.

Most of the Rs had both a father and a mother present in their life. Thus, findings may not be applicable to young adults who grew up in a single-parent household.

Further, the present study did not examine the influence of peer communication on self-esteem. Many studies (e.g., Pipp & Robinson, 1985) have documented the influence of both peer and parent relationships on adolescent self-esteem. Although such an investigation lay outside the scope of the present study, obviously communication with both peers and parents may influence the self-esteem of young adults.

SUGGESTIONS FOR FUTURE RESEARCH

Research addressing how perceptions of overall family interaction patterns, rather than just perceptions of parental communication, influence self-esteem could contribute to our understanding of these phenomena.

The discipline could benefit from a study examining young adults not in college. As stated before, our results cannot be generalized for all young adults because those attending college may have a different level of self-esteem and different communication patterns with parents.

It is the researchers' contention that a longitudinal study would contribute to the growing research on self-esteem of young adults. It would be interesting to see if the models represent the paths of influence at other stages of life.

The growing research on self-esteem could also benefit from qualitative study examining the issue of perceived family communication. Interviews would allow for a detailed examination of how the individuals socially construct perceived parental communication.

CONCLUSION

According to Chaffee and Berger (1987), much of the research on family communication "rests upon the optimistic assumption that behavior can be both understood and improved" (p. 99). Despite its limitations, the present study contributes to our understanding of family communication by offering a more complex and perhaps more accurate picture of how parental communication relates to self-esteem of young male and female adults. This research provides the basis for meaningful preliminary models depicting the influence of perceived parental communication on young adults' self-esteem.

NOTES

1. Chartier and Chartier (1975) based their research on previous examinations of adolescents', rather than young adults', self-esteem. Subsequent scholars reporting data on young adults' self-esteem also drew from prior examinations of adolescents as well as examinations of young adults, as available. The present authors acknowledge we are following in this tradition and base many of our research questions on research completed with adolescents as well as research completed with young adult respondents.

2. The cognitive/intellectual type of involvement is based on the amount of mentally stimulating activities the child is exposed to by the parent (e.g., giving books, cognitive games). Personal involvement refers to attending a child's activities (e.g., conferences, plays, recitals). The third type of involvement, behavioral involvement, refers to the parent's actual, observable behavior toward the child (e.g., the parent may help his/her child with homework).

3. For the complete manuscript, including research analyses, please contact the first author.

REFERENCES

Adams, G. R., Gullotta, T. P., & Markstrom-Adams, C. (1994). *Adolescent life experiences* (3rd ed.). Pacific Grove, CA: Brooks/Cole.

Adler, A. (1932). *The practice and theory of individual psychology.* New York: Harcourt, Brace and Company.

Adler, P., Kless, S., & Adler, P. (1992). Socialization to gender roles: Popularity among elementary school boys and girls. *Sociology of Education, 65,* 169–187.

Alain, M. (1989). Do what I say, not what I do: Children's reactions to parents' behavioral inconsistencies. *Perceptual and Motor Skills, 68,* 99–102.

Avison, W. R., & McAlpine, D. D. (1992). Gender differences in symptoms of depression among adolescents. *Journal of Health and Social Behavior, 33,* 77–96.

Barber, B. K., Chadwick, B. A., & Oerter, R. (1992). Parental behaviors and adolescent self-esteem in the United States and Germany. *Journal of Marriage and the Family, 54,* 128–141.

Bardwell, J., Cochran, S., & Walker, S. (1986). Relationship of parental education, race, and gender sex-role stereotyping in five-year-old kindergartners. *Sex Roles, 15,* 275–281.

Barrett-Lennard, G. T. (1964). *Relationship Inventory.* Armidale, Australia: University of New England Press.

Bem, S. (1974). The measurement of psychological androgyny. *Journal of Consulting and Clinical Psychology, 42,* 155–162.

Blake, P. C., & Slate, J. R. (1993). A preliminary investigation into the relationship between adolescent self-esteem and parental verbal interaction. *School Counselor, 41,* 81–85.

Boldizar, J. (1991). Assessing sex typing and androgyny in children: The children's sex role inventory. *Developmental Psychology, 27,* 505–513.

Bollis-Pecci, T. S., & Webb, L. M. (1997, November). *The Memphis family perceptions instrument: Tests for validity and reliability.* Paper presented at the meeting of the National Communication Association, Chicago. (ERIC Document Reproduction Service No. ED 409 598)

Brage, D., Meredith, W., & Woodward, J. (1993). Correlates of loneliness among Midwestern adolescents. *Adolescence, 28,* 685–693.

Brand, H. J., Crous, B. H., & Hanekom, J. D. M. (1990). Perceived parental inconsistency as a factor in the emotional development of behavior-disordered children. *Psychological Reports, 66,* 620–622.

Bruner, J. (1990). *Acts of meaning.* Cambridge, MA: Harvard University Press.

Buri, J. R., & Dickinson, K. A. (1994, May). *Comparison of familial and cognitive factors associated with male and female self-esteem.* Paper presented at the annual meeting of the Midwestern Psychological Association, Chicago. (ERIC Document Reproduction Service No. ED 369 022)

Buri, J. R., Kirschner, P., & Walsh, J. M. (1987). Familial correlates of self-esteem in young American adults. *Journal of Social Psychology, 127,* 583–588.

Buri, J. R., Murphy, P., Richtmeier, L. M., & Komar, K. K. (1992). Stability of parental nurturance as a salient predictor of self-esteem. *Psychological Reports, 71,* 535–543.

Bush, K. R. (2000). Separatedness and connectedness in the parent-adolescent relationship as predictors of adolescent self-esteem. *Marriage and Family Review, 30,* 153–180.

Bush, K. R., Peterson, G. W., & Cobas, J. A. (2002). Adolescents' perceptions of parental behaviors as predictors of adolescent self-esteem in mainland China. *Sociological Inquiry, 72,* 503–526.

Bynum, M. K., & Durm, M. W. (1996). Children of divorce and its effect on their self-esteem. *Psychological Reports, 79,* 447–450.

Caldera, Y., Huston, A., & O'Brien, M. (1989). Social interactions and play patterns of parents and toddlers in feminine, masculine, and neutral toys. *Child Development, 60,* 70–76.

Cardinali, G., & D'Allura, T. (2001). Parenting styles and self-esteem: A study of young adults with visual impairments. *Journal of Visual Impairment and Blindness, 95,* 261–271.

Chaffee, S. H., & Berger, C. R. (1987). What communication scientists do. In C. R. Berger & S. H. Chaffee (Eds.), *Handbook of communication science* (pp. 99–122). Newbury Park, CA: Sage.

Chalfant, D. (1994). Birth order, perceived parental favoritism, and feelings toward parents. *Individual Psychology, 50*(1), 52–57.

Chartier, J., & Chartier, M. R. (1975). Perceived parental communication and self-esteem: An exploratory study. *Western Journal of Speech Communication, 38,* 26–31.

Chubb, N., Fertman, C., & Ross, J. (1997). Adolescent self-esteem and locus of control: A longitudinal study of gender and age differences. *Adolescence, 32,* 113–128.

Cooper, J. E., Homan J., & Braithwaite, V. A. (1983). Self-esteem and family cohesion: The child's perspective and adjustment. *Journal of Marriage and the Family, 45,* 153–159.

Coopersmith, S. (1967). *The antecedents of self-esteem.* San Francisco: Freeman.

Crowley, S. L., & Taylor, M. J. (1994). Mothers' and fathers' perceptions of family functioning in families having children with disabilities. *Early Education and Development, 5,* 213–225.

DeHart, T., Murray, S. L, & Pelham, B. W. (2003). The regulation of dependency in parent-child relationships. *Journal of Experimental Social Psychology, 39*(1), 59–67.

Demo, D. H., Small, S. A., & Savin-Williams, R. C. (1987). Family relations and the self-esteem of adolescents and their parents. *Journal of Marriage and the Family, 49,* 705–715.

Desselle, D. D., & Pearlmutter, L. (1997). Navigating two cultures: Deaf children, self-esteem and parents' communication patterns. *Social Work in Education, 19,* 23–31.

Enger, J. M., Howerton, D. L., & Cobbs, C. R. (1994). Internal/external locus of control, self-esteem, and parental verbal interaction of at-risk black male adolescents. *Journal of Social Psychology, 134,* 269–274.

Fagot, B. (1978). The influence of sex of child on parental reactions to toddler children. *Child Development, 49,* 459–465.

Fagot, B., & Lienbach, M. (1989). The young child's gender schema: Environmental input, internal organization. *Child Development, 60,* 663–672.

Felson, R. B., & Zielinski, M. A. (1989). Children's self-esteem and parental support. *Journal of Marriage and the Family, 51,* 727–735.

Fischer, S., & Fischer, R. L. (1986). *What we really know about child rearing.* New York: Basic Books.

Fitzpatrick, M. A., & Badzinski, D. M. (1994). All in the family: Interpersonal communication in kin relationships. In M. L. Knapp & G. R. Miller (Eds.), *Handbook of interpersonal communication* (2nd ed., pp. 726–771). Thousands Oaks, CA: Sage.

Fitzpatrick, M. A., & Vangelisti, A. L. (Eds.). (1995). *Explaining family interactions.* Thousand Oaks, CA: Sage.

Freud, S. (1870). *A general introduction to psychoanalysis.* New York: Simon & Schuster.

Gardner, F. E. M. (1989). Inconsistent parenting: Is there evidence for a link with children's emotional problems? *Journal of Abnormal Child Psychology, 17,* 223–233.

Gecas, V., & Schwalbe, M. (1986). Parental behavior and adolescent self-esteem. *Journal of Marriage and the Family, 48,* 37–46.

Green, A. W. (1995). Self-esteem associated with coping behaviors of adolescents in divorced/single parent families with implications for school counselors. *Dissertation Abstracts International, 56*(07), 2564A. (UMI No. AAT9536632)

Haney, P., & Durlak, J. A. (1998). Changing self-esteem in children and adolescents: A meta-analytical review. *Journal of Clinical Child Psychology, 27,* 423–434.

Harris, I. D., & Howard, K. I. (1983). Correlates of perceived parental favoritism. *Journal of Genetic Psychology, 146,* 45–56.

Harter, S. (1985). *Manual for the self-perception profile of children.* Denver: University of Denver.

Harter, S. (1990). Processes underlying adolescent self-concept formation. In R. Montemayor, G. Adams, and T. Gullotta (Eds.), *From childhood to adolescence: A transitional period?* Newbury Park, CA: Sage.

Herz, L., & Gullone, E. (1999). The relationship between self-esteem and parenting style: A cross-cultural comparison of Australian and Vietnamese Australian adolescents. *Journal of Cross-Cultural Psychology, 30,* 742–761.

Hoglund, C. L., & Bell, T. S. (1991, August). *Longitudinal study of self-esteem in children from 7–11 years.* Paper presented at the annual meeting of the American Psychological Association, San Francisco. (ERIC Document Reproduction No. ED 341 932)

Huang, L. N. (1999). Family communication patterns and personality characteristics. *Communication Quarterly, 47,* 230–243.

Kiracofe, N. M., & Kiracofe, H. N. (1990). Child-perceived parental favoritism and birth order. *Individual Psychology, 46,* 74–81.

Kirkpatrick, L. A., Waugh, C. E., Valencia, A., & Webster, G. D. (2002). The functional domain specificity of self-esteem and the differential prediction of aggression. *Journal of Personality and Social Psychology, 82,* 756–767.

Klein, H. A., O'Bryant, K., & Hopkins, H. R. (1996). Recalled parental authority style and self-perception in college men and women. *The Journal of Genetic Psychology, 157,* 5.

Lanza-Kaduce, L., & Webb, L. M. (1992). Perceived parental communication and adolescent self-esteem: Predictors of academic performance and drop-out rates. *ACA Bulletin, 82,* 1–12.

Leaper, C., Anderson, K. J., & Sanders, P. (1998). Moderators of gender effects on parents' talk to their children: A meta-analysis. *Developmental Psychology, 34,* 3–27.

Leondari, A., & Kiosseoglou, G. (2000). The relationship of parental attachment and psychological separation to the psychological functioning of young adults. *Journal of Social Psychology, 140,* 451–466.

Levine, T.R., & Wheeless, L. R. (1990). Cross-situational consistency and use/nonuse tendencies in compliance-gaining tactic selection. *Southern Communication Journal, 56,* 1–11.

Loeb, R. C., Horst, L., & Horton, P. (1980). Family interaction patterns associated with self-esteem in preadolescent girls and boys. *Merrill-Palmer Quarterly, 26,* 3, 205–217.

Lum, K., & Char, W. (1985). Chinese adaptation in Hawaii: Some examples. In W. Tseng & D. Y. H. Wu (Eds.), *Chinese culture and mental health.* Orlando, FL: Academic Press.

Luthar, S. S., & Quinlan, D. M. (1993). Parental images in two cultures: A study of women in India and America. *Journal of Cross-Cultural Psychology, 24,* 186–202.

Margolin, L., Blyth, D. A., & Carbone, D. (1988). The family as a looking glass: Interpreting family influences on adolescent self-esteem from a symbolic interaction perspective. *Journal of Early Adolescence, 8,* 211–224.

McLeod, J. M., & Chaffee, S. H. (1972). The construction of reality. In J. Tedeschi (Ed.), *The social influence processes* (pp. 50–59). Chicago: Aldine-Atherton.

Michaelieu, Q. (1997). Female identity, gendered parenting, and adolescent women's self-esteem. *Feminism and Psychology, 7,* 328–333.

Midgett, J., Ryan, B. A., Adams, G. R., & Corville-Smith, J. (2002). Complicating achievement and self-esteem: Considering the joint effects of child characteristics and parent-child interactions. *Contemporary Educational Psychology, 27,* 132–143.

Munford, M. (1994). Relationship of gender, self-esteem, social class, and racial identity to depression in blacks. *Journal of Black Psychology, 20,* 157–174.

Murrell, S. A., & Stackowiak, J. G. (1967). Consistency, rigidity, and power in the interaction patterns of clinic and nonclinic families. *Journal of Abnormal Psychology, 72,* 265–272.

Neale, A. (1986, November). *Parental favoritism and intergenerational helping.* Paper presented at the meeting of the Gerontology Society of America, Chicago.

Nielson, D. M., & Metha, A. (1994). Parental behavior and adolescent self-esteem in clinical and nonclinical samples. *Adolescence, 29,* 525–541.

Niemi, R. (1968). A methodological study of political socialization in the family. *Dissertation Abstracts International, 28*(12), 5120A. (UMI No. 68-7683)

Noller, P., & Callan, V. J. (1990). Adolescents' perceptions of the nature of their communication with parents. *Journal of Youth and Adolescence, 19,* 349–362.

Openshaw, D. K., Thomas, D. L., & Rollins, B. C. (1984). Parental influences of adolescent self-esteem. *Journal of Early Adolescence, 4,* 259–274.

Owens, K. O. (1995). *Raising your child's inner self-esteem: The authoritative guide from infancy through the teen years.* New York: Plenum Press.

Papini, D. R., Farmer, F. F., Clark, S. M., Micka, J. C., & Barnett, J. K. (1990). Early adolescent age and gender differences in patterns of emotional self-disclosure to parents and friends. *Adolescence, 25,* 959–975.

Peterson, G. W., Southworth, L. D., & Peters, D. F. (1983). Children's self-esteem and maternal behavior in three low-income samples. *Psychological Reports, 52,* 79–86.

Pipp, S., & Robinson, J. D. (1985, April). *Adolescents' constructs of self, parents and peers.* Portions of this paper presented at the meeting of the Society for Research in Child Development, Toronto. (ERIC Document Reproduction Service No. ED 270 704)

Pleck, J. (1981). *The myth of masculinity.* Cambridge, MA: MIT Press.

Pomerleau, A., Bolduc, D., Malcuit, G., & Cossett, L. (1990). Pink or blue: Environmental gender stereotypes in the first two years of life. *Sex Roles, 22,* 359–367.

Pyant, C. T., & Yanico, B. J. (1991). Relationship of racial identity and gender-role attitudes to black women's psychological well-being. *Journal of Counseling Psychology, 38,* 315–322.

Quatman, T., & Watson, C. M. (2001). Gender differences in adolescent self-esteem: An exploration of domains. *Journal of Genetic Psychology, 162,* 93–118.

Reid, B. V., & Valsiner, J. (1986). Consistency, praise, and love: Folk theories of American parents. *Ethos, 14,* 282–304.

Reuter, T. P., & Webb, L. M. (1992, November). *Young adults' self-esteem and perceived parental communication: A re-examination.* Paper presented at the annual meeting of the Speech Communication Association, San Antonio, TX.

Ritchie, L. D., & Fitzpatrick, M. (1990). Family communication patterns: Measuring intrapersonal perceptions of interpersonal relationships. *Communication Research, 17,* 523–544.

Rosenberg, M. (1965). *Society and adolescent self-image.* Princeton, NJ: Princeton University Press.

Scheck, D. C., & Emerick, R. (1976). The young male adolescent's perception of early child-rearing behavior: The differential effects of socioeconomic status and family size. *Sociometry, 39,* 39–52.

Scheck, D. C., Emerick, R., & El-Assal, M. M. (1973). Adolescents' perceptions of parent-child relations and the development of internal-external control orientation. *Journal of Marriage and the Family, 35,* 643–654.

Schor, E. L., Stidley, C. A., & Malspeirs, S. M. S. (1995). Behavioral correlates of differences between a child's assessment and the parents' assessment of the child's self-esteem. *Developmental and Behavioral Pediatrics, 16,* 211–219.

Segrin, C., & Menees, M. M. (1996). The impact of coping styles and family communication on the social skills of children of alcoholics. *Journal of Studies on Alcohol, 7,* 29–33.

Smith, M. D., & Self, G. (1977). *The influence of gender difference on perceptions of self-esteem: An unobtrusive measure.* Paper presented at the annual meeting of the Southwestern Sociological Association, Dallas. (ERIC Document Reproduction Service No. ED 144921)

Socha, T. J., & Stamp, G. H. (Eds.). (1995). *Parents, children, and communication: Frontiers of theory and research.* Mahwah, NJ: Erlbaum.

Spence, J., & Hall, S. (1996). Children's gender-related self-perceptions, activity preferences, and occupational stereotypes: A test of three models of gender constructs. *Sex Roles, 35,* 659–691.

Stevenson, H. W., Lee, S., Chen, C., Lummis, M., Stigler, J., Fan, L., & Ge, F. (1990). Mathematics achievement of children in China and the United States. *Child Development, 61,* 1053–1066.

Sturkie, K., & Flanzer, J. (1987). Depression and self-esteem in the families of maltreated adolescents. *Social Work, 32,* 491–496.

Thomas, C. E., Booth-Butterfield, M., & Booth-Butterfield, S. (1995). Perceptions of deception, divorce disclosures, and communication satisfaction with parents. *Western Journal of Communication, 59,* 228–245.

Tims, A. R., & Masland, J. L. (1986). Measurement of family communication patterns. *Communication Research, 13,* 5–17.

Turner, L. H., & West, R. (2002). *Perspectives on family communication* (2nd ed.). Boston: McGraw-Hill.

Vangelisti, A. (1993). Communication in the family: The influence of time, relational prototypes, and irrationality. *Communication Monographs, 60,* 42–54.

Vella, M. L., Persic, S., & Lester, D. (1996). Does self-esteem predict suicide after controls for depression? *Psychological Reports, 79,* 1178.

Walitzer, K., & Sher, K. (1996). A prospective study of self-esteem and alcohol use disorders in early childhood: Evidence for gender differences. *Alcoholism: Clinical and Experimental Research, 20,* 1118–1124.

Watkins, D., Dong, Q., & Xia, Y. (1997). Age and gender differences in the self-esteem of Chinese children. *Journal of Social Psychology, 137,* 374–379.

Wenk, D., Hardesty, C. L., Morgan, C. S., & Blair, S. L. (1994). The influence of parental involvement on the well-being of sons and daughters. *Journal of Marriage and the Family, 56,* 229–234.

Wrobel, G. (1990). The self-esteem of transracially adopted adolescents. *Dissertation Abstracts International, 51,* 08B. (UMI No. AAG9029718)

Wu, Y., & Smith, D. (1997). Self-esteem of Taiwanese children. *Child Study Journal, 27,* 1–9.

Zervas, L. J., & Sherman, M. F. (1993). The relationship between perceived parental favoritism and self-esteem. *Journal of Genetic Psychology, 155,* 25–33.

EMERGENCY DRESS

Sherryl Kleinman

As I help my mother unpack during her yearly visit to Chapel Hill, I open the closet door of the bedroom and discover I've forgotten to remove my clothes to make way for hers. I know I've now given her an opportunity to scrutinize what she finds.

"Pants, pants, pants," she mutters, shoving the hanging legs away from each other, searching for one— just one—item cut of whole cloth, a stretch of material without a crotch. The scritch-scratching of the hangers across the metal bar makes my fillings ache.

"But Ma, I have *lots* of pants," I tell her, as if my varied selection will make up for my lack of girl clothes. Can't she see how far I've come since my teenage years, when I lived in two pairs of jeans? Now there's black rayon and gray crepe, dark blue corduroy, smooth beige cotton, purple linen. I'm practically a clothes horse!

"What if there's an *occasion*," she says, "and you don't have a dress? You've got to have *one*. To be prepared." Her eyes look down to the floor, searching the smattering of shoes with one-inch soles and no discernible heels. "And a pair of pumps," she adds.

To my mother my closet is a house without a fire alarm, a bathroom without band-aids, a door without a dead bolt.

"What occasion would come up?" I ask, knowing my question will sound stupid.

"Anything," she answers. "A function."

So she is not talking about weddings, surprise parties, or New Year's Eve, but a Gathering of Professors where the men will wear suits and the women will wear dresses. I've been a professor for twenty years, but she's smart enough not to generalize from me to professors-at-large, confident that I'm the odd woman out.

I am a difficult daughter for my mother. She sees it as a personal failure that I am happy with the same haircut for eleven years. "And somehow you managed to find the only man in America who is just like you!" she says.

Michael likes the short hair on my head and the long hair on my legs and under my arms. He agrees that we don't need the State to make our relationship real.

"Not owning a dress is too much," she says, and demands we go to the mall right then to buy me an all-occasion emergency dress. I sigh and say, "Let's think about it tomorrow."

PART VI

EDUCATIONAL AND PROFESSIONAL CONTEXTS

EXCLUDING GENDERS

A Case Study in Organizational Conflict

Margaret Cavin

CALIFORNIA STATE UNIVERSITY, LONG BEACH

If we were to compare the life of the average white middle-class female and male in the United States during the nineteenth and twentieth centuries, we would see that men's and women's condition changed dramatically in many respects. Suffrage, property rights, child custody, and career opportunities are just a few of the areas in which parity between men and women has grown. Though far from sharing equal status, the advances women and men have made in the United States have led many to conclude that the worst of the gender inequities is over. Lest we feel complacent in our gains, Margaret Cavin's article should remind us that old power struggles continue and the arguments of oppression are still voiced loudly, even in the places we might least expect to hear them. Cavin's report of the content in a "male only" class in a private college alerts us to how easily the arguments that have advanced the cause of gender equality can be silenced. She demonstrates to readers that stereotypes of silent, submissive, and suppressed women are still being promoted as the appropriate condition of females.

In her report, Cavin takes the reader to the heart of the clash between a paradigm of the past and one of the present—between issues of tradition, hierarchy, and power held by a small group of white males, and the forces for change, inclusion, and participatory governance. For the reader interested in taking an active role in making social and policy changes, this article suggests strategies to effect change within a well-entrenched and -supported system. The author's description and analysis of events is both frustrating and hopeful.

QUESTIONS FOR DISCUSSION

- *Note how some of the strategies used to help females gain power-equity are used by those in power to erode that equity. Is Cavin's an unusual experience? Have you seen other examples?*
- *Consider how the power structure of the institution functions to silence males' and females' voices. What would happen if these voices were allowed to be heard?*

- *Regarding the content of the class under debate, consider what stereotypes are being cultivated and how the students in and outside the class are attempting to reinforce or fight those stereotypes.*
- *Consider how you would feel and what you would do if you discovered that such a course was being offered at your institution. What would you do about it, if anything?*

S ome time ago, a story was reported on National Public Radio outlining the details of a bitter fight between the administration of Boston College and one of its tenured faculty. Mary Daily, who calls herself a radical lesbian feminist, had been teaching a gender-exclusive class to female students for several years until one male threatened to sue the school if he was not allowed to join or enroll in the class. When Boston College told Daily that she had to accept male students, she said she would rather retire. To her surprise, the administration took her turn of phrase literally, locked her out of her office, and began sending her retirement benefits. While the events and outcomes are different, the issues of my story that follows are exactly the same as the issues in this news story. Exactly the same arguments were used, exactly the same labels were thrown around, only my story is exactly opposite.

Organizational structure and communication methodologies have undergone substantial changes in recent years. Researchers in these areas have laid the groundwork for entirely new approaches to workplace communication, negotiation, and relationships. Organizations are discovering the value of nonlinear, multivoiced paradigms in which each member of an organization has the potential to be heard and decisions are based on the merit of the idea rather than the location of the idea. Of course, this situation occurs more neatly in theory, and many organizations resist change and continue to function more traditionally. One organization that is at the forefront of the resistance is the focus of this article—a small, private, religiously affiliated university that I identify as Sunrise University.

Sunrise University steadfastly stands against the impending tide of change. In a recent test of its very traditional approach, battle cries like "We're going to the wall with this one!" and odd threats like "Our alumni [might] mistakenly believe that we are, as a university, taking an egalitarian political position which is unbiblical!" were mixed with claims of department sovereignty and warnings of a conspiracy to overthrow the long-held principles and distinctiveness of the university. The drama created around this test captivated the attention of the entire school. It seemed to strike at the heart and soul of the university. It was ground zero for a clash between a method of the past and a method of the future. That being so, I thought (once I had recovered from the fallout) it would make an interesting case study. What makes it interesting is that all the key issues were present: (1) Sunrise is a perfect example of a traditional hierarchical organization; (2) a trial run of a faculty town hall was in its infancy; (3) a conflict arose over gender fairness due to a strong patriarchal presence; (4) I used some of the available feminist and postmodern approaches to try to create a site of discourse; and (5) in the end, I failed, highlighting some useful lessons.

Sunrise University is a private, nationally ranked university featuring legitimate programs while holding firmly to its past as a biblically based university. Entering students are required to show evidence to support that they are Christians, and are required to take 30 units of Bible and theology. Foundational to their particular view of Christianity is the belief that patriarchy should be the method of operation in all of their institutions. (I did not know this when I was hired to teach at this particular university; I discovered it when I raised the issue of gender exclusion.) A patriarchal structure is one in which an individual (male) is in authority over the other individuals. Decisions are handed down in a linear fashion, many times with no explanation or discussion. This structure comes from the belief that all the way back to Adam and through his descendents to Noah, decision making was constructed this way. These men were perceived as "fathers" to the human race. Many Evangelicals believe that this structure exists in the church, as well as any other organizational form, and extends to the family structure in the home.

Sunrise University is a patriarchal and hierarchically structured university that is governed ultimately by a board of directors with no faculty representation. Power clearly emanates down through a top-heavy administration. In the fall of 1996, I agreed to serve as the Arts and Professions Representative on the Steering Committee of a newly formed university faculty governance Townhall. This is an elected position chosen by all of the faculty within a given school. Faculty governance was and is a subject of great importance that historically had not been part of our experience at Sunrise University. It was our goal to ease the faculty into governance slowly within our restrictive culture. It was during this time that I became aware of a clear trend toward gender exclusion in various contexts on campus and, with that, a whole rhetorical structure of male dominance. In this essay I will explain the process I used, which began with feminist critique of course materials, speeches, and flyers, and how that process led to the steps I took through the university structure to effect elimination of gender exclusion in a particular university setting.

Rhetorical criticism is a process of examining words as "symbolic acts" of power (Kenneth Burke) that may lead a particular audience or group of people to choose particular physical actions. Historically, there are many examples of the power of speech to effect change in an audience. Classic examples are Hitler's hate speech, Lincoln's Gettysburg Address, Roosevelt's Fireside Chats, and King's "I Have a Dream" speech. The changes in thinking and acting then lead to new and different symbolic acts, and the cycle continues. The theory behind this is that our words and our actions are inextricably linked. The language we use does say something about what we believe, how we perceive others, choices we make on which we act, and so on.

Feminist criticism examines language to discover if a speaker is reinforcing a particular power structure that is in place or if the speaker is offering a shift to a different group's being in power or, perhaps, is offering equality of power for all. This could be a white-male-dominated structure, for example, but is not exclusive to a particular sex. Feminist criticism is interested in discovering if any group is dominant over another, if the language used supports equality among individuals, or if a speaker is communicating a new system or paradigm of power that is different from the existing one. Language analysis seemed appropriate to apply in this case, because the issue was that one group was potentially being granted favoritism and special privileges over another.

"AUTHENTIC MANHOOD" CLASS: A MALE MOVEMENT TRAINING SITE

The problem of gender exclusion first came to my attention when a male former student came to my office and expressed his concern about a class being taught in the theology department titled "Authentic Manhood." Female students were forbidden to take the class because, as one faculty member put it, "men need time to themselves so they can be better in their relationships with women." Each student in the class was required to complete journal packets that were developed much like workbooks. These bound documents included course lecture material, articles, and space for personal responses to class discussions. My former student wanted me to examine his journal and use the information with discretion. After reading the journal as a rhetorical critic, I concluded that the information was problematic on several levels.

The first and most obviously ironic point of interest was the clearly homoerotic suggestive images present in the workbook journal. It is ironic because the institutional stance on homosexuality is that it is a sin and a "lifestyle" of homosexuality is to be condemned as such. As the reader looks through the book, though, images of men with overdeveloped muscles posing with each other and alone appear to be dominant. These images easily bring to mind the muscle-bound characters of Tom of Finland, drawings that are clearly targeted to gay male visual interest.

Moving from the visual to an analysis more textual, I discovered articles printed in the journal that advocated a specific perspective regarding child/parent relationships. The notes constructed an image of the mother, titled "The Legacy of Mother," that described the role of mother with terms such as "engulfment" and "abandonment." Among the rather cluttered and often confusing collection of odd stories and even odder illustrations were statements like "Typically the deepest wounding comes from extremes, where we receive either too much or too little of mother." The author (I assume the instructor) goes on to write that mothers must try to separate from their sons, but concludes, "it takes more than mother's willingness to make this separation, it takes other men to assist." The relationship with the mother is explained in extremes of engulfment or abandonment implying no other dimension relevant. The material describes the engulfing mother as manipulating with guilt, discouraging independence, and molding her son into "mother's little man." Boys then are described as reacting to this engulfing in one of two ways: rebellion or compliance. The compliant boy becomes a pleaser, a placator. The rebellious boy becomes afraid of commitment or may become violent in order to get even with women. Abandoning mothers cause boys to have problems in forming healthy attachments to women. In either case, the problems are the mother's fault. Because the fault lies with the mothers, boys must separate themselves from their mothers. One classroom exercise asks the males to say good-bye to their mothers. Instructions include "let the wounded boy in you speak," "tell her good-bye." The point of the exercise is that to become a man, the boy must leave his mother; a male cannot be a man and still have a close relationship with his mother.

The relationship with the father is explained very differently. For example, the instructor gives subsequent handouts titled "A father's presence is so magical!" "A father's influence is so powerful!" "A father's legacy is so wonderful!" "A father's calling is so awesome!" and "A father's absence is so devastating!" On this page, the instructor states, "Dad's absence is a curse. It's death." He writes also, "Whether active or absent, involved or indifferent, he lives in our core. He permeates our being. He shapes our soul. He impacts our personality. He indwells my heart. He touches my life." The rhetorical perspective created is that male students need to recognize their mothers as engulfing or abandoning and, further, that they should seek distance from their mothers and union with their fathers. Their mothers are responsible for the ills they encounter in life in adult relationships, and whether bad or good, their fathers are vital for their growth and success as grown men.

Researching the situation further, I discovered that the instructor also used Robert Bly's (1990) teachings in *Iron John* as foundation for his class. Robert Bly, acclaimed poet and winner of the National Book Award, started the male movement as a backlash against early feminist movements. He travels across the country speaking to male conferences about "male grief" and all the problems of being a contemporary male. He teaches that men should be better parents but goes on to assert that men who are raised by mothers only become too "soft" as a result. In the book *Male/Female Roles: Opposing Viewpoints,* Fred Pelka (1995) states:

> It is distressing, but not surprising that Bly's barely sublimated misogyny strikes such a chord among so many men. Bly and his followers celebrate their gathering to seek "a new vision" of masculinity. But Bly's ideas of masculine and feminine are cut from the same old sexist cloth, and his anger and distrust of women seem hardly cause for celebration. (p. 173)

It seemed evident that the "Authentic Manhood" class was creating an advocacy environment for a patriarchal and misogynic political agenda disallowing any counterviewpoints.

At a later date, I obtained the text being used in the class, which was titled *Recovering Biblical Manhood and Womanhood: A Response to Evangelical Feminism,* edited by John Piper and Wayne Grudem (1991). In the first chapter, John Piper states, "I hope it will be obvious that my reflections are not the creation of an independent mind, but the fruit of a tree planted firmly in the soil of constant meditation on the Word of God" (p. 32). This statement communicates that his writings are not from his own "independent mind" but are instead direct from God. This premise creates a situation in which students must either accept this one position or question the authority of God. Clearly there is no balance with alternative points of view given. The book is constructed around these theses:

> At the heart of mature masculinity is a sense of benevolent responsibility to lead, provide for and protect women in ways appropriate to a man's differing relationships. At the heart of mature femininity is a freeing disposition to affirm, receive and nurture strength and leadership from worthy men in ways appropriate to a woman's differing relationships. (pp. 35–36)

The male students were being taught that men and women were to relate to each other in clearly defined roles, and that those roles were God given and Sunrise approved.

In addition to the problems created with a political agenda being taught in classes, I discovered that this was a senior-level class in which students did not have to complete exams or write research papers and were allowed to choose their own grade for themselves. While there might be some "fluff" classes in which students were not required to take exams or write research papers, all other classes at least required a professor to give a grade based on clear criteria established in a syllabus. The Authentic Manhood class allowed males to receive three hours of credit for an upper-division class in which they could choose their own grade while females at the same school were not provided the same "opportunity." This seemed to be an issue relevant to Title IX, which requires universities to provide equal access to all students. In fact, Title IX of the Education Amendments of 1972 reads, "Title IX prohibits sex discrimination against any participant in an educational program or activity that receives federal funds." My personal concern regarding our Title IX compliance added to my increasing interest in seeking some form of remedy to the situation. A second issue, along with some comments from my students in class, confirmed my desire to act.

EXCLUSIONARY CHAPELS AND CONFERENCES: PROMISEKEEPERS ALIVE AND WELL ON CAMPUS

Not long after I was introduced to the "Authentic Manhood" class, I began to see posters appear across campus featuring a picture of an "erect" sword with the heading, "'Men: Sharpening Your Sword' Men's Conference" along with a quotation from scripture, Proverbs 27:17, which states, "As iron sharpens iron, so one man sharpens another." Aside from the entertainment value offered by such a clearly phalocentric illustration and the amusement regarding the irony of a school deeply steeped in the ideas of the religious right where homophobia reaches epidemic proportions, the posters proved to be useful in my classes as we began to examine the functions and outcomes of keeping women from sites of "worship."

I acquired taped sessions of the speeches given at several of the men's chapels. When I analyzed them rhetorically, I discovered more disturbing information. For example, one speaker (a male faculty member from the department of psychology), stated:

> We [men] are a hunted species. We are the species when God decides to make a change, we are the ones that God is going to use to make a change. I firmly believe that. I believe that women are spiritually discerning and somewhat more sensitive to God's leading than we are. But I also believe that when God wants to change the world, when God is going to incorporate change, He is going to use men. (taped speech, Fall 1996)

This quotation communicates to the male students gathered for "worship" that women should be marginalized in issues of leadership, that they are unworthy to be used of God. It confirms these young men's attitudes that they enjoy, by virtue of their sex, special treatment from God and a special "burden" of leadership responsibility. This same faculty member continued:

> And I'm here to tell you that what turns a woman on, what makes a woman tick, not necessarily physically, but what is going to draw her closer to you is if she believes you are some spiritual giant or you allow yourself to share too much emotionally with them. You start sharing deep levels or they believe you're super spiritual, it's just as if two girls walked in this room completely naked right now. That's what it does to them, it's the same effect. (taped speech, Fall 1996)

In this quotation, women are also taken together, stripped of their individuality, as objects waiting to be turned on by a male disclosure, a kind of religious aphrodisiac. The speaker never attempts to make his speech persuasive by claiming empirical or any other independent verification. Had he tried to collect such data, he would have discovered it to be a daunting task. In all my preparations for my class on gender communication, I have never discovered anything that would substantiate such claims that women typically become sexually aroused when men use religious language or perform religious acts.

In a different speech by another male faculty member, this time from the department of theology, the speaker explained to the all-male audience that some women had "threatened" to attend the "Men Only" chapel. The speaker went on to assert that had the women shown up, they would have been asked to leave. Again, this is a clear statement to the men present that the women are to be the "absent other," to be feared and to be removed when issues of importance are discussed.

Without an exclusive environment, these hurtful, inaccurate, and dehumanizing comments would, most likely, not be made. These chapel services were little more than breeding grounds for male backlash ideology. The young men attending the meetings were attending not a debate or a public forum or even a rally; they were attending a worship service. A worship service, in their particular environment, centers the authority of God in the pulpit. Any man standing in such a position is rarely questioned afterward and almost never openly challenged. The "male only" chapels gave me the impression that Sunrise University was institutionalizing the dogma of the male movement, a formal commitment to an ideology that had the potential to jeopardize the university's legitimacy.

Additionally, Sunrise is a Christian university; students are required to attend a certain number of chapels. Gender exclusionary chapels occurred during this time as special additions and provided males more opportunities to meet the chapel requirement than females. Once again, I was faced with the fact that my university was supporting a lack of equitable opportunities for its female students (by far the majority of Sunrise's population), and again, the issue of Title IX compliance concerned me.

The mounting discrimination evidenced by the "Authentic Manhood" class and the exclusionary chapels convinced me to pursue an organizational remedy. I purposefully chose to take an approach that mirrored the rather obsolete organizational structure of Sunrise rather than fight against the structure and the problem at the same time. The fairness issue seemed to me the most immediate. Working to undermine a rising backlash mentality would be something I would have to do in my classroom, student by student. I realized, even then, that I could never effect that kind of change in an environment like Sunrise.

COMMUNICATION PROCESS: STEPPING ON THE TURF OF REAL MEN

I first chose to work through the organizational network structure and communicate through the established proper procedure which, in my mind, meant taking the issue to the chair of my department. Because of the serious nature of academic freedom and responsibility, I felt it was necessary, when I posed the issue to him, to make clear that it was not my desire to criticize or target a particular class or the way a professor taught that class, but that my concern was a larger issue of equal access provided to all students in university-sanctioned classes and activities. Academic freedom has to do with freedom of speech but does not protect a faculty member's right to discriminate against a student. For example, a teacher may make statements in class, choose controversial textbooks, and the like, but academic freedom does not allow a teacher to say he or she does not want to let students take a class based on their sex, race, or similar factors. So this was not an issue of academic freedom. I was not critiquing the course materials or the chapel speeches in order to tell speakers they could not express an opinion or could not choose a particular text for a class. I was, however, critiquing the view communicated about women and men.

Once I had communicated my concerns to my department chair, he presented my concerns to the dean and vice provost, who then brought them to the attention of the general assembly of chairs. Later, he returned to me and stated that my concern was somehow dropped in the meeting in favor of a discussion regarding academic rigor. He then recommended that if I still felt strongly about the situation, I should find another way to communicate my point of view.

I sent an email to the Chaplain of Student Ministries and explained my concerns regarding the exclusionary chapels. Rather than respond to me directly, he passed my email on to the Director of Women's Ministries, and she answered me with the following:

> We feel no need to adjust our Women's Ministries program to look like the men's program. Our programs reflect the Lord's leading for us, and theirs reflects the Lord's leading for them. We feel it is not only appropriate, but we applaud their initiative and desire to schedule men only chapels. We are exclusive in our events, and they are exclusive in theirs to respond to exclusive needs.

I then responded to her by explaining that I was not concerned with whether there were women's or men's programs on campus, but rather, that there should be no gender-based privileges on a university campus. I stated that when there is exclusion, there is mystery, misinterpretation, and dishonesty. There is much research to point out the potential problems with purely homogeneous groups, such as the potential for groupthink. This kind of segregated class allows for an environment in which identification through disclosure can occur between participants and lead to participants' pointing out differences between them as a group and the "other" (those who are not part of the group), particularly when a specific political agenda is being perpetrated through the encounters. She did not respond to my email, but rather the director of chapels responded by asking me to meet with him for coffee. When we met, he said he had no intention of talking to me, but rather, he would "listen" to my concerns. I expressed them, and he then said, "Margaret, let me ask you a question. If we are not supposed to have gender exclusive classes and chapels, then why did Christ select 'male only' disciples?" Needless to say, the meeting concluded with unsatisfactory results.

I did not stop at that point, but rather, I then went to the University Legal Counsel for a clarification of my understanding of Title IX. He explained to me that he knew nothing of classes or chapels that were exclusive but that it was true that the university was bound by Title IX. He said he did not have a copy of the law, but he gave me a copy of a letter of exemption, on file with the Board of Education, that applies to hiring procedures and does not offer any exemption allowing gender exclusive programs beyond those already in place in Title IX.

I began to realize that communicating through the traditional, entrenched organizational network might not prove effective, but I decided to continue to work within that frame, shifting only to an even more institutional level. Since the issue was a subject that affected all classes and university-sanctioned activities, I thought it proper to bring it before the newly formed university Townhall in my role as the School of Arts and Professions Representative. I explained to the Townhall Steering Committee that I intended to raise the issue at the next meeting, and information in the form of a statement was subsequently sent out through email to all faculty. My statement asking for a vote regarding gender exclusion read as follows:

> I intend to move that Sunrise University undergraduate and graduate faculty should discontinue and forever cease the practice of gender discrimination and exclusion in its academic and religious programs. This motion would in effect prohibit any class designated as a "Men's Only" or "Women's Only" course offering. It would also prohibit any chapel labeled "Men Only" or "Women Only." It is my belief that these practices which have occurred in both chapel and the classroom, are a violation of Title IX mandates as well as a moral violation of Christian standards. It is for these reasons I will make the above motion. For further information, you may reference Title IX laws as well as a letter of exemption which is on file with the Department of Education on behalf of Sunrise University. Please note the existence of "Men Only" chapels which are heavily advertised throughout campus and the existence of a current course offering which excludes women.

The above motion was sent to all faculty a week prior to the next Townhall Meeting at which the issue would be raised. During the week intervening, I received several calls from male faculty members asking me not to raise the issue, and one male faculty member left a note on my desk that read:

> I'm a little nervous about the issue on men's assemblies scheduled for this afternoon. I hope we're careful about what we say. I'm wondering if this is a no win situation. The Lord knows we have a lot of wimpy men in the country. Are women hurt when men talk about how to be better men? I have a copy of an article I got a couple of days ago on the theme, that when men do what's right, women profit. Another thought: I got an email on an investment session for women staff and faculty members. If that is all right for women, why isn't it all right for men to get together?

In spite of these messages, I proceeded as scheduled, and on the day of the Townhall, November 11, 1996, faculty attendance was at a record high (63 needed for a quorum, 81 were present), and the room was filled with not only faculty, but staff and administrators as well, including the president of the university. As the representative for the School of Arts and Professions, I sat at the front of the room with the other representatives from the other schools (Humanities, Sciences, Student Affairs/Library, Business/Continuing Studies, Theology, Psychology, and Intercultural). I chose to remain sitting with the panel rather than standing at the lectern when speaking in order to communicate an attitude of equality and collaboration.

In my speech, I began by explaining that I felt honored bringing this issue before the faculty because I have tremendous respect for the idea of faculty governance. I then outlined my main points: I gave a brief history of the series of events that led to my motion and then explained my general concern regarding the situation. I stated:

> When any group is systematically excluded from an activity a statement is made to the group excluded. The statement is this: "We don't want your presence." That statement brings with it many more negative statements like: "You are not desirable, You are of little use, Your ideas are irrelevant, You don't deserve the information which is provided to others, etc." There are also other unspoken statements made to those who are included. . . . I have listened to some of the meetings held on this campus and have found that many of these statements were not only understood by virtue of the segregation, but were confirmed by the speakers in the texts in their speeches. (Cavin speech, Townhall, November 11, 1996)

I supported my statement by giving some examples from chapel speeches, keeping the names of the speakers anonymous in order to avoid embarrassing anyone directly in the meeting. In the end I made it very clear that I was not against the discussion of gender specific topics, but rather I was speaking only to the exclusion of women or men from the official programs of the university, that I was primarily concerned that we should comply with the law, and that we should take care not to create an unfair and artificial environment of masculine superiority.

At the conclusion of my speech, the chair of the department that offered the "Authentic Manhood" class (a well-known local pastor) rose to his feet and came to the front of the room, stood at the lectern (a well-known symbol of "godly" authority in the church), and stated, "I am hurt by what you have said. You have built a case rather than building unity in Christ. Your method is fracturing. You are using the format like secular schools." He then pointed his finger at me and stated, "Margaret, you want power, institutional power." Then he addressed the representatives in general and said, "I am pained at the committee response. You are not following the biblical model. The unity of spirit should be your priority." He then asserted, "We have had a very positive response to the class as women are willing to forego their legal rights and allow men to have the class."

The president of the university stood at the back of the room and apologized to me for being "stonewalled" by the organizational process. The faculty then began to respond by expressing diverse opinions on the topic, all the way from arguing that men and women should be free to have separate classes to agreeing with my motion, until the provost stood and moved to table the discussion and form a committee to investigate the matter further. The Townhall Steering Committee (the representatives) could determine the Gender Exclusion Committee member selection. A vote was taken, and a majority agreed that this was the best solution.

COMMUNICATION BACKLASH:
REAL MEN HAVE REAL STRENGTH

At the next Townhall Steering Committee, the committee (all men except for myself) began to discuss who should be selected for the Gender Exclusion Committee. At the conclusion of the Townhall Meeting, faculty had been given a sign-up sheet and those interested in serving on the committee to investigate the situation could volunteer. Individuals rushed to sign the sheet, and many laughed that this was the first committee on which faculty had been eager to serve. Now it was the task of the Steering Committee to decide who would be selected among those who had signed the sheet. The men on the Steering Committee made it very clear that they felt it would be wrong for me to serve on the committee. They then ruled out a second woman who they claimed was "too abrasive" and would create hard feelings among the larger faculty if she were selected. Once the smoke had cleared, the members of the committee were predominantly individuals who were politically in favor of gender exclusion. This was clear because they had stood and stated their viewpoints very clearly at the Townhall Meeting. It is interesting to note that one of the first lessons I discovered in the process was that the viewpoints were not distinguished by gender; rather, there were men who saw the potential problems with gender exclusion and women who did not. At the conclusion of our Steering Committee meeting, having formulated the Gender Exclusion Committee, I was feeling very discouraged that anything productive would come from this particular newly formed committee. However, there were many surprises awaiting me as the situation unfolded.

Surprise No. 1

An intense and heated discussion erupted on campus in chapels, classes, in the student newspapers, and in other communication forums. Unfortunately, I was misquoted when interviewed for the student newspaper on several occasions. Some examples were that I wanted unisex bathrooms and dorm rooms and that I was planning to stop Promisekeepers from having "Men Only" meetings. Promisekeepers is a national Christian male organization that exists for the purpose of developing male character and returning men to their "rightful" place as "head of the home." In any case, this subject was the primary focus of the campus for several months. It seemed clear that this was an issue that struck to the very heart of the social, relational, and political core of the institution. I think I had not realized the brimming tension waiting to explode the moment someone dared to light the fuse of discourse.

Surprise No. 2

Meanwhile, the newly formed Gender Exclusion Committee asked the Department of Theology to respond with scripture to the issue I had raised at the Townhall

Meeting. A theological committee was then formed, and they wrote a document that was submitted to all university faculty with the intention of discussing the points at the next Townhall Meeting. Overall, the authors stated that gender exclusive classes and chapels are "consistent with biblical principles and are grounded in Sunrise's religious tradition and mission as a university, and a basis exists for exemption from Title IX restrictions." They then defended the following three points. First, men and women are different from one another. The second point they made was that faculty and administration have a responsibility to meet the needs of students, thus accomplishing university goals. The third and final point they made was that the "spirit of Christian love, unity, honor, and respect for others must characterize all activities at Sunrise University." Scripture was used to substantiate the importance of expressing love, unity, honor, and respect. However, the only scripture that they used to support gender exclusion was Titus 2:1–15, in which Titus (a pastor) is instructed to teach principles of relationships to men and women. In the document the authors claim, "This passage also indicates that some instruction was carried out in gender-exclusive groups and through role modeling (vv. 4–5), though the New Testament does not go into extensive detail about the logistics of such instruction." In fact, the scripture noted does not go into any detail about instruction and never mentions in any way gender exclusionary teaching, and the situation in Titus is describing a pastor and church situation (which the authors of the theology document themselves noted), not a university.

At the second Townhall Meeting on March 3, 1997, I made several points to the university faculty regarding the theology document. First, I explained that it was inappropriate for the Gender Exclusion Committee to "farm out" the work to the Theology Department. Instead, the committee should have first decided if Sunrise was in fact in violation of Title IX and then, if they decided that we were, they should approach the university faculty in the Townhall to determine whether we as a faculty wanted to try and circumvent the law of the land. If the faculty determined that they did not want to comply with Title IX, then the committee might want to approach any departments that anticipate having exclusive classes to respond with a document that supports those classes and that clearly excuses their program from that law. I pointed out that Title IX exists to teach us how to live with the demands of gender differences without hurting one another. I also explained that, from a rhetorical perspective, the theology document only builds a case for the belief in gender differences. It does not build a case for gender exclusion. I stated:

> We cannot support excluding men and women from university academic and religious life based on the fact that men and women are different. This document does not give any scriptural support for gender exclusion. I encourage each of you to look up each and every scriptural citations in this document and examine them for yourselves. It is fine, as I said before, to have classes and chapels that deal with gender differences. But there are no grounds in my opinion, including religious, to not allow an individual to attend these

classes and chapel on the basis of their sex. This motion is not about gender differences, it is about gender exclusion. (Cavin speech, Townhall, March 3, 1997)

Several other arguments by faculty in favor of gender exclusion were raised at the Townhall meeting as well. One was that the class "Authentic Manhood" met disclosure needs of the male students. They argued that it is difficult for men to discuss personal "dark" issues in front of women, and they need a private environment that allows them to share freely. I pointed out that the role of the university is to educate students, not provide therapy. I also argued that it is irresponsible for a university to give credit (especially upper-division credit) for therapy sessions. I stated:

> If we interpret educating the whole person as providing students with therapy, we run the risk of creating a narcissistic therapeutic culture which seeks only that which makes them "feel good." If we embrace this therapeutic culture we may leave behind the hard work of preparing our students for a lifetime of intellectual pursuit. (Cavin speech, Townhall, March 3, 1997)

A second argument that was made was that while at that time there existed no comparable class for women (e.g., "Authentic Womanhood"), that might be a solution. I responded to this by stating that this was the response to race issues in the Civil Rights Movement. Historically, in fact, many Christians built a case, based on scripture, to keep the races separate. It has been found unconstitutional to do so in this country. More general discussion among faculty concluded with the Gender Exclusion Committee's being charged to research the subject thoroughly and to present a position in favor of or against gender exclusion to the faculty at the next meeting in May.

Surprise No. 3

Several weeks before the final Townhall Meeting of the year, scheduled for May 5, 1997, the Gender Exclusion Committee contacted me to explain that after several months of research and deliberation they were going to recommend a motion to the faculty in the following form:

> We move that all academic curricula at Sunrise University (including chapels and conferences with required attendance) shall be open to both genders.

The motion was almost identical in nature to the one I had presented at the beginning of the academic year. This came as a surprise, especially in light of the position of the members on the committee initially. However, the committee's research and discussions had brought them to this conclusion. In order for the committee to place their motion on the floor, I had to be willing to withdraw my motion. On May 5, 1997, in the presence of another record attendance, I stood and read the following statement:

> After examining the motion the committee presented, the end result is precisely what I called for in my motion, and since there is no need for two similar motions to be on the floor at the same time, I withdraw mine and lend my support to the committee's motion. (Cavin speech, Townhall, May 5, 1997)

At that time, pandemonium broke loose in the room. One faculty member from the Department of Theology stood and stated that if the faculty voted for this motion, "any ideology could be put in place." He explained, "An egalitarian viewpoint could be taught to our students and our alumni would mistakenly believe that we are as a university taking an egalitarian political position which is unbiblical." This statement struck to the heart of the issue. An egalitarian view holds that men and women should be considered equal with each other in all ways, including leadership.

Another theology faculty member stood and pointed out that if a university faculty vote was taken against gender exclusion, then their department would simply decide to override the vote and act autonomously, offering the class in spite of the outcome of the university faculty decision. He claimed that the Department of Theology was "sovereign." This seemed to strike to the heart of the political issue as well, in that some viewed themselves as "sovereign" or independent when in fact a university should be grounded in "dialogue" between disciplines, particularly when involved with university-wide policies and issues.

At that time, communication became very confusing, voices speaking over others; swiftly one demanded a vote, a second was offered, and without further discussion, a vote was taken. The motion raised by the Gender Exclusion Committee was defeated by a 4 to 1 margin. The meeting was over.

ANALYSIS

The convergence of an institutional problem of gender exclusion and male backlash phenomenon with a traditional hierarchical organizational structure should have provided an opportunity to dismantle one while calling into question the other. The gender exclusion issue pointed to, mirrored, and threatened a larger political system of university patriarchal and hierarchical power. It seems clear that incorporating communication and rhetorical skills through the traditional organizational network system does not work in the face of such power. In fact, it only served to entrench the power structure further. When those in power saw the issue defined, clarified, and brought to light, it led them to protect and enforce the power structure further. In using the traditional linear mode of organizational communication, all opportunities were lost, the problem was exacerbated, and the power structure was validated.

In her article "Gaining a Voice: Feminist Organizational Communication Theorizing," Patrice M. Buzzanell (1994) examines the need for feminist study of organizational communication. She explains that much of organizational research has been from a cause–effect linear approach because this is perceived as direct and rational (male). She writes:

> Because linear thinking assumes that there is one best way to live and conduct organizational activities, it creates oppositional thinking, whereby we lapse into forgetting that there are alternatives. As a result, other (female) values and definitions of organizational effectiveness often pose deviant and "incorrect" alternatives to social and organizational situations. (p. 358)

She believes, with others, that examining multiple interpretations explained through narratives can enhance organizational communication, stories of lived experiences in the workplace (p. 367).

I adopted what Buzzanell (1994) calls a "liberal feminist perspective," which seeks to use the system to achieve voice rather than denying it or trying to overthrow it (pp. 372–373). Once I began to seek voice in the Townhall, however, I was perceived by many as attempting to seek "redress" and "overthrow" the current system. According to my understanding of Buzzanell's template, I failed because I did not fully appreciate the effectiveness of the liberal feminist perspective. Had I used this perspective with more strategic communication forethought, I might have achieved a difference in the outcome.

In the book *The Organizational Woman,* Haslett, Geis, and Carter (1996) discuss specific "liberal" strategies women can use to work within the organization that can potentially lead to change and success. One way is to informally network with various individuals within the workplace in order to receive suggestions and gain support before information is communicated formally. It is useful to build alliances rather than "crusading" alone. This also allows people to have an opportunity to think about the issues, articulate their viewpoints in a nonthreatening environment, and give their support for the ideas presented. This alliance, contrary to some forms of feminism, needs to include both men and women. In retrospect, I believe that I might have been more successful had I developed an alliance in this manner.

OUTCOME: REAL MEN WHO PRAY TOGETHER STAY TOGETHER

As a result of the process, not only is there an "Authentic Manhood" class, but because of the great popularity of the class with males on campus, there is now an additional class titled "Biblical Manhood." Periodically an "Authentic Womanhood" class is offered that uses the same textbook as the male class and embraces the same political agenda. Exclusionary chapels continue to exist, and in fact, soon I began to see posters on campus reading "Sunrise Women, You Are Abba's Daughters." Again, rhetorically, there is the interesting metaphor of women as "daughters" or more specifically, children. Historically, perceiving women as children has indicated a position for women that suggests they are not mature and are unable to care for themselves. I believe that this class is offered periodically in order to give a nod to the issue of Title IX and protect the university from lawsuits. Although this may well technically meet criteria given by Title IX, I do not believe it is honoring the letter or intent of the law. However, in any case, Title IX was only one part of the issue. I communicated this issue to the Sunrise faculty because I believe that any form of exclusion, discrimination, or segregation should not exist in an educational environment. It should not exist for persons based on their gender or race.

It is interesting to note the general response of students and faculty to the exclusionary classes and chapels. One faculty member in the English Department asked the female students why they were so silent regarding the issue I had raised. The general response was that they did not care about the subject because they did not see how the classes or chapels affected them or their relationships with men in any way. Some said that they in fact thought the class was a good class for males because they learned to take their "responsibilities" toward women more seriously and to be "leaders." Overall, many women on campus in fact support and encourage the men to take the class and go to "male only" chapels because they want the men to "lead them." Many of the women at Sunrise are seeking men who will be an "authority" over them in all areas, including spiritual, relational, physical, and so on. I have male students from time to time in my classes who express pressure from females to "perform" in this way. I say this to point out that individuals from both genders exacerbate the problem. I must say that there is a small minority of students in my classes who communicate a different perspective and welcome opportunities for men and women to be seen and treated with respect as equals. They are, however, a very small group.

Once the dust had cleared, I also found that many faculty were irritated with me for having raised the issue because they felt I had squandered my opportunity to speak on their behalf in the faculty Townhall regarding issues such as pay. They felt the issue of gender equality was not very important and should not have been a priority. Their reaction may be explained by attributing a subconscious motivation to their attitudes. It could be that there is a group backlash fantasy at work here, and a real effort is also at work to maintain the parameters of that narrative. The fantasy includes Sunrise as a place where men can return to a system where the rule of the day is authority and where men need only give male voice to an idea and it becomes truth by virtue of that masculine authority. Everything in this group fantasy world is sharply defined and ordained by a male god so that there is no need for a dialectic exchange of multiple voices where other perspectives are invited. The fantasy world is a final utopia where subjectivity has been banned and all live on the word (logos) that falls from the mouths of men.

CONCLUSION

In a chapter titled "Men's Psychological Development: A Relational Perspective," Stephen J. Bergman (1995) explains that men are taught to separate themselves from their mothers from the time they are very young in order to establish their own sexual identities. They may spend their entire lives reinforcing and communicating how they are different from initially their mother and later any woman, in order to maintain their identities. They do this many times at great expense to a "primary desire for connection with others" (p. 72). Bergman also explores modern men's groups and expresses several concerns with them. One problem he has is that men need to "break out of the tired concept of separation/individuation and strong independent male role and identity as prelude to relationship and learn about mutual relationship, which means not only developing it in ourselves but fostering it in others" (p. 88). Berman goes on to point out:

> In my work with men, it is clear that they are comfortable with each other—there is a lot of laughing and finding common experience. It is in the next step, when the genders face each other across the room, that the conflicts through difference arise, the feelings deepen, and the vital work—inevitably moving through the process of male dread and female anger, toward mutuality—gets done. (p. 88)

Bergman concludes:

> No amount of us men learning how to be warriors alone together or jumping out of airplanes alone or together, or seeing our fathers as human-sized will help us learn to relate to women, or perhaps even learn what is meant by "mutual." Male-male work, if it stays male-male, may fragment energy and deflect power, seeding violence and destruction in the process. The missing piece, the learning and empowering piece, is to do that which is new to our age: bring men and women back from their enclaves into the creative space called relationship. (p. 88)

Bergman's point is that the real challenge for the future is not more same-sex exclusion, but a coming together of the sexes in order to dispense with mystery about each other and build relationships based on understanding and respect. This will potentially benefit both men and women when this can occur. This is a worthy challenge for the future, to bring men and women together into the "creative space called relationship"; and only then can we begin to understand what is truly "authentic" personhood.

REFERENCES

Bergman, S. J. (1995). Men's psychological development. In R. F. Levant & W. S. Pollack (Eds.), *A new psychology of men.* New York: Basic Books.

Bly, R. (1990). *Iron John: A book about men.* Reading, MA: Addison-Wesley.

Buzzanell, P. M. (1994). Gaining a voice: Feminist organizational communication theorizing. *Management Communication Quarterly, 7,* 339–383.

Haslett, B., Geis, F. L., & Carter, M. R. (1996). *The organizational woman: Power and paradox.* Norwood, NJ: Ablex.

Pelka, F. (1995). Men do not need to become more manly. In D. Bender, B. Leone, & J. Petrikin (Eds.), *Male/female roles: Opposing viewpoints.* San Diego: Greenhaven Press.

Piper, J., & Grudem, W. (Eds.). (1991). *Recovering biblical manhood and womanhood: A response to evangelical feminism.* Wheaton, IL: Crossway Books.

Title IX, Education Amendments of 1972 (Title 20 U.S.C. Sections 1681–1688). Available: http://www.dol.gov/dol/oasam/public/regs/statutes/titleix.htm

Titus 2:1–15, *New American Standard Bible.*

GENDERED AUTHORS, GENDERED LEARNING

Patricia MacCormack

ANGLIA POLYTECHNIC UNIVERSITY

MacCormack is interested in the relationship between a person and a given communication message or text. At first glance, many students may not find this idea to be inherently interesting. However, with further thought, this relationship deserves some consideration as it can provide some interesting insights. Why do people respond to the same text (such as a book, television show, movie, or greeting card) in different ways? Why does one person relate to a particular character in a television show while another person has no feelings about the character at all? What makes a text feminine or feminist? What makes it "male"?

Questions such as these can lead students to probe more deeply their own reactions and responses to various texts. As related to gender, discussions can be centered on the responses of men and women to the same text and the variation of responses within the sexes. The article is written from the point of view of a specialist in English literature, but the questions posed in the article can easily be adapted to any text in any situation and will lead to productive discussions.

QUESTIONS FOR DISCUSSION

- *Where does meaning lie—in the mind of the viewer or in the object viewed?*
- *Does the sex of the viewer account for differences in perception?*
- *How do texts (written and visual material) shape the gender of the viewer?*
- *Do the sexes differ in the way each processes visual information? Do males focus on certain aspects and females on others?*

Have you ever watched a television program and liked a character based on the gender identification you have with him/her? Have you ever then acted in a way that could be described as influenced by that character? Where is the gender influence in your reading? Do you read the character in a particular way because you are a girl or boy, woman or man—or is the character informing the ways in which you are a girl or boy, woman or man?

This article will explore the ways in which texts interact with readers and facilitate the ways in which subjects interact with each other. Here, a *text* refers to any form of communication that we are exposed to in culture—television, books, magazines, films, the Internet. Traditionally, texts exist as objects that refer only to themselves. They are seen to hold meaning independent of their readers. Many literature departments continue this understanding of texts by asking the student to look for "authorial" intent, or what the author means in her/his text. However, Roland Barthes (1977) and Michel Foucault (1977) ask the reader to look instead at the way the reader, rather than the author, *makes* meaning in texts. Roland Barthes claims the author is dead; Michel Foucault claims the author never existed as such. Both theorists ask readers of texts to acknowledge the ways in which they, as gendered and culturally constructed subjects, import their own meanings into a text. When we disagree with our friends about certain texts—what they mean, what we like or dislike about them—we are expressing ourselves as creator, rather than decipherer, of meaning in these texts. Barthes sums up this idea by claiming "In the multiplicity of writing, everything is to be *disentangled*, nothing *deciphered*" (p. 148). Whereas deciphering suggests finding a truthful meaning within the language of a text, disentanglement instead refers to finding certain meanings in texts that are based on the reader, the time and place the reader exists within, even the faculty and teacher of the text.

Traditional analyses of texts refers to deciphering them based on three underlying beliefs about the text:

1. The text is an expression of private ideas.
2. The author is a master/creator/reference point of the text.
3. The relationship between the text and the author's aim is a one-to-one relationship.

Barthes altered these three critical concepts, replacing them with three problems:

1. The fundamental ambiguity of the text, its potential meanings
2. The impossibility of ever knowing what an author is informed by in his/her writing, let alone what our own minds are informed by when we read and comprehend
3. The plurality of meaning in any system that includes author, text, *and* reader

Rather than deciphering the somewhat impossible puzzle of a singular meaning in an author's work, Foucault and Barthes instead encourage us to disentangle meaning in the text based on its situatedness

- in our hands (*who* are we?)
- in our time (*when* are we?)
- in our classroom (*where* are we, which *subject*, which *teacher*?)

Meaning as a singular concept is altered after Foucault and Barthes to more closely align with what we would understand today as *opinion*. But we should not think opinion is simply "what I think today." Opinion is a reflection of our history, our cultural situatedness (where we are located) and the particularities of our bodies (our gender, race, sexuality, class). This does not mean that all readers who are female will necessarily have the same opinion about a text—for example, whether it is sexist or not. Rather, the many intersections of subjectivity—race, class, sexuality, gender, history—mean that very few people will share an identical opinion about the meaning and, more important, the effects of a text.

- Do you know anyone who appears *the same* as you?
- Does he/she share the same opinions about texts?
- What do you think creates the differences in opinions from people who are the same gender, race, or even in the same classroom as you?

What this form of opinion creates is an idea of specificity in the world, where meaning and its effect as it is incarnated in texts can never be predicted, because to predict the effect of a text (i.e., what it means) would be to claim that all subjects are the same. Here we have the transferal of a text as a "thing" we study and then leave alone, to a producer of meaning in the world.

Foucault (1977) poses these very queries when he interrogates what he calls the "author-function." Instead of thinking of the function of the author as being the means by which we can "find out" what the text means, the function of the author for Foucault is the way in which the text is applied to our reading. Our idea of the author informs our reading.

- Do you like to know the gender of authors?
- Why do you think the gender of the author is important?
- Is it always important? For example, is it important for a feminist text to be written by a woman? Does it matter only sometimes, all the time, or never?

Foucault (1977) suggests we transfer our questions about texts from who the author is to what we make of the texts. No longer the tiresome repetitions:

- "Who is the real author?"
- "Have we proof of his authenticity and originality?"
- "What has he revealed of his most profound self in his language?"

New questions will be heard:

- "What are the modes of existence of this discourse?"
- "Where does it come from; how is it circulated; who controls it?"

- "What placements are determined for possible subjects?"
- "Who can fulfill these diverse functions of the subject?" (p. 138)

We have all probably been in classes where the first questions are heard, and in some classes, like history, these may be pertinent. But let us take the second set of questions and look at them individually to begin to understand what "disentanglement" refers to.

1. **"What are the modes of existence of this discourse?"** Here a text is interrogated twofold: the modes of existence of this discourse refer to how the text was produced and how it is read. A mode of existence is contingent on time and culture. We now read African American literature and feminist literature, whereas one hundred years ago these texts were not in existence. Therefore, it is because of our current culture, not because African Americans and feminists were not writing, that we are enabled to read these texts. However, these texts are still not considered entirely "mainstream," so their mode of existence still has a long way to go before they achieve the status of importance they demand.

Mode of existence refers also to what Foucault in *The Order of Things* (1966/1994) calls an "episteme." An episteme is a stream or genre of knowledge. Science is a different episteme to English literature; ideas about language, authorship, and truthfulness are entirely different between faculties. On a social level, our opinions not simply about texts but about their mode of existence will differ. A feminist student may claim that the mode of discourse we know as "modern science" was only enabled by the exclusion of female scientists for a long period in the history of science, whereas a traditional student may have come to learn this discourse as truthful. Therefore, a traditional scientist will interact differently with the scientific texts and community—perhaps not questioning them—than will a more suspicious feminist scientist. Another example: In Australia the white legal system, another form of text, is understood to be the law that regulates all Australian culture. Many indigenous Australian people believe in their own traditional law. Thus, two forms of law exist simultaneously in Australia although the government only recognizes one. One form of law affects white Australians, but more than one affects some indigenous Australians. A discourse's history, its place in culture and within individuals, enables the particularities of its existence, which then regulate the effect it has on an individual. The way indigenous Australians interact with one another, and with white Australians, is a reflection of the particular form of law they are using. The concrete ways in which our bodies interact with one another here depends on the form of text we are thinking about, using, and believing in different situations.

2. **"Where does it come from; how is it circulated; who controls it?"** The control of a form of text is important because unless we have a certain amount of control over a text, we are powerless to change it. In traditional culture, white, male,

upper-class people were on the whole the creators of texts that affect all people, such as science or the law. Now, however, these texts are being infiltrated by different kinds of people who see a need to change the texts because the texts then change the way we live. Native inhabitants and even female lawyers, doctors, and teachers sometimes utilize traditional texts in different ways, therefore creating new spaces for the inclusion of their people. The way a feminist lawyer uses the law creates a different interaction between herself, her client, and the court than a conventional lawyer reading the law.

3. "What placements are determined for possible subjects?" Think about the following questions: What is your favorite television show? Are you in that show? Or is there someone who could be you? How many placement potentials do you see in the show? Is everybody in the show like you? If so, is that one of the features that makes you like the show? If not, is the diversity what you like about the show? To what extent do you identify with the subjects in the show, and to what extent do you identify with a desire to be like the subjects in the show? Are you able to identify with many characters, some of whom are like you, some of whom are seemingly unlike you?

There is a common understanding in film, television, and written literature that identification is only available to the most "obvious" and through the most similar characters to those characters whom the viewer most resembles. Do you ever consider the possibility that we can identify with those who do not immediately resemble ourselves? For example, Laura Mulvey's influential film essay "Visual Pleasure and Narrative Cinema" (1975, 1990) claims that only men are able to identify as male protagonists when watching films and that women must either identify with the women-as-objects on-screen (itself a problematic assumption) or "become" men to identify with male characters.

Suggesting that a woman is only able to identify with another woman insinuates that a viewer (or reader) is a stable and completed subject. Rather, I would suggest that any act of interaction with a film, a book, or even a scientific theory brings with it a certain power to form the subject who reads it. So Foucault's question "What placements are determined for possible subjects?" refers to many things. It refers to the possible subjectivity of the author and her/his world. It refers to the many available characters with which a reader could identify, either across gender and race or in conformance with the reader's race and gender. The question also refers to the state of the subject in relation to the constitutive power of the text to inform the subject's own self. When we read a glossy magazine and feel pressure to have *that* body or *those* shoes, we are reconstituting our ideas of our own femaleness or maleness. On a more academic level, when we read texts that radically alter the way we think, our idea of our own being in the world may be altered, hence speaking "I" may be different from the moment before. Our subject placement, in

Foucault's words, has changed. We, as individuals, have many "possible subjects" in us. How many different people, or even your pets, do you identify with, in feelings, in image, in thought, each day?

4. **"Who can fulfill these diverse functions of the subject?"** This question relates to the ideas I ended the previous paragraph with, but another "subject" should be considered here. Not only is the subjectivity of the reader important, but also the subjectivity of the discourse is vital in understanding the discursive power of a text. For example, science is a discourse that claims to rely on truthful statements and objective practices in order to speak knowledge. A novel is a text that claims pure fantasy as its aim. It creates many subjects in its story; it does not wish to impact on daily life in the same way as science (indeed novels are often seen as an "escape" from daily existence). *We* as readers must be two different subjects when we read each of these epistemes because the epistemes themselves are different forms of discourse—they themselves could be like different subjects of discourse, and certainly their language refers to different subjects. When we read a scientific text about the newest HIV breakthrough or a possible AIDS cure, we are different from the reader of a Mills and Boon romance. Not only must we think about different things and within different contexts, but also we almost have to speak different languages. The language of a scientific textbook is different from the language of a novel.

Science is probably a more "difficult" discourse for everyday people to deal with. It often requires a standardized level of education to comprehend, which in turn requires certain access to money to go to college or to purchase books. Different cultures access science differently. Chinese medicine is a science that is entirely different from Western medicine. So the "who" fulfilling the diverse functions of the subject is a specific "who." A "who" refers to a certain culture, socioeconomic level, and depending on the politics of the company or the episteme in question, gender or race (remember most CEOs are still white men). This means that the reader is a specific "who" as well, one who may never enter the episteme of science as a practitioner, or one who is expected to. The subjectivity of the episteme is determined often by its own ability to engender change and access to many readers. Michael Payne (1997) states, "Epistemes both enable and limit the production of knowledge, not simply by external, institutional or political manipulation but by their own determination of the extent of possible intellectual production" (p. 45). Many epistemes are particularly resistant to change. The ability to make meaning in a text enables that text to be altered, as discussed above. So when a feminist teacher, for example, interacts with a text by teaching her/his students her/his opinion of that text, the students may, as a result of the text, interact in a more feminist way with other texts *and* with other people.

Elizabeth Grosz (1995) asks, "What makes a text feminine or feminist?" She comes up with four answers. I would like to reapply these answers, as I did with Foucault's answers earlier, to our understanding of the ways in which reading constitutes our own knowledge and us. Grosz's answers are: "(1) The sex of the author; (2) the content of the text; (3) the sex of the reader; and (4) the style of the text" (p. 11).

In order to work through these four responses, I will first propose definitions for the terms "feminist" and "feminine." In the context of learning and reading, "feminine" could refer to anything that is either traditionally aligned with women or anything by which women themselves would choose to be defined. A feminine text may be a text written for, about, or by women, but also a text that may be read as marginal or nondominant. Like knowledge, the term "feminine" comes to refer to something that is historically as well as culturally contingent. Thus, a feminine text now may not always be so. Similarly, a feminist text refers to specifically political challenges to dominant modes of patriarchy. A feminist text takes as its central aim a desire to disrupt or disentangle patriarchal knowledge that may otherwise go uninvestigated or be unquestionably taken as truthful. A feminine or feminist text is a form of *"minoritarian"* text. According to Deleuze and Guattari (1987), a minoritarian is any person or thing that does not hold the established position of power—this includes women despite their population being higher than men. For Deleuze and Guattari, "Majority implies a state of domination" (p. 291). The sex of the author does not make the meaning of the text but may contextualize the meaning of the text for the reader, for the time and place the text is being read within. The reader of the text as maker of its effect, however, is the way by which the text becomes interactive with others. Only when two opinions about a text are shared can different meanings be formed.

The content of the text is similarly open to contingency in its meaning, although this may not always be clear. We are ready to argue over our opinions of a television show text, but less game to argue over the contents of a math textbook. Why? The content has, in both cases, been authored as such. Our role as readers of gender, race, and color is visible when responding to the television show; we do or do not like something because of the way it represents our society or us. A math textbook is less clear in relation to the ways in which it represents gender. But it does represent gender in its content. How? By presenting knowledge that claims to be gender-free, a math textbook claims there is no gender in its knowledge, which covers over the history of math as traditionally a white male field of discovery.

Think about the statistics of math professors in universities. Do you estimate they would be more male or female dominated? What effect do you think this knowledge would have on your understanding of math? Some? None? All of these questions have an effect on the way we as readers comprehend the content of a book, whether the book obviously lends itself to such gendered reading, such as a feminist book, or seems unrelated, such as a math textbook. In order for us to read in a gendered context as feminist rather than simply masculine or feminine, we must ask questions of gender of all forms of knowledge, not simply the obvious ones. This form of inquiry of all knowledge leads to Grosz's third answer, which refers to the gender of the reader. If the reader is a minoritarian, the specificity of his or her minoritarianism will affect his or her reading in unique combinations. If the reader is a majoritarian, the interrogation of the text may be different. The male, white reader may wish to align himself with the minoritarian by taking an interest in feminist texts or texts that explore racial, sexual, and cultural difference. In this way, certain readers can begin to alter their readership by actively wishing to change their position. Similarly, certain minoritarians may become majoritarian—for example, a female scientist may not always be a feminist scientist if she practices her science in a traditional manner.

The style of the text, Grosz's fourth answer, is the most similar to the disentanglement of Barthes. "Style" is a particularly ambiguous word because it refers to the genre or episteme of the text; the text's author and the reader's understanding of the author; the time and place of the text's creation and the time and place of the current reading; the reader's gender, race, sexuality, culture, mood; and endless other specifics of the reader; the way in which the text is being taught, whereby the lecturer becomes another form of author. What the style refers to is the absolute unpredictability of any authentically truthful meaning in a text. This does not mean that nothing in a text is true, but only that all truth presented in a text is a contingent truth that relies on many factors both within and outside its medium to make it meaningful.

When Barthes encourages us to disentangle texts, he does not mean this to happen once. Disentanglement may occur repetitively and endlessly. Most important, disentanglement can and does occur between two people rather than simply at home privately and alone. All communication is a form of disentanglement when ideas are being produced rather than opinions being forced. Although the above definition of the meaning of texts can be frustrating and unclear, a lack of answers, of singular meanings, and of right and wrong comprehension is no lack at all. It rather proliferates meaning in every person's understanding of a text. Rather than referring to "anything goes," it refers to a validation of every reader's making of meaning and a volition for people to share those meanings; hence, any person's opinion of a text is itself a text that is up for analysis, interpretation, and interaction.

Two hundred years ago white middle- and upper-class heterosexual men made meaning, reproduced meaning, and taught how meaning is understood. Today, however, this idea of singular meaning asks the question "meaning for whom?" New questions follow, and members of every gender, race, and culture are able to make meaning based on their own lived experiences. This is not a wild or unaccountable version of reading. For each meaning that a person makes, his/her reasons for formulating such meaning are sought. Meaning, however, loses its power of "oneness," which loosens one kind of person's control over its inception and reproduction. The style of a text becomes the ways in which such a text can be disentangled between people rather than within a person. Reading authors, as readers, we come to understand reading as a flux-process rather than linear action.

READING AS THE PRODUCTION OF MEANING

How does a text produce meaning, and what is the difference between the production of meaning and simply meaning as existing in a book? When we think of a book, we think that book sits in the library containing the meanings it has. If we do not like what a book says, we can simply return it to the shelf and ignore it. Or can we? When we read or view a text, the meanings it forms in our head, mingled with the specificity of our subjectivity, is not extractable. We cannot unread a text, can we? Even if we disagree with a text, then, we have made—or produced—a meaning from that text simply because we have thought about it. This will necessarily be different from the meaning our classmates have made about the same text.

- Think of a text you dislike.
- Are you still able to think about that text, form an opinion of it?
- What is that opinion?
- How does your opinion differ from the opinions of others around you?

The fact that texts make us think new things, whether or not we like them, reflects the constituting powers of texts. What this means is that we are not simply a certain gender, race, or even body. Our ability to be a certain gender, race, and body comes from our understanding of what these terms *can* mean. When we think "gender," we are only able to think what we know from culture, and at its broadest level culture is nothing more than an interlocking mesh of texts—television, film, books, but also science, the law, and even speech. There is no "gender" outside of culture, and hence there is no "gender" purely outside of texts. However, we should not think, simply because we only understand concepts like "gender" or "race" through culture's texts, that these understandings are clear, immediate, or even comprehensible. D. N. Rodowick (1997) emphasizes, "Our relationship to the image is neither determined nor dialectical" (p. 209). Although we come to think terms such as "gender" through culture, we certainly do not all think them the same, or even accept them. There is instability at the very heart of texts whereby no text can ever predict its reader's response, and therefore texts provoke, more than meaning, mediation between people, opinions, and reception.

This is why a thoughtful study of authorship as being made within individuals is so important. When we feel we are being discriminated against, it is not because there is something hurtfully untrue about us being said, but because the cultural representation of "us" is so limited, and the pervasive "reading" of certain bodies, black, female, poor, is offensive. *We* are not offensive, but the "authorship" of our bodies (as stupid or violent or passive or other stereotypes) per se is offensive. By vocalizing our readings and opinions of texts, we are creating more alternative readings of those texts, and hence our interaction with others becomes a diversifying sharing of opinions rather than a closing off of potential readings.

Returning to Deleuze, I want to claim that the practice of reading is like the practice of "being"—a series of interchanges that sees each entity aligning itself with the other (text/author-reader) to produce a variable that both constitutes the text and the reader as a result of the effect of the other. This form of effect that changes and creates is really more an "affect," a full alteration of the reader and the text rather than simply a reading and comprehension. Rosi Braidotti (2000) explains Deleuze's definition of such affect as "a folding-in of external influences and a simultaneous unfolding outwards of affects" (p. 159). When we read, the way texts affect us folds outward from book to self. It changes the way we think, it forms our opinions, and it makes us behave differently. Simultaneously, we fold our own affects (thoughts, opinions, moods, identification as gendered) inward to create meaning in the text. This is why texts have different meanings for different people. It is what forms our own opinions, which to a certain extent are already formed before we pick up a book. It is what creates diversity in meaning in the classroom and in the world. Diversity nourishes gender studies, because gender itself refers to more than one gender, hence more than one way to read, more than one way to be affected by reading, and more than one way to respond.

REFERENCES

Barthes, Roland. (1977). The death of the author. *Image-music-text* (Stephen Heath, Trans.). London: Fontana Paperbacks.

Braidotti, Rosi. (2000). Tératologies. In Ian Buchanan & Claire Colebrook (Eds.), *Deleuze and feminist theory*. Edinburgh: University of Edinburgh Press.

Deleuze, Gilles, & Guattari, Félix. (1987). *A thousand plateaus: Capitalism and schizophrenia* (Brian Massumi, Trans.). Minneapolis: University of Minnesota Press.

Foucault, Michel. (1977). What is an author? *Language, counter-memory, practice: Selected essays and interviews* (Donald Bouchard, Ed.). Oxford: Basil Blackwell.

Foucault, Michel. (1994). *The order of things: An archaeology of the human sciences*. New York: Vintage Books, Random House. (Original work published 1966)

Grosz, Elizabeth. (1995). *Space, time and perversion: The politics of bodies*. Sydney: Allen & Unwin.

Mulvey, Laura. (1975). Visual pleasure and narrative cinema. *Screen*, 16.

Mulvey. Laura. (1990). Afterthoughts on "Visual Pleasure and Narrative Cinema" inspired by *Duel in the Sun*. In E. Ann Kaplan (Ed.), *Psychoanalysis and cinema* (pp. 24–35). New York: Routledge.

Payne, Michael. (1997). *Reading knowledge: An introduction to Barthes, Foucault, and Althusser*. Malden, MA: Blackwell.

Rodowick, D. N. (1997). *Gilles Deleuze's time machine*. Durham and London: Duke University Press.

NONVERBAL COMMUNICATION, YOUR APPEARANCE, TRADITIONAL STEREOTYPES

A Fashion Alert!

Kelly Quintanilla

TEXAS A&M UNIVERSITY, CORPUS CHRISTI

Although we learn from childhood that we should never judge a book by its cover, few would argue that we are constantly making assumptions about people based on the limited data of initial interaction. The initial stimuli generated by a new other is filtered and interpreted through several lenses. Gender filters and role expectations, for instance, suggest how males and females should dress to fulfill particular social roles. Using male standards of power and their relationship to fashion, Kelly Quintanilla compares the different fashion rules for professional women and men in the United States as she considers the potential suppression of women's professional and corporate power through fashion. Although her emphasis is on the disadvantages females may experience in light of gender-dictated professional fashion, Quintanilla cautions her male readers that the fashion and pharmaceutical industries are beginning to destabilize the empowered male's professional image through their promotion of the young, muscular, thick-haired corporate male model.

QUESTIONS FOR DISCUSSION

- *How does the author define "professional" attire?*
- *How does the author's notion of what constitutes clothing appropriate for a professional job interview coincide with your own perceptions of appropriate attire for job interviews, as an interviewee and interviewer?*
- *Do you agree with the author's descriptions of expectations of fashion for male and female interviewees? If not, how do they differ, and to what do you attribute the differences?*

- *Another point worth considering as you read this piece is the potential disadvantages fashion poses for males. For instance, given the highly competitive nature of job markets, might fashion provide a means for individuals to distinguish themselves? If an ability to set oneself apart from other qualified candidates is an advantage, might the limited options for males' professional attire be a detriment to males' pursuit of employment?*
- *In comparing males' professional garb to females', the author acknowledges that both are swathed in attire that often is not very comfortable—panty hose and heels for women, neckties and suit coats for men—noting that there seems to be more discomfort inherent in females' professional clothing. Do you think this conclusion accurately depicts the state of men's professional clothing choices? (Hint: You may want to consider, for example, how dark trousers and a suit coat in the midday heat of a sweaty August day compare to a sleeveless, loose-fitting, ankle-length cotton dress.)*
- *Consider the complex relationship of gender and fashion to the economics and politics of fashion. How, for example do these relationships influence gender socialization and reinforcement of gender roles and stereotypes? How might the politics of fashion contribute to the perpetuation of gender differences within corporate cultures?*

Recently I served on a discussion panel following a "Dress for Success" fashion show. During the discussion, a career services expert advised the student audience, "Women should wear a business suit with a skirt, not pants, to the first round of job interviews, and men should not wear earrings." "Isn't this the twenty-first century?" one of the students inquired. "Do those rules still apply?"

As I began to formulate my response, I had a flashback to my first job fair ten years before. As my male classmates and I strolled across campus, I was feeling very confident in my sharp new business suit. However, I quickly began to notice that this trip differed from the countless other trips I had taken with these classmates. Unlike the previous trips, I was having difficulty keeping up. Usually we were dressed in casual attire, but today we were dressed "professionally." For me this meant high-heeled pumps, which hindered my walking. I could not proceed at the same rapid pace as my male counterparts in their flat dress shoes. Furthermore, my narrow skirt restricted the length of my stride. My classmates were all in pants. The fact that my purse continually had to be readjusted, as it slid from my shoulder, also slowed my pace. The men did not have this worry; their pants had pockets. My outfit did not have pockets, so I needed a purse for my wallet, keys, and lipstick. There I was—the picture of the modern women, dressed in clothing that restricted my movement, clothing that sent a message that I was less active and less powerful. I was sending this message via nonverbal communication. Nonverbally, I was communicating that I could not keep up.

WHAT IS NONVERBAL COMMUNICATION?

According to Knapp and Hall (1997, p. 5), "To most people the phrase nonverbal communication refers to communication effected by means other than words (assuming words are the verbal element)." Nonverbal messages can be sent in many ways. One can send a nonverbal message through tone of voice, gestures, touch, smell, and more. In addition, objects such as clothing, uniforms, shoes, makeup, jewelry, purses, and briefcases send nonverbal messages about the person wearing them.

In the above example, I was communicating through a specific type of nonverbal communication known as demeanor. Demeanor is "the way one presents and conducts oneself" (Henley, 1977, p. 83). Demeanor is often used to show such things as class and power differences. By wearing our business attire, my classmates and I were trying to send the message that we belonged in a "professional" class.

Nonverbal communication plays a critical role in the job interviewing process. When you walk into a job interview, the interviewer has very little information from which to judge your competence. In most cases the only information the interviewer has is your resume and the impression that you make during the interview. That impression is based largely on the nonverbal components of your interview. According to White (1983), "an estimated 65 percent of the hiring decision is based on nonverbal aspects of the interview" (p. 16). Josette Veltri, director of an image consulting firm, estimates that "55–80% of the first impression you make is visual" ("Job Seekers Should," 1995, p. 6).

How long does it take an interviewer to form an impression? It depends on who you ask. Virginia Sullivan, president of Image Communication International in New York City, only gives the interviewee 3 seconds to make that first impression ("It's a Look," 1995). Other experts estimate candidates have from 10 seconds to 16 minutes to show their competence (Martin, 1995; Repinski, 1999; "Initial Minutes," 2000). Regardless of whether the candidate has a few seconds or a few minutes to form a positive impression, it is clear that nonverbal communication plays an important role in the interviewing process, since not much information can be conveyed verbally in such a short amount of time.

This brings us back to the business suit. All of my classmates and I were dressed in business suits; therefore, we were all communicating nonverbally that we were in a "professional" class. But we may not have been communicating that we belonged to the same class. The differences between my classmate's male suit and my female suit conveyed traditional male and female stereotypes. According to Ivy and Backlund (2000), "Stereotypes can be useful, but they are often too general, exaggerated, inaccurate, and unfavorable, and they are very difficult to dislodge" (p. 69). When I entered my interview, I was nonverbally sending the stereotyped message that I, as a woman, was less active and less powerful than my male colleagues. These sorts of traditional stereotypes may help explain why interviewers still prefer male candidates over female candidates (Guerrero, DeVito, & Hecht, 1999).

WOMEN'S FASHION: A LOOK BACK

To understand how clothing can be used to convey traditional stereotypes, it is important to take a historical look at the fashion industry. Historically, women's clothing has reinforced the traditional stereotype of the less active, less powerful female. In the work *American Beauty,* Lois Banner (1983) identifies fashion phases throughout U.S. history. One item that was used during several fashion phases was the corset. A corset, according to Webster's Dictionary, is "a stiffened girdle worn to shape the figure." The corset was used to pull women in so they could achieve the desired appearance. "Throughout most of the century, from the 1820's on, the stylish circumference was eighteen inches, a waist measurement so out of line with normal body dimensions that most women could achieve it only by tightening their corsets" (Banner, 1983, p. 48). Attempting to create an 18-inch waist, the same size as the diameter of an official basketball hoop, may sound impossible, but for fashion's sake, these women tried. As Scarlett O'Hara shows us in *Gone with the Wind,* one woman would hang onto a bedpost as an another woman pulled the corset as tight as possible, to the point of pain, and then secured it. It is not surprising that this practice had negative consequences. Corseting was "a practice that caused headaches and fainting spells and may have been the primary cause of uterine and spinal disorders wide spread among nineteenth-century women, as many contemporary doctors and reformers contended" (Banner, 1983, p. 48). The modest Southern belle, a model of femininity, has repeatedly been portrayed as very fragile and powerless. One way this image has been communicated nonverbally is through fainting spells. In reality the modest Southern Belle fainted due to reduced lung capacity, rather than a fragile disposition. High levels of physical activity were nearly impossible when one's corset was properly secured. In addition to nonverbally communicating that these women were less active and powerful than their male contemporaries, the corset also communicated sexual desirability by accentuating the waist. Throughout history articles of clothing such as foot bindings, stiletto heels, false eyelashes, and push-up bras have been used to communicate sexual desirability by accentuating whatever feature was considered fashionable at the time.

The corset is just one of many nineteenth-century fashion items used to create the image of "the fragile and submissive maiden of the Victorian stereotype" (Banner, 1983, p. 43). Believe it or not, this fragile look was so desired that it became fashionable to look ill. Although the corset did not remain a part of twentieth-century fashion (thank goodness!), the Victorian standard of beauty and fashion has not been completely abandoned. In fact, "working women continue to wear a 'uniform' reminiscent of the shirt waist of the 1890s or the dress of the 1920s" (Banner, 1983, p. 290).

WOMEN'S WORKPLACE FASHION

I think most of you will agree that articles of clothing such as the corset did nonverbally communicate a stereotypical message of women as less powerful and less active, but that was then and this is now. Times have changed. According to Dunn (1997), the changes resulting from the increase of women in the workplace are among the most dramatic of the century. A 1995 Bureau of Labor statistic revealed that 45% of all paid workers are women (cited in Dunn, 1997, p. 1). Clearly women's roles have changed, but the stereotypical, nonverbal messages of their clothing have not. In a 1970s clothing advice book, *The Woman's Dress for Success Book,* Molloy (1977) states, "Business people simply do not take women as seriously as they take men" (p. 77). However, he assures us that women can take steps to correct this problem. The first step is for women to "adopt a business uniform" (Molloy, 1977, p. 34). This professional business uniform, which I was wearing in the opening example, is nothing more than a male business suit with more confining and restrictive features. Specifically, women are advised to wear a knee-length skirt instead of pants, 1- to 2-inch pumps instead of flats, and a loose bow tie instead of the traditional tie.

According to *Career World* (White, 1983), since the time Molloy first described the ideal women's business suit, standards have relaxed. But these standards are not so relaxed as to include pants. As White points out, "Young women should continue to choose skirts over pants, tailored over dressy styles" (p. 17). When job interviewers were asked what they look for in the first 10 seconds of a job interview, the majority echoed Molloy's advice: "I expect a woman to be wearing a suit or a dress" (Mattera, 1992, p. 122). Although *The Complete Idiot's Guide to Successful Dressing* (Repinski, 1999) claims women no longer need to follow "the classic dress for success mode" (p. 12), the author recommends a suit with pants only for companies with a casual dress code. If there is any doubt about the dress code, skirts are recommended over pants. Stewart and Cash (1997) sum up the skirt issue with their advice to female interviewees: "Select a business suit or jacket with a skirt rather than slacks. Pant suits were once very controversial, then seemed to gain acceptance in many organizations, particularly government agencies and not-for-profit groups, and have now declined" (p. 250).

Why do all of these interviewers and authors advise female candidates to wear the traditional business uniform? Simply put, it communicates the desired nonverbal message. As Edwards (1998) states, "It's a more professional look" (p. 52). Businesswomen who follow Molloy's recommended fashion advice are labeled as "smartly businesslike" ("The Right Suit," 1988, p. 150) or "close to perfect" ("It's a Look," 1995, p. 186).

Women who stray from the traditional business suit are seen as communicating negative messages. For example, a woman wearing a tightly tailored dress, a revealing slit, or sexy hose risks sending the message that she is a flirt or an airhead ("The Right Suit," 1988; "It's a Look," 1995).

As noted above, Molloy (1977) recommended that women wear knee-length skirts. This length was challenged in the 1980s, when the fashion industry pushed to replace the knee-length skirt with a mini skirt as part of the female business uniform. It seems that the female business suit of the 1970s, which nonverbally communicated less activity and less power was not aligned closely enough with the traditional female stereotype; therefore, sex appeal was added through the mini skirt. Just as the corset accentuated the waist, the mini skirt accentuated the legs. In regard to this change to the mini, an article in *Working Woman* claimed, "The aim of the '80s short skirts is to fit into the suit. Today's short skirt is not a statement of anything more than fashion" (Twidale, 1987, p. 72). But as Bettiner Berch (1987) points out, "American women were being force fed fashion that changed dramatically and arbitrarily each season on the spinach principle: even if you don't like it, it's good for you" (p. 26).

Women did reject the mini skirt in the 1980s, but it resurfaced as part of the business uniform in the 1990s. In fact, the central theme of a 1999 episode of the popular sitcom *Ally McBeal* centered on the appropriateness of mini skirts in the workplace. McBeal, an attorney, fought to wear mini skirts in court when a male judge deemed them unprofessional. Similarly, when her boss complained about mini skirts at work, Cathy, the title character of a comic strip, states, "When we wore pants, men didn't respect us because we looked too 'militant' . . . when we wore long skirts, men didn't respect us because we were too 'frumpy' . . . For 15 years, we've been buying and discarding clothes trying to find a respectable balance between femininity and professionalism and we are sick of it!! If you can't keep your eyeballs where they belong, it is your problem!!" Cathy then privately informs her friend, "Never underestimate the fury of a woman who just paid to have all her clothes shortened" (cited in Ivy & Backlund, 2000, p. 410). In keeping with traditional stereotypes, Cathy is worried about the cost of updating her wardrobe, not the larger issues raised by her statement.

For women in the twenty-first century, the advice concerning mini skirts is mixed. Although Mattera (1992) believes that rules on hemlines are becoming more relaxed, Madeline R. Weeks, fashion director, recommends "no micro minis; nothing shorter than seventeen inches" (cited in "It's a Look," 1995, p. 188).

It is clear that making the business uniform more feminine does not communicate a nonverbal message of equality, but what sort of message does a more masculine business suit send? Women who stray from the traditional female business suit for the traditional male suit are also seen as communicating negative messages. For example, women who wear male business suits with pants, flats, and standard ties are viewed as "too severe" ("The Right Suit," 1988, p. 150) or "kind of a drag" ("It's a Look," 1995, p. 187). By dressing in the identical professional uniform of their male colleagues, these women do not communicate equality in their performance. In fact, even when a woman does wear the suggested female business suit, she may gain some points in professionalism, but she may also lose points in other areas. For example, research by Lennon and Miller (1984) revealed that when businesswomen wear blazers, they are perceived as more respectable but less likable. Similarly, Sweat and Zentner (1985) reported that although the classic suit makes a woman appear more professional, it also makes her seem less approachable.

Regardless of whether women are wearing mini skirts or knee-length skirts, wearing a skirt rather than pants does restrict a woman's ability to move. A straight skirt limits the length of one's stride. It also makes sitting more difficult. A woman in a skirt must be more aware of her posture for fear her hemline will reveal too much leg. This is not a concern for men or women in pants. A knee-length skirt accentuates the calf, while a mini skirt accentuates the entire leg. In either case, skirts are more revealing than pants. Showing skin seems out of line for a business professional, but in line with traditional stereotypes.

Appropriate footwear is another part of Molloy's business uniform. Both Molloy's *The Woman's Dress for Success Book* (1977) and *The Complete Idiot's Guide to Successful Dressing* (Repinski, 1999) recommend a classic pump. Repinski reports that the increased height provided by high heels may provide for more powerful nonverbal communication by placing men and women eye-to-eye. However, she does add that "any confidence the heels bestow will be quickly undermined if you look as though you are going to topple over or the overall look is remotely suggestive" (p. 115). Furthermore, just as varying from the classic business suit can result in negative labeling, so can varying from the classic pump with its 1- to 2-inch heel. A women wearing stiletto heels may be labeled "too ditsy," and a women in flats may be seen as "too casual" ("It's a Look," 1995, p. 188).

Like the skirt, pumps (even pumps with small heels) are far less comfortable than flats. Heels decrease walking speed. They make it more difficult to stay balanced and to carry heavy loads. If comfort breeds confidence, as Repinski (1999) suggests, then clearly pumps have a negative effect on those wearing them. In general, the pumps and skirts of the female business uniform present a nonverbal image of a less active, less powerful, and more sexual business professional than do suits with pants and flats. Like the corset, the female business uniform restricts physical activity and accentuates sexually desirable body parts. It reflects the traditional female stereotype.

MEN'S FASHION

So far we have talked a lot about the traditional female stereotype as it relates to the history of female fashion and the female business suit, but what about the men? The history of fashion for American men is quite simple. "American men did not follow fashions" (Banner, 1983, p. 233). As far back as 1857, it was reported that dark suits were the custom for American men, and not much has changed in the working world (Banner, 1983). Although the ideal for male beauty has taken a few turns over the last two centuries (from small and pale to portly and prosperous to athletic and strong), the uniform of the professional working man has remained remarkably the same.

In a modern community, in which time has a commercial value, what was needed was a simple costume that could easily be put on and off. The suit with shirt and tie fit such a purpose well, and so it had developed (Banner, 1983, p. 234). The vast majority of "dress for success" books and articles written for male job seekers give the same advice—namely, the applicant should wear a dark suit, a white or ivory shirt, and a tie (Stewart & Cash, 1997; Cantore, 1998; Repinski, 1999; White; 1983). Some variations on this theme are permitted. For example, White (1983) tells male job seekers that shirts and ties can be livelier than Molloy recommended. But overall, the male business uniform is a fashion standard.

When wearing the standard male business uniform, job applicants nonverbally communicate professional status. Their movements are not restricted by uncomfortable shoes, straight skirts, or hemlines that may ride up to embarrassing heights. Furthermore, male applicants can enhance their power and status nonverbally through the color of their tie. Stewart and Cash (1997) suggest a dark suit, solid white shirt, and a "contrasting, but not 'wild' tie" (p. 249). The color of the tie can be used to nonverbally communicate confidence and power. For example, during the 1980s red ties were known as power ties.

Like females who stray from the standard, males who do not follow the standard dark suit, white shirt, and tie may be labeled as rebellious, unprofessional, and/or have their sexuality questioned. For example, excessive jewelry and tattooing of any kind is not acceptable. *The Complete Idiot's Guide to Successful Dressing* states:

> Men aren't allowed much adornment, at least from nine to five. Cuff links are one of the tiny bits of glimmer they're permitted to wear in the office. . . . Also acceptable are wedding and conservative rings, like signets and college rings. Collar pins and tie clips are your call (they're reportedly fading in popularity), but bracelets and necklaces are pushing the envelope. (Repinski, 1999, p. 112)

As for earrings, "one or more earrings may negatively affect some interviewers" (Stewart & Cash, 1997, p. 249). Jewelry still does not fit into the traditional male stereotype.

In today's changing world there are, of course, companies that do not subscribe to this standard. Steven Grasse, CEO of Gyro Worldwide, stated, "If they wear a suit, they're automatically out because it means they don't know enough about us. The more tattoos and body piercing, the better I like you" (cited in Brown, 1998, p. 19). But the image, the stereotype of the professional, successful, powerful, and active businessman, is fairly well ingrained in the American psyche. That stereotype does not include tattoos or piercings.

For the men reading this essay, who may feel more confident than many women about the nonverbal messages your appearance is sending, a fashion alert is also warranted. Although a man's professional attire does send a message of more activity and more power than a woman's attire, advertisements from both the fashion and the pharmaceutical industries are attempting to restructure the nonverbal messages associated with male appearance. The current onslaught of advertisements pushing products such as Rogaine and Propecia to stop hair loss or increase hair growth come with no guarantees, but they do include a long list of side effects. One of the most damaging of these side effects is the nonverbal message that baldness or hair loss equals a loss of youthfulness and attractiveness. In a youth-obsessed, looks-oriented culture such as the United States, that can equate to a loss of power. Although Michael Jordan may still be able to say "Bald is beautiful," for the majority of balding men in this society the old adage that men get more distinguished with age may be changing.

Still, it is safe to say that the traditional male stereotype is one that lends itself more easily to the business world than the traditional female stereotype. Mike Brady worked, while Carol Brady stayed at home with the kids. According to Remland (2000), wearing the proper business attire nonverbally communicates motivation in an employment interview. This is good news for both male and female applicants who follow their respective dress for success guidelines. Unfortunately for the female applicants, only the "masculine" attire communicates assertiveness (Remland, 2000, p. 347), thereby giving the male candidate the edge. For those who believe Oscar Wilde's claim that a well-tied tie is the first serious step in life, women seem somehow left out of the serious world of business.

CONCLUSIONS

In the future, we may not need to be as concerned about dressing for success. According to a survey of 3,700 U.S. executives, "87.1% believe suits and ties (and, one can hope, skirts and nylons) will disappear from corporations in ten years" (cited in Fisher, 1998, p. 300). If that does occur, then maybe the traditional stereotypes that accompany the male and female business suits will disappear as well. But for now, you may have formed your own answers to the questions posed by the student at the Dress for Success fashion show. "Isn't this the twenty-first century? Do those rules still apply?" As for me, I must admit I have always worn a business suit with a skirt and heels to all my job interviews. Even though I am aware of the nonverbal messages I am sending, I still fear the interviewer might misread my change in attire to "less professional female" as opposed to "equally active and powerful employee."

READING RESPONSES

1. Look at the objects you are wearing at this moment. What nonverbal message are you sending?
2. Cut a rope or string to a length of 18 inches (the ideal waist size of the nineteenth-century women). Wrap it around your waist. Try to make the ends meet. Imagine being corseted to this size.
3. Role reversal: Spend one class session dressed in the professional attire of the opposite sex. Men, slip on a straight skirt and heels. Women, try on a pair of wing tips and a tie. Try sitting, standing, walking, and running. What did you learn from this experience?
4. Go to a local department store and check out the ties. Select a tie you think nonverbally communicates each of the following: power, wealth, sense of humor, common joe, and nerd. What feature(s) of each tie communicated these characteristics to you?
5. Are mini skirts appropriate for the workplace? What nonverbal messages do they send?
6. When you see someone with tattoos and piercings, what nonverbal message do you take from their appearance? Do you think your classmates agree with your perception? Do you think the person with the tattoos and piercings is intentionally trying to send this message?
7. Women should wear skirts and pumps to job interviews. Men should not wear earrings or other piercings to job interviews. Do these rules still apply? Should they still apply? What advice would you give job applicants?

REFERENCES

Banner, L. (1983). *American beauty.* New York: Knopf.

Berch, B. (1987, March). Early feminist fashion. *Ms.,* p. 24.

Brown, E. (1998, February 23). The job interview. *Forbes,* pp. 18–20.

Cantore, J. (1998, February). Interview tips. *Career World,* pp. 22–23.

Dunn, D. (1997). Introduction to the study of women and work. In D. Dunn (Ed.), *Workplace/women's place: An anthology* (pp. 1–13). Los Angeles: Roxbury.

Edwards, A. (1998, February). Dress off! *Essence,* p. 52.

Fisher, A. (1998, November 23). Ask Anne: Readers sound off on clothes, cows and staying sober. *Fortune,* p. 300.

Guerrero, L., DeVito, J., & Hecht, M. (1999). *The nonverbal communication reader: Classic and contemporary readings* (2nd ed.). Prospect Heights, IL: Waveland Press.

Henley, N. (1977). *Body politics: Power, sex, and nonverbal communication.* New York: Simon & Schuster.

Initial minutes of job interviews are critical. (2000, January). *USA Today*, p. 8.

It's a look, but . . . will it get the job? (1995, March). *Mademoiselle*, pp. 186–189.

Ivy, D., & Backlund, P. (2000). *Exploring GenderSpeak: Personal effectiveness in gender communication* (2nd ed.). New York: McGraw-Hill.

Job seekers should dress for success. (1995, January). *USA Today*, pp. 6–7.

Knapp, M., & Hall, J. (1997). *Nonverbal communication in human interaction* (4th ed.). Harcourt Brace.

Lennon, S. J., & Miller, F. G. (1984). Salience of physical appearance in impression formation. *Home Economics Research Journal, 13*, 95–104.

Martin, V. E., Jr. (1995, October). Preparing for the on-campus interview. *Black Collegian*, pp. 74–77.

Mattera, J. (1992, June). Three things an interviewer looks for in the first 10 seconds of your interview. *Glamour*, p. 122.

Molloy, J. (1977). *The woman's dress for success book.* New York: Warner Books.

Remland, M. (2000). *Nonverbal communication in everyday life.* Boston: Houghton Mifflin.

Repinski, K. (1999). *The complete idiot's guide to successful dressing.* New York: Alpha Books.

The right suit for a job interview. (1988, March). *Glamour*, p. 150.

Stewart, C., & Cash, Jr., W. (1997). *Interviewing: Principles and practices* (8th ed.). Boston, MA: McGraw-Hill.

Sweat, S., & Zentner, M. A. (1985). Attributions toward female appearance styles. In M. R. Solomon (Ed.), *The psychology of fashion* (pp. 321–355). Lexington, MA: Lexington Books.

Twidale, H. (1987, September). Career clothes change shape. *Working Women*, 68–74.

White, A. (1983, March). Will your clothes say "Hire me?" *Career World*, pp. 16–18.

ASSIGNING RESPONSIBILITY FOR WORKPLACE BEHAVIOR

Sexual Harassment as a Form of Organizational Communication

Frances J. Ranney

WAYNE STATE UNIVERSITY

Theories of why sexual harassment occurs in the workplace and who is responsible for it abound. In this article, Frances Ranney separates these theories into three categories: sexual harassment as desire; sexual harassment as power; and sexual harassment as part of the structure of the organization. Ranney draws from two court cases from the past decade—that of Theresa Harris, a manager whose case against her male boss went to the Supreme Court, and Kerry Ellison, an IRS employee whose case against a male coworker was won at the Appeals Court level— to illustrate these perspectives on sexual harassment.

The cases discussed and the theories highlighted demonstrate the complexities of identifying and dealing with sexual harassment in the workplace. Only after the facts of the cases are related and through Ranney's explanation of the theories do we achieve some clarity as to how sexual harassment can occur despite a corporate culture that is hypersensitive to the legal responsibility to prevent it, and the potential repercussions to them if they fail to do so. Just when readers think they now have a handle on how to distinguish between what is and is not a case of sexual harassment, the author offers an example from her own work experience for readers to consider in light of the theories and cases previously discussed.

Readers who are interested in furthering their understanding of how sexual harassment can occur despite an organization's efforts to prevent it may want to explore standpoint theory. This theory explains how women experience organizational communication and cultures differently than men, which ultimately can contribute to vastly different interpretations of communication behaviors in the workplace.

QUESTIONS FOR DISCUSSION

- *The author discusses only cases of sexual harassment in male-female superior-subordinate situations. Can sexual harassment occur in female-*

male superior-subordinate, or female-female and male-male superior-subordinate re-
lationships? If so, how? If not, why?

- *How might the issue of race, ethnicity, or sexual orientation influence perceptions of*
  sexual harassment?

- *In your own employment history or that of others you know, are you aware of examples*
  that might be considered sexual harassment?

- *Was there a time of confusion or uncertainty as to how to describe or what to call an*
  action you were uncomfortable with?

- *Which of the theories would best describe that situation? If the actions of that person*
  were discussed with a supervisor or with peers, how did they treat you? As a victim?
  As mistaken? Were your perceptions supported, discounted, or negated?

- *Finally, after reading this article, how might you talk to someone who told you of being*
  sexually harassed on the job? What would you say?

Theresa Harris and her boss weren't getting along. Charles Hardy, the president of Forklift Systems where Harris worked as a manager, really wanted a man in her job. He had a habit of responding to her ideas by saying "You're a woman, what do you know?" He had even called her a "dumb ass woman" in front of the other, nonmanagement employees. He liked to "joke around" at work and would often ask the women, including Harris, to get pennies out of his front pants pocket, or ask them to pick up things he'd thrown on the floor in front of him so he could make sexual remarks about their clothing. Harris was the only female manager in the company, and the only woman who ever complained about Hardy's "jokes."

Kerry Ellison, an IRS agent who lived in California, had a different problem. Sterling Gray, another agent, wanted to go out with her, but she wasn't interested. Gray wouldn't give up and started writing her long letters, including one that said, "I cried over you last night and I'm totally drained today. Never have I been in such constant term oil [sic]." Ellison asked friends to let him know she wasn't interested, and when she was sent to another state for training she hoped he would forget about her. But she received a three-page, single-spaced letter from him at her hotel, even though her location had supposedly been kept confidential by her supervisor.

Both Harris and Ellison ended up filing sexual harassment lawsuits against their employers, and both eventually won—Ellison at the Appeals Court level in 1991, and Harris at the Supreme Court in 1993. The behavior they encountered at work seems surprising, given how sensitive businesses and workers have become about the issue of sexual harassment. Though many Americans were not very aware of the issue before 1991, when Anita Hill testified before the Senate Committee that eventually appointed Clarence Thomas to the Supreme Court, sexual harassment had been outlawed nearly thirty years earlier by the Civil Rights Act of 1964. The Supreme Court heard its first sexual harassment case in 1986, before Thomas was appointed to the Court, but during the time that he was the director of the Equal Employment Opportunity Commission—ironically enough, the government agency in charge of enforcing the Civil Rights Act.

There are many theories about why sexual harassment occurs in the workplace and about who (or what) is responsible for it. Whether we think of any particular event as a case of sexual harassment is based not only on how we define "harassment," but also on what kinds of behaviors we think of as "sexual." Most people would believe that physical activities ranging from kissing to intercourse are sexual, but would differ about whether less obvious activities such as touching or brushing against someone are. We also differ on whether verbal activities such as compliments or invitations to sexual activity, or threats when sexual activity is refused, constitute sexual harassment acts. Furthermore, definitions of acceptable behavior vary from place to place; some workplace cultures, as Matts Alvesson and Yvonne Due Billing (1997) point out, will tolerate far more sexualized behaviors than others (p. 122). Finally, how we define sexual harassment is important because our definitions tell us not only what we believe sexual harassment is, but also who is responsible for it.

Theories about sexual harassment can be separated into at least three categories, based on the ways they define the term:

1. Sexual harassment occurs because an individual wants to engage in sexual activity with another who does not want to do so (what I call "sexual harassment as desire").
2. Sexual harassment occurs because an individual wants control over another and uses sexual means to exercise it ("sexual harassment as power").
3. Sexual harassment occurs because an organization is structured in such a way as to allow certain individuals to exercise power over others by sexual means ("sexual harassment as structural").

You can see that the first category places responsibility for sexual harassment on the individuals involved, whereas the third places responsibility primarily on the organization. The second theory places responsibility on either the individual or the organization, or both. The following sections examine these categories separately before discussing their significance in the conclusion.

SEXUAL HARASSMENT AS DESIRE

The Kerry Ellison case provides an example of what may be interpreted as sexual harassment based on desire. Sterling Gray wanted to date Ellison and, as the judge who wrote the opinion in this case noted, might look to some people like "a modern-day Cyrano de Bergerac" who, like the character in the French story, was a heroic, comic, and hopeless romantic (and therefore a character who elicited sympathy). If this situation were simply a matter of Gray's desire for Ellison, it would also be a strictly personal problem that Ellison would be primarily responsible for resolving by somehow communicating to Gray that he should leave her alone. In fact, that's what she tried to do, first by refusing his invitations and then by asking a friend to intervene.

Neither of her strategies was successful, though research has shown they are typical of most women who experience sexual harassment (Riger, 1995, p. 221; Herrick, 1999, pp. 275–276). Research in the fields of sexual psychology and linguistics might point to some reasons why. One study of "women's resistance messages"—what women say to men when they don't want to escalate their sexual involvement with them—shows that women and men can generate reasonable, yet completely contradictory, interpretations of those messages, especially when they are rather indirect. Direct messages, such as "I don't want to do this," are usually interpreted uniformly by both sexes. But less direct resistance messages, such as "I don't have any protection," can also make men believe that a woman is actually consenting to sex and asking him to supply the protection himself (Motley & Reeder, 1995, p. 367).

That might lead us to think that women should simply learn to be more direct (or that men should learn to interpret women's statements more accurately). Linguists, however, have noted that many women prefer a less direct speech style than is typical of men, and for logical reasons. In Motley and Reeder's psychological study, for example, the women preferred indirect messages because they feared that men would think they were "prudes" or become angry if they used a direct resistance message (p. 368). Deborah Tannen, in *Talking from Nine to Five* (1994b), analyzed the results of these typical male and female communication differences and concluded that we need to learn to value all different kinds of speech in the workplace if we want to equalize opportunities. However, in other work (1994a), she has noted the difficulties in acting on this recommendation, given that differences in signaling meaning "work to the disadvantage of members of groups that are stigmatized in our society, and to the advantage of those who have the power to enforce their interpretations" (pp. 7–8).

If sexual harassment is an individual problem based strictly in romantic or sexual desire, who is responsible for it? Some people have claimed that in male-female interaction it is the woman's responsibility to behave and dress modestly in order to avoid giving men the impression that she is available sexually. In fact, the first Supreme Court sexual harassment case held that a woman's speech and dress were significant factors in deciding whether she had been sexually harassed (*Meritor*, 1986, p. 6). More recent legal opinions have even argued that there is such a thing as "welcome harassment," when a woman somehow signals that she is available sexually or deserves to be harassed (Ranney, 1998, p. 164). It is not uncommon to believe that, as conservative political figure Phyllis Schlafly once put it, "a virtuous woman is rarely harassed" (quoted in MacKinnon, 1987, p. 25). Therefore, although it may be the man's responsibility to interpret messages correctly, the woman may be seen as sending sexual messages even if she thinks she is merely going to work.

SEXUAL HARASSMENT AS POWER

Theresa Harris's case is an example of sexual harassment that can be interpreted as an exercise of power. The harasser in this case, Charles Hardy, never suggested that Harris become involved with him sexually. However, he was the owner and president of the company and therefore could have fired or demoted any woman who refused to participate in his "games." Since the women at Forklift Systems were all subordinate to Hardy, they could have believed they had little choice about whether to cooperate with him, though in court some of those women testified that they didn't mind Hardy's jokes.

The power hypothesis has been advanced most effectively by Catharine MacKinnon, a feminist legal scholar and activist whose 1979 book *Sexual Harassment of Working Women* was influential in convincing the Supreme Court to recognize sexual harassment as a violation of the Civil Rights Act. MacKinnon's legal argument was that sexual harassment was not a personal problem but a violation of civil rights, because women who are harassed at work have a hard time doing their jobs and sometimes quit their jobs because of it—or are fired when their work performance suffers. Support for this hypothesis comes from research that shows what most people already realize—that women generally have less structurally conferred power in work organizations than men do and are more frequently harassed (Riger, 1995, p. 214).

One study of same-sex harassment claims the idea that sexual harassment is a power issue is based in "stereotypes" of men and harassers and as "the power brokers in organizations" (Farley, 1978, cited in DuBois, Knapp, Faley, & Kustis, 1998, p. 732). But these same researchers acknowledge that same-sex harassment occurs far less frequently than male-female harassment and add, "It is important to keep in mind that [sexual harassment] is usually not motivated by sexual attraction or sexual intentions. In fact, [it] is most often the result of factors related to power and dominance" (pp. 732–733). It is also true that the overwhelming majority of sexual harassment targets are female (Townsley & Geist, n.d.).

Who can be held responsible when harassment is seen as an exercise of power? Certainly, it is more likely in such cases that the harasser, rather than the target, will be held responsible as an individual. But such is not reliably the case; Hardy was not held responsible for his actions until the case went to the Supreme Court. Instead, Harris was blamed for being too sensitive to Hardy's behavior. The lower court believed that her sensitivity was due to her position as a manager who wanted to be accorded more respect than the nonmanagement employees (*Harris*, 1992, p. 5). Those nonmanagement employees who, you remember, did not object to Hardy's jokes were described by the court referee as "conditioned to accept denigrating treatment" (p. 6). But the referee did not think that either the conditioning or the denigrating treatment was illegal.

Because Hardy was the president and owner of Forklift Systems, it is hard to separate his responsibility from that of his company. In many cases, though, when nonowner supervisors harass their subordinates, the company is held responsible. Legally, this responsibility hinges on the belief that companies should control their employees' behavior and that any person who is a supervisor in a company is a direct representative, or "agent," of the company itself. The phrase used in court opinions when a company is held responsible for sexual harassment is that it either "knew or should have known" that its agent was violating its sexual harassment policy—and therefore should have stopped it (*Carr,* 1994, p. 1009).

But how does a company know, and how does it—or can it—control the behavior of all its employees? To discuss these questions, we can turn to descriptions of sexual harassment as a function of an organization's structure.

SEXUAL HARASSMENT AS STRUCTURAL

The theory that sexual harassment is inherent in the nature and structure of organizations and thus nearly inevitable is the most radical and controversial of these three theories. Patrice Buzzanell (1995) provides a description that clearly links organizational structure both to workplace discrimination against women and to communication processes. As she points out, the usual structure of American workplaces is based on a hierarchical system that has traditionally and overwhelmingly favored males who, in 1995, still held 97% of all top management jobs (p. 329). Trying to resolve this inequity by placing women in top jobs, Buzzanell says, has failed because such strategies don't change the nature of the organization itself. Women who are placed in such jobs must therefore behave like men in order to succeed; furthermore, many such women are perceived as "tokens" who have not succeeded because of any personal merit but because of luck or the company's need to satisfy affirmative action requirements (p. 330). According to Buzzanell, the "glass ceiling" (the invisible barrier women encounter when they try to move up the corporate ladder) is the product of the ways we talk about men, women, and the workplace itself. We thus "'do gender' in our organizing processes," including our communication processes (p. 328).

Buzzanell's theory is consistent with research that shows women are disadvantaged at work because they are often excluded from the informal communication networks that provide men with information vital to success in a workplace (Gilbert & Ones, 1998, p. 686). One study found, for example, that women have trouble getting mentors because the men who could mentor them sometimes believe women are less suited for advancement or fear that they will become physically attracted or romantically involved with their protegees—and then be accused of sexual harassment (p. 689). Ironically, then, men's fears of false accusations lead women to be excluded from the information they need to advance; they thus remain in the subordinate positions where they can be more easily victimized by harassers who want to exert power over them.

Another reason women fail to advance as rapidly or as far as men in work organizations is because they seem to lack what organizations reward—commitment to the organization itself. In order to seem committed, employees must be willing to "work long hours when necessary, to relocate, and to place a greater importance on the interest of the firm than on personal interests when the two are in conflict" (Allen, Russell, & Rush, 1994, p. 445). The structure of most American families is such that, despite the entrance of most married women and women with children into the workforce, women are still primarily responsible for child care and housework. Diane Eyer notes in her book *MotherGuilt* (1996) that women still do 75% of housework and 70% of child care, and that the presence of a husband actually adds five hours of domestic duties to a woman's workload (p. 27). It is not surprising, then, that it is harder for most women to look "committed" than it is for most men.

Complicating matters further is the finding that managers are more likely to reward work performance that they believe is due to internal causes, such as ability and effort, than performance they believe is due to external causes, such as luck or the "ease" of a task—and that when women perform well at work their managers tend to attribute their success to external causes. Men's success is more likely to be attributed to their own ability (internal causes). When employees fail, the beliefs are completely reversed: When women fail, managers believe it is because of their own (lack of) ability, but when men fail, managers more often believe it is due to (bad) luck or some other external factor (Allen et al., pp. 446–447). Given this complex of assumptions, if a woman claims that her work is suffering because of an external factor such as harassment by a coworker, it is easier for her manager to believe that her poor performance is due to her own incompetence.

It would seem, therefore, that women (and members of racial minorities as well) are placed in a triple bind by the very structure of the organizations in which they work. Unable to demonstrate the "commitment" an organization demands because of their greater family responsibilities, they may be perceived as successful by luck but as failures by nature. Further, they are unable to gain access to the information they need to succeed because that information is "owned" by more powerful males who may not share it because they fear their mentoring of women will bring about charges of sexual harassment. One result of this triple bind is that women generally remain in less powerful structural positions where they are more likely to become the targets of harassment.

CONCLUSION

What can we conclude about the nature of sexual harassment and its place within the communication structures and processes of an organization? Buzzanell (1995) believes that most theories come up short precisely because they take the nature of organizations (their hierarchical structures and their ability to control the behavior of their employees) as a given, thus restricting the focus of organizational change to surface issues (p. 327). Merely adding women to the top of the hierarchy is not enough, she says, to change the organizations themselves. Instead, ways of talking about organizations and the place of men and women within them simply maintains the hierarchy that disenfranchises groups such as women and racial minorities (p. 335). Solutions that assume women will bring "different" values to organizations, such as a more "caring" orientation that may value competition less than connection, simply result in women "doing 'women's work' in the organization," she claims (p. 331). A hotel manager who spoke to one of my business communication classes recently illustrated Buzzanell's position when he said that his hotel chain likes to hire women into management positions because women are "good at creating a home away from home."

Gilbert and Ones (1998) suggest that, in order to equalize opportunities for women and minorities, organizations should restructure themselves along a "multi-cultural" rather than "plural" model. The plural model, they say, is one that attempts to hire more women and minorities simply to comply with affirmative action requirements and expects them to "fit in" with the existing corporate culture. The multicultural model sees diversity as both a moral and a business imperative—it is simply right morally and rewarding economically to change the culture of the organization (pp. 692–693). What all this research suggests is that such change can only come about through communication, through changing not only the ways communication takes place and the participation of women and minorities in communication processes such as mentoring, but also through the ways we talk about organizations and their members. Buzzanell (1995) suggests that we replace the traditional hierarchical model, often referred to metaphorically as a "ladder," with another model that would use the metaphor of a "web" (p. 342). Presumably, in organizations seen and talked about as webs, different segments and their members would be intricately linked without preferences given to particular members or segments based on gender or race. Gilbert and Ones refer to this form as "true structural integration" and believe it "may be one of the last areas for integration of women and people of color to occur" (pp. 700–701).

How optimistic can we be that changing the ways we communicate in organizations or the ways we talk about organizations, men, and women can reduce or eliminate workplace sexual harassment? Given the factors that work against change in organizations and the triple bind to which women are subject in them, we could just as easily claim that sexual harassment is not simply a *function* of organizational communication structures but a *form* of organizational communication itself—one of the ways that an organization communicates to its employees their place, roles, and opportunities for advancement. What do you think?

CASE STUDY: CAN SEXUAL HARASSMENT BE AVOIDED?

The story below is true and is provided so that you can think about and discuss the issues presented above. It doesn't come from a court case, but from my own work experience in the business world. To protect some people involved who were and are colleagues and friends of mine, I've changed some details. The questions that follow the case study are based not only on the background information I've given you, but also on the questions that my students have asked about this scenario in class. Though the situation was eventually resolved satisfactorily, the outcome could have been very different if I had made different choices. Those choices were difficult for me, but far less difficult than those made by people, mostly women, who are faced with more extensive and long-lasting harassment. I hope this case study will help you to consider seriously the alternative hypotheses offered by the scholars discussed above and to think about what options for behavior, and responses to behavior, organizational structures and communication processes make possible for their employees.

Part One: The Work Assignment

I was a single parent in my mid-30s, working as an account assistant for a company that provided tax advice to its customers. Most of those customers were businesses, but we also advised some of their individual executives. It was not, therefore, unusual when I received a call from one of the account managers, Mr. Haskins, asking me to call an executive who wanted some assistance in opening a tax shelter investment.

I had heard about this executive before; he was notorious for asking lots of questions and worrying excessively about his finances. I had never done any work for him before, though, and had never met him. I called him, introduced myself, and began to explain what he needed to do. He did ask a lot of questions, but he was quite pleasant. After about 5 minutes of conversation, we had covered all the bases as far as I was concerned, so I made a move to end the conversation. However, he continued to talk.

He asked me a few personal but innocent questions. The account manager had told him I was thinking about going back to college for an advanced degree, and he asked about that. He also seemed to know that I was a single mother, and asked about my children—their ages and so on. In all, we talked for about 20 minutes, far more than necessary. I managed to end the conversation finally and hung up, a little irritated at wasting my time on cocktail party small talk. I recorded the 20 minutes in my time record for billing purposes and went on to my next task.

Part Two: The Follow-up

Even though I thought my business with this customer was finished, he called me the next day. He asked a simple question about his tax shelter and then began to talk about himself. He told me he had a condo in a resort area and that his wife was there for a vacation. He told me about his consulting work and also about some modeling he had done for business ads. Several national companies had used his photo, he said, because he had "executive good looks." I cut the conversation shorter this time and hung up more irritated than the day before, beginning to understand why everyone referred to this customer as a pain.

The next day he called again. He had one or two new business questions but again spent more time talking about himself. This time he told me he had been an athlete in high school and college, saying "I've worn a few jock straps in my time." I began to feel very uncomfortable and managed to politely end the conversation. I also began to wonder how to keep him from calling daily and mentioned the situation briefly to the account manager, Mr. Haskins. Though I didn't give him the details of the conversations, I did report them to another male manager, John, who was a close friend. He just laughed.

The next day I received another call. After asking a simple question about his tax shelter, he told me that he wasn't sure he could handle the details himself and that he wanted me to travel to his bank, about an hour from my home, and open the tax shelter for him. To thank me, he said that he would buy me dinner (our customers would frequently take us out for business meals). The only day he was available was the next Friday, December 31.

Part Three: The Resolution

I couldn't decide what to do. It was not odd for a customer to make small talk on the phone, but not for more than 5 minutes or so. It was not unusual for me to travel to a customer's city to help with financial transactions, but not for something as simple as this one. It was not unusual for customers to provide meals for us, but lunch was more common than dinner. I had worked in this office for 10 years and had never refused an assignment, so I talked to John about what to do. He told me I should go to dinner and just put up with the guy. "You don't have to kiss him or anything," he said. "Just turn him down graciously."

After two days and two more phone calls, I finally decided I could not go through with the trip. I went to a female account manager, Ms. Martin, and described the situation. She was disgusted by the customer's behavior and asked me to bring her all the paperwork I'd done so she could reassign the job. I did so and never heard anything from the customer again.

A few days later, Mr. Haskins came by my office and apologized for the customer's actions. "I never thought he would do anything like that," he said, "though come to think of it, he did ask me what you look like." I made a joke of it. "What did you say?" I asked. "Madonna?"

Weeks later, my friend John brought the incident up again. "You really didn't need to worry about that guy," he said. I told John I didn't think I should have to go out on dates with the customers as part of my job. "What's the big deal?" he asked. "That customer is a little crazy, but he has good reasons for it. We all think he has posttraumatic stress disorder from serving in Vietnam."

"What makes you think that?" I asked.

"Let me put it this way," John said. "He's the only customer we have who always carries a gun in his briefcase."

"Wait a minute!" I said. "You knew he carried a gun, and you knew I would refuse any advances he might have made, and yet you told me to go to dinner with him?"

"Well, sure," he answered. "I mean, he *carries* a gun, but he wouldn't *use* it."

Questions for Your Consideration

As you think about and discuss these questions in class, keep in mind the theories about what sexual harassment is and who can be held responsible for it. Are individuals, both harassers and their targets, responsible? Or are their organizations responsible, or the structure of the organizations itself? Does harassment come about because individuals have personal flaws or because the structure of their workplaces forces them to establish positions of power based on gender? If we had seen our workplace as a "web" rather than as a "ladder," would this situation not have arisen, or have been handled differently? In the case above, what options for behavior were available to all the parties involved, and why did they behave the way they did? You may be interested in reading the sexual harassment cases cited or some more recent Supreme Court cases, including the *Burlington Industries* (1998) and *Faragher* (1998) cases listed in the References.

REFERENCES

Allen, Tammy D., Russell, Joyce E. A., & Rush, Michael C. (1994). The effects of gender and leave of absence on attributions for high performance, perceived organizational commitment, and allocation of organizational rewards. *Sex Roles, 31*, 443–464.

Alvesson, Maats, & Billing, Yvonne Due. (1997). *Understanding gender and organizations.* London: Sage.

Burlington Industries, Inc. v. Kimberly B. Ellerth. (1998). U.S. Lexis 4217.

Buzzanell, Patrice M. (1995). Reframing the glass ceiling as a socially constructed process: Implications for understanding and change. *Communication Monographs, 62,* 327–354.

Carr v. Allison Gas Turbine Division. (1994). 32 Fed. Rep. 3rd Ser. 1007 (7th Circ.).

DuBois, Cathy L. Z., Knapp, Deborah E., Faley, Robert H., & Kustis, Gary A. (1998). An empirical examination of same- and other-gender sexual harassment in the workplace. *Sex Roles, 39,* 731–749.

Ellison v. Brady (1991). 924 Fed. Rep. 2d Ser. 8712 (9th Cir.).

Eyer, Diane. (1996). *MotherGuilt: How our culture blames mothers for what's wrong with society.* New York: Random House.

Faragher v. City of Boca Raton. (1998). 524 U.S. 775; 118 S. Ct. 2275; U.S. Lexis, 4216.

Gilbert, Jacqueline A., & Ones, Deniz S. (1998). Role of informal integration in career advancement: Investigations in plural and multicultural organizations and implications for diversity valuation. *Sex Roles, 39,* 685–704.

Harris v. Forklift Systems, Inc. (1992). 976 Fed. Rep. 2nd Ser. 733 (6th Cir.).

Herrick, Jeanne Weiland. (1999). "And then she said": Office stories and what they tell us about gender in the workplace. *Journal of Business and Technical Communication, 13,* 274–296.

MacKinnon, Catharine A. (1979). *Sexual harassment of working women: A case of sex discrimination.* New Haven, CT: Yale University Press.

MacKinnon, Catharine A. (1987). *Feminism unmodified: Discourses on life and law.* Cambridge, MA: Harvard University Press.

Meritor Savings Bank v. Vinson. (1986). 477 U.S. Sup. Ct. 57.

Motley, Michael T., & Reeder, Heidi M. (1995). Unwanted escalation of sexual intimacy: Male and female perceptions of connotations and relational consequences of resistance messages. *Communication Monographs, 62,* 354–382.

Ranney, Frances J. (1998). Posner on legal texts: Law, literature, (economics), and "welcome harassment." *College Literature, 25,* 163–183.

Riger, Stephanie. (1995). Gender dilemmas in sexual harassment: Policies and procedures. In Sherri Matteo (Ed.), *American women in the nineties: Today's critical issues* (pp. 213–234). Boston: Northeastern University Press.

Tannen, Deborah. (1994a). *Gender and discourse.* New York: Oxford University Press.

Tannen, Deborah. (1994b). *Talking from nine to five: How women's and men's conversational styles affect who gets heard, who gets credit, and what gets done at work.* New York: Morrow.

Townsley, Nikki C., & Geist, Patricia. (n.d.). The discursive enactment of hegemony: Sexual harassment and academic organizing. OCLC First Search: Periodical Abstracts. Available: http://newfirstsearch.oclc.org

BULLIES ON THE ADULT PLAYGROUND

Josie Duke

UNIVERSITY OF NORTH CAROLINA—CHAPEL HILL

The bar, by cultural definition, is a "hook-up" place—a place where men go to pick up women, and women go to be picked up by men. If you are single and at a bar, you are telling the world you are in search of a potential mate. For women with different motivations, the bar scene turns into a game reminiscent of dodge ball—deflect the hits and duck, cover and run from hostile players. Some men do not understand when they have fouled, when I'm taking my penalty shot, and when they have struck out. Some only care about the win, and the game is not over unless they dictate it is over.

I love to go dancing with my girlfriends. But once we hit the floor, the "shadow dancers" try to infiltrate our team and make a game of one-on-one. Shadow dancers are men who will generally approach women from behind and start dancing with them. These mystery guests will bump and grind the woman to obtain her attention in hopes of getting her to play along. I used to respond with "Sorry, I have a boyfriend." Like a good girl, I was taught that rejection must be followed with a justification. But sometimes this justification is not good enough. "I don't see him dancing with you now. His loss." "Okay, I just don't want to dance with you." That line has never worked for me because now they want to know why. "Why are you here then?" Translation: "Why are you here if you do not want to dance with men?" Deeper translation: "I'm a man, and you should want to dance with me." Ding, ding: jerk alert! Plan A: explanation, failed. Switch to Plan B: escape.

My friends and I will rehearse simple signals for help. Time to send out the SOS: rub elbow, rub elbow. Within a few minutes a teammate is by my side. "I'm going to the restroom. Please come with me." Translation: "I know you want to leave this loser. Tell me all about it in the restroom, where we will wait 10 minutes to dodge this creep." I have used many lines to avoid men's persistence from the truth ("I'm here only to have a good time with my friends") to blatant lies ("I need to call the babysitter and check up on my little Samantha.") None of them work because *no* explanation is good enough. The cultural motivation has been defined: You are heterosexual, looking to hook up.

If I am dancing with a female partner, the men are more vicious. The polite ones will ask, "May I dance with you?" "Sorry, I'm with her, and we only dance with each other." The guy will then try to nudge himself between my partner and me. We are forced to move somewhere else. If the guy follows, we point to our male friend, "We're with him." His translation: "Oh, you're not lesbians." He goes to our friend and apologizes to him and tells him how lucky he is.

I have never received a direct apology in a bar. Rather, my male friends receive the apology for me. For example, I was playing pool with some friends, and a guy walks over to me, places his hands on my waist and shoulder, and tells me, "I like the way you move." I give him the dirtiest look I can muster, which means: "Get your freakin' hands off me." He takes it as: "Your pool partner must be your boyfriend." He walks over to my pool partner; "I'm sorry, man—I didn't know" and walks away. He invades my space, but my male friend gets the apology.

Men have often tried to appease my nonexistent boyfriend. Another time, a guy asked me if he could buy me a drink. "I don't drink." He translates this to: "You must have a boyfriend." He shifts his eyes, searching for any other guy within two feet of me and shakes the hand of my male friend next to me. "She's so beautiful, hell, I will buy you the drink. She's worth it. What are you drinking? Sorry for moving in on your girl."

Sports bars are the only bars where I do not run into much trouble. Some men will directly question my reason for being there. After all, I am penetrating men's territory. They will ask me how much I really know about football or why I am watching sports. But mostly their attention is on another game, and I do not have to worry about playing the typical bar games. I know men's motivation in going to the sports bar do not involve me.

Bar games are power games, and men tend to have the advantage. Unless a man is by her side, the woman is perceived to be "fair game" and a "willing" participant. Many of these games seem innocent enough; however, they reflect a darker side of our culture that perpetuates men's violence against women. These experiences in a bar demonstrate how a woman's "no" is not respected and how she is still regarded as men's property. Underlying all of this is fear—fear of men's violence—which affects the actions of both men and women. Why do women make nice excuses? Why do men apologize to women's boyfriends?

Some may argue that women who do not like being bullied at the bar can always choose not to go. However, women should not have to put up with being bullied and be denied a public space. They should not have to develop elaborate defensive strategies like hiding in restrooms. They should be able to put an "end" to the game before it even begins and have their desires respected. Women should be mutual playmates and not boys' playthings. The rules need to change.

PART VII

MEDIA INFLUENCES ON GENDER COMMUNICATION

ON THE INTERNET, EVERYBODY WORRIES THAT YOU'RE A DOG

The Gender Expectations and Beauty Ideals of Online Personals and Text-Based Chat

Michele White

WELLESLEY COLLEGE

The evolution of the Internet has given rise to much discussion about the potential advantages and disadvantages of a medium that allows users to interact in the virtual safety of cyberspace. One feature of the medium that provides a sense of personal security is the absence of personal sensory data—visual, vocal, and olfactory. In essence, computer mediated communication (CMC) offers users the otherwise impossible option of synchronous interaction during which time no physical aspects of participants are empirically revealed. Ultimately, that which is disclosed about the self and which we can learn about the other can be highly controlled or manipulated. This apparent blessing of the medium also brings with it a host of problems, such as finding the "right" mate and then determining if that person really is who he/she claims to be.

According to Michele White, inscribed within the discourse of discovery is a larger issue of concern: the reinforcing of gender stereotypes and gender expectations. White's article intersects the gender-stereotypical modes of self-presentation and the technology of cyberspace to explore how the medium and the messages conveyed reveal the gender-related fear and paranoia of society in general. In addition, she suggests this fear and paranoia may be inflamed and escalate through the process of trying to determine a communicant's "true" identity in CMC.

QUESTIONS FOR DISCUSSION

- *If you engage with strangers in chat rooms, how important is it for you to know their "true" gender identity? Why?*
- *How do you know if you can believe people in cyberspace when they reveal their gender?*
- *How do you endeavor to discover a cyber stranger's "true" gender identity?*
- *How do you reveal your gender identity to strangers in cyberspace?*
- *What does your own concern with identifying a cyber stranger's gender identity tell you about your own stereotypes about gender?*

In this article, I argue that many online settings reinforce traditional ideas about the body and gender. Accessible versions of gender theory by such authors as Butler, de Lauretis, and Mulvey are used to demonstrate how bodies are produced and regulated in virtual settings. The application of their work indicates that the desire to categorize all Internet users as either male or female continues to be reinforced despite pronouncements like "On the Internet, Nobody Knows You're a Dog."[1] Gibson's (1984) sci-fi literature suggests a similar unknowable body. In his novel, cyberspace allows users to escape their material existence as well as the "prison" of their own flesh. Early narratives about the Internet in magazines like *Mondo 2000* and *Wired* have also implied that there would be no sexism, racism, homophobia, ageism, and classism online because users left their bodily conditions and participated in a virtual setting where any identity was possible. According to Senft (1996), there has been a recent surge "in sociological writing about cyberspace, one that suggests that online life is the ideal spot to experiment with hypothetical identity-making." Individual users may declare that online settings provide "an interesting way to explore my sexuality" (Green_Guest, 18 June 2000). However, these proposals have failed to consider that all users engage in the virtual setting from an already culturally produced and regulated gender position (Butler, 1993).

A close visual and textual reading of Yahoo!'s Personals and Profiles system, with an emphasis on the men seeking women (M4W) part of this service, and Stanford and Placeware's LambdaMOO, will demonstrate how conventional ideas about binary gender and body ideals are continually reinscribed online. The desirability or even worth of certain bodily characteristics is maintained by requests for particular types of bodies and comments about users' descriptions. Many online systems perpetuate visual pleasure, or the individual's enjoyment of objectifying and erotic viewing, even though the body is largely produced through text. Particular attention will be paid to the stereotyped ways that users describe their bodies and the kinds of problems that overtly sexual descriptions produce. For instance, men's desires to locate aesthetically pleasing partners are linked to fears that each description of a beautiful woman is actually "Some fat white guy claiming to be a woman" (Beige_Guest, 23 January 1999). On Yahoo!'s Personals, the inability to differentiate between "real" women and escort services also produces certain crises in desire.

YAHOO!

Yahoo! began in 1994 as David Filo and Jerry Yang's list of favorite links (Yahoo!a). Yahoo! is now described as "the first online navigational guide to the Web" (Yahoo!b). It is one of the many portals that provide such free services as search engines, Web-based email, chat forums, instant messaging, shopping, classified advertisements, and news so that users will make the site their default Web page or use it frequently.[2] According to *PC World*, "AltaVista, Excite, Infoseek, Lycos, Microsoft's Internet Start, Netscape's Netcenter, Snap, and Yahoo" are the "eight major portal contenders" (Lake, 1998). If "surfing" the Net has been conceptualized as a confusing process of "moving" from site to site, where users can lose track of their "location" or how reliable a vendor is, then portals offer a clearly named and visually similar setting in which users are promised convenience, reliability, and stability. Yahoo! Wallet, which allows users to personalize their services and store credit card information online, is described as "Quick, Simple, Secure" (Yahoo!d). The names of personalized services, such as the Yahoo! Companion "browser toolbar that gives you quick access to your favorite Yahoo! features" (Yahoo!e), suggest the move from the anonymous user to a more intimate, loyal, and friendship-oriented relationship with the portal. This personalization comes at a cost because Yahoo! requires users to submit their email address as well as information about their occupation and gender in order to get a Yahoo! ID and password.

Users may choose to employ Yahoo! Personals because the site provides a sense of stability through its welcoming messages, which address the user by name or alias, and the familiar red logo that appears on each page. However, Yahoo!'s Personals and Profiles system also forces all users to communicate within a demarcated gender position that they ostensibly "select." The growing trend to make users specify binary gender suggests that it is a natural aspect of all actions. Teresa de Lauretis (1987, pp. 11–12) argues that marking the "M" or "F" on forms results in the "M" and "F" categorizing, ordering, and shaping our identity. After marking the form, we represent ourselves as that gender. Users could write their online identity in many different ways, but systems like Yahoo! make binary gender an implicit aspect of identity formation in the virtual setting. Yahoo!'s sign-up form explains that "this information will help us personalize various areas of Yahoo! with content that is relevant to you" (Yahoo!f).

Recent feminist scholarship has argued that there is no essential bodily type or set of desires that women share (Butler, 1989; de Lauretis, 1984; Fuss, 1989), but Yahoo!'s comments suggest that relevance is determined by such criteria as gender. Through this process, such social representations as gender are "accepted and absorbed by an individual as her (or his) own representation, and so becomes, for that individual, real, even though it is in fact imaginary" (de Lauretis, 1987, p. 12). This means that the culturally constructed ways that women express their femininity (emotional, shy, weak, and nurturant) and men express their masculinity (unemotional, aggressive, strong, and potent) are deemed to be natural.

When Yahoo! Personals users write an advertisement, they must identify themselves as either a "Man" or "Woman" and express a preference for either a "Man" or "Woman" even though users can seek "Penpals/Long Distance" and "Activity Partners" where the gender of the person isn't necessarily a factor. The possibility that gender isn't a selection criterion for some users and identifying as bisexual are com-

pletely negated by this process.[3] The main link for posting advertisements may be titled "Find a friend or a mate," but the structure of Yahoo!'s site clearly privileges relationships in which gender is an important selection factor. Yahoo! underscores their
investment by positioning the gender categories near the top of the form that users
employ in order to post an ad. There is no way to self-select out of gender, even
though users may choose "Prefer not to say/No Answer" to the "Ethnicity,"
"Education," "Employment," and "Religion" categories.[4] This suggests that ethnicity
may not always be considered an important aspect of relationships, or that there may
even be a position outside of ethnicity, but gender is a natural and necessary part of
all communication. Binary gender is also supported in the Profiles system, where
most users choose to describe their "Sex" as either "Male" or "Female" on the form
even though users can select "No Answer." The organization and categories of
Yahoo! Profiles suggest that binary gender is necessary information about all individuals, there is no position outside of binary gender, and a user's only choice is to not
answer even though feminists and queer theorists have argued that binary gender
unnecessarily fits many types of bodies and subject positions into a limited set of categories (Bornstein, 1994, 1998; Feinberg, 1998; Fausto-Sterling, 1985).

Users must also identify their "body type" by selecting "Slim/Waif-ish,"
"Slender/Average," "Athletic/Fit," "Healthy/Slightly overweight," or "Large" from
the form. The importance of body type is underscored by the many ads from men
with a stated preference for slender or thin women.

> Successful, Very Joyful DWPM, 55 Young, 6'4, 190lb, Eclectic Interests, ISO Soulmate:
> Tall, N/S, Slender, Inner/Outer Beauty, To Young 53. (charming_odyn, 2000)
>
>> Just a quick note; If you are 30 # and up over weight, then I probably wouldn't be in-
> terested. . . (frank916, 2000)

The ways that users describe themselves are also regulated. There are frequent
advertisements in which men chastise women for not describing and depicting
themselves properly.

> WHAT IS IT??? I have placed a couple ads, exchanged photos with a few "ladies" and
> went on to meet "someone" who did not resemble the picture in any way, shape or form!
> Are there ANY attractive, shapely women using these personals who are bright, healthy,
> sober, dress nicely and have never been on Jerry Springer? Is anyone reading this who
> couldn't model clothes for Roseanne ?? . . . . isn't "rubenesque, BBW, working-on-it, or
> just a few pounds over her senior prom size." (ultraman_41042, 2000)

The terminology used by advertisers suggests that there are ideal forms of bodies as well as undesirable bodies. "I get tired of looking at the ads by women that
have 'healthy/slightly overweight' in them" (Chem_teacher_98, 2000). Very few of
the ads express a desire for larger women. Advertisers that express an interest in
BBW, or big beautiful women, support normative desire because they often describe

their attraction as unusual. The stereotype that larger women are "desperate" for any relationship and are more sexually available than other women is perpetuated by the disproportionate number of advertisers who are only looking to have erotic encounters with BBW. This desire is different from the motivation of most BBW.

> I am a BBW who would like to find a friend. If it leads to more then great if not I have still found a new friend. I am not interested in a casual sexual encounter, so if you are there is no need to respond. (sanjosesweet, 2000)

All women's "right," irrespective of body type or other attributes, to have relationships and sexually fulfilling experiences is troubled by the representations in the M4W section of Yahoo! Personals.

Women's abilities to communicate within this forum and even their status as women is disturbed by the way that Yahoo! Personals functions. The frequent solicitations that many male advertisers receive from pornography Web sites and escort services have made men doubt that responses are from "real" women. One male user asks "Where has the love disappeared to . . . . All I have seen was paysites, and escorts replying [to] my ads for true love. I am tired of seeing these ads, thinking it was a woman . . . I was searching for, to find out that it wasn't" (hardwood4u_94306, 2000). Some ads from men looking for women, including sexually explicit requests, express a fear that respondents won't be women. "You cannot be a homosexual, crossdressing male hoping to win over us straight guys" (StorytellerJon, 2000). This erasure of individual women is supported by the many advertisements for porn sites and escort services in the W4M section. Yahoo! doesn't address these issues. Instead, it validates the Personals site by offering expert advice and testimonials on the opening page.

Yahoo! encourages the user, who is "Still skeptical?" to "Read these Success Stories" (Yahoo! 2000). Polls and other devices are designed to attract users and instruct them about the appropriate kinds of behavior and desire that occur within relationships. For instance, the gender distinctions that are asserted in Yahoo! Personals are supported by Dr. John Gray's weekly "Mars Venus LuvFact" where he makes such claims as "men have stronger erotic reactions to visual stimuli than most women do" (Gray, 2000). Gray's column, as well as much of the material on Yahoo! Personals, privileges heterosexual relationships.

Material on other parts of the portal site, including the misty representation of a Caucasian family on Yahoo! Wallet, depicts users as young, white, and heterosexual. Other people certainly use these services, but they have remained underrecognized by the system (Yahoo!g). During most of this study, the photographs of couples in the Success Stories section depicted light-skinned heterosexual relationships.[5] Only one of these couples appeared to be Hispanic. None of the people represented seemed to be of African or Asian decent. Yahoo! may allow users to search for different kinds of relationships, but the photographs, adorned with hearts and wedding rings, suggest that Personals' "success stories" are about heterosexual relationships and marriages. These representations create a hierarchy in which heterosexuality and whiteness are coded as better and more "successful" than other types of bonds.

It wasn't until early June of 2000 that photographs of gay, lesbian, and black success stories appeared on the Personals page. The images functioned differently than the other testimonials because they illustrated Yahoo! Polls. "Which of the following people do you hope your child will turn out to be like?" (8 June 2000) appeared near a photograph of a black couple and their child. "Do you think gay marriage should be legal?" was juxtaposed with a gay couple. The "gay marriage" poll and the "accompanying" testimonials seemed to be related to Lesbian and Gay Pride events that are organized around the anniversary of the Stonewall riots. Each of the testimonials that "accompanies" the poll mentions a marriage or "union," but they aren't adorned with wedding rings. The rights of heterosexual unions remain legally and socially uncontested, but the rights of gay and lesbian couples are denied in many states and, as if contesting the new representations on the Success Stories page, by the voters in the Yahoo! poll.[6] Through such devices, Yahoo! Personals demarcate appropriate bodies and desires, as do the depictions on LambdaMOO.

LAMBDAMOO

MOOs, or multiuser object-oriented worlds, are part of a group of text-based gaming and social settings that also includes MUCKs, MUDs, MUSHes, MUSEs, MUX, and Talkers. LambdaMOO is the oldest MOO; it was supported by Xerox and has been Internet accessible since October of 1990 (Curtis, 1992). Stanford University and Placeware Incorporated now support the MOO, which currently has 4,810 characters (LambdaMOOa). MOOs have been social as well as research settings, and Curtis, who was one of the key designers of the system, has written about LambdaMOO (Curtis, 1992, 1993). Other scholarly works have also considered the relationship between gender and identity formation on MOOs (Bruckman, 1993; Cherny, 1994; Dibbell, 1998; Stone, 1995; Turkle, 1995; White, 1999). Most of these authors have not considered the ways that LambdaMOO's programming encourages the construction of gendered bodies and descriptions that seem to render real attributes. The production of a kind of visual pleasure on MOOs is particularly interesting because these systems are completely text-based. There is no physically embodied interaction between people on MOOs, and there is no specific "real" space in which interactions take place.

LambdaMOO users interact with one another and the detailed textual setting through the manipulation of a character. Users can personalize many of the details of their character by using a set of computer commands. Each character is also recognizable because it has a unique name that the user has chosen. The text that provides some context or details about the character is known as its "description," and the user sets it by typing the command "@describe me as <description>." Any character can read this description after the user has set it. Guests have more limited options, because a user only manipulates a guest for a short amount of time, but users can also write descriptions as a way of personalizing their more temporary virtual bodies.

Some members of the MOO community render their virtual bodies and believe that other characters are the equivalent of physical individuals. Character descriptions often include such details as age, height, weight, body type, eye color, hair color, and type of clothes.[7] This practice may have been encouraged by the example that LambdaMOO's Help system provides with information about how users can employ the @describe command. In this example, the user named "Munchkin" types the command "@describe me as 'A very fine fellow, if a bit on the short side'" (LambdaMOOb). The user is conflated with the character by typing "describe ME" in order to produce a character description. The Help system example is meant to explain how this MOO command works, but it also suggests that community conventions require a character description that provides such physical details as height. This example doesn't encourage the production of characters that are based on objects, places, immaterial concepts, or ideas, even though a character could be a shoe, a country, or a mood. The differences between the textual character and the user who types the commands, which can often be quite extreme, are hidden by what appears to be the "truth" of physiognomy-oriented character descriptions.

> Abraxas
> A slim 5'9 fellow who enjoys biking, golf and Windows programming. So go ahead and ask: "What do you do for fun?" (hmm) I enjoy watching Dave, and try not to get mugged when waiting for tickets. :) (Abraxas, 1998)

> Lavender_Guest
> Jeff, 23, 5ft10, low 200, brown/blue. (14 December 1998)

> Green_Guest
> Karen. 31, 5-8. Slender, brown eyes, round face, wide mouth, very dark brown hair. I am the secretary for the owner of a local retail store. (24 December 1998)

The use of gender on MOOs also helps to collapse the differences between a character and a user because it supports the illusion that character descriptions depict "real" bodies. The Help text for @describe, which specifies that Munchkin is a "fellow," encourages users to gender virtual bodies. Most users choose to depict their characters as either male or female, even though they can use the programming to gender themselves as neuter, either, Spivak, splat, plural, egotistical, royal, and 2nd. A fairly typical breakdown of the gender of characters on LambdaMOO was "109 males (54%), 67 females (33%), and 23 others (11%)" (Stetson, 2000). All characters must have a gender, which they usually select, but features such as race, the age of the user, and the user's socioeconomic class need not be chosen or indicated in the character's description.[8] This suggests that gender is a virtual as well as physical requirement for having any form of MOO identity. These positions are continually confirmed because gender information is provided when characters virtually look at each other.[9]

Users employ the "Look" command to navigate their characters through the textual system because this is the most common way to access information about MOO settings and characters. The Look command is listed in the introductory Help text for LambdaMOO as one of "the first five kinds of commands you'll want to know" (LambdaMOOc). The ability to textually look allows users to preserve the presumed naturalness of the material body. To look is, after all, "to ascertain by the use of one's eyes" (*Merriam Webster Dictionary*, 1998). The Look is a privileged term in MOO systems, even though characters communicate and comprehend the MOO setting by reading and writing texts. The Look command and the option that informs characters when another character "looks you over" work together to form a setting in which characters clearly gaze at gendered virtual bodies.

This process of MOO gazing makes certain characters, particularly characters that are gendered as female, into a kind of object that can be looked at, admired, and controlled. Consistent and inexplicable bouts of being virtually looked at suggest that character attributes are being tabulated and patrolled by the larger community. "Being gazed upon can be pleasurable or painful: there are times when we enjoy being watched or photographed or filmed by others but there are also times when being watched or recorded makes us feel acutely embarrassed, persecuted even" (Walker & Chaplin, 1997, p. 97). Virtually looking and gazing are too often the terrain of male identified characters. A disproportionately high number of male characters "own" the programmed features that make other forms of looking, such as @peruse, @kgb, @fbi, @scope, glance, @peep, @gawk, see, and @examine, available to the general MOO community. The names of these commands emphasize the surveillant properties of looking. Female characters are more likely to be the object of these virtual looks. Frequent messages, which are visible to all users, from female characters that are being virtually looked at and discussions about this topic in public rooms and MOO mailing lists make the community aware of the different ways that male and female characters are viewed. Ironic descriptions, such as "I have gigantic breasts. Please hit on me relentlessly" (Technicolor_Guest, 11 June 1999), also demonstrate the different ways that male and female characters are treated on MOOs.

Sexual and provocative guest descriptions have become such a regular and popular part of LambdaMOO that the "Silly/Stupid/Salacious-Guest-Description" mailing list was set up so that users could "Post stupid, silly, ridiculous, absurd guest descriptions here for the enjoyment of all" (LambdaMOOd). Some of these descriptions seem to be written by characters in order to entertain the list readers. "Hi! I am Loki. I logged on as a guest and entered a goofy description just so I could post it here for all to see!" (Plaid_Guest, 7 December 1998). However, the tendency to repost guest descriptions, for others' "enjoyment," that feature erotic female bodies provide users with another forum in which they can regulate beauty ideals and enjoy textually generated visual pleasure.

Beige_Guest
Busty, blonde, bombshell. (30 December 1998)

Olive_Guest
A HOT SEXY BABE IN HER LATE TEENS, 19 TO BE EXACT. SHE HAS LONG BROWN HAIR AND BIG BROWN EYES. SHE'S WEARING SHORTS AND A TIGHT TANK TOP THAT SHOWS OFF HER BELLY. SHE'S FEEL-ING EXTRA HAPPY TONIGHT. (6 December 1998)

When a guest described herself as "late 30s bi-female, wearing a tight red minidress and 4 inch heels" with "a black leather collar tightly around her neck. Females only please," a user established age, sexuality, and gender appropriate behavior by comment-ing "late 30's wearing that kind of getup? ewww. And you claim to be bi, then want fe-males only. Stupid cunt" (Pichu, 2000). Such blatantly condemnatory comments may encourage other users to repress alternative forms of expression and to produce stereo-typed bodies that remain within conventional systems of desire. Even humorous com-ments reinforce the existence of visual pleasure and act as a cunning reminder that women are looked at and evaluated. For example, "A Beautiful woman with a pink tank top and turquoise miniskirt" made a character's "eyes hurt" (ACW, 2000).

We all learn about how we should look and be looked at through such forums. Such structures as the cinema have created a system of belief in which particular kinds of desires and visions of the body are fulfilled. Mulvey (1986) has argued that the subject of the gaze is male, assisted by an implicit association with the camera's viewpoint, while its object is female. "Cinematic codes create a gaze, a world, and an object, thereby producing an illusion cut to the measure of desire" (p. 208). MOOs create a similar set of seemingly real illusions. Female guests have "huge breasts," nar-row waists, and are often half clad in a "short skirt" (6 December 1998). The produc-tion of such stereotyped bodies may be in reaction to the ways that this formula is sometimes disrupted. Every character's position as the object of the virtual look is an important and as yet unexplored aspect of MOO culture. Overtly sexual male guest descriptions, which render characters that are "hard and horny" (Purple_Guest, 4 Jun 1999) with genitals that are "the envy of most men" (Guest, 16 May 2000), may dis-turb the presumed naturalness of match-ups between male and female characters and attract the erotic gaze of other males. The almost complete absence of hypersexual descriptions among male characters on LambdaMOO, where only male guests seem to have erotic descriptions, suggests that these descriptions don't represent an appro-priate masculinity, offer an identity that users are willing to sustain with less anonymity, or attract a desired gaze.

The ability to "look" at character descriptions, which have detailed physiog-nomic attributes, produces a kind of visual terrain in text-based settings. The inability to know what users look like is counteracted by the ways that MOOers depict themselves inside and outside of the system. There is a variety of Web pages where users can see and post their photographs of MOOers (Everett, Fiegel Wolfe, MOOGallery). Some users announce or even advertise their Webcams, where other people can see them MOOing. In these cases, the textual bodies of MOOers appear to be verified by photographic proof. Despite such documentation, which of course can never fully link any MOO character to an offline identity, many users continue to argue that there are no female MOOers. "We're all fat pasty guys here" (Red_Guest, 28 April 2000). Another commonly held position is that "skinny women don't exist on MOO, they're all fat and ugly" (Blue_Guest, 28 April 2000).

Such notions justify the constant evaluation of female MOOers on mailing lists and in public forums. The ability to write bodies into being seems to have encouraged the continued manipulation of these illusions for other users' pleasure. For instance, the Real MOO Gallery offers "some of our friends as we'd like to see 'em" (Everett). On this site, the images of MOOers are put into fantastical configurations. It is not surprising that most of the images of women are presented in near-nude or erotic poses, including bondage outfits, mermaid fantasies, and magazine layouts, that make female bodies visible and available to the male gaze. On LambdaMOO, such empowered gazes are met with a female character that provides "Someone to stare at" (Pink_Guest, 20 June 2000), "glances up shyly then looks down again" (Russet_Guest, 22 May 2000), has "sleep in her eyes" (Matte_Guest, 5 June 1999), or "an innocent look" (Copper_Guest, 6 June 1999). This suggests that the mastering gaze also produces a corollary passive female model. The fascination with being visual online rather than having visual pleasure can entice "the other into submission" (Salecel & Žižek, 1996, p. 3). The mastering gaze of certain characters and the voyeuristic terminology of MOO commands perpetuate a series of limiting identity constructs on the MOO as well as in other settings.

CONCLUSION

These examples show how some programmers and Internet users adopt stereotypes from the material world. These conventions are used to try to resolve the ambiguous properties of online communication. If meeting online has provided a variety of dilemmas, including the problem of identifying "real" women, then Yahoo! provides greeting cards that try to express and then stabilize this experience. One "card" depicts a woman worrying about online identity. She asks, "Remember meeting an interesting man and wondering if he was married? Now you meet an interesting man in a chat room . . . and wonder if he's a man" (Yahoo!i). This card appears to have reversed the often-expressed concern that men pretend to be women online. However, the card also questions representations of women because the thumbnail preview illustrates the image of a woman with the question, "Is He a Man?" This question may be asked about the depicted woman and suggest that she is a man. The woman may also ask it about some other person.

Users react to these "problems" with identifying gender in different ways. A user may state that "I'm hopelessly hetero" but "as long as they can *play* a good woman here it really doesn't matter" (Videx, 1996). Other users feel that their heterosexual position is compromised by "mistakenly" having an online relationship with someone of the same sex. These "problems" with correlating gender identity and physical body parts reflect larger social issues. The presumed differences in demeanor between men and women are continually challenged by such things as the *Maury Povitch* television episode "Is This Person a Man or a Woman?" where viewers tended to incorrectly identify the sex of contestants. Films like *Paris Is Burning* and *Boys Don't Cry* document the violence that people like Brandon Teena, who was brutally murdered, face when their gender presentation is different from what society has deemed acceptable. Yahoo! attempts to provide users with a way to resolve similar uncertainties with online identification. A "card" depicts an open photo booth with the text "Glad to have met you online. A picture would be nice." Users' worries about gender masquerades and demands for visual verification suggest that identity remains unstable in virtual settings (Doane, 1991).

MOO users' fascination with what other MOOers look like and "cards" that ask for a record of a user's physiognomy suggest that on the Internet, everybody worries that you're a dog. The focus on particular kinds of physical attributes in Yahoo!'s Personals and LambdaMOO is one way that computer communication reinforces stereotypes. Online communication could allow us to establish new modes of self-representation and communication. However, the technologies that this article describes are more likely to repress alternative forms of communication. This doesn't mean that the technology has to produce such effects. Instead, it suggests that all users and programmers should consider the specific ways that cultural codes and computer programming function before reproducing them online.

NOTES

1. Peter Steiner's "Nobody Knows You're a Dog" statement and cartoon are often reproduced on Web sites and in other forums. Peter Steiner, *The New Yorker,* 5 July 1993, p. 61.
2. Yahoo! launched its nationwide classified services, including personals, on 10 February 1997. The classifieds had already become one of its most popular services on Yahoo Metro sites (San Francisco, Los Angeles, Chicago, New York, Washington DC, Boston, Austin) (Yahoo!c).
3. Users who read Yahoo! personal advertisements can choose to read those ads directed toward men and women at the same time, but there is no standard way that users can identify their ungendered or bisexual desire.

4. The bottom of the form also has spaces in which users must specify if they smoke, drink, or have children.
5. Twenty-nine testimonial letters were presented. Twenty of them were accompanied by photos.
6. In the "gay marriage" poll, 55% of participants answered "No" (Yahoo!h).
7. There are a number of ways that guests can also be used to establish a fixed identity. Some guest users choose to use the same description every time that they log in as a guest. Other users simply label the guest with a name, such as Sue or Ben, that makes it seem like this is their "real" name.
8. Users who don't set their character's gender by typing "@gender <gender>" will have their gender remain as "neuter." If a character sets gender to something other than one of the ten gender choices, then the system uses "neuter" pronouns. A few characters have circumvented the neuter pronominal markers by programming their own set of gender pronouns.
9. These confusions make alternative gender identification less stable than the male and female positions. Despite these gender biases, some characters persist in identifying as an alternative gender.

REFERENCES

Bornstein, K. (1994). *Gender outlaw: On men, women, and the rest of us.* New York: Routledge.

Bornstein, K. (1998). *My gender workbook: How to become a real man, a real woman, the real you, or something else entirely.* New York: Routledge.

Bruckman, A. (1993). *Gender swapping on the Internet.* Retrieved June 6, 2000 from the World Wide Web: http://www.cc.gatech.edu/fac/Amy.Bruckman/papers/

Butler, J. (1989). *Gender trouble: Feminism and the subversion of identity.* New York: Routledge.

Butler, J. (1993). *Bodies that matter: On the discursive limits of "sex."* New York: Routledge.

Cherny, L. (1994). Gender differences in text-based virtual reality. In *Cultural performances: Proceedings of the Third Berkeley Women and Language Conference.* Retrieved June 27, 2000 from the World Wide Web: http://www.usyd.edu.au/su/social/papers/cherny2.html

Curtis, P. (1992). *Mudding social phenomena in text-based virtual realities.* Paper presented at the conference on Directions and Implications of Advanced Computing, sponsored by Computer Professionals for Social Responsibility. Retrieved June 6, 2000 from the World Wide Web: ftp://ftp.lambda.moo.mud.org/pub/MOO/papers/DIAC92.txt

Curtis, P. (1993, May). *MUDs grow up.* Paper presented at the Third International Conference on Cyberspace. Retrieved June 6, 2000 from the World Wide Web: ftp://ftp.lambda.moo.mud.org/pub/MOO/papers/MUDsGrowUp.txt

de Lauretis, T. (1984). *Alice doesn't: Feminism, semiotics, cinema.* Bloomington: Indiana University Press.

de Lauretis, T. (1987). *Technologies of gender: Essays on theory, film, and fiction.* Bloomington: Indiana University Press.

Dibbell, J. (1998). *My tiny life: Crime and passion in a virtual world.* New York: Holt.

Doane, M. A. (1991). *Femmes fatales: Feminism, film theory, psychoanalysis.* New York: Routledge.

Fausto-Sterling, A. (1985). *Myths of gender: Biological theories about women and men.* New York: Basic Books.

Feinberg, L. (1998). *Trans liberation: Beyond pink or blue.* Boston: Beacon Press.

Fuss, D. (1989). *Essentially speaking: Feminism, nature, and difference.* New York: Routledge.

Gibson, W. (1984). *Neuromancer.* New York: Ace Books.

Lake, M. (1998, August). The new megasites: All-in-one web supersites. *PC World.* Retrieved May 17, 2000 from the World Wide Web: http://www.pcworld.com/top400/article/0,1361,7202,00.html

Mulvey, L. (1986). Visual pleasure and narrative cinema. In P. Rosen (Ed.), *Narrative, apparatus, ideology: A film theory reader.* New York: Columbia University Press.

Salecel, R., & Žižek, S. (1996). Introduction to *Gaze and voice as love objects.* Durham, NC: Duke University Press.

Senft, T. (1996). Introduction: Performing the digital body: A ghost story. *Women and Performance, 17.* Retrieved December 2, 1999 from the World Wide Web: http://www.echonyc.com/~women/Issue17/introduction.html

Stone, A. (1995). *The war of desire and technology at the close of the mechanical age.* Cambridge, MA: MIT Press.

Turkle, S. (1995). *Life on the screen: Identity in the age of the Internet.* New York: Simon & Schuster.

Walker, J. A., & Chaplin, S. (1997). *Visual culture: An introduction.* Manchester, UK: Manchester University Press.

White, M. (1999). Visual pleasure in textual places: Gazing in multi-user object-oriented worlds. *Information, Communication, and Society, 2*(4).

INTERNET REFERENCES

Abraxas. type "look ~Abraxas" Retrieved December 21, 1998 via telnet: LambdaMOO, lambda.moo.mud.org 8888

ACW. *Silly/Stupid/Salacious-Guest-Descriptions. Retrieved May 11, 2000 via telnet: LambdaMOO, lambda.moo.mud.org 8888

charming_odyn. Yahoo! personals california. Retrieved May 8, 2000 from the World Wide Web: http://personals.yahoo.com/display/personals?cr=California&cc=personals&cf=&cs=time+2&ce_g=Man&ce_p=Woman&rl=yes&ct_hft=table

Everett, R. An alternative plane of existence on LambdaMOO. Retrieved June 7, 2000 from the World Wide Web: http://idt.net/~everett3/main.html

Falc. LambdaMOO hall of presidents. Retrieved June 7, 2000 from the World Wide Web: http://www.welcome.to/moogallery/

Fiegel Wolfe, A. LambdaMOOer homepages. Retrieved June 7, 2000 from the World Wide Web: http://www.illuminatrix.com/andria/gallery.html

frank916. Yahoo! personals california. Retrieved May 8, 2000 from the World Wide Web: http://personals.yahoo.com/display/personals?cr=California&cc=personals&cf=&cs=time+2&ce_g=Man&ce_p=Woman&rl=yes&ct_hft=table

Free On-Line Dictionary of Computing. Multi-user dimension from FOLDOC. Retrieved November 27, 1998 from the World Wide Web: http://wombat.doc.ic.ac.uk/foldoc/foldoc.cgi?Multi-User+Dimension

Gray, J. Yahoo! personals – Dr. John Gray – Looking for love. Retrieved June 2, 2000 from the World Wide Web: http://personals.yahoo.com/info/drgray/12.html

Hammer Silly/Stupid/Salacious-Guest-Descriptions. Retrieved December 6, 1998 via telnet: LambdaMOO, lambda.moo.mud.org 8888

hardwood4u_94306. Yahoo! personals – california. Retrieved May 17, 2000 from the World Wide Web: http://personals.yahoo.com/display/personals?ct_hft=detailnp&nncss=&pncss=&tot=1&cc=personals&cr=California&search=cc%3Dpersonals%26ck%3Dhardwood4u_94306%2B%2B%2B%26za%3Dand%26cpcy%3D%26cr%3DCalifornia%26cs%3Dtime%2B2%26ncss%3D&cids=personals-0958576296-421361&rpre=0&position0.x=11&position0.y=6

LambdaMOOa. type ";length(players())" after becoming a programmer. Retrieved June 17, 2000 via telnet: LambdaMOO, lambda.moo.mud.org 8888

LambdaMOOb. type "help @describe" Retrieved January 2, 1999 via telnet: LambdaMOO, lambda.moo.mud.org 8888

LambdaMOOc. type "help introduction" Retrieved January 2, 1999 via telnet: LambdaMOO, lambda.moo.mud.org 8888

LambdaMOOd. type "@examine *silly" Retrieved May 24, 2000 via telnet: LambdaMOO, lambda.moo.mud.org 8888

Loki. *Silly/stupid/salacious-guest-descriptions. Retrieved December 6, 1998 via telnet: LambdaMOO, lambda.moo.mud.org 8888

Merriam Webster Dictionary. WWWebster dictionary - Search screen. Retrieved January 2, 1999 from the World Wide Web: http://www.m-w.com/cgi-bin/netdict

Pichu. *Silly/stupid/salacious-guest-descriptions. Retrieved April 28, 2000 via telnet: LambdaMOO, lambda.moo.mud.org 8888

sanjosesweet. Yahoo! personals. Retrieved June 8, 2000 from the World Wide Web: http://personals.yahoo.com/display/personals?ct_hft=table&ce_eth=&ce_rel=&ce_sm=&cl_age=&ch_age=&ck=bbw&za=and&g=&cs=time+2&ce_body=&ce_dr=&ce_art=&ce_ser=&ce_dan=&ce_din=&ce_fam=&ce_mov=&ce_mus=&ce_out=&ce_pho=&ce_spi=&ce_spo=&ce_the=&ce_tra=&ce_g=Woman&ce_p=Man&rl=&rs=&ra=&rpe=&rpa=&p=&cc=personals&cr=&cf=

Stetson. feature object, type "genwho" Retrieved June 1, 2000 via telnet: LambdaMOO, lambda.moo.mud.org 8888

StorytellerJon. Yahoo! personals. Retrieved June 9, 2000 from the World Wide Web: http://personals.yahoo.com/display/personals?ct_hft=detailnp&position=5&cc=personals&rpre=2&nncss=&pncss=40G0a&tot=36&cids=personals-0957370314-143711,personals-0957155100-284442,personals-0957136162-922362,personals-0956958483-871712,personals-941399816-15722,personals-923455008-12137&search=cc%3dpersonals%26ck%3dhomosexual%26ce%5fp%3dWoman%26ce%5fg%3dMan%26za%3dand%26cpcy%3d%26cr%3d%26cs%3dtime%2b2%26ncss%3d40V0a&cr=

ultraman_41042. Yahoo! personals. Retrieved June 8, 2000 from the World Wide Web: http://personals.yahoo.com/display/personals?ct_hft=detailnp&nncss=&pncss=&tot=1&cc=personals&cr=Virginia&search=cc%3Dpersonals%26ck%3Dultraman_41042%26za%3Dand%26cpcy%3D%26cr%3DVirginia%26cs%3Dtime%2B2%26ncss%3D&cids=personals-0959009099 033137&rpre=0&position0.x=14&position0.y=5

Videx *BDSM. Retrieved October 23, 1996 via telnet: LambdaMOO, lambda.moo.mud.org 8888

Yahoo!a. Yahoo! – Company history. Retrieved June 6, 2000 from the World Wide Web: http://docs.yahoo.com/info/misc/history.html

Yahoo!b. Mayor Giuliani, Yahoo! auctions and Macy's unveil the NYC 2000 fashion auction. Retrieved June 6, 2000 from the World Wide Web: http://docs.yahoo.com/docs/pr/release529.html

Yahoo!c. Buy it, sell it, find it on Yahoo! classifieds: Yahoo! rolls out national classifieds service. http://docs.yahoo.com/docs/pr/release81.html (6 June 2000).

Yahoo!d. Yahoo! wallet. Retrieved May 12, 2000 from the World Wide Web: http://wallet.yahoo.com/

Yahoo!e. Yahoo! – Help companion. Retrieved June 28, 2000 from the World Wide Web: http://help.yahoo.com/help/us/companion/companion-01.html

Yahoo!f. Welcome to Yahoo! Retrieved July 1, 2000 from the World Wide Web: http://edit.yahoo.com/config/eval_register?.intl=&new=1&.done=&.src=ym&partner=&promo =&.last=

Yahoo!g. Yahoo! personals—Success stories. Retrieved May 12, 2000 from the World Wide Web: http://personals.yahoo.com/info/testimonials.html

Yahoo!h.Yahoo! personals poll. Retrieved June 6, 2000 from the World Wide Web: http://polls.yahoo.com/public/archives/14856907/p-pers-68?m=r

Yahoo!i. Yahoo! greetings. Is he a man? Retrieved June 19, 2000 from the World Wide Web: http://greetings.yahoo.com/greet/send?.id=152001966&.catu=/browse/Any_Occasion/Computers_and_Internet/

CREATING SUPPORT AND SOLVING PROBLEMS IN ONLINE SUPPORT GROUPS

Toward a Context-Based Perspective of Gender Differences in Communication Styles

Mary Walstrom

UNIVERSITY OF ILLINOIS, URBANA–CHAMPAGNE

Much of the discussion in which we engage about gender and communication begins from the assumption that, generally, females and males tend to differ in their communication styles. These differences are born of the socialization practices that characterize males' communication as the norm and females' as different. According to Mary Walstrom, assuming a styles perspective on gender communication may be counterproductive to understanding how language functions.

In this piece, Walstrom challenges readers to take a context-oriented perspective in analyzing the variations between males' and females' language use. The author's central claim is that the context in which communication occurs, in conjunction with gender, will have a direct influence on the language choices of participants. Walstrom demonstrates her thesis through a discourse analysis of participants in an online eating-disorder support group. Operating within a communication environment that provides safety for those who are averse to revealing their body results in blending socially prescribed communication behaviors of females and males. Ultimately, through the strategy of blending language styles typically ascribed to females and males, participants were able to optimize trust building and facilitate problem solving. Based on her analysis, Walstrom concludes that approaching gender communication from a context-based perspective will afford communicators more flexibility in language choice and, consequently, greater potential for achieving communication goals in a variety of communication interactions.

QUESTIONS FOR DISCUSSION

- *How would you characterize your style of communication: more or less female or male?*

- *Do you find yourself relying on your gender-socialized style in certain situations while in others you adopt the style of a gender other than yours? If so, describe some of the different situations and your gender communication adaptations.*
- *In the case of the eating-disorder support group described in the article, how do you think the channel of communication in conjunction with the topic of discussion might have influenced gender communication choices?*

I n classrooms, corporate offices, living rooms, and online chat rooms, women and men often experience communication breakdowns because of differences in their language use. While these differences may be taken as destiny—as if women were from Venus and men from Mars (Gray, 1992)—I suggest a more flexible view. Although research has shown that the sexes communicate in distinct styles, studies have also evidenced—and researchers advocate—versatility in speakers' style use. Such versatility is important for successfully achieving myriad interactional goals: answering a professor's question, asking for a promotion, settling a marital dispute, or forming online friendships. I suggest that gender-based conceptions of communication styles—namely, as "female" and "male"—may constrain speakers' understanding of language use, as well as its benefits. In this article, I advocate replacing a gender-based view of communication styles with one that is context-oriented. From this perspective, communication styles may be seen as a single pool of linguistic resources that speakers may use to achieve mutually negotiated purposes in particular sites. In this article, I encourage you to apply this perspective practically—to develop versatility in using communication styles—to enjoy greater satisfaction in achieving the purposes of your everyday interactions.

I support and illustrate a context-oriented view of communication styles through a discourse analysis of an exchange from an online eating-disorder support group. I demonstrate how group participants merge various features of female and male communication styles to accomplish the therapeutic aims of this forum. Rather than introduce new, perhaps equally limiting terminology, I continue to use throughout my analysis the terms "female" and "male" to refer to communication styles that group participants use. However, the thrust of this article is to offer a fresh approach to understanding communication styles—as context-specific resources rather than sexed-based traits. Central to this approach is a view of communication styles as practical tools available to all speakers—female or male—for effectively achieving the aims of everyday interactions and creating speaking contexts that are respectful and welcoming for all (that is, safe).

Below, I first expand on the rationale for this article, elaborating on the limitations I see with a gender-based conception of communication styles. I also discuss how our increasing Internet-based culture presents ways to apply a context-oriented perspective of communication styles. I then synthesize research on communication styles, highlighting their respective goals and linguistic features. This review serves as a backdrop for my analysis of ways online eating-disorder support group participants merge female and male communication styles to accomplish the threefold purpose of their forum. In closing, I propose ways college students may begin to broaden their communicative style use, as well as offer discussion questions to prompt your creative expansion on my suggestions.

FROM A GENDER-BASED TO A CONTEXT-ORIENTED PERSPECTIVE OF COMMUNICATION STYLE

I propose a context-oriented alternative to a gender-based conception of communication styles to reverse popular views of women's and men's language use as inherently different or otherwise difficult to change. Research has shown that much overlap exists between women's and men's communication styles; however, these commonalties are glossed by widespread labeling of these styles as "female" and "male." A problem with this terminology is that speakers may become strict style users—using the style associated with one's sex—perpetuating the essentialist view that the sexes are "supposed to be different" (Gray, 1992, p. 10). However, strict style users may find that their abilities to make effective, rewarding communicative choices are impaired (Trenholm & Jensen, 1996). Moreover, strict style users may begin to value the style they prefer over the other. Such a bias may make these speakers less open to the opinions of those who use the style they devalue, or cause them to feel incompetent or unsafe using it. Granted, it may be challenging to reverse contextual norms that reward the use of certain communication styles by women and men. For example, male style—associated with power and authority—tends to prevail in many institutional contexts (offices, schools, public debate, etc.), and deviance from that style may yield negative consequences (e.g., to not be taken seriously). However, I suggest skilled versatility in using communication styles may appear attractive to, and be more widely accepted by, greater numbers of persons because of the benefits of this competency. For example, speakers who can strategically merge features of female and male communication styles may show more openness to the opinions of others and be more likely to achieve context-specific purposes.

With our rapidly expanding use of Internet-based forms of interaction, now is an opportune time to practice broadening one's skill in using female and male communication styles. One way many Internet users, wittingly or unwittingly, engage in such activity is in adopting different male or female personas while conversing online. For example, studies of online interactions of many types (e.g., discussion forums, chat rooms, and MUDs/MOOs) show that people often adopt multiple gender identities (Turkle, 1995). To succeed in doing so, one typically draws on either female or male communication styles, which are generally taken by others as indicating female or male persons, respectively (Herring, Johnson, & DiBeneddetto, 1995). The ability to represent oneself as a particular gender through communication style use is also enhanced online as this bodiless environment lessens the likelihood that contrived identities may be challenged. This ability to "try on" a gender identity online by manipulating one's use of female and male communication styles indicates the useful environment that the Internet offers for expanding one's communication style versatility.

GENDER-BASED PERSPECTIVES OF COMMUNICATION STYLES: F2F AND ONLINE

Extensive research on women's and men's communication has shown that each group tends to use distinct styles, each with its own aim (Wood, 2001). The primary goal of female communication style is to cultivate supportive, intimate relationships based on equality. This aim is achieved through expressive forms of communication (Trenholm & Jensen, 1996). For example, female style features the sharing of personal experiences and the disclosing of feelings. A central goal of male communication style is to establish control, independence, and a superior social status (Wood, 2001). This aim is accomplished through instrumental types of communication (Trenholm & Jensen, 1996). For example, male verbal style involves factual exchanges focusing on practical outcomes, displays of knowledge and skill, and attempts to assert one's views and talents as superior to others.

Linguist Deborah Tannen (1990) characterizes female style as "rapport-talk" and male style "report-talk" (p. 77), terms that highlight their distinct goals. Tannen claims that misunderstandings and conflicts occur when men and women do not attend to these differences. She also explains it is difficult to become more flexible in style use, as each gender has been socialized (e.g., by families and peers) to prefer the style associated with their sex. Another difficulty Tannen notes in broadening one's versatility in style use relates to the double bind such changes present. For example, the interpersonal intimacy conveyed by female style may be taken by men as a threat to their independence, and the independence-asserting role of male style may be seen by women as a threat to intimate relationships. However, Tannen encourages men and women to attempt to understand and learn each other's "genderlect" (p. 297) to decrease clashes resulting from misunderstood communicative goals.

The goals of female and male communication styles have been demonstrated in research on women's and men's storytelling practices. The relational goal of female style appears in women's nontraditional storytelling forms, such as kernel-storying (Kalcik, 1975) and spinstorying (Langellier & Peterson, 1992). Stories are built collectively and focus on everyday events and shared feelings. The structure of these storytelling modes emerge as the length and direction of development are spontaneously negotiated among tellers. The fluid, collaborative nature of these forms of women's storytelling fosters relations of solidarity and harmony (i.e., equality). The independence- and status-oriented goals of male communication style are hallmarks of traditional storytelling practices (e.g., public performances), mainly observed among men (Langellier & Peterson, 1992). Typically told by a single speaker, these stories revolve around a remarkable or tellable event (e.g., a achievement or an adventure). The structure of traditional stories is linear, whereby sequences of actions culminate in a climax or point. Traditional stories also emphasize the performance skill of the teller, and thus often contain humor as well as dramatic dialogues and actions. Through the exclusive speaker control and orchestrated structure of traditional stores, tellers assert autonomy and boost their social ranking.

The central aims of male and female communication styles are accomplished by speakers through various communication strategies. I now turn to a discussion of these features, as well as their respective strengths and liabilities. In addition, I briefly review research on communication style use online to contextualize the analysis of support group interaction below.

Female and Male Communication Styles: F2F Contexts

According to Wood (2001), the relational- and equality-seeking goals of female communication style are achieved as participants invite others' contributions, show interest in and understanding of others' perspectives, equitably share talk time (e.g., conversational floor, [Edelsky, 1981]), and build on each others' topics, especially by matching experiences. Female style also involves nonverbal signs of appreciation of others' contributions (e.g., back channeling). Finally, female style includes tentatively framed statements, such as hedges ("perhaps, maybe") and tag questions ("You agree, right?"), to show respect for others' views and promote dialogue. Male communicative style contains an alternative set of strategies, which serve its aims of establishing autonomy, control, and status. Speakers employing this style seek control over conversational flow through interruption and changing topics. Moreover, male style focuses on instrumental activities such as problem solving or advice giving. The direct, assertive nature of male style—seen in commands ("Stop that")—conveys authority. Finally, nonverbal signs of understanding or appreciation within a male style are minimal (Wood, 2001). It is important to keep in mind that the features of each style may accomplish the goal of the other (Tannen, 1990). For example, the sharing of a matching experience may aim to outshine the experience of another rather than convey equality. Likewise, changing the topic may be done to make space for a new conversational participant rather than to exercise interactional control. Ultimately, the meaning of a speaker's style use is collectively negotiated and determined by interactants in particular contexts.

Each style is also associated with benefits and liabilities (again depending on context-specific understandings of style use). The benefits of female communicative style include strengthening relational networks and creating respectful and welcoming speaking contexts. Male style benefits involve efficiently accomplishing tasks, as well as presenting one's expertise in important evaluative contexts (e.g., classrooms or work settings). Concerning the drawbacks, female communicative style may indicate indecisiveness, subordinate status, and a lack of knowledge or confidence. Male style may convey hostility and close down communicative channels. Moreover, male style may produce risky communicative contexts—that is, threaten the face of one or more interactants. The concept of face entails two dimensions, our desire to have our wants recognized and appreciated as well as not infringed upon (Brown & Levinson, 1987). When face is threatened—such as by criticism (characteristic of male style)— speakers feel humiliated, and often withdraw from interaction. Research suggests that understanding differences between female and male communication styles and becoming more versatile in their use enable one to maximize the benefits and limit the liabilities of each.

Female and Male Communication Styles in Online Contexts

Research on men's and women's communication online has shown that each group continues to use predominately male and female communication styles, in both face-to-face and online contexts. For example, Sullivan (1996), in a comparative study of online support groups for breast and prostrate cancer survivors, observed extensive female style use in the former group and male style use in the latter. The strengths and liabilities of female and male styles have been evidenced in online research as well.[1] As in face-to-face interaction, communication researchers have called for flexibility in using communication styles online, specifically to incorporate more female style (Spender, 1995). A leading reason for this shift is to promote more equitable communication. For example, in online forums, male verbal style tends to predominate, seen in participants' routine exchange of insults and challenges (known as "flaming"). Consequently, many persons hesitate to participate in online forums and may leave them entirely (Anderson, 1996; Ebben & Kramarae, 1993; Herring, 1994, 1996; Herring et al., 1995; Kramarae & Taylor, 1993; Morahan-Martin, 1999). Alternatively, in women-only forums, female style tends to be favored, and the use of politeness strategies (e.g., tentative expressions) and affective expressions (verbal and symbolic) prevails. As a result, participants enjoy a safe communicative environment—one that is hospitable and inviting to all (Baym, 2000; Winter & Huff, 1996; Sharf, 1997; Walstrom, 1999, in press).[2]

CONTEXT-BASED VERSATILITY IN COMMUNICATION STYLES ONLINE: AN ANALYSIS

Below I present a discourse analysis of one exchange between women participants in alt.support.eating-disord (ASED), a public online forum for those struggling with eating disorders (mainly anorexia and bulimia). This exchange is excerpted from a longer thread, including an initial post (that introduces a topic) and all replies to that post.[3] The exchange selected for the present analysis stood out as a rich example of the skillful weaving by ASED participants of female and male communication styles to meet the purpose of the online forum. This purpose is stated in the ASED Frequently Asked Questions (FAQ) document: to serve as a resource for those seeking support, information, and recovery (ASED, 2000). An additional dimension of this purpose came to light through my analysis of the structure of ASED interaction—specifically, women's use of female and male communication styles. Through merging these styles, women accomplish the overall goal of the former—egalitarian, supportive relationships—and a particular function of the latter—problem solving. These relational and instrumental activities appear to be key in furthering the third facet of the ASED purpose: to facilitate recovery.

To provide you with a foundation for understanding this qualitative discourse analysis, I briefly overview this method of inquiry. I also highlight its strengths to help you appreciate the rich insights it can offer communication researchers. Discourse analysis entails the study of the micro-level structure of talk, focusing on interactants' coordinated use of various communicative strategies (such as turn-taking and interruptions). Through closely examining typically brief sequences of interaction, discourse analysts seek to capture social actions accomplished through language (e.g., showing support or challenging a position), going beyond those explicitly stated (e.g., asking for help). The meaning of these actions, as noted earlier, IS understood to be collaboratively negotiated and accomplished by interactants in specific contexts. Discourse analysts strive to grasp these situated meanings, avoiding to the extent possible preconceived understandings of participants' interaction.

Discourse analysis is especially useful in that it enables researchers to illuminate realms of meaning that often escape the awareness of interactants (in speaking or writing). This close method of examination also detects what otherwise may be glossed in content- or quantitative-based studies of larger expanses of talk. Another asset of discourse analysis is that interpretations are grounded in demonstrable instances of the phenomenon being studied—such as communicative style use—which readers can trace and evaluate themselves. In following the exchange analyzed below, I invite you to join me in entering into dialogue with two ASED participants as a participant-observer/researcher. In taking an active role in interpreting participants' communicative style use, you may better appreciate and understand the unique strengths of discourse analysis as a tool for making sense of everyday communication. You may also more solidly grasp a central argument of this article—to demonstrate the advantage of developing proficiency in versatile communication style use.

I now turn to an analysis of an ASED exchange in which I trace how participants merge features of female and male communication styles to achieve the purpose of this particular site. In Example 1, I highlight how ASED participant Karla uses female and male communication styles to present a twofold problem she encounters in both face-to-face (f2f) eating-disorder support groups and one-on-one therapy. I call attention to ways Karla invokes these styles to seek and maintain egalitarian, supportive relationships with ASED participants and to engage in problem posing. I also discuss how these activities broadly further Karla's ongoing pursuit of recovery.

Example 1[4]
```
01   I've been to this a few times - I always seems to feel extra self-concious
02   in groups, because I feel like everyone is judging the extent of my
03   sickness based on my appearance. If I feel fat one day, I feel guilty for
04   claiming to have an eating disorder. If I restrict for a while, then I
05   feel more sick and more eligible for the title of "eating disordered". I
06   think I prefer individual therapy, but I've been having trouble calling my
07   therapist lately. I don't feel like I'm skinny enough to deserve
08   treatment. Why do I feel this way? Does anyone else have this problem?
09   Karla
```

Karla begins her post by indicating her prior visits to—and seeming participation in—the ASED forum ("I've been to this a few times"). This introduction enables Karla to indicate a prior connection to ASED participants and an interest in sustaining it. Karla immediately identifies a dilemma she is facing, effectively posing a problem. She shows that in f2f support groups she constantly evaluates her appearance negatively and senses that others are doing the same ("I always seem to feel extra self-conscious in groups, because I feel like everyone is judging the extent of my sickness based on my appearance."). Given my own participation in and extensive study of ASED interaction, I've observed that the stating of an eating-disorder-related problem in this context generally solicits help for solving it. Besides problem posing, Karla also displays an interest in close relationships with ASED participants. For example, she discloses her feelings—specifically, negative self-evaluations—indicating a desire for intimacy.

Karla continues problem posing by revealing a second struggle she deals with in f2f support groups. She does so by outlining the logic underlying her negative self-evaluations (feelings). For example, Karla shows that she links assessments of the degree of her eating disorder to being qualified to claim that she has one ("If I feel fat one day, I feel guilty for claiming to have an eating disorder. If I restrict for a while, then I feel more sick and more eligible for the title of 'eating disordered'.").

Moreover, she states that the way she evaluates her appearance (as fat or, ostensibly, thin, ["more sick"]) determines, and, at times curtails, her right to participate in ("be in")—and to ostensibly receive help from—f2f support groups. Karla's sharing of her thought process facilitates problem solving, as she offers ASED participants additional important details for helping her resolve her dilemma. At the same time, Karla's continued disclosure of her feelings invites intimate relationships with ASED participants.

Continuing problem posing and relationship building, Karla relates how her troublesome feelings persist in one-on-one therapy. Although Karla expresses a preference for this context over f2f support groups ("I think I prefer . . ."), she shows that she faces the same problem in this setting. For example, Karla indicates that her negative evaluations of her appearance determine, and undermine, her right to receive help from her therapist ("I don't think I'm skinny enough to deserve treatment"). Here Karla engages in problem posing as she develops and restates her dilemma, again revealing the logic at its core. She also does relational work in disclosing emotions that convey an interest in intimacy. Next, Karla focuses on problem posing in explicitly and assertively soliciting help from ASED participants. Specifically, she asks for reasons for her troublesome feelings ("Why do I feel this way?"). She also invites input from those who have experienced her dilemma ("Does anyone else have this problem?"). In her latter request, Karla demonstrates an interest in building supportive, symmetrical relationships, as she recruits perspectives that would revolve around shared struggle.

In sum, Karla uses male and female communication styles to build close, egalitarian relationships with ASED participants and pose a problem she faces in therapeutic contexts. In engaging in these activities, Karla also shows her aim to achieve the recovery-related purpose of the group. That is, she seeks connections with and help from others to expand her access to recovery-promoting resources (f2f support group and therapy).

In Examples 2.1–2.4, I attend to ways one respondent, Tara, blends male and female communication styles to help Karla solve her problem and to develop a close, egalitarian relationship with her. Tara engages in problem solving by offering Karla potential insight into her negative evaluations and in asserting an approach to dealing with them. Tara builds a symmetrical, close relation with Karla by showing her strong interest in and identification with Karla's feelings. This latter process is especially salient in Example 2.1.

Example 2.1[5]
41 karla,
42 I know exactly what you mean! I just started posting to this group
43 recently, and its the most I've ever done to talk to anyone. The
44 thought of talking to others (in person where they can see me and how
45 fat I am) who are, in my opinion, are alot sicker than me terrifies me.

46   That's why I was glad to find this group (it is more private—no one

47   can see me, they can only get a small window into my feelings).

Tara begins her reply by expressing solidarity and equality as she identifies with Karla's problem. For example, Tara expresses enthusiastic interest in and precise understanding of Karla's post ("I know exactly what you mean!"). Tara builds symmetrical relations by offering a closely matching account of Karla's problem, drawing on her ideas about f2f eating-disorder support groups and her participation in ASED. For example, Tara shows she believes that if she attended a f2f group, other (ostensibly thinner) participants would judge her size, like she does, as fat ("The thought of talking to others [in person where they can see me and how fat I am] . . . "). Given Tara's strong fear about this possibility ("The thought of talking to others . . . terrifies me"), she indicates that she exclusively discusses her eating disorder in the ASED forum ("I just started . . . "). Tara also specifies why she prefers ASED to f2f groups: The online environment enables her to conceal her physical appearance and to control others' access to her feelings ("That's why I was glad . . . ," lines 46–47). By stressing these dimensions of the ASED forum, Tara supports her claim to identify with Karla's problem. In other words, Tara shows her strong concern about (possible) negative evaluations of her appearance by f2f support group participants. In expressing common ground and mutually disclosing feelings, Tara cultivates with Karla a close relationship based on equality.

In Example 2.2, Tara continues to build such a relationship by further identifying with Karla's problem, extending their shared territory to include trouble seeking one-on-one therapy. Tara also reveals a likely origin of her difficulty pursuing this form of treatment. This form of information facilitates problem solving by contributing to Karla's pursuit of reasons for her feelings.

Example 2.2

48   I am also afraid to talk to a therapist because they would probably

49   laugh me out of the office. I'm not sure what causes this feeling,

50   maybe self-doubt or low self esteem. I'm not an expert, but I can

51   certainly relate with your feelings.

Tara does relational work by matching Karla's struggle contacting a therapist (lines 06–07). For example, Tara shows she is afraid to seek one-on-one therapy ("I am also afraid to talk to . . ."). Tara's fear stems from her expectation that a therapist would not take her effort to seek treatment seriously. Here Tara displays solidarity as she suggests that, like Karla, she does not deserve clinical treatment. Tara goes beyond relation building to problem solving in offering information to Karla. This information, based on her personal experience, appears geared toward Karla's request for help understanding her problem ("Why do I feel this way?" in line 08). For example, Tara shows that she has traced a possible source of the way she questions her eligibility for help from a therapist: "self-doubt or low-self esteem." In sharing her theory, she builds on the reason Karla has identified for her problem: feeling fat ("1 don't feel I'm skinny enough to deserve treatment"). By hedging ("maybe") and qualifying of the scope of her knowledge ("I'm not an expert"), Tara indirectly offers rather than authoritatively prescribes her theory as an explanation for Karla's feelings. Generally, presenting alternative versions of others' feelings may be taken as a threat to face, as this practice violates individuals' exclusive rights to define their internal experiences (Buttny, 1993; Peräkylä & Silverman, 1991). In offering an explanation based on personal experience, Tara avoids this potentially face-threatening act, bolstering relational harmony. Tara enhances such a relation by displaying solidarity. For example, Tara reaffirms that she shares Karla's feelings, even if her layperson explanation does not shed light on Karla's experience ("I'm not an expert, but I can certainly relate to your feelings").

In Example 2.3, Tara extends the scope of her problem-solving efforts, going beyond offering information to prescribing action for Karla to take. At the same time, she couches her advice in displays of intimacy and support. In doing so, Tara helps maintain interpersonal closeness, which may be threatened by her assertive call for action.

Example 2.3
52   Call your therapist, maybe one on one would be easier for you right now.
53   Then, when you are ready to face others, you can give it a shot.
54   Good luck :)
55   tara

Tara boldly directs Karla to seek immediate help for her problem ("Call your therapist"). As a potential incentive for action, Tara offers Karla a reason for taking her advice—namely, that seeing a therapist may be less threatening for her than attending f2f support groups ("maybe one on one would be easier for you right now"). In addition to advocating change, Tara also encourages Karla's continued and future work on her eating disorder. For example, Tara predicts that, after time in one-on-one therapy, Karla will be prepared to attend f2f support groups. By projecting Karla as "ready" to do so, she suggests that Karla will overcome the preoccupations that she struggles with in the group context. Through helping Karla envision success in this way, Tara assists Karla in solving the twofold problem she aired in her post. At the same time, Tara contributes to solving Karla's larger struggle—overcoming an eating disorder. That is, by encouraging her to continue therapy and f2f support group attendance, Tara assists Karla in her ongoing pursuit of recovery.

Tara also engages in relationship building in this concluding segment of her post. She does so by mitigating in various ways the possible face threat inherent in her assertive call for Karla to act. For example, Tara shows sensitivity toward Karla's feelings by offering advice directed toward easing Karla's distress ("maybe one on one would be easier for you . . .”). Tara also presents her advice in a way that suggests she believes Karla will find it acceptable and helpful. For example, Tara portrays Karla as successfully attending her f2f support group at some future point in time (“when you are ready to face others, you can give it a shot”). In addition, Tara conveys intimacy through a symbolic expression of friendliness (shown in a smiley face emoticon). Finally, by wishing her well (“Good luck”), Tara seems to express interest in a continued relationship with Karla, perhaps in the form of a progress report of her support group attendance.

CONCLUSION

In this analysis of one ASED exchange, I outlined ways in which group participants richly draw on women's and men's communication styles to build close, egalitarian relationships and engage in problem solving. Women use myriad features of female style to achieve their relational goal, and use selected features of male style to accomplish the instrumental task of problem solving. Each of these activities can be seen as supporting the broader, collective aim of the ASED forum—to assist participants in overcoming an eating disorder. Thus, this analysis demonstrates ASED participants' versatile use of women's and men's communication styles to meet the purposes of this context, as stated by women themselves—to serve as a resource for support, information, and recovery. Moreover, through extensive female style use, women create a safe place—an inviting and respectful communicative climate—for collective coping activity. One way participants' sense of such a climate may be inferred is by the absence of insults or criticism in this exchange—a consistent trend I've observed across ASED exchanges.

The strengths of male and female styles, as noted above, seem to be optimized in this exchange as well. For example, women conduct a crucial goal-oriented task, cultivate egalitarian relationships, and create a context that invites all to engage in these activities. Yet I see potential benefit in participants' increased use of a component of male communicative style: assertiveness. For example, with this strategy, women may more efficiently intervene and help remedy each other's eating-disorder-related practices. A need for such intervention is suggested in Tara's reply, as she leaves unaddressed Karla's apparent starving behavior (“If I restrict for a while” in line 04). Through increased directness, ASED participants may also more readily advocate changes in action, as effectively done by Tara: “Call your therapist” (line 52). The confronting of eating-disorder practices is a valued feature of f2f eating disorder support groups (Jones, 1992). This assertive activity may assist ASED participants in meeting the recovery-oriented purpose of their forum. Granted, extensive assertiveness can threaten intimacy, as it may be taken as “flaming.” Preventing this outcome can be difficult online in the absence of nonverbal information that could soften a call for change (unless supplied by an emoticon, such as a smiley face). However, it seems clear that ASED participants highly value and successfully maintain a safe on-line communicative environment through extensive female style use. Therefore, in-corporating increased assertive statements may be less likely to jeopardize the respectful nature of the ASED communicative context.

This analysis aims to illustrate a context-oriented alternative to a gender-based view of communication styles. That is, group participants pooled and flexibly em-ployed features of male and female communication styles to effectively accomplish the purposes of the ASED forum. With this context-oriented perspective of communica-tion styles, I hope to have equipped you to begin developing versatility in drawing on communication styles to maximize their respective strengths—relationship building and problem solving. I see two strong benefits for college students to acquire this com-petency. First, increased versatility in style use may enable you to assist peers struggling with psychological afflictions, such as alcoholism, depression, and eating disorders. Although these conditions are widespread among college students, campus health services are often poorly equipped to deal with them. Health educators at the University of Michigan have called attention to this problem: "Colleges and universi-ties often act as if their students don't suffer from mental illnesses . . . they inundate students with information about physical health services, but say little about mental health services" (Berman, Strauss, & Verhage, 2000, p. B9). Students who are versatile in using communication styles—namely, using their features to show support *and* solve problems—have at their disposal a powerful tool. They may be able to help others, and themselves, cope with mental illnesses—both online and in f2f contexts.

Second, college students skilled in flexible communication style use may be more likely to achieve the purposes of many everyday interactional contexts. For ex-ample, an aim common to family dinner tables, classroom group discussions, and corporate team meetings is effective problem-solving activity. Accomplishing this aim may be enhanced by speakers' dual use of female and male styles to build egali-tarian, supportive relationships while solving problems. As shown in the present analysis, various features of female style may be blended with problem-solving activ-ity to create a safe communicative climate while attending to serious issues in need of remedy. Students who excel in employing female and male communicative styles with versatility are likely to find increased satisfaction and positive outcomes in many everyday interactions.

NOTES

1. See Herring's (1994, 1996; Herring et al., 1995) extensive analyses of male and female communicative styles within several academic discussion lists for rich examples of their respective strengths and liabilities.

2. Clinicians are increasingly recognizing how online support groups offer participants safe spaces for online therapy. For example, online therapist and support group facilitator Colon (1996) notes that these forums offer a feeling of safety, resulting in participants feeling less inhibited to examine aspects of themselves or issues that they might hesitate to explore in a face-to-face group. The present analysis demonstrates how women actively create and value a safe online context through myriad features of female communicative style.

3. The original thread of the analyzed exchange contained five replies.

4. All posts appear in original form (including typos and spacing), pseudonyms replace all real names, and potentially identifying information has been changed.

5. Replies are numbered sequentially, following the initial post to which they respond. For example, the number "10" is assigned to the first line of the first reply that responds to the initial post ending on line "09."

REFERENCES

Alt.support.eating-disord (ASED). (2000). *Frequently asked questions (FAQ)*. Online document: http://www.glitterkitty.net/asedfaq/group.html

Anderson, J. (1996). Not for the faint of heart: Contemplations on Usenet. In L. Cherny & E. R. Weise (Eds.), *Wired women: Gender and new realities in cyberspace* (pp. 126–140). Seattle: Seal Press.

Baym, N. (2000). *Tune in, log on: Soaps, fandom, and on-line community*. Thousand Oaks, CA: Sage.

Berman, S. M., Strauss, S., & Verhage, F. (2000, June 16). Treating mental illness in students: A new strategy. *Chronicle of Higher Education*, p. B9.

Brown, P., & Levinson, S. (1987). *Politeness: Some universals in language usage*. Cambridge: Cambridge University Press.

Buttny, R. (1993). *Social accountability in communication*. London: Sage.

Colon, Y. (1996). The public forum: Chatt(er)ing through the fingertips: Doing group therapy online. *Women and Performance, 17*(9), 205–215.

Ebben, M., & Kramarae, C. (1993). Women and information technologies: Creating a cyberspace of our own. In J. Taylor, C. Kramarae, & M. Ebben (Eds.), *Women, information technology, and scholarship* (pp. 15–27). Urbana, IL: Center for Advanced Study.

Edelsky, C. (1981). Who's got the floor? *Language in Society, 10*, 383–421.

Gray, J. (1992). *Men are from Mars, women are from Venus*. New York: HarperCollins.

Herring, S. (1994, June). *Gender differences in computer-mediated communication: Bringing familiar baggage to the new frontier*. Keynote paper presented at the American Library Association Annual Convention, Miami.

Herring, S. (1996). Posting in a different voice: Gender and ethics in computer-mediated communication. In C. Ess (Ed.), *Philosophical perspectives on computer-mediated communication* (pp. 113–145). Albany: State University of New York Press.

Herring, S., Johnson, D. A., & DiBeneddetto, T. (1995). "This discussion is going too far!": Male resistance to female participation on the Internet. In K. Hall & M. Buchholtz (Eds.), *Gender articulated: Language and the socially constructed self*. New York: Routledge.

Jones, A. (1992). Community self-help groups for women with bulimic and compulsive eating problems. *British Review of Bulimia and Anorexia Nervosa, 6*(2), 63–71.

Kalcik, S. (1975). "... like Ann's gynecologist or the time I was almost raped": Personal narratives in women's rap groups. *Journal of American Folklore, 88*, 3–11.

Kramarae, C., & Taylor, J. (1993). Women and men on electronic networks: A conversation or a monologue? In J. Taylor, C. Kramarae, & M. Ebben (Eds.), *Women, information technology, and scholarship* (pp. 52–61). Urbana, IL: Center for Advanced Study.

Langellier, K. M., & Peterson, E. E. (1992). Spinstorying: An analysis of women storytelling. In E. C. Fine & J. H. Speer (Eds.), *Performance, culture, and identity* (pp. 157–180). Westport, CT: Praeger.

Morahan-Martin, J. (1999). Males, females, and the Internet. In J. Gackenbach (Ed.), *Psychology of the Internet: Intrapersonal, interpersonal, and transpersonal implications* (pp. 169–193). San Diego: Academic Press.

Peräkylä, A., & Silverman, D. (1991). Reinterpreting speech-exchange systems: Communication formats in AIDS counseling. *Sociology, 25*, 627–651.

Sharf, B. (1997). Communicating breast cancer on-line: Support and empowerment on the Internet. *Women and Health, 26*, 65–85.

Spender, D. (1995). *Nattering on the Net: Women, power, and cyberspace*. North Melbourne: Spenifex Press.

Sullivan, C. (1996, November). *Cancer support groups in cyberspace: Are there gender differences in message functions?* Paper presented at the Speech Communication Association Convention, San Diego.

Tannen, D. (1990). *You just don't understand: Women and men in conversation*. New York: William Morrow.

Trenholm, S., & Jensen, A. (1996). *Interpersonal communication*. Belmont, CA: Wadsworth.

Turkle, S. (1995). *Life on the screen: Identity in the age in of the Internet*. New York: Simon & Schuster.

Walstrom, M. K. (1999). *"Starvation is who I am...": From eating disorder to recovering identities through narrative co-construction in an on-line eating disorder support group*. Unpublished doctoral dissertation, University of Illinois, Urbana-Champaign.

Walstrom, M. K. (in press). "You know, who is the thinnest": Combating surveillance and creating safety in coping with eating disorders online. *CyberPsychology and Behavior*.

Winter, D., & Huff, C. (1996). Adapting the Internet: Comments from a women only forum. *American Sociologist, 27*, 30–54.

Wood, J. (2001). *Gendered lives: Communication, gender and culture* (4th ed). Belmont, CA: Wadsworth.

LIONS, TIGERS, AND LITTLE GIRLS

Representations of Gender Roles
in *Power Rangers: Wild Force*

Mark Borchert
CARSON-NEWMAN COLLEGE

Whether it's Bugs Bunny and Bullwinkle, or Scooby Doo and the Simpsons, cartoons have been a staple of U.S. television culture for several generations. Children (of all ages) often spend their Saturday mornings in front of the television, engrossed in the antics of animated life forms locked in a battle of wits, muscle, or superhuman power. The main characters or stars of the cartoons may be people, animals, machines, or alien beings. Regardless of their form, they all share one thing in common: Their genders are distinguished and distinctive.

The influence of television on role formation and behavior is a significant area of interest to mass communication scholars. In this article, Mark Borchert analyzes a popular cartoon in order to discover how gender roles are constructed, communicated, and ultimately reinforced or challenged. His analysis reveals a pattern of gender presentation that suggests traditional male-female stereotypes are embedded in the verbal and nonverbal aspects of the cartoon, thereby reinforcing a patriarchal ideology. With the help of his 6-year-old daughter, however, Borchert discovers that the transparent gender messages of the cartoon may be negotiated or opposed by children as they bring their own experiences and preferences to the cartoon's characters.

QUESTIONS FOR DISCUSSION

- *Make a list of the cartoons you watched regularly when you were a child. Identify the gender assigned to characters and their typical behaviors. Were there cartoon characters that challenged or resisted gender stereotypes? If so, how?*
- *Consider the author's description and interpretation of the episodes he analyzed. Given his observations, are there other gender stereotypes that he might have included in his discussion?*

■ *Watch an episode of* Power Rangers. *Identify features of the cartoon episode that support Borchert's findings. Can you find any aspects of the cartoon that might refute his conclusions?*

■ *Compare a contemporary cartoon, such as* Power Rangers, *with a popular cartoon of ten, twenty, or thirty years ago. Do gender depictions of cartoon characters appear to have changed? If so, how? If not, what has remained constant?*

M uch of my media research involves analyzing FCC rulings or considering the implications of technological innovations in communication. So, although it seemed logical to me, my 6-year-old daughter found it very curious to discover me taking notes as I watched *Power Rangers: Wild Force* one Saturday morning. "What are you doing, Daddy?" she queried.

"I'm watching *Power Rangers* to find out what it tells us about men and women and how they should act," I responded.

Satisfied with that simple explanation of media content analysis, she slid in next to me on the couch. For the next half-hour, we watched as spandex-clad women and men kicked and karate-chopped their way to victory over the forces of evil.

Although *Power Rangers* is new to my 6-year-old, it is not a new program. The franchise is in its tenth season, and the original show, *Mighty Morphin' Power Rangers,* was a global phenomenon. The initial series combined fighting sequences from a 1970s Japanese children's program, *Zyu Rangers,* with the adventures of a team of American "teenagers with attitudes."[1] According to many television critics, the show quickly became one of the most popular children's programs of all time (Meyer & Tsiantar, 1994; Everett, 1995).

Although the program now has morphed into *Power Rangers: Wild Force* and offers higher production values, many elements of the original show remain. The series is still marked by numerous martial arts fighting sequences. Actors in rather silly monster costumes continue to play the villains. The protagonists still transform from American teenagers into faceless superheroes, distinguishable by the color of their outfits. In their current incarnation, the Rangers are empowered by their animal totems (a lion, an eagle, a shark, a tiger, and a bison), and their leader is a young man raised in the jungle. The Princess Shayla of the ethereal island of Animarium now guides the Rangers. When her magical fountain begins to bubble, she knows that evil Orgs, the soulless enemies of humanity, are attacking.

My daughter was delighted to discover that one of the Power Rangers had the same name as she. "Look, Daddy, Alyssa is White Tiger. She's tough!" exclaimed my daughter, as we watched her new hero kick an Org in the face.

MIXED MESSAGES

As I watched my daughter become enthralled by *Wild Force,* I wondered what the show taught her about the roles of women and men in society. Of the five Rangers, two are women. Although neither is the leader of the team, they participate fully in rescuing the Earth from the evil Orgs. Alyssa has mastered the martial arts, and she joins the male characters in the mêlées with their enemies. My daughter's reaction suggests that the program provides a model for tough women, partners with men in defending the rights of others from wrongdoers (albeit using quite violent means).[2]

If this is the message of *Power Rangers* concerning gender, it is not the only message. In my content analysis of twelve consecutive episodes, I found numerous and conflicting portrayals of gender roles in *Power Rangers: Wild Force.* In some cases, the female characters play active protagonists with key leadership parts in the efforts of the heroic team. In other cases, women are victimized or objectified as the Saturday-morning stories unfold. Newcomb and Hirsch (2000) discuss the polysemic nature of television, its ability to present multiple and conflicting messages. They describe television as a "cultural forum" offering a "multiplicity of meanings," some reactionary and repressive, others subversive and even emancipatory. They argue that although the resolutions of television stories are often predictable and formulaic, the issues and viewpoints represented in many, even innocuous, series are complex, contradictory, and open to interpretation. Many perspectives surface in the telling of a story, and a single television program can offer multiple and competing understandings of gender, power, and the role of women and men in society.

Consider *Power Rangers: Wild Force* in this light. In an episode titled "A Father's Footsteps," Alyssa is presented as a strong character. The episode begins with Alyssa easily defeating two male Power Rangers in a martial arts practice session, just as she has done "every day for the last four months." A newspaper article then reveals that she has won a college scholarship based on her perfect grade-point average. Through a series of flashbacks, the program focuses on Alyssa's struggle between pursuing her dreams of studying science at a university or following in her father's footsteps by practicing the martial arts. In this episode, Alyssa is clearly the protagonist. As her father comes to visit her at school, he is disappointed to discover that Alyssa has skipped class. His disappointment, however, soon fades as he sees his daughter using her martial arts skills in defense of the Earth. In this episode, a favorite with my daughter, Alyssa plays the key role in the Rangers' defeat of the Orgs. She is presented as an active leader in the group, a character with physical and intellectual skills, and the appropriate heir of her father's mantle. Although in the end, her father's approval proves key to Alyssa's happiness and the program's resolution, the show offers a forum for wrestling with traditional understandings of gender roles and the patriarchy. Although the conclusion is formulaic and predictable, the show, as

Newcomb and Hirsch suggest, presents complex and contradictory messages about the power and place of a young woman in the contemporary world.

An episode titled "Three's a Crowd" offers an alternative perspective on gender. In this program, a wedding-dressed Org captures brides, while Danny (a Latino), the shy Black Ranger, competes for the attention of Kendall, a beautiful wedding coordinator. This episode presents women as either victims or sexual objects, or both at once. The Rangers' foe in this show is an Org that transforms brides into manikins, objectifying them and adding them to his collection. In the context of battling this monster, Danny glances at Kendall and is entranced by her beauty. Almost immediately, he faces a competitor for Kendall's affection. Although not a Power Ranger, the other young suitor is wealthy and handsome (as well as blonde and fair-skinned), and the story line focuses on the implicit tension between the two men.

Each suitor offers Kendall a bracelet. Danny makes her a friendship bracelet; his rich opponent presents her with a diamond one. In this context, a relationship with the wedding coordinator is a trophy to be won. Like the brides-turned-manikins, the contest is for possession of her. Kendall's own role is primarily that of the defenseless victim. Initially, she is injured in an attack by the wedding-dress Org. On crutches and with bandaged head, she comes to cheer for the Black Ranger in his battle with evil. In battle, when he thinks about her, Black Ranger's powers are weakened and he is repeatedly knocked to the ground. In his distress, she suddenly appears from behind a wall. He shouts, "No Kendall, get away from here. It is not safe." She responds, "Don't worry about me. I understand everything. You must fight to defend the Earth. I am behind you all the way." Raising her right arm, she shows him that she has chosen to wear his friendship bracelet. In her vulnerable condition, she is once again attacked and predictably defended and rescued by Danny. Black Ranger had won on two levels: not only had he defeated evil, but he had won his prize.

Contrary to the storybook ending in which the handsome prince rides off with his beautiful prize, Black Ranger and Kendall have no hopes for a "happily ever after." In this episode, the affection these two feel for one another distracts Black Ranger from his true mission, to defend the Earth. After pledging her allegiance to Black Ranger, Kendall must relinquish any connection to him. In the final scene of the episode, she releases Black Ranger to his mission. His only response is "I need to stay focused. Thank you for understanding." Black Ranger then turns back to join his friends as Kendall stares longingly at him, clutching the friendship bracelet to her heart. Without looking back, Danny rejoins the team, and together the Rangers leave happily.

In this episode, women are not complex characters or the focus of the story. They are sexual objects to be captured, rescued, won, and possessed. In fact, the heroic status of the Black Ranger relies on the helplessness and dependency of women. These two episodes present very different messages.

THE RANGE OF POWER

Although various perspectives on gender emerge in the adventures of the Power Rangers, not every perspective carries equal weight. One central and continuing message, for example, is the "natural" leadership of Cole, the Red Ranger. Young, white, handsome, and muscular, Cole is the alpha male of the Wild Force. His animal totem is the lion, the king of the beasts. Although the story line presents him as the newest member of the group, his leadership role within the team is immediately underscored through visual cues. Cole is the first character introduced in the title sequence, and whenever the Rangers are transformed into fighting superheroes, he takes the central position in a V-shaped formation. When the team members combine their powers to create a unified weapon, it is the Red Ranger that wields it, once again flanked on either side by his subordinate team members. Just as he is the visual centerpiece of the group, his point of view and exploits are central to most stories. After the death of his parents, Cole was raised by jungle dwellers and among the animals. His relationships with his family's killer, animals, other team members, and the memory of his parents animate many of the stories. The dialogue of the series also communicates his leadership position. For example, after all the Power Rangers have been defeated by an Org, Cole asserts, "I can't give up. I'm the leader." Finding strength in these words, he destroys the monster.

The visual elements, dialogue, and story line of many episodes present a similar message about gender and authority. Natural leadership abilities reside within the strong, white, male figure. "Red Ranger is the leader. He's the head," my 6-year-old asserted after watching an episode titled "Lionheart." Why is this the case? Why doesn't the White Ranger, Alyssa, lead the team? At one point, Princess Shayla, the Wild Force's spiritual guide, explains, "As the lion is the king of the jungle, so is his chosen Ranger the leader of the team." The program suggests that it is only "natural" and "realistic" that an assertive, muscular male leads the team. Media scholars like John Fiske (1987) suggest that the claim of "realism" does not reflect a connection with unquestionable facts of life; rather, it suggests a program's adherence to the conventions and socially acceptable beliefs of a culture. It appears "natural" because it emulates, rather than challenges, the status quo. Seen in this context, Cole's role on the show reflects the dominant ideology of our society, the assumption that just "as the lion is king of the jungle," strong men are our natural leaders.

The only challenge to Cole's authority comes from Taylor, the Yellow Ranger. She is an outspoken and assertive young woman, the first person chosen as a member of the Wild Force. An episode titled "Click, Click, Zoom" explores the potential leadership role of Taylor in the group. This episode begins with the Red Ranger, Cole, rejecting a rulebook, a Power Rangers' manual written by Taylor. "We only need one rule, teamwork," Cole insists. Frustrated by his rejection of her rules and her potential leadership, Taylor storms off. She soon encounters an Org shaped like a camera. In the ensuing struggle, the monster photographs Taylor, capturing her body. Now an invisible victim, Taylor must be rescued by Cole. Ultimately, she is freed by the Red Ranger and acknowledges his natural leadership of the group.

In some ways, Taylor's words and personality offer an alternative to the dominant ideology. Her presence and assertiveness suggest that a woman, as well as a man, could serve as a leader of the group. Other elements of the show, however, challenge this perspective. The Rangers, for example, do not respond to Taylor's directives as they do to Cole's words. In many instances, her actions are presented as endangering rather than saving the group. Although she presents an oppositional message, it is a perspective undercut by the story line, the series' visual cues, and ultimately Taylor's own words. As she resolves her confrontation with Cole, she calls him "leader."

Gramsci (1971) and other critical scholars note that within a society various messages are in constant competition. This struggle goes on in political debates, theatrical presentations, works of literature, and even children's television programs. Just as Cole and Taylor vie for leadership of the Rangers, the alternative messages implicit in the stories of the Wild Force compete for the audience's acceptance and acknowledgment. The term *hegemony* expresses the notion that within a program, a text, or a society, different messages exist and compete. The term also suggests that one set of messages has greater persuasive power. In fact, one perspective is often unquestioned; it is presented as the natural, commonsense alternative. This preferred message has dominance over the alternative readings or interpretations. In the context of *Power Rangers: Wild Force,* the dominant message about gender is quite clear. Although women and men may share some measure of power, it is appropriate that men hold the ultimate authority. When a woman seeks to assert her authority, the show suggests that she is ineffective and even dangerous. Thus, the dominant message of the show reinforces the status quo of a patriarchal society.

In the business realm, the world of religion, the political arena, and even our educational system, the distribution of power and authority between men and women is never equal. In our current social systems, men continue to hold the most powerful positions and receive the greatest compensation for their work, and yet many times, this inequity appears appropriate and natural. Althusser (1971) suggests that ideology—our belief system about our real conditions of existence—structures and sustains unequal relationships of power. Belief systems may appear natural and commonsense, yet they position the individual in structures of dominance and subordination. In fact, it is because they appear natural that they maintain their powerful hold on us. "Those who are in ideology," Althusser writes, "believe themselves by definition outside ideology. . . . Ideology never says, I am ideological" (p. 175). Taylor may speak in assertive tones and place demands on the group, but the prospect of her authority over the team seems strangely unnatural and discomforting. The reactions of the other Rangers to Taylor, the key images in the show (all of which present Cole in a central position), and the story line itself invite rejection of Taylor's ideas and acceptance of traditional notions of male power. In this way, *Power Rangers* sustains the dominant ideology, reinforcing conventional understanding of the distribution of power between the sexes.

Although a central message of the program naturalizes the authority of men over women, the text is not "closed" to other interpretations. Hall (1980) maintains that the meaning of a media text involves two distinct processes: the "encoding" of the text in its production and the "decoding" of the program during its reception. Audience members filter the messages presented by a program through their own life experiences and beliefs, and they may arrive at alternative interpretations or "readings" of the meaning of a show. Although a program may appear to reinforce the values of the status quo, an audience member might come away with a negotiated or oppositional interpretation. A viewer might ignore the dominant message and embrace a secondary theme that resonates with her or his life experiences. In their play, children constantly reinterpret mediated stories, changing the characters to meet their needs and the plot lines to fit with their circumstances. For my own daughter, the role of Alyssa captivates her. After watching a show, she speaks of nothing but White Tiger's actions, even if the character has played only a minor role in that episode. As an active interpreter, she devises new meanings for Alyssa's activities and statements, and she carefully explains to others why Alyssa is the most powerful of the Rangers. Although the central message of the program reduces the range of power offered to women, perhaps my daughter finds the resources within this media text for a limited challenge to its implicit hierarchy.

CONCLUSION: A PARENT'S RESPONSE

As a parent, it is difficult to find much that is edifying about *Power Rangers*. Violence is presented as the answer to conflicts. Stereotypes abound, and the show's message reinforces traditional gender roles. In addition, I cannot help being disturbed by the commercialism of the program.

As I completed my research, I asked my daughter what she thought was the message of the show. "What did you learn from *Power Rangers*?" I asked. "You don't just have to play with Barbies," she explained.

Ultimately, the central message may be less about the distinctions between men and women and more about its creators' desire to cast us all in the role of consumers of children's toys. For a decade, Power Ranger merchandise has filled the toy aisles, and the series has invited children "to play along" by purchasing action figures. In fact, many scenes in the show look like toy commercials. The animals within the show (the lion, shark, eagle, and so on) resemble mechanical playthings rather than actual beasts, and monsters, robots, and animals battle one another in toylike fashion.

Interestingly, whenever we roll by the toy section of the store, my daughter springs into action when she sees Power Ranger products. She has accurately decoded one of the messages of the show: "Buy Power Ranger toys." She pores over the toys, looking at each one, describing its characteristics, noting the special features included in each box. But before long, she begins a search for White Tiger. Carefully she examines each box on each shelf from the front to the back. This process can last up to ten minutes. Not surprisingly, Red Ranger abounds, but White Tiger, Alyssa's character, cannot be found. My daughter's shoulders slump as we leave the toy section without a find, but I leave the store wondering, "Had she found it, would I have bought it for her?" Would you?

NOTES

1. In the opening sequence of the 1995 show, the evil Rita Repulas emerges from her prison shouting, "After 10,000 years, I'm free. It's time to conquer Earth." In response, the benevolent Zordon advises his robot companion, "Alpha, Rita's escaped. Recruit a team of teenagers with attitudes."
2. In fact, the original series was noted for its violent content. With its action-packed fighting scenes, the series boasted not the 25 acts of violence per hour of an average children's program, but 211 acts per hour (Cooper, 1994).

REFERENCES

Althusser, Louis. (1971). Ideology and ideological state apparatuses (Notes toward an investigation). In *Lenin and philosophy and other essays* (B. Brewer, Trans.). New York: Monthly Review Press.

Cooper, R. (1994, December 11). Toys are a source of violence. *Dallas Morning News*, p. J6.

Everett, Shu-Ling. (1995). Mirage multiculturalism: Unmasking the Mighty Morphin Power Rangers. *Journal of Mass Media Ethics, 11*, 28–40.

Fiske, John. (1987). *Television culture.* New York: Methuen.

Gramsci, Antonio. (1971). *Selections from the prison notebooks of Antonio Gramsci* (Quintin Hoare & Geoffrey Nowell Smith, Eds. and Trans.). New York: International Publishers.

Hall, Stuart. (1980). Encoding/decoding. In Stuart Hall, Dorothy Hobson, Andrew Lowe, & Paul Willis (Eds.), *Culture, media, language.* London: Hutchinson.

Meyer, Michael, & Tsiantar, Dody. (1994, August 8). Ninja Turtles, eat our dust. *Newsweek*, pp. 35–35.

Newcomb, Horace, & Hirsch, Paul. (2000). Television as a cultural forum. In *Television: The critical view* (6th ed., pp. 561–573). New York: Oxford University Press.

INDEX